mote
arfare

Remote Warfare

NEW CULTURES OF VIOLENCE

Rebecca A. Adelman
and David Kieran, Editors

University of Minnesota Press
Minneapolis
London

The University of Minnesota Press gratefully acknowledges the financial support provided for the publication of this book by the Dresher Center for the Humanities at the University of Maryland, Baltimore County.

Excerpts from Mikkel Brixvold, *Så efterlades alt flæskende* (Copenhagen: Lindhardt and Ringhof, 2014), are reprinted with permission of the author.

Published by the University of Minnesota Press
111 Third Avenue South, Suite 290
Minneapolis, MN 55401-2520
http://www.upress.umn.edu

ISBN 978-1-5179-0747-1 (hc)
ISBN 978-1-5179-0748-8 (pb)
A Cataloging-in-Publication record for this book is available from the Library of Congress.

Contents

Acknowledgments

This book is one product of a friendship and intellectual connection that began serendipitously more than a decade ago. We are both committed to analyzing the multifaceted ways that Americans make sense of their nation's wars and asking what is at stake, culturally and politically, in that sense-making. Over the years, our work on these questions has proceeded along frequently intersecting and sometimes overlapping trajectories. Our friendship and collaboration developed over the course of many emails, phone conversations, exchanges of work in progress, appearances together on panels, and the ingestion of a significant amount of dim sum.

Although this volume emerged initially from our shared interest in creating space for new kinds of conversations about remote warfare, many others have contributed to its realization. This project began as a special issue of the *Journal of War and Culture Studies*. We were thrilled that the editors, particularly Rachel Woodward, were as excited as we were by a set of linked articles on this topic, and they translated their enthusiasm into unwavering support. Contributions from David M. Walker, Fabio Cristiano, and Daniel Grinberg inspired and enlivened our thinking about the potential for scholarship on remote warfare.

We were pleased to receive so many excellent proposals in response to our initial call for papers, which we took as an indication of the vibrant, multidisciplinary scholarship querying the cultures of remote warfare not just in the context of U.S. militarism and imperialism but in a global frame as well. That response led us to contemplate the project that ultimately became this volume. We owe many thanks to our contributors, who produced thoughtful essays, stuck with us through many rounds of revision and peer review, and responded to our entreaties and questions with patience and good humor.

From our first conversation with Dani Kasprzak at the annual meeting of the American Studies Association in 2017, working with the University of Minnesota Press has been a pleasure. Dani shepherded this project through the early stages of development and peer review, then Pieter Martin took over and ably guided the manuscript through the final stages. We also benefited from the efforts and expertise of Anne Carter and Jason Weidemann. Our copy editor, Ashley Moore, helped us produce a more readable book, and Amy Zimmer prepared the index.

Completing this project also depended on the support of mentors who have stood by us for many years, including Wendy Kozol, Jennifer James, and Melani McAlister; our colleagues at the University of Maryland, Baltimore County, and Washington & Jefferson College; and our spectacular friends, loving families, and astonishing partners, Jason Tremblay and Emma Gilmore Kieran. We count ourselves overwhelmingly fortunate to be surrounded by so many people who have cared for, encouraged, and supported us for so long.

Introduction

Rethinking Killing at a Distance

REBECCA A. ADELMAN AND DAVID KIERAN

On March 13, 2018, President Donald J. Trump announced that his "new national strategy for space recognizes that space is a war-fighting domain, just like the land, air, and sea." Tantalizingly, he added, "We may even have a Space Force."[1] Critics unsurprisingly derided the proposal as the latest example of the president's penchant for uninformed bombast. CNN's Jim Acosta called it a proposal "right out of 'Star Wars'" and mused that it might have come "because he's so close to Hollywood." But other analysts were less dismissive. Moments later, for example, Phil Mudd, former director of the CIA's Counterterrorist Center and the FBI's National Security Branch, told Wolf Blitzer, "We already look at space as a potential instrument of war. If you look at the ability potentially in the future of delivering weapons from space, I know there are people who won't like it, but you have to acknowledge you wouldn't have been able to believe 150 years ago we'd need an Air Force."[2] Its pithiness notwithstanding, this assertion reminds us that the horizons for remote warfare are always receding, and that forms of warfighting that might once have seemed un-, or only, imaginable have rapidly become commonplace.

Over the months that followed, the notion of a space force elicited both mockery and serious policy consideration. In June, when the president signed the "Memorandum on National Space Traffic Management Policy," he insisted, "When it comes to defending America, it is not enough to merely have an American presence in space. We must have American dominance in space," and officially called for the

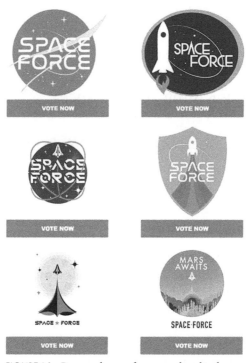

FIGURE I.1. Proposed space force merchandise logos.

creation of a space force.[3] Perhaps unsurprisingly, the administration quickly sought to monetize this initiative, offering a commemorative coin and surveying supporters regarding which of six space force logos they preferred (Figure I.1).[4] But the ostensible seriousness with which the president and his supporters regarded the prospect of a space force found its equal and opposite reaction among skeptics. For example, Comedy Central's satirical news program *The Daily Show with Trevor Noah* ran a segment in which supporters interviewed at a Trump rally came across as wide-eyed dunces who embraced the space force primarily because it "sounded cool."[5] At the same time, however, news reports lent credibility to the idea that space would be a new frontier for warfighting, if not to the plan for the space force itself. The *New York Times,* for example, cited an intelligence assessment that indicated that Russia and China would be able to "shoot down American

satellites within two to three years," with potentially catastrophic ramifications for U.S. military operations.[6] In August 2019, the space force
proposal came closer to being realized, with the formal establishment
of the U.S. Space Command.[7]

Throughout the debate, however, historically minded journalists
pointed out that Trump was hardly the first president to consider the
military applications of space technology. As an article on Space.com
pointed out, "The idea of a separate Space Force goes all the way back
to Eisenhower."[8] Indeed, Eisenhower both called for "the peaceful use
of space" and highlighted "the need to assure that full advantage is
taken of the military potential of space."[9] Lyndon B. Johnson signed a
treaty restricting the United States from, among other things, "establishing military bases on the moon."[10] Ronald Reagan's Strategic Defense Initiative—nicknamed Star Wars by its critics—famously sought
to use satellites to prevent a nuclear attack.[11] And Barack Obama was
president when the Air Force's Boeing X-37B "space plane" made its
first flight.[12] Indeed, the Space Command was not entirely new. As *Politico* pointed out, it had "existed in another form from 1985 to 2002."[13]

We suggest that the story of the space force should not be dismissed
merely as the latest musings of a president with a penchant for hyper-
bole and a loose relationship with the truth. Instead, we take both the
serious policy debates and the popular responses it provoked as the latest reminders of two realities about remote warfare. The first is that it
is central to modern state-sponsored violence. As philosopher Elaine
Scarry reminds us, the central goal of warfare is to "out-injure" and
ultimately kill.[14] In modern warfare, the acts of killing and injuring often happen in the absence of physical proximity, as belligerents deliver violence on others from distances that might range from a few feet
to several thousand miles. The second is that the promise and peril of
these kinds of violence have been and remain a continuing preoccupation of politicians, policy makers, defense intellectuals, activists, and
purveyors of popular culture. The essays gathered here interrogate the
cultural and political dimensions of these realities. Moving beyond the
questions of tactical efficacy and morality that tend to dominate debates
about remote warfare, they contemplate instead how various actors
have interpreted and responded to the centrality of violence delivered
from a distance to modern warfare.

Plausible, Possible, and Thinkable: Approaches to Remote Warfare in Culture and Scholarship

Debates about remote warfare have orbited around three major questions. The first pertains to strategic and tactical efficacy: Does a belligerent's ability to kill from a distance enhance the likelihood of victory? The second relates to the experience of war for combatants and civilians: Does the nature of war, of injuring and being subject to injury, change substantially when the mechanism of injury is delivered remotely, and if so, how, and what is at stake in those shifts? The third, finally, is ethical: Under what circumstances, if any, is killing at a distance justifiable?

Efforts to address the first two questions have preoccupied scholars writing about conflicts ranging from the Peloponnesian War to the Syrian Civil War, and they intersect with broader debates about the effects of technology. Scholars wonder, that is, whether new technologies—and the apparent superiority that they provide belligerents who can deliver violence from greater distances than their opponents—fundamentally alter the nature of warfare, and whether those technologies are sufficient to sway the outcome.[15] As Fernando Echeverria Rey cautions, to engage in these questions risks a problematic embrace of technological determinism, which, he argues, "aims to explain the transformations of warfare from the point of view of technological innovation, simplifying the otherwise complex dynamics of war into a single element."[16] He contends that it is dangerous to assume that "the introduction of a new weapon generates an automatic adaptation of tactics," a position that necessarily "entails a certain simplification of the complex reality of warfare."[17]

Nonetheless, the historiography of warfare is replete with assertions that new capabilities to kill or injure from a distance have remade combat, well before the advent of the computerized technologies that draw so much critical attention today.[18] A few examples illustrate the durability and pervasiveness of these debates. Historians of the medieval period, for instance, have long queried the effects of archery. Chuck Lyons writes that the longbow, first deployed by the British in the 1300s, "would transform medieval warfare and help England dominate the richer and more powerful France for much of the Hundred Years' War"; Andrew Ayton disagrees, however, emphasizing the significance of the projection and cannot be exhausted through taking action in the world or by factual accumulation: there is always another level to the imaginary, more potential dangers to preempt, other nightmares to locate and eliminate."[46] These forms of militarized violence continually proliferate enemies for the state to target. This means that the critical task of responding to innovations in war making is virtually endless but also crucial. This work requires a rejection of the state's own depictions of remote warfare and a continual reconsideration of scholarly assumptions about it.

Curiously, official portrayals of remote warfare and scholarly critiques of it often align in descriptions of its disembodiment, each portraying remote warfare—for different purposes—as a practice that happens with minimal human input.[47] Key explanatory texts like P. W. Singer's *Wired for War: The Robotics Revolution and Conflict in the 21st Century* and Adam Rothstein's *Drone* provide helpful industrial and technical details about the machines that we send to war, but they also intimate that humans, as machines become more advanced, are reduced to mere supervisors, always on the verge of superfluity or obsolescence.[48] For example, Rothstein describes the drone as follows: "The drone is deeply serious, bringing with it the politics of death. It is also cryptic, a bit beyond our understanding, within our world but outside of our vision. It is something built by humans, but humans we don't know."[49] Yet as Kevin McSorley argues, "politics is written in war through the very specific idiom of violently injuring human bodies."[50] This is obviously true for the people who become its casualties, but it also holds for the people who perpetrate done violence: war still requires bodies, no matter how distant or lopsidedly mediated the connections between them might become. Relatedly, Christine Sylvester makes an "axiomatic" observation that "war is experienced through the body, a unit that has agency to target and injure others in war and is also a target of war's capabilities."[51] The contributors to this volume remind us that despite pervasive discourses about the increasingly disembodied nature of contemporary warfare—circulated by government, media, and academic sources alike—war remains a profoundly corporeal phenomenon, and they work to account for the full range of humans involved in remote warfare.[52]

Just as discourses of technologized warfare can occlude the central role of bodies in prosecuting it, so too can the rhetoric of "remote warfare" obscure the surprising intimacies that such conflicts generate.[53] In the chapters that follow, contributors theorize the body as a channel for actions, memories, ideas, experiences, affects, emotions, and sensations in militarized environments. Fundamentally, both technologies and fantasies of remote warfare are designed to maximize the distance between operators and targets. At the same time, they also function as conduits that link—violently—the various participants in these conflicts, reshaping their identities, experiences, and subject positions. Indeed, the work of defining and maintaining state identity is a crucial element of war making, as Carl Schmitt and others have noted.[54] Yet the divisions between friend and foe, us and them, are rarely stable; in practice, and over time, they are often proved fluid and contingent. Carlo Galli, for example, has written about the historical evolution in constructions of the "enemy" in Western thought. He argues that the twentieth century witnessed the collapse of distinctions between criminals and enemies, and civilians and military personnel, while the conceptualization of war expanded so much that we now believe it possible to wage it against "peoples, races, ideologies, societies, forms of life and modes of production."[55]

Yet even as the ambit of warfare broadens in this indiscriminate way, discourses about new weapons technologies hinge on the promise that increasingly sophisticated sensors, machines, and systems will enable users to find, distinguish, and eradicate enemies more efficiently and "safely." But not all enemies have characteristics that identify them as such and, moreover, not all enemies are distant.[56] Beyond their limited utility in distinguishing others who are threatening from others who are not, technologies of remote warfare can often inaugurate at least a partial collapse of the categories of victim and perpetrator, as in the case of Agent Orange casualties or, more recently, in the case of sound and pressure waves from explosions.[57] Chapters in this volume, with their attention to unexpected intimacies and points of contact on the landscape of remote warfare, take up the challenges posed by these new dialectics of identity.

Recently, critical attention to the power dynamics structuring remote warfare has focused on relations of verticality. Theorizing this axis of domination is crucial, but air war is only one of the many forms that militarized remoteness takes. Verticality in warfare is predicated on a strict separation between the powerful parties above and the relatively powerless parties below. In this model, weaponry is the only thing that connects them, and the people firing the weapons are the only actors who possess any agency. This depiction captures the lopsided distributions of force and mortality that remote warfare engenders, but most writings on verticality privilege the perspective of the more powerful entity—usually the state and its agents. Even critical views like those presented in Thomas Hippler's *Governing from the Skies: A Global History of Aerial Bombing,* which provides a detailed history of this practice, focus largely on the perspective of the state, which means that in descriptions of this type of remote warfare, the people and lands below appear almost exclusively as targets rather than beings or inhabited places.[58]

Other scholars, however, have challenged such emphases. In her *Aerial Aftermaths: Wartime from Above,* Caren Kaplan writes, "The conventional binary between distance and proximity and its related oppositions—objective and subjective, global and local, unfamiliar and familiar, strange and intimate—may be culturally and historically specific to Western modernity, but even within that narrow register of human experience, there is ample evidence of greater nuance and possibility than those bluntly contrasted extremes."[59] Contributors to *Remote Warfare* seek out precisely such alternative experiences, expanding their foci beyond the vertical to consider remote warfare as a profoundly multidirectional phenomenon and querying the types of identity formation that happen on that terrain. In the asymmetrical and nonlinear conflicts that characterize the twenty-first century, the geography of war is increasingly amorphous and the effects of remote warfare are rarely confined to a single "battlefield," if such a thing can even be said to exist as a discrete geography. Consequently, we argue for the necessity of a broader range of disciplinary perspectives and the type of nuanced cultural analysis that a humanities framework can provide.

Visions, Intimacies, Reconfigurations: The Chapters

Remote Warfare gathers twelve essays into three sections, each engaging a particular dimension of these new cultures of remote warfare. Chapters in the first section, "Visions," explore various ways of anticipating, imagining, and conceptualizing remote warfare. The first chapter, by Michael Zeitlin, explores the prehistory of drones in the aviation writings of Italian general and head of aviation Giulio Douhet (1869–1930) and William "Billy" Mitchell (1879–1936), who is widely regarded as the father of the U.S. Air Force. Writings by these key aviation theorists, Zeitlin argues, enable us to trace the genealogies of technology and imagination in remote warfare from the weapons of the early twentieth century to the unmanned combat aerial vehicles of the present. Indeed, in the immediate aftermath of the First World War, both Douhet and Mitchell speculated that airplanes would soon fly without pilots and would be controlled by radio signals, transforming the conduct of fighting war at a distance. In particular, Douhet and Mitchell predicted that aerial warfare would erase the distinction between civilians and combatants entirely. In doing so, they anticipated one hundred years ago the central dilemma of contemporary remote warfare: in the twenty-first century, the U.S. military justifies drone warfare on the grounds that it can precisely target the enemy, but that still leaves an essential problem largely unsolved, which is how to distinguish the enemy from the other people among whom he or she lives. The expansion of drone warfare in the twenty-first century, Zeitlin concludes, repeatedly affirms the rightness of their predictions.

In many ways, Douhet and Mitchell prefigured the questions that David Buchanan addresses in the next chapter, in which he analyzes the image of the warrior that has solidified in American literature since September 11, 2001. This preferred image and narrative of war, he argues, completes a traditional scapegoat cycle in which the warrior absolves the nation of its guilt for violence. However, Buchanan notes that this vision of a traditional warrior—one who goes to war and is wounded vicariously for a hungry audience—may be incompatible with the remoteness of modern warfare and the ethics of contemporary warrior behavior. Himself a distance-based warrior in the U.S. Air Force, Buchanan explores a recent trend in American war literature: the attempt to borrow from Native American warrior societies and purification rituals. Such appropriation, it seems, reflects a dire need in American war culture to update a warrior ethos as the warrior moves farther and farther away from the warzone. Buchanan closes with an analysis of N. Scott Momaday's *House Made of Dawn* and the U.S. Air Force Academy's new warrior ethos curriculum. In the end, Buchanan wonders "whether a more democratic and realistic approach to the representation of war experience is one that refuses to privilege combat witness at all" and so expands our conceptualizations of warriors beyond the narrow frame of violence.

While Buchanan emphasizes the lived experience of making war from a distance, Jens Borrebye Bjering and Andreas Immanuel Graae interrogate academic and popular epistemes of remote warfare via an analysis of *Homeland,* perhaps the most iconic popular depiction of American antiterrorist work. The series follows a young female CIA agent, Carrie Mathison, and Bjering and Graae track its evolution. Over the course of its first four seasons, the show that began by problematizing the interpretation of an archive of raw, homeland security–related intelligence transformed into a text that problematizes the intelligence archive itself. Bjering and Graae interpret this development as a reaction to the new challenges faced by the intelligence community in the age of population-scale computerized surveillance. To do this work, they employ Jacques Derrida's theorization of the archive in *Archive Fever: A Freudian Impression* and argue that present-day intelligence operations have abandoned any attempt at a hermeneutic approach to the interpretation of potentially vital pieces of data. Instead, Bjering and Graae demonstrate that new intelligence practices substitute interpretation with something more sinister: the destruction of any data point that might, now or in the future, turn out to be even remotely threatening to the security or interests of the United States. The story arc of *Homeland* reveals that this predatorial strategy of instant destruction is intimately connected to the ability to conduct remote airstrikes at will anywhere on the planet, making the drone into an anti-hermeneutic tool that destroys, rather than interprets, archives.

Nike Nivar Ortiz offers the section's final analysis of a vision of remote warfare, that generated by a development unfolding alongside the evolution that Bjering and Graae document: the movement of military-borne surveillance technologies into the domestic sphere. In this chapter, Ortiz focuses on Persistent Surveillance Systems, a private company founded in 2004, and notes that its military-grade persistent surveillance tools have been implemented on a trial basis in cities like Ciudad Juárez, Mexico; Baltimore, Maryland; Dayton, Ohio; and Compton, California. The commercial success of these military technologies in the domestic sector entails heavy costs for marginalized groups, as they have mostly been deployed in urban areas with large populations of people of color. Perhaps the most troubling aspect of this deployment, Ortiz argues, is that these surveillance technologies run on sophisticated algorithms that are beyond civilian comprehension. In essence, they calculate criminality within an expansive field of vision and based on the algorithmic analysis of data that would otherwise be unnoticeable or seem insignificant to the human eye or mind. Ortiz's theorization reveals that tools like persistent surveillance technology not only affect the day-to-day lives of people but also reconfigure an individual's social contract with the state. Ultimately, Ortiz asks readers to consider the political and cultural challenges that arise when military technology originally developed to battle enemies abroad becomes so easily translatable to the supposedly "friendly" domestic sphere. For Ortiz, this translation compels us to ask, What does it mean to be a citizen in the twenty-first century? And how is it different from being an enemy of the state?

Taken together, the chapters in "Visions" reveal the myriad actors involved in the work of imagining remote warfare, and the variegated conceptions of it that result from these processes. "Intimacies," the second section, charts the sometimes unexpected relationships and connections engendered by remote warfare, a degree of interactivity belied by the term itself. Confronting, and undermining, common critical presumptions about the distancing effects of remote warfare, chapters in this section instead consider the forms of proximity it creates. First, Michael Richardson explores the possibility that drone interfaces generate affective connections between operator and target, noting that research into drone warfare operations and their consequences for pilots has largely debunked the mythology of a video game mentality that lends itself to reflexive violence. Despite this, however, Richardson argues that this vision of drone warfare continues to possess a cultural currency that muddies the ground for debate about its costs and consequences. The surface similarities between killing by drone and gaming—the view through a screen, the controllers that drive the interfaces, the pressing of a button to fire—obscure the crucial differences and disjunctures that sever the sutures binding drone warfare and video games. This chapter addresses the processes of mediation within intimately distant acts of killing, their entanglement with video games, and the ways in which traumatic affects generate, circulate, and manifest in gaming responses to drone warfare. It does so by analyzing two serious games—*Killbox* (DeLappe and Biome Collective 2015) and *Unmanned* (Molleindustria and Munroe 2012)—to show how each deploys gaming techniques and aesthetics to tease out the nuanced mediations and traumatic affects inherent to remote war. As Richardson unknots drones and games, he reveals a clearer picture of how drone warfare operates, a view that enables a more precise accounting for the affective tensions and paradoxes through which publics understand this mode of war and participants experience it.

Keeping with the question of the relationship between realities and representations of remote warfare, Tim Jelfs turns to depictions of lethal violence in American literature and uses these to anchor an actor-network theory–inspired critical analysis of the concept of remote war. Drawing on the work of leading ANT theorist Bruno Latour, Jelfs ranges widely across the canon of modern American war writing and cultural history. He proposes that contemporary accounts of the distancing effects of remote war may fail to do justice to the complexity of interactions between the humans and nonhumans that wage it. Instead, Jelfs suggests that the networks of the human and nonhuman rendered in American war writing from Mark Twain to Tim O'Brien more closely approximate reality. These texts reveal that the relationship between humans and the nonhuman means they have devised for killing is best understood as a dialectic of the remote and the intimate. Moreover, Jelfs argues that unorthodox examples of war writing—such as Officer Darren Wilson's 2014 grand jury testimony detailing the killing of Michael Brown on the streets of Ferguson, Missouri—demonstrate that war itself may be far less "remote" from the United States than Americans sometimes imagine.

In her reading of the vast archive of cultural and media production around the killing of Osama bin Laden, Annika Brunck queries the various kinds of remoteness—a concept she expands beyond its technological implications to include spatial, cultural, and psychological dimensions—operative within them. She analyzes the roles that narratives of finding and capturing bin Laden have played in discourses of remote warfare in general and the War on Terror in particular. She situates the wars initiated by the George W. Bush administration in response to the 9/11 attacks as a case of remote warfare but considers, like Jelfs, how impressions and relations of remoteness were actively constructed. Brunck traces how narratives about bin Laden as evil mastermind initially worked to counteract the remoteness inherent in the War on Terror, thus preserving public support for the campaign. She then goes on to argue that, as the years went on and bin Laden remained elusive, this discursive strategy no longer worked, making the remoteness of the War on Terror visible and opening it up for criticism. Ultimately, the chapter shows that the successful killing of bin Laden in 2011 briefly collapsed the paradigm of remote warfare only to paradoxically affirm it afterward.

While the preceding chapters in this section trace various constructions of remoteness, the final chapter of "Intimacies" departs from the American context to trace the formation of the "veteran"—a figure complicated by the dialectics of remoteness and intimacy that define contemporary wars—as a legible social category in Denmark. To do this work, Ann-Katrine S. Nielsen explores these relations in contemporary literature by Danish veterans. Nielsen begins from the premise that as Danish foreign policies have been increasingly (re)militarized during the 1990s and 2000s, the veteran has emerged as a unique figure. She focuses her analysis on two prominent texts. The first is the novel *Mikael* (2014), by Dy Plambeck, an author, journalist who reported from Afghanistan, and partner of a veteran. The second is a collection of poems, *Så efterlades alt flæskende* (2014), by Iraq veteran Mikkel Brixvold. Nielsen argues that these texts forge an encounter with the war as something other and more than a remote (media) spectacle. By focusing on embodiment and affective encounters, these texts raise the specter of war in a gesture that haunts the returned veteran but also the reader and a Danish nation-state hesitantly adjusting to its new role as a belligerent. These works reveal that the (post)war experience cannot be contained by the body of the individual veteran but perpetually seeps into civil society.

Cataloging the diverse relationships inaugurated by remote warfare—beyond those that arise directly between the killer and the killed—the chapters in "Intimacies" reckon with their cultural consequences. Chapters in the final section, "Reconfigurations," build from this inventory to develop analyses that contradict determinist frameworks for understanding remote warfare, offering instead reconfigurations that chart forms of resistance, protest, and creativity that arise in its interstices. These analyses attend directly to the suffering that remote warfare causes but seek to foreground the myriad ways that people who live under that violence engage with and survive it. First, Syed Irfan Ashraf and Kristen Shamas offer an ethnographic account of the prevalence of death within geographies subjected to remote warfare. Ashraf and Shamas utilize critical and phenomenological perspectives on communication (processes of constructing shared meaning) to examine two case studies of remote warfare in which this meaning-making nexus around space, bodies, and death was necropolitical. In these two case studies—aerial bombardment and cluster munitions in Lebanon (2006–8), and drone warfare in Pakistan (2008)—remote warfare operated to maintain a deathly regime over which bodies could be destroyed with impunity. They examine the operations of necropolitics that construct certain spaces as terrains where inhabitants can permissibly be killed. Notably, in comparing the processes of necrospatialization and resistance in the two case studies, they detect nothing novel or unique about the necrospatializing capacity of drones. Their study of the efforts by residents of those places to resist subjugation uncovers a mixed record of resistance and the possibility that endeavors to communicate, mediate, and make meanings around death might also advance necropolitics.

Owen Coggins, in the next chapter, also queries the mixed outcomes of protest against remote warfare as he examines ambivalent representations of violence in sonic antidrone activism. Specifically, Coggins investigates the politics of a series of performances and protests in which artists and activists used droning music, sound, or noise to protest military or surveillance drones. Exploring the concept of sonic "target audiences," the chapter considers sound and technology in contemporary mediascapes that confuse and conflate entertainment technology and mediated warfare. Coggins argues that drone music can create a powerful field of ambivalent ambience in sound, mobilizing confusion and failure to produce a potential aura of critical unease in the absence of clear moral definition. Yet he also notes that these resistant actions are drawn into this vagueness and uncertainty. Analyzing five protests staged between 2013 and 2015, Coggins argues that performers' and protesters' appeals to the homonymic different meanings of the word *drone,* along with other juxtapositions, highlight moral binaries. Moreover, he contends that drone sound provided an accessible way for symbolic communities to form as they turned aspects of war machines, including recordings of the sounds they make, against war. Throughout, noise was mobilized to evoke a sense of ineffability and unease, or of disruption. Coggins ultimately proposes the concept of "resistant ambi(val)ence" as a way to understand this atmosphere of unease and its mixed resistant potential.

While these protests are typically organized by civilian actors, Brittany Hirth turns to warfighters' perspectives and their strategies for resisting media depictions of the battles they fight. Hirth resurrects the absurd tradition as a lens to read two soldiers' personal narratives: Anthony Swofford's *Jarhead* (2003) and Chris Kyle's *American Sniper* (2012). Hirth argues that the narrative techniques of parody and black humor, two features of the absurd literary tradition, might enable veterans to write of battle traumas that would be inexpressible in conventional language. Swofford parodies the media's televised portrayal of the technologically precise, "clean" Persian Gulf War, which does not reflect the collateral damage of bombing that he witnessed, and employs black humor to emphasize the threat of death that lingered despite the war's being conducted mostly by air. Similarly, Kyle's memoir of his time as the most "lethal sniper in U.S military history," during which he operated in tandem with airstrikes in the Iraq War, reflects the same conventions of the absurd tradition in his parodying of war as a game and the black humor that enables him to cope with writing about battle experience. This reading of the parody and black humor within Swofford's and Kyle's narratives illuminates the ethical stakes of the Gulf War and the Iraq War, juxtaposing the media's sanitized portrayal of these conflicts to the humor that provides an emotional analgesic for the veteran compelled to write his or her story.

While Hirth weighs the affordances and limitations of the absurd as counter to the violence of remote warfare, Sajdeep Soomal's closing chapter explores the possibilities of the fanciful, weighing two visions of an architecture against drones and an uncovering of the racial, architectural logics that underpin the subcontinental postcolony. Soomal examines two texts. The first is an Urdu-language folkloric cartoon titled "Kabhi Drone, Kabhi Dengue" (Sometimes drone, sometimes dengue) that stages a conversation between a dengue-carrying mosquito and an American Predator drone. The second is Shura City, an experimental architectural proposal for a drone-proof smart city by new media feminist artist Hiba Ali and architect Asher J. Kohn.

Reading the folkloric cartoon, Soomal asks what lessons we might derive from the unlikely encounter between the mosquito and the drone. Demonstrating how new threats to the postcolony and its citizenry resonate with older state-structuring antagonisms, he inquires whether we can find shelter from the drone in the postcolony without reproducing the paradigmatic figure of the terrorizing *dacoit*. In the second half of the essay, Soomal thinks with Ali and Kohn to consider how paradigms of speculation, securitization, extraction, privacy, and surveillance are endemic to contemporary building-development projects. Studying the artists' satirical, corporate video pitch for Shura City, he shows how the drone-proof smart city can quickly turn into its own techno-securitized, neoliberal state—one that is destined to replicate the same structuring logics as the old postcolony. An architecture against drones quickly turns into an architecture against *dacoits*.

The chapters in "Reconfigurations" do not idealize the cultural practices and productions that they describe but instead provide an assessment of their transformative potentials alongside an accounting of the ways they might be constrained by the structural violences of remote warfare. Taken together, these chapters prompt us to consider what remote warfare means for those who wage it and those who endure it, whether they reside in the United States or abroad. Variously, they ask, What are the cultural preconditions for remote warfare? How does living with remote warfare transform the cultures that perpetrate it or suffer under it? How might cultural production capture or obscure the experience of remote warfare? How are audiences and spectators implicated in remote warfare by their consumption of its artifacts? To what extent can cultural production offset, impede, or resist the violence of remote warfare? As they build on an emerging body of research, they point to the necessity of continually engaging those questions, and hint at novel strategies for pursuing that work.

Presumably, given the increasing separation between civilian and military populations in the United States, most of this book's readers will only ever experience remote warfare in a mediated way, as spectators, consumers of media or popular culture, which leaves us powerless and empowered at once. Yet it is equally likely that the enduring centrality of militarism to U.S. culture and foreign policy means that remote warfare will continue apace, even as it evolves to embrace new technologies and unfold in new geographies. A willingness to work in and through this uncertainty is thus a necessary hedge against our complicity in forms of violence to which we might object. By refusing the appeal of the easiest solution to these problems, these authors point to new directions for inquiry, creativity, and—if we are so inclined—resistance.

Notes

1. "President Trump Delivers Remarks to Members of the Military," Federal News Service, March 13, 2018; Claudia Grisales, "With Congressional Blessing, Space Force Is Closer to Launch," National Public Radio, August 11, 2019, https://www.npr.org/2019/08/11/743612373/with-congressional-blessing-space-force-is-closer-to-launch.

2. "Democrats Blast Republicans for Shutting Down Trump-Russia Probe; Interview with California Congressman Eric Swalwell; Trump Examines Border Wall Prototypes in California; President Trump Fires Rex Tillerson; Trump: 'Something Very Positive Could Happen' with North Korea," *The Situation Room,* CNN, March 13, 2018.

3. Elizabeth Howell, "Trump's Space Force Push Reopens Arguments about Military in Space," Space.com, June 20, 2018, https://www.space.com/40942-trump-space-force-reopens-military-debate.html. See also "Remarks by President Trump at a Meeting with the National Space Council and Signing of Space Policy Directive-3," White House, June 18, 2018, https://www.whitehouse.gov/briefings-statements/remarks-president-trump-meeting-national-space-council-signing-space-policy-directive-3/.

4. White House Gift Shop, "#4 Coin Pre-order, Space Force, Historic Moments in World History Coin Collection, Title: President Donald J. Trump," White House, 2018, https://www.whitehousegiftshop.com/product-p/space-force-coin.htm; Gina Martinez, "President Trump's Campaign Is Asking Supporters to Vote on a Space Force Logo," *Time,* August 9, 2018, http://time.com/5363058/donald-trump-campaign-space-force-logo/.

5. "In Trump's Universe, Everyone Loves 'Space Force,'" *Daily Show,* Comedy Central, June 26, 2018, http://www.cc.com/video-clips/7bw209/the-daily-show-with-trevor-noah-in-trump-s-universe--everyone-loves--space-force-.

6. According to the *Times,* this capacity that would have potentially catastrophic ramifications for "aircraft carriers in the Persian Gulf, drones in the skies above Yemen and fighter jets over Syria[, and] American ground troops on patrol in Afghanistan." Helene Cooper, "Pence Advances Plan to Create a Space Force," *New York Times,* August 9, 2018, https://www.nytimes.com/2018/08/09/us/politics/trump-pence-space-force.html. A year later, National Public Radio quoted Secretary of Defense Mark Esper's comment that space "is now a

warfighting domain. Not because we made it that way but because the Russians and Chinese are making it that way." Grisales, "With Congressional Blessing."

7. Jacqueline Feldscher, "Trump Establishes New Military Space Command," *Politico,* August 29, 2019, https://www.politico.com/story/2019/08/29/trump -military-space-command-1693825.

8. Howell, "Trump's Space Force."

9. Howell, "Trump's Space Force"; Dwight D. Eisenhower, "Statement by the President on Releasing the Science Advisory Committee's 'Introduction to Outer Space,'" March 26, 1958, American Presidency Project, https://www.presidency .ucsb.edu/node/234597; Dwight D. Eisenhower, "Special Message to the Congress Relative to Space Science and Exploration," April 2, 1958, American Presidency Project, https://www.presidency.ucsb.edu/node/234638; Cooper, "Pence Advances Plan"; Howell, "Trump's Space Force."

10. Sarah Kaplan, "Trump Floats Idea of 'Space Force,'" *Washington Post,* March 13, 2018, https://www.washingtonpost.com/news/speaking-of-science/wp /2018/03/13/trump-floats-idea-of-space-force/. For discussion of this treaty, see Dana J. Johnson, "The Impact of International Law and Treaty Obligation on United States Military Activities in Space," *High Technology Law Journal* 3, no. 1 (1988), 33–80; and Senate Subcommittee on Space, Science, and Competitiveness, *Reopening the American Frontier: Exploring How the Outer Space Treaty Will Impact American Commerce and Settlement in Space,* 115th Congress, 1st session (2017), https://www.govinfo.gov/content/pkg/CHRG-115shrg29998/pdf /CHRG-115shrg29998.pdf.

11. Cooper, "Pence Advances Plan"; Howell, "Trump's Space Force"; Ronald Reagan, "Statement by Principal Deputy Press Secretary Speakes on Antisatellite Weapons Testing," August 20, 1985, American Presidency Project, https:// www.presidency.ucsb.edu/node/260454. For a similar perspective from an official in the Reagan administration defense department, see William E. Furniss, "President Reagan's Strategic Defense Initiative," *University of Toledo Law Review* 16 (1984): 149–55. For one example of the political debate over the Strategic Defense Initiative, see Jeffrey R. Smith, "Reagan Announces a New ASAT Test," *Science,* September 6, 1985, 946; and Sidney D. Drell, Philip J. Farley, and David Holloway, "The Reagan Strategic Defense Initiative: A Technical and Strategic Appraisal," *Arms Control Today* 14, no. 6 (1984): 12. For a cultural history of American interests in such weapons, see H. Bruce Franklin, *War Stars: The Superweapon and the American Imagination* (Amherst: University of Massachusetts Press, 2008).

12. Kaplan, "Trump Floats Idea"; "X-37B Orbital Test Vehicle," U.S. Air Force, September 1, 2018, https://www.af.mil/About-Us/Fact-Sheets/Display/Article /104539/x-37b-orbital-test-vehicle/; Mike Wall, "Gotcha! US Air Force's Secretive X-37B Space Plane Spotted by Satellite Tracker," Space.com, August 21, 2018, https://www.space.com/41565-x-37b-space-plane-skywatcher-photos-otv5 .html; and Kiona Smith-Strickland, "What's the X-37 Doing up There? The Air Force Isn't Saying, So We Asked Other Spaceplane Experts," *Air and Space,* February 2016, https://www.airspacemag.com/space/spaceplane-x-37-180957777/.

According to Smith-Strickland, "It's clear that any technologies tested [aboard] will have some military application."

13. Feldscher, "Trump Establishes."

14. Elaine Scarry, *The Body in Pain: The Making and Unmaking of the World* (Oxford: Oxford University Press, 1985), 89. Scarry notes that this fact is often elided in "strategic and political depictions of war" (12).

15. Fernando Echeverria Rey, "Weapons, Technological Determinism, and Ancient Warfare," in *New Perspectives on Ancient Warfare,* ed. Garrett G. Fagan and Matthew Trundle (Leiden: Brill, 2010), 22.

16. Rey, 23.

17. Rey, 21.

18. Rey, 22.

19. Chuck Lyons, "Simple but Deadly: In the Century before Guns, the Longbow Brought a Lethal Efficiency to Medieval Warfare and Gave England an Early Advantage in the Hundred Years' War," *MHQ: The Quarterly Journal of Military History* 22, no. 4 (2010): 10–11; Andrew Ayton, "Arms, Armour, and Horses," in *Medieval Warfare: A History,* ed. Maurice Keen (Oxford: Oxford University Press, 1999), 205.

20. Robert P. Broadwater, *Civil War Special Forces: The Elite and Distinct Fighting Units of the Union and Confederate Armies* (Santa Barbara, Calif.: Praeger, 2014), 88, 92. Historian Earl J. Hess, for example, explains that if the rifles' "increased range led contemporaries to predict revolutionary changes in warfare" and "historians later accepted this view and established it as a standard interpretation in Civil War historiography," what is in fact the case is that however far such rifles *could* shoot, "fighting usually took place at very close ranges during the Civil War, far less than is required to argue that the long-range capability of the rifle musket was felt in combat." That is, Hess rejects the technological determinist claim. Earl J. Hess, *Civil War Infantry Tactics: Training, Combat, and Small-Unit Effectiveness* (Baton Rouge: Louisiana State University Press, 2015), xi–xii. Hess takes up this controversy at length in *The Rifle Musket in Civil War Combat: Reality and Myth* (Lawrence: University of Kansas Press, 2015).

21. Tami Davis Biddle, *Rhetoric and Reality in Air Warfare: The Evolution of British and American Ideas about Strategic Bombing, 1914–1945* (Princeton, N.J.: Princeton University Press, 2004), 3. According to Biddle, the ways that the United States and the United Kingdom have answered those questions remained contentious for scholars throughout the twentieth century. She writes, "Controversy and emotional intensity have always surrounded the very concept of long-range or 'strategic' bombing. The concept implies that aircraft carrying bombs to an enemy's 'vital centers' can undermine its ability and will to fight. The idea is simple enough, yet few other claims about military power have provoked so many debates, or aroused so much intensity of feeling, both inside and outside the military" (2–3).

22. Biddle, 238, 239–44.

23. Gian Gentile, *How Effective Is Strategic Bombing? Lessons Learned from World War II to Kosovo* (New York: New York University Press, 2001), 169.

24. Thomas A. Keaney and Eliot A. Cohen, *Gulf War Air Power Survey Summary Report* (Washington, D.C.: U.S. Government Printing Office, 1993), ix, https://apps.dtic.mil/dtic/tr/fulltext/u2/a273996.pdf; Gian P. Gentile, *How Effective Is Strategic Bombing? Lessons Learned from World War II to Kosovo* (New York: New York University Press, 2000), 169, 188.

25. See, for example, Wesley K. Clark, *Waging Modern War: Bosnia, Kosovo and the Future of Combat* (New York: Public Affairs, 2002), 432. See also Clark, 117, 424. Biddle concludes, "it is probably too early to judge the efficacy of precision air attack as a political tool" (*Rhetoric and Reality*, 300). Gentile is more critical, arguing that "the American-dominated NATO air campaign over Yugoslavia demonstrates that problems still exist with the use of strategic bombing in war and conflict" (*How Effective?*, 191).

26. Dave Grossman, *On Killing: The Psychological Cost of Learning to Kill in War and Society* (New York: Back Bay Books, 2009), 107.

27. Grossman, 107–8.

28. Grossman, 108.

29. See, for example, Wayne L. Chappelle et al., "Symptoms of Psychological Distress and Post-traumatic Stress Disorder in United States Air Force 'Drone' Operators," *Military Medicine* 179, no. 8 (2014): 63–70; and Chappelle et al., "An Analysis of Post-traumatic Stress Symptoms in United States Air Force Drone Operators," *Journal of Anxiety Disorders* 28, no. 5 (2018): 480–87.

30. On the "voyeuristic intimacy" that drone operators feel with their targets, see Matthew Power, "Confessions of a Drone Warrior," *GQ*, October 23, 2013, https://www.gq.com/story/drone-uav-pilot-assassination.

31. "'Will I Be Next?' U.S. Drone Strikes in Pakistan," Amnesty International, October 21, 2013, https://www.amnestyusa.org/reports/will-i-be-next-us-drone-strikes-in-pakistan/.

32. Robert Greenwald, dir., *Unmanned: America's Drone Wars* (Culver City, Calif.: Brave New Films, 2013).

33. James Igoe Walsh and Marcus Schulzke, *Drones and Support for the Use of Force* (Ann Arbor: University of Michigan Press, 2018), 3, 6.

34. Peter L. Bergen and Daniel Rothenberg, eds., *Drone Wars: Transforming Conflict, Law, and Policy* (New York: Cambridge University Press, 2015). Bradley J. Strawser, ed., *Killing by Remote Control: The Ethics of an Unmanned Military* (Oxford: Oxford University Press, 2013), has a similar overall effect.

35. Doubtless, *Drone Wars* makes a novel contribution by including personal narratives from people directly affected by drone warfare, whether as perpetrators or targets. Yet even as these autobiographical accounts add crucial detail and complexity to theoretical debates, they may also stymie the process of making intellectual decisions about how to proceed, because personal experience can be so rhetorically unassailable.

36. Grégoire Chamayou, *A Theory of the Drone*, trans. Janet Lloyd (New York: New Press, 2013), 17.

37. Consequently, many scholars inspired by Chamayou tend to seek remedies for the violent excesses of drone warfare in alternative practices of meaning

making, such as art. See, for example, Kathrin Maurer, "Visual Power: The Scopic Regime of Military Drone Operations," *Media, War and Conflict* 10, no. 2 (2017): 141–51.

38. Chamayou, *Theory of the Drone*, 71.

39. Chamayou, 77, 107.

40. Power, "Confessions of a Drone Warrior."

41. Currently, the active-duty U.S. military numbers 1.29 million people, which amounts to less than 0.5 percent of the population. "Demographics of the U.S. Military," Council on Foreign Relations, April 24, 2018, https://www.cfr.org/article/demographics-us-military.

42. Mary L. Dudziak, *Wartime: An Idea, Its History, and Its Consequences* (Oxford: Oxford University Press, 2012), 132. See also David Kieran, *Signature Wounds: The Untold Story of the Military's Mental Health Crisis* (New York: New York University Press, 2019), 89.

43. Andrew Bacevich, *Breach of Trust: How Americans Failed Their Soldiers and Their Country* (New York: Metropolitan Books, 2013), 13.

44. Lyons, "Simple but Deadly," 10–11. See also D. J. Gallo, "Unfriendly Confines: The Unsung History of America's Low-Key Hooliganism," *Guardian*, October 18, 2017, https://www.theguardian.com/sport/blog/2017/oct/18/unfriendly-confines-the-unsung-history-of-americas-low-key-hooliganism; "Obama's Speech on Drone Policy," *New York Times*, May 23, 2013, https://www.nytimes.com/2013/05/24/us/politics/transcript-of-obamas-speech-on-drone-policy.html.

45. Importantly, some researchers have begun to think beyond conventional questions about, methodologies for studying, and intellectual framings of drone warfare, a development that we hope will expand thinking on remote warfare more generally. These scholars have cleared new and crucial intellectual space for the work of this collection, which theorizes remote warfare as an experience that has been foreshadowed, abetted, and contested through cultural production. As we conceptualized this collection and worked with the authors, we were inspired by the work of Jamie Allinson, Peter Asaro, Keith Feldman, Caren Kaplan, Lisa Parks, and Ian Shaw, among others. Jamie Allinson invokes the concept of necropolitics to recenter the matters of race and colonialism into conversations on drone warfare; Jamie Allinson, "The Necropolitics of Drones," *International Political Sociology* 9, no. 2 (2015): 113–27. Peter Asaro asks crucial questions about the conditions under which drone operators labor in an attempt to capture the particularities of the "bureaucratized killing" that they undertake; Peter M. Asaro, "The Labor of Surveillance and Bureaucratized Killing: New Subjectivities of Military Drone Operators," *Social Semiotics* 23, no. 2 (2013): 196–224. Keith Feldman critiques the turn toward humanitarian visual practices, as evidenced in the art installation *Not a Bug Splat*, in antidrone activism; Keith P. Feldman, "#Notabugsplat: Becoming Human on the Terrain of Visual Culture," in *The Routledge Companion to Literature and Human Rights*, ed. Sophia McClennen and Alexandra Schultheis Moore (London: Routledge, 2016), 224–32. Ian Shaw theorizes technologies like drones and surveillance systems as elements of an emerging machine-driven Leviathan; Ian G. R. Shaw, *Predator*

Empire: Drone Warfare and Full Spectrum Dominance (Minneapolis: University of Minnesota Press, 2016). Lastly, Lisa Parks and Caren Kaplan describe their approach to the edited collection *Life in the Age of Drone Warfare* as "critical humanities, post-structuralist, and feminist," and the text reveals the potential of such conceptual and methodological frameworks; Lisa Parks and Caren Kaplan, introduction to *Life in the Age of Drone Warfare*, ed. Lisa Parks and Caren Kaplan (Durham, N.C.: Duke University Press, 2017), 7.

46. Joseph Masco, *The Theater of Operations: National Security Affect from the Cold War to the War on Terror* (Durham, N.C.: Duke University Press, 2014), 196, 36.

47. Alison Williams speaks, for example, of a "reality gap between the discursive rendering of UAVs [unmanned aerial vehicles] as omnipresent and the active requirement for a corporeal element within this assemblage." Alison J. Williams, "Enabling Persistent Presence? Performing the Embodied Geopolitics of the Unmanned Aerial Vehicle Assemblage," *Political Geography* 30 (2011): 385.

48. P. W. Singer, *Wired for War: The Robotics Revolution and Conflict in the 21st Century* (New York: Penguin, 2009); Adam Rothstein, *Drone* (New York: Bloomsbury, 2015).

49. Rothstein, 113.

50. Kevin McSorley, "Towards an Embodied Sociology of War," *Sociological Review* 62, Suppl. 2 (2014): 108. McSorley also addresses the question of embodiment in drone warfare (120–21).

51. Christine Sylvester, *War as Experience: Contributions from International Relations and Feminist Analysis* (New York: Routledge, 2013), 5.

52. See, for example, Sarah Maltby, "The Dis/embodiment of Persuasive Military Discourse," *Journal of War and Culture Studies* 5, no. 1 (2012): 33–46. Maltby focuses on the NATO practice of Psy Ops leafleting, which we might think of as a softer form of remote warfare.

53. For a consideration of the sensory intimacies begotten by occupation, see Gil Z. Hochberg, *Visual Occupations: Violence and Visibility in a Conflict Zone* (Durham, N.C.: Duke University Press, 2015).

54. On the ways that the presence of enemies animates the political life of the state, see Carl Schmitt, *The Concept of the Political,* 1932, trans. George Schwab (Chicago: University of Chicago Press, 2007).

55. Carlo Galli, "On War and the Enemy," *CR: The New Continental Review* 9, no. 2 (Fall 2009): 208.

56. For example, reflecting on the rise of so-called domestic terrorists, Piotr Szpunar notes a shift in discourse and representation, observing that these figures used to be constructed as readily identifiable and ineluctably different "others" but are now increasingly depicted as "doubles" for regular citizens, virtually impossible to identify until it is too late. Piotr M. Szpunar, "From the Other to the Double: Identity in Conflict and the Boston Marathon Bombing," *Communication, Culture and Critique* 9, no. 4 (2016): 577–94.

57. On the debate over Agent Orange, see Edwin A. Martini, *Agent Orange: History, Science, and the Politics of Uncertainty* (Amherst: University of

Massachusetts Press, 2012), esp. 197–237. On traumatic brain injury, see J. Martin Daughtry, "Thanatosonics," *Social Text* 32, no. 2 (2014): 25–51. Daughtry argues that the damaging power of sound in warfare provides a phenomenological and embodied link between the perpetrators and victims of this kind of violence. Traumatic brain injury from blast exposure is caused by pressure waves; these also travel indiscriminately.

58. Thomas Hippler, *Governing from the Skies: A Global History of Aerial Bombing,* trans. David Fernback (London: Verso, 2017). The kinds of nuanced and expansive views of aerial targeting and its ideological, geopolitical, and legal frameworks that collections like *From Above: War, Violence, and Verticality* provide are crucial touchstones for our thinking about this book. Peter Adey, Mark Whitehead, and Alison J. Williams, eds., *From Above: War, Violence, and Verticality* (Oxford: Oxford University Press, 2013).

59. Caren Kaplan, *Aerial Aftermaths: Wartime from Above* (Durham, N.C.: Duke University Press, 2018), 22.

PART I

VISIONS

CHAPTER 1

"An Entirely New Method of Conducting War at a Distance"

The First World War and the
Air War of the Future

MICHAEL ZEITLIN

> The attempt . . . has been made by many peoples in many ages to
> injure or destroy an enemy by injuring or destroying an image of
> him, in the belief that, just as the image suffers, so does the man,
> and that when it perishes he must die. . . . This belief in the
> sympathetic influence exerted on each other by persons or things
> at a distance is of the essence of magic.
>
> —James Frazer, *The Golden Bough* (1922)

> Nor can the battlefield any longer be limited to actual combatants.
>
> —Giulio Douhet in 1921

Giulio Douhet, Billy Mitchell, and the Prehistory of Drones

Any genealogy of contemporary drone warfare is traceable to the
prophecies and premonitions of the era of the First World War and the
desire to kill a distant enemy from a remote location. This desire is fundamental to the work of two major aviation theorists of the early
twentieth century, the original visionaries of our unmanned combat
aerial vehicles (drones). Giulio Douhet (1869–1930), Italian general and
head of aviation, published *The Command of the Air* (1921) while serving in Benito Mussolini's Ministry of War.[1] His book on "the probable
aspects of the war of the future" was translated into French, German,
Russian, and English and "widely disseminated in western military

establishments" throughout the 1920s and 1930s.[2] An American edition of Douhet's treatise appeared in 1942 and was reissued in 1983 by the Office of Air Force History in its series USAF Warrior Studies, the editors noting the institution's long-standing engagement with Douhet's work: "A translation of *The Command of the Air* was available at the Air Service Tactical school as early as 1923."[3]

Douhet's American counterpart, William ("Billy") Mitchell (1879–1936), widely regarded as the father of the U.S. Air Force, published *Winged Defense: The Development and Possibilities of Modern Air Power—Economic and Military* in 1925. This is a detailed vision, inspired by Douhet, of how "great contests for control of the air will be the rule in the future."[4] Such contests would include (as he accurately predicted) "area bombing" by "great masses of airplanes"; ground-strafing operations flown by specially designed, heavily armored, low-flying aircraft; the ever-increasing power of air-dropped explosives; and the free deployment of incendiaries and poison gases. Preserving the safety of the pilot was a paramount anxiety in such scenarios. A veteran combat aviator himself, Mitchell foresaw a battle sky filled with pilotless, all-metal aircraft squadrons remotely controlled by radio signals (see later in this chapter).[5]

Douhet and Mitchell also foresaw and fully accepted a major new consequence of the coming air war. As airplanes increase their capacity to carry tons of bombs into the air, precision bombing would give way to "area," "saturation," "carpet," and "shuttle" bombing.[6] Technical advances in aviation physics and engineering would sanction this wider definition of the terrestrial target, a matter affecting both tactics and politics. As Douhet's and Mitchell's British disciple Major Oliver Stewart put the matter in 1936, "There is no aspect of modern warfare about which politicians and people in the Services are less inclined to speak openly than the line of demarcation between what is and what is not a legitimate bombing objective."[7] For Stewart, Douhet, and Mitchell, the future of airborne munitions would erase this "line of demarcation" completely. The targets of aerial bombardment would include not only factories, railways, and troop compounds but whole urban areas, some expanding to the borders of the metropolis itself. The global air war of the future, that is, would entail the killing of massive numbers of civilians who, in being members of the nation-state at war, would no longer be thought of as innocent. As Stewart impatiently explains, "There can be no doubt that a town in any industrial civilization, is a military objective: it provides the sinews of war; it houses those who direct the war; it is a nexus of communications; it is a centre of propaganda; and it is a seat of government . . . the aerial bombardment of open towns will probably, almost certainly, be a feature of any future war."[8] Douhet had grasped this aspect of realpolitik more than a decade earlier: "Do not believe that tomorrow the enemy will make any distinction between military forces and the civilian population."[9] Nor will total war's imperial expansion of the battlespace be limited to "industrial civilizations." It will also extend to "air operations connected with the military campaigns in Egypt, Sinai, the Western Desert, Darfur, Palestine, Arabia, Mesopotamia, and in Macedonia."[10]

The American wars in Iraq, Afghanistan, Yemen, and elsewhere continue to demonstrate the reach of such early twentieth-century conceptions of aerial warfare into "the colonial present."[11] In what follows, I explore the extent to which the aerial tactics of the current drone campaigns of the Forever War on Terror are continuous with this expansion of the battlespace and this erosion of "the line of demarcation between what is and what is not a legitimate bombing objective." The current dream of "target selection perfected to the point of assassination" can do little, in fact, to control or restrain the centrifugal effects and indiscriminate lethality of aerial assaults.[12]

Radial physics, images, and patterns are fundamental to Douhet's and Mitchell's conception of surveillance, reconnaissance, and preemptive attacking power as only the air force can sustain and project it. If, for Mitchell after the First World War, "the former isolation of the United States is a thing of the past" given the enemy's imminent ability to fly its bombers across the ocean, "the only defense against aircraft is by hitting the enemy first." He notes, "All of the great countries of the world are now organizing their air power for striking their adversaries as far away from their own countries as possible."[13] In order to prepare itself for this new reality, the nation needed to extend its power of surveillance far beyond its own borders in a web of "aviation centers" linked by "wireless telegraphy": "Radiating out from these aviation centers are listening and operation posts all along their coasts and even out at sea, so that any hostile aircraft approaching will be promptly reported." "Considering our possible emergencies in the future," Mitchell continues—anticipating wars with Japan and Russia—the system should be extended to "the Hawaiian Islands," "the Philippine Islands," and (with Canada's cooperation) "Alaska."[14] This paranoid conception of total perimeter defense, hyperalertness, and maximal striking reach underlies the current ambition to achieve both coverage and precision by destroying enemy objects wherever they can be electronically detected, even objects moving at supersonic speeds.[15]

The Line of Aim

For French theorist Paul Virilio (1932–2018), "the line of aim" defines the path of the missile (whether stone, arrow, spear, bullet, or rocket) from the eye of the shooter to the intended target. In its most advanced current manifestations, the line of aim, starting "from the eye" and "passing through the peep-hole and the sights and on to the target object," is primarily a form of digital "photo-analysis" and live-feed "military cinematography."[16] For Douhet and Mitchell, the line of aim—in their own near future—would be calculated by means of radio signals and surveillance photography, a cinescopic conception of "an entirely new method of conducting war at a distance."[17]

"It is possible," Mitchell imagined, "for an airplane to fly along and control by radio several other airplanes which have no human beings in them and which may be made to drop their bombs on a city."[18] Eventually a coordinating human pilot would not be necessary: each machine of the squadron would "fly without a pilot by means of commands transmitted from the ground through electro-magnetic waves."[19] Extending from radio stations on the ground to the air wing aloft, the line of aim would multiply and fan out from the squadron's bomb and gun sights, covering as comprehensively as possible the target-rich environment below. Airplanes transfigured into radio bombs flying in formation are renamed to match their new form and function: "*Aerial torpedoes* which are really airplanes kept on their course by gyroscopic instruments and wireless telegraphy, with no pilots on board, can be directed for over a hundred miles in a sufficiently accurate way to hit great cities."[20] These "*gliding bombs* can be directed to their objectives from a distance; that is, a bombarding airplane can launch a bomb which has wings and glides. Its course is controlled by a gyroscope which acts on its rudder so that it will go in the desired direction. It may also be controlled by radio."[21]

The technical problem of how to guide these self-propelled missiles "in the desired direction," as the battle unfolded rapidly and unpredictably in the air, produced the first provisional and, for the moment, somewhat blurry notion of the intelligent camera lens. "These airplanes are equipped with cameras that are snapped by the device that would drop the bomb. The photograph indicates where the bomb would hit."[22] Mitchell does not say explicitly that these cameras might be controlled by radio signals or that their captured images might be transmitted across "the ether." Nevertheless, the idea of the airborne camera inherent in this prehistory of drones implies some latent conception of magical visual immediacy.[23] Thus might the command center transcend its ground-level view of operations and surmount the logistics of a soon-to-be-obsolete paradigm: dangerous surveillance missions flown by vulnerable pilots in slow-moving observation aircraft, followed by dark-room photographic development, image interpretation by intelligence officials, and the planning of return missions to drop bombs on targets that may well have moved in the interim.[24]

In sum, the quest for visual immediacy inherent in Mitchell's conception of the radio plane conjures the idea of the machine or the missile that can see. For Virilio, the "innovation of eyeless vision" in the missile-mounted camera or the "'sight machine' aboard an intelligent satellite" anticipates the full "automation of perception" in the drone campaigns to be conducted automatically by artificial intelligence: "Why tire yourself when everything runs without human intervention?"[25]

As Harun Farocki has observed, an original conception of the machine that can see, as in the cruise missile and smart bomb of the 1980s and 1990s, was represented in early cinema's deployment of the *phantom shot*. The first phantom shots were "film recordings taken from a position that a human cannot normally occupy . . . for example, shots from a camera that had been hung under a train."[26] In the Orwellian year of 1984, as Virilio describes it, the ability to go *live* with phantom eyesight represents the military's resolute "conquest of the image."[27] In every generation or weapons epoch, the line of aim connecting the eye with the object to be destroyed extends itself at the speed of the state's most advanced surveillance and weapons systems—that is, "at the speed of thought" and vision.[28]

Killing at the Speed of Thought

A brief history of the modern death wish can be found in Sigmund
Freud's "Thoughts for the Times on War and Death" (1915), written
while two of his sons were serving in the Austrian army during the
First World War, with a third son soon to volunteer.[29] Freud cites *Le
Père Goriot*, a novel by Honoré de Balzac, in which the idea of killing
someone by mental power alone is traceable to "a passage in the works
of J. J. Rousseau where that author asks the reader what he would do
if—without leaving Paris and of course without being discovered—he
could kill, with great profit to himself, an old mandarin in Peking by
a mere act of will. Rousseau implies that he would not give much for
the life of that dignitary. '*Tuer son mandarin*' has become a proverbial
phrase for this secret readiness, present even in modern man."[30] Here
the fantasy of killing at a distance is based on the same "principle governing magic, the technique of the animistic mode of thinking . . . the
principle of the 'omnipotence of thoughts.'"[31] The voodoo doll is su-
perfluous: primitive man in Freud's account believed that he could put
a hex on the enemy and so kill him by thoughts alone—by remote control, as it were. The enemy is merely plucked from the imaginary field
and destroyed in a burst of the ego's "secret injurious powers."[32] The
fulfillment of wishes here is both "prompt" and, "like the ancient Athe-
nian code of Draco," fatal: the ego "knows no other punishment for
crime than death. And this has a certain consistency, for every injury
to our almighty and autocratic ego is at bottom a crime of *lèse-majesté*
[insulting the monarch]."[33] "It is fortunate," continues Freud in 1915,
"that all these wishes do not possess the potency that was attributed to
them in primaeval times; in the cross-fire of mutual curses mankind
would long since have perished, the best and wisest of men and the
loveliest and fairest of women with the rest."[34]

In this last phrase, Freud struggles unsuccessfully to negate the
knowledge that hides in plain sight within his objective description of
the escalating world war:

> Not only is it more bloody and more destructive than any war of other
> days, because of the enormously increased perfection of weapons of at-
> tack and defence; it is at least as cruel, as embittered, as implacable as
> any that has preceded it. It disregards all the restrictions known as

International Law, which in peace-time the states had bound themselves to observe; it ignores the prerogatives of the wounded and the medical service, the distinction between civil and military sections of the population, the claims of private property. It tramples in blind fury on all that comes in its way, as though there were to be no future and no peace among men after it is over. It cuts all the common bonds between the contending peoples, and threatens to leave a legacy of embitterment that will make any renewal of those bonds impossible for a long time to come.[35]

Freud would have had any number of events to draw on for this analysis, beginning with the fall of Brussels and the burning of Louvain, Belgium, in August 1914. As American war journalist Richard Harding Davis reported from the scene, this was "war upon the defenceless, war upon churches, colleges, shops of milliners and lacemakers; war brought to the bedside and the fireside; against women harvesting in the fields, against children in wooden shoes at play in the streets. At Louvain that night the Germans were like men after an orgy."[36] In accordance with German general Erich Ludendorff's doctrine of "total war," Belgian civilians "like flocks of sheep [were] rounded up and marched through the night to concentration camps."[37] Others were taken as hostages and executed in reprisal for often merely alleged attacks by the *franc tireurs,* the practice, planned in advance, justified thus: "War cannot be conducted merely against the combatants of an enemy state but must seek to destroy the total material and intellectual (*geistig*) resources of the enemy."[38] The year 1915 also saw Germany's campaign of unrestricted submarine warfare and the sinking of the *Lusitania,* Britain's attempt at a total marine blockade of Germany, and the use of chlorine gas first by the Germans at Ypres in May and then by the British in September, with phosgene and mustard gas deployments soon to come. In 1915 the Turks began a campaign of "race extermination" in Armenia that would produce a million corpses.[39] Such events helped make credible Freud's theory of "the death drive" and the claim that human beings en masse were, "like primaeval man, a gang of murderers," acting out their "unconscious wishful impulses" under the direction of the state's primal fathers.[40] Freud chides his reader that such a reckoning of the human primate at war should neither shock nor surprise: "In reality our fellow-citizens have not sunk so low as we feared, because they had never risen so high as we be-lieved."[41] If given the absolute power to kill his distant enemies at the drop of a thought, modern man would show himself to be no different in essence from his primitive ancestors.

The Freudian "autocratic ego," as aviation in the early twentieth cen-tury was quick to grasp, had no better throne from which to survey this mass of remote groundlings to be annihilated than the cockpit of the airplane.[42] In what Virilio terms "the aerialization of human vi-sion," the ego's literal elevation alone transforms the ground below into the 100 percent target space.[43] Strapped to an airplane rigged up with its bombs and machine guns, "man," we might say with Freud, "has, as it were, become a kind of prosthetic God. When he puts on all his auxiliary organs he is truly magnificent."[44] The ability to kill from an elevated distance thus becomes more potent and less restrained than at any previous time in history.

With the war's first August, German zeppelins bombed the residen-tial areas of Antwerp and Liège, killing hundreds of civilians indis-criminately. By 1917 zeppelins yielded to Gotha bombers flying in diamond formation in broad daylight, above the range of British anti-aircraft guns. The dead on the ground included schoolchildren at their desks. As one eyewitness reported, "There came to London yes-terday the nearest vision of modern warfare that it has yet known":

> Many of the little ones were lying across their desks, apparently dead, and with terrible wounds on heads and limbs, and scores of others were writhing with pain and moaning piteously in their terror and suffering. . . . Many bodies were mutilated, but our first thought was to get at the injured and have them cared for. We took them gently in our arms and laid them out against a wall under a shed. . . . Some mothers were almost insane with grief, and when they couldn't find their own children would rush through the bodies looking for them, and when you remember that there was a hole in the roof four feet deep and covering the whole area of the classroom it will be understood what that meant.
>
> The worst part of our task was the last—that of picking up the mutilated fragments of humanity.[45]

Such is the First World War context from which the futurist visions of Douhet and Mitchell emerged. When advanced industrial "nations are at war, everyone takes a part in it: the soldier carrying his gun, the woman loading shells in a factory, the farmer growing wheat, the scientist experimenting in his laboratory," and (they failed to add but fully understood) the children at their desks.[46]

In sum, "to have command of the air means to be in a position to wield offensive power so great it defies human imagination," writes Douhet, showing nonetheless that his own "power of human foresight" was quite capable of forming "some conception of the magnitude aerial offensives may reach in the future."[47] As an extension of the nation's industrial power, airplanes will drop metal cylinders filled with explosives, incendiaries, poison gases, toxic chemicals, and biological agents. "Aerial warfare will be intense and violent to a superlative degree."[48] Douhet also understood that when bombs disperse from twenty thousand feet above heavily populated industrial cities, whatever they hit in their random radial patterns becomes the legitimate target.

What the Present Is Preparing for the Future

Douhet impresses in the sustained and realistic manner in which, during and after the First World War, he "ask[s] of the present what it is preparing for the future."[49] He anticipates in all of its essential particulars, for example, the Nazi attack on Gernika in April 1937, a war experiment that would serve as the prototype of aerial attacks in the coming global war:[50]

> Take the center of a large city and imagine what would happen among the civilian population during a single attack by a single bombing unit. For my part, I have no doubt that its impact upon the people would be terrible. Here is what would be likely to happen to the center of the city within a radius of about 250 meters: Within a few minutes some 20 tons of high-explosive, incendiary, and gas bombs would rain down. First would come explosions, then fires, then deadly gases floating on the surface and preventing any approach to the stricken area. As the hours passed and night advanced, the fires would spread while the poison gas paralyzed all life. By the following day the life of the city would be suspended; and if it happened to be a junction on some important artery of communication traffic would be suspended.
>
> What could happen to a single city in a single day could also happen to ten, twenty, fifty cities.[51]

Xabier Irujo of the University of Nevada, Reno, and the Center for Basque Studies gives the indispensable account of what happened at Gernika on market day, April 26, 1937, the day of Hitler's birthday parade in Berlin. His account reads as though directly from Douhet's pages:

> For the first time in Europe, an entire city was reduced to rubble by an aerial attack. For the first time, an attack on an undefended civilian population was conceived as a war experiment intended to measure the impact of the raid on the morale of the enemy by inflicting the maximum number of casualties and the greatest material damage. . . . Flying abreast in close formation through an aerial corridor, successive waves of bombers dropped their cargoes over the urban area, using a carefully calculated mixture of incendiary and high-explosive shells, while fighter planes kept the surviving civilians on the ground under constant machine-gun fire.[52]

Before the attack, the raid's chief planner, German air force colonel Wolfram von Richthofen (a cousin of the Red Baron), had studied the effects of incendiary bombs on wooden buildings destroyed at Eibar in a previous raid.[53] Given the predominance of its wooden structures and its political value as a symbol of democracy, Gernika was the perfect target for fascist terror bombing. Moreover, "the town was completely undefended (no antiaircraft batteries protected the town), and the weather was perfect for the attack. It was a tranquil spring day, with the kind of conditions that German pilots called *Flugwetter*, or 'flying weather.'"[54] Just as, with Leni Riefenstahl, "the preparations for the Party Congress [at Nuremburg in September 1934] were made hand in hand with the preparations for the camera work," the German air command staged Gernika as a spectacle to be captured on film.[55] Commander in chief of the Luftwaffe Hermann Göring "only wanted to be able to show the picture of a town completely destroyed by the action of the air force as proof that this deadly capability was exclusive to the Luftwaffe, not the artillery or navy."[56] The before-and-after photographic record was used to plan further attacks.

As an expression of the new aerial warfare, Gernika was merely the hope of a bigger war—a war in which the Nazis did not see their own cities burning.[57] Douhet had known better that the future would be dominated by "that Air Force which succeeds in dumping the largest quantity of bombs in the shortest time," and for the moment he believed, or expediently claimed, that Italy, "thanks to the ingenuity and initiative of His Excellency the Honorable Balbo[,] . . . is ahead of all other nations."[58] But he also knew that in Germany, England, America, Japan, and Russia, as in Italy, the chemist in his laboratory "leans over his test tubes in quest of ever more powerful compounds."[59] Billy Mitchell too feared that his Cassandra prophecies were not being sufficiently heard or believed. "The European War was only the kindergarten of aviation," he warned.[60]

Gazing into this future with Douhet and Mitchell, we thus "catch a glimpse of the heights of atrocity to which aerial warfare may reach," heights as limitless as the narcissistic death wishes of the air force commanders, as a key eyewitness, Hermann Rauschning, was in a position to note.[61] Here he recalls one of Hitler's loud rants in 1934: "I have no scruples, and I will use whatever weapon I require. . . . Aerial attacks, stupendous in their mass effect, surprise, terror, sabotage, assassination from within, the murder of leading men, overwhelming attacks on all weak points in the enemy's defence, sudden attacks, all in the same second, without regard for reserves or losses: that is the war of the future. A gigantic, all-destroying blow. I do not consider consequences; I think only of this one thing."[62] Another eyewitness, Friedrich Reck-Malleczewen, records a rumor making the rounds as the German army, stalled in the "snowy wastes" before the Volga, laid siege to Stalingrad in January 1942: "A spectre is rising out of the snowy wastes of Russia, the spectre of retaliation, and my honest countrymen are now trying to drown out their growing fear by believing in miracles that will change everything. They have hopes for a gas which will destroy all life in a large country in ten seconds, and a fantastic 'atom bomb,' three of which would suffice to sink the British Isles."[63] Such intoxicating visions of destruction were, for the moment, barely deferred by technical impediments. August 6 (Hiroshima) and 8 (Nagasaki), 1945, demonstrated that whatever could be imagined could in fact be done, even as the military mind, in its "excess of spirits," continued to dream of ways to move from atom to hydrogen bombs and beyond.[64]

Bombing and Strafing in the Counterinsurgency War

The race for aerial supremacy in the work of Douhet and Mitchell takes for granted the lethal contestation and perhaps mutual destruction of the most highly advanced industrial nations on the planet. But their work also includes a vision of asymmetrical warfare by which such powers would deploy their air forces to conquer and subjugate colonial insurgencies within their own empires. The need to "win hearts and minds" appears nowhere in Mitchell's account of aerial policing and colonial policy for the nation that enjoys aviation supremacy:

> In Mesopotamia, Iraq as it is called, the air force handles the military occupation of the country in a manner similar to that in which armies have in the past. The result of this occupation has been very satisfactory. The airplanes fly over the country at will, are able to put down uprisings quickly, transport troops to places where they are needed on the ground, and to cover much more country with less effort than is possible by other means.
>
> To demoralize an enemy unprovided with aircraft or not well provided with aircraft, against savage tribes or poorly organized levies, attack aviation has a tremendous effect.[65]

The Italians, as Mitchell and of course Douhet well knew, were the first to use airplanes to bomb and strafe civilians in the Italo-Turkish War of September 29, 1911–October 18, 1912.[66] For Filippo Marinetti, the founder of Italian futurism, this massacre of civilians on the ground was "the most beautiful aesthetic spectacle of [his] existence."[67] The future was to be filled with such breathless "aerovisions": "Skimming the surface of the ground, [the pilot] decapitates a hundred women with his right wing, then, banking, makes another pass, decapitating another thousand lined up along the 'vibrating rails.'"[68]

A groundling himself amid a mass of spectators numbering in the tens and even hundreds of thousands, Marinetti first imagined machine-gun strafing upon seeing the Wright Flyer at Le Mans in 1908. This fantasy of mass murder by airplanes was foundational to the thirty-year string of futurist manifestoes that would follow.[69] This scenario is typical: "Between my feet I have a tiny machine gun that I can fire by pushing a steel button. . . . Look down, straight down, among the masses of greenery, the riotous tumult of that human flood in flight! . . . But you are numberless! . . . And we might use up our ammunition and grow old in the slaughter! . . . Let me direct the fire! . . . Up 800 meters! Ready! . . . Fire! . . . Oh! the joy of playing billiards with death! Continue the massacre!"[70] With the First World War, forward-firing machine guns were synchronized to shoot their bullets through the propellers of the front-mounted aero engine. The 47-shot Lewis gun was soon succeeded by the Vickers, its 500 and then 650 rounds per minute pouring forth, as renowned American fighter ace Captain Eddie Rickenbacker reported, "in streams" and "hurricanes of flaming bullets."[71] The reports of Rickenbacker and other famous combat aviators of his time show how obsessed they were with machine-gun strafing. Royal Air Force ace captain Alan Bott reports that the fighter pilot's initial discovery that he could wreak havoc on the ground with his machine guns was essentially accidental, and that the killing of groundlings was, at first, understood by the pilots as a species of "guerilla work" falling outside prevailing rules of engagement.[72] It would not take long, however, for the practice to become standard operating procedure. As pilots discovered in themselves "a desire to swoop down and panic the Boche," they developed a flair for "the free-lance ground stunt . . . to relieve boredom by joyous pounces on Brother Boche."[73] Canadian ace Billy Bishop, in his terrifying memoir *Winged Warfare* (1918) (terrifying in the glimpse it offers into the interior of the killing mentality), concurs: "It is great fun to fly very low along the German trenches and give them a burst of machine-gun bullets as a greeting in the morning, or a good-night salute in the evening. They don't like it a bit. But we love it; we love to see the Kaiser's proud Prussians running for cover like so many rats."[74] For Rickenbacker, the merciless strafing of groundlings is also an invariably thrilling experience:

> All the boys came home overjoyed with the scurrying troops on the ground that had been thrown into great confusion by the attack of the aeroplanes. This ground strafing is probably the most exciting sport in aviation and one that is attended with comparatively little danger to the pilot. The aeroplanes swoop down so swiftly and are so terrifying in the roar of their engines and the streams of bullets issuing forth from two rapid-fire guns that an ordinary soldier always looks for a hole

rather than for any weapon of defense. . . . I could imagine the terror and helplessness my single presence inspired among the slow moving troops below. I was having the time of my life.[75]

Strafing became so tactically important that British ace James McCudden predicted, "We shall . . . have heavily armoured scouts carrying a large amount of machine-gun ammunition, who will fly continuously behind the enemy lines harassing the enemy infantry and making them live practically underground during the day. These machines will fly at a height of a few feet and at such a great speed that the chances of a hit, except by the lucky bullet, will not be frequent."[76] Here he anticipates the development of such ultimate strafing weapons as the A-10 Warthog, the Douglas AC-47 ("Puff the Magic Dragon"), the AC-130 Spectre Gunship, and the AH-64 Apache helicopter, whose hideous capabilities in the wars in Iraq and Afghanistan can be seen on YouTube.[77]

In plotting a series of points "on the graph curve showing the evolution of the character of war" in the twentieth and twenty-first centuries, Douhet and Mitchell help us trace the technological and imaginary genealogy of aerial warfare from the Wright Flyer of 1903–9 to the U.S. military's unmanned combat aerial vehicles of the present, the Reapers, Hunters, Stalkers, Ravens, Wasps, and Global Hawks of the Forever War on Terror.[78] The U.S. military justifies drone warfare on the basis of the precision it is able to achieve in targeting the enemy. But that still leaves an essential problem largely unsolved as asymmetrical warfare unfolds in Syria, Afghanistan, Yemen, Somalia, and beyond: how to pluck out the enemy from amid the people he or she lives among. David Stockton reports that the U.S. government's list as of May 2018 of specially designated nationals (SDNs) is "a staggering 1,132 pages long. By our reckoning it lists in excess of 500,000 foreign evil doers of one type or another. The fact that it takes 221 pages just to get through the 'A's' in its alphabetical listing—owing to the prevalence of Ali's, Abdul's, and Ahmed's—is perhaps indicative of the nature and scope of Washington's SDN dragnet."[79]

Drones are used to target some of these SDNs, but drones are only a small part of the United States' vast military and intelligence operations involving thousands of personnel and countless conventional military "assets."[80] Moreover, the high-resolution visual capabilities of onboard scopes and cameras have not prevented identities from being mistaken as military operations continue to unfold in a counterinsurgency war "that places the local population at the centre of its operations."[81]

This basic reality was exposed with the WikiLeaks release of gunsight footage taken during the Baghdad airstrike of July 12, 2007, in which two U.S. AH-64 Apache helicopters, using 30 mm cannon fire, killed twelve to eighteen people, including two journalists. Two children were also wounded in the attack.[82] Discussing another notorious case of mistaken identity, the February 21, 2010, U.S. attack in Khud, Afghanistan, that left "at least 23 people dead and more than a dozen wounded, including three children: all civilians," Derek Gregory illuminates a "mode of visual apprehension that is culturally constructed and prescriptive." He notes, "Within such a space of constructed visibility, it was virtually impossible for the victims of the attack to be seen as civilians until it was too late."[83] And as Robert Kaplan has observed recently, the latest American weapons, "equipped with GPS sensors and a guidance system," continue to be quite capable of "hitting 'precisely the wrong place' and killing and mutilating a family of women and children on the Afghan steppe as a consequence."[84]

One hundred years ago, Douhet and Mitchell predicted that aerial warfare would erase the distinction between civilians and combatants entirely. They continue to be right as drone warfare expands in the twenty-first century.

Notes

1. Giulio Douhet, *The Command of the Air* (1921), trans. Dino Ferrari, reprinted in USAF Warrior Studies (1942; Washington, D.C.: Office of Air Force History, 1983).

2. "Editors' Introduction," in Douhet, ix.

3. "Editors' Introduction," viii–ix.

4. William Mitchell, *Winged Defense: The Development and Possibilities of Modern Air Power—Economic and Military* (1925; Mineola, N.Y.: Dover, 2006), 9.

5. Mitchell, 8. In the meantime, human pilots in need of boosted protection were far from obsolete: "In 1919 we devised a super-bomber, capable of going 1300 miles without landing, to carry two four thousand pound bombs, and to be able to land or hit the ground at a speed of one hundred miles an hour without smashing up" (Mitchell, 185).

6. See Richard Overy, *The Bombing War: Europe 1939–1945* (New York: Penguin, 2013); and Xabier Irujo, *Gernika, 1937: The Market Day Massacre* (Reno:

University of Nevada Press, 2015). Irujo notes, "Flying abreast in close formation through an aerial corridor, successive waves of bombers dropped their car-
goes over the urban area, using a carefully calculated mixture of incendiary
and high-explosive shells, while fighter planes kept the surviving civilians on
the ground under constant machine-gun fire." He also observes, "The German
pilots called this strategy 'shuttle bombing' and 'carpet bombing,' because the
objective was to completely devastate an area by dropping as many bombs as
possible within an aerial corridor in successive waves of planes" (Irujo, vii, 78).

7. Oliver Stewart, "The Doctrine of Strategical Bombing," *Journal of the
Royal United Service Institution* 81, no. 521 (February 1, 1936): 95.

8. Stewart, 97–98.

9. Douhet, *Command of the Air*, 188.

10. Stewart, "Doctrine of Strategical Bombing," 100.

11. See Derek Gregory, *The Colonial Present: Afghanistan, Palestine, Iraq*
(Malden, Mass.: Blackwell, 2004).

12. K. Anderson quoted in Derek Gregory, "From a View to a Kill: Drones
and Late Modern War," *Theory, Culture and Society* 28, nos. 7–8 (2011): 190. See
Physicians for Social Responsibility, *Body Count: Casualty Figures after 10
Years of the "War on Terror"* (Washington, D.C.: Physicians for Social Responsibility, 2015), https://www.psr.org/wp-content/uploads/2018/05/body-count.pdf;
Wikipedia, s.v. "Casualties of the Iraq War," last modified January 1, 2020,
https://en.wikipedia.org/wiki/Casualties_of_the_Iraq_War; Wikipedia, s.v. "Civilian Casualties in the War in Afghanistan (2001–Present)," last modified January 26, 2020, https://en.wikipedia.org/wiki/Civilian_casualties_in_the_war_in
Afghanistan(2001–present).

13. Mitchell, *Winged Defense*, ix, 213, 216. H. G. Wells had foreseen the military implications of this imminent possibility in *The War in the Air* (1907). Louis
Blériot flew across the English Channel on July 25, 1909. Charles Lindbergh's
transatlantic flight took place on May 20, 1927. Italian Black Shirt and Secretary
of State for Air Italo Balbo led a squadron of twenty-four seaplanes from Rome
across the Atlantic Ocean to Chicago, site of the world's fair in celebration of "a
century of progress," a flight of 6,100 miles undertaken in seven stages, completed on July 16, 1933. See "Italy Is Jubilant at Feat of Fliers," *New York Times*,
July 16, 1933. For rich discussion of this history, see two books by Robert Wohl:
A Passion for Wings: Aviation and the Western Imagination, 1908–1918 (New
Haven, Conn.: Yale University Press, 1994) and *The Spectacle of Flight: Aviation
and the Western Imagination, 1920–1950* (New Haven, Conn.: Yale University
Press, 2005). Douhet and Mitchell foresaw the need for a state of permanent
war readiness in which the air force would have some of its planes "kept constantly in the air, so that in the future, the country that is ready with its air force
and jumps on its opponent at once will bring about a speedy and lasting victory" (Mitchell, *Winged Defense*, 10).

14. Mitchell, *Winged Defense*, 21, 218.

15. Mitchell and Douhet anticipate what Bjering and Graae in this volume call
the "predatory mania of extermination and destruction" inherent, for example,

in Carrie the Drone Queen's "desire" (in the television series *Homeland*) "to sit in front of the monitors in her living room in order not to miss anything." Her *"predatory antihermeneutics"* unfolds as a desire "to kill every possible threat before it even materializes as a subject of analysis or interpretation." Marlena Baldacci and Brad Lendon, "Chinese Student Sentenced to a Year in Prison for Taking Photos of Naval Base," CNN, February 7, 2019, https://www.cnn.com /2019/02/06/us/chinese-student-photographs-military-base/index.html. Veronica Stracqualursi, "US Successfully Tests Missile Defense System in Hawaii," CNN, December 10, 2018, https://www.cnn.com/2018/12/11/politics/us-aegis -missile-defense-test-successful/index.html.

Optical capture of the object on screen can mean its almost instant vaporization in spacetime reality, a tour de force of megalomania first achieved in the 1980s. According to Paul Virilio's account in *War and Cinema*, "Last summer, on 5 July 1983, an American KC-135 aircraft fitted with a laser system shot down a Sidewinder missile travelling at 3,000 kilometres an hour."

"Scan. Freeze frame."

Paul Virilio, *War and Cinema: The Logistics of Perception* (1984), trans. Patrick Camiller (New York: Verso, 1989), 111. This desire for instantaneity continues to flow along the line of the asymptote. As Derek Gregory observes in his 2011 essay, "The time from finding to engaging emergent targets is now 30–35 minutes; the Air Force aims to reduce this to less than two minutes, and Cheater (2007: 12) envisages it being 'compressed to seconds by 2025'" ("From a View," 196).

16. Virilio, *War and Cinema*, 3, 93, 99.

17. Mitchell, *Winged Defense*, 11.

18. Mitchell, 164–65. See the futurist image of the "city with its aeroplane on a leash" in "F. T. Marinetti, from the Catalogue of the Exhibition *Aeropittura/Aeroscultura/Arte sacra futurista,* Offices of the 'Gazzetta del Popolo,' Turin, February 19, 1938," in *Futurism in Flight: "Aeropittura" Paintings and Sculptures of Man's Conquest of Space (1913–1945),* ed. Bruno Mantura, Patrizia Rosazza-Ferraris, and Livia Velani, published to accompany the exhibition at the Accademia Italiana delle Arti e delle Arti Applicate, London, September 4–October 13, 1990 (London: Aeritalia, Società Aerospaziale Italiana, 1990), 207.

19. Douhet, *Command of the Air,* 64n.

20. Mitchell, *Winged Defense*, 6, emphasis added.

21. Mitchell, 164, emphasis added.

22. Mitchell, 165.

23. For James Frazer, magical thinking assumes "that things act on each other at a distance through a secret sympathy, the impulse being transmitted from one to the other by means of what we may conceive as a kind of invisible ether, not unlike that which is postulated by modern science for a precisely similar purpose, namely, to explain how things can physically affect each other through a space which appears to be empty." Frazer, *The Golden Bough: A Study in Magic and Religion* (1922), abridged ed. (London: Macmillan, 1987), 12.

24. The enduring futility of these logistics in the American war in Vietnam is exposed in Stephen Wright's incomparable novel *Meditations in Green* (Toronto:

Bantam Books, 1983). "He reached forward, turned the crank on his right, and the film, unrolling from a reel on the left, moved smoothly across a long rectangle of illuminated glass. The military name for this task was image interpreter. Griffin was required to translate pictures into letters and coordinates that were instantly telexed to such important addresses as III MAF, 1AIRCAV, 25DIV, III MAG, MACV, CINCPAC, and most impressive, JCS. The data went round and round and where it came out he preferred not to hear. A camera fixed in the belly of a Mohawk OV-1A had collected today's images during a morning break in the weather above a sector of suspected hostile activity approximately fifty kilometers southwest of Griffin's stool. His job was to interpret the film, find the enemy in the negatives. He turned the crank. Trees, trees, trees, trees, rocks, rocks, cloud, trees, trees, road, road, stream, stream, ford, trees, road, road. He stopped cranking. With a black grease pencil he carefully circled two blurry shadows beside the white thread of a road. Next to the circles he placed question marks. Road, road, road, road, trees, trees, trees. His eyes felt hard as shells, sore as bruises. Trees, trees, trees, trees. Wherever he put circles on the film there the air force would make holes in the ground" (40).

25. Virilio, *War and Cinema*, 3; Paul Virilio, *Ground Zero*, trans. Chris Turner (London: Verso, 2002), 33; Jake Carter, "12 Ways AI Is Shaping the Drone Industry," Dronelife, July 6, 2018, https://dronelife.com/2018/07/06/12-ways-ai-is-shaping-the-drone-industry/.

26. Harun Farocki, "Phantom Images," trans. Brian Poole, text based on a talk delivered at ZKM, Karlsruhe, Germany, 2003, in *Public 29: Localities*, ed. Saara Liinamaa, Janine Marchessault, and Christine Shaw, Fine Arts/Cultural Studies Program at York University, Toronto (Winnipeg: Hignell Book Printing), 13. The Nazis' dumb and eyeless V-1 buzz bombs and V-2 rockets represent in this sense a stage already surpassed by Douhet's and Mitchell's prophetic imaginations and the visual intelligence of the early cinema. "Like Fascism itself," as Theodor Adorno described them, "the robots career without a subject. Like it they combine utmost technical perfection with total blindness. . . . 'I have seen the world spirit,' not on horseback, but on wings and without a head.'" Theodor Adorno, *Minima Moralia: Reflections from Damaged Life*, trans. E. F. N. Jephcott (1951; London: Verso, 1978), 55. Only the defense against the buzz bombs and V rockets possessed the ability to "see" in this period (radio detecting and ranging [radar]).

27. Virilio, *War and Cinema*, 110. David Finkel's *The Good Soldiers*, which follows the American army into its notorious 2007 surge in Iraq, describes how "the conquest of the image" is now virtually absolute: "A bright white blimp called an aerostat . . . floated high above the FOB [forward operating base] with a remote-controlled camera that could be focused on whatever might be happening a thousand feet below. Day or night, the aerostat was up there, looking down and around, as were pole-mounted cameras, pilotless drones, high-flying jets, and satellites, making the sky feel at times as if it were stitched all the way up to the heaven with eyes." David Finkel, *The Good Soldiers* (New York: Farrar, Straus and Giroux, 2009), 30.

28. Herbert quoted in Gregory, "From a View," 196. Restraint upon this desire is now not so much technical as bureaucratic: complains one unmanned aerial vehicle pilot, "Requests for permission to strike [must] pass through 'echelons of staffs sitting above me, like owls in trees' (West, 2011: 89)" (quoted in Gregory, "From a View," 196).

29. Peter Gay, *Freud: A Life for Our Time* (New York: W. W. Norton, 1988), 352.

30. Sigmund Freud, "Thoughts for the Times on War and Death," in *The Standard Edition of the Complete Psychological Works of Sigmund Freud*, trans. James Strachey, vol. 14, *On the History of the Psycho-analytic Movement* (London: Hogarth, 1957), 298. *Tuer son mandarin* is fully continuous with the "video games staged in simulacra of Afghanistan [that] show stylized landscapes prowled solely by 'insurgents' or 'terrorists' whose cartoonish appearance makes them instantly recognizable; the neo-Orientalism of these renditions is a matter of dismal record" (Gregory, "From a View," 198).

31. Sigmund Freud, *Totem and Taboo: Some Points of Agreement between the Mental Lives of Savages and Neurotics*, in *The Standard Edition of the Complete Psychological Works of Sigmund Freud*, trans. James Strachey, vol. 13, *Totem and Taboo and Other Works* (London: Hogarth, 1955), 85.

32. Sigmund Freud, "The Uncanny," in *The Standard Edition of the Complete Psychological Works of Sigmund Freud*, trans. James Strachey, vol. 17, *An Infantile Neurosis and Other Works* (London: Hogarth, 1955), 247. The mental or imaginary visibility of the enemy in this sense produces "a special kind of intimacy that consistently privileges the view of the hunter-killer"—Gregory's apposite description of the drone pilot's monitor view of "a killing space" that no longer "appears remote and distant" ("From a View," 193).

33. Freud, "Thoughts for the Times," 297.

34. Freud, "Thoughts for the Times," 297.

35. Freud, 278–79.

36. Richard Harding Davis, "Horrors of Louvain" (*New York Tribune*, August 30, 1914), in *World War I and America: Told by the Americans Who Lived It*, ed. A. Scott Berg (New York: Library of America, 2017), 39.

37. Davis, 39.

38. Barbara Tuchman, *The Guns of August* (1962; New York: Ballantine Books, 1990), 202; quotation in Tuchman, 382.

39. Henry Morgenthau, U.S. ambassador to the Ottoman Empire, to Robert Lansing, counselor for the U.S. State Department, July 16, 1915, in "'A Campaign of Race Extermination': Istanbul, July 1915," in Berg, *World War I*, 169.

40. Freud, "Thoughts for the Times," 297. See also Freud's *Group Psychology and the Analysis of the Ego* (1921) in *The Standard Edition of the Complete Psychological Works of Sigmund Freud*, trans. James Strachey, vol. 18, *Beyond the Pleasure Principle, Group Psychology and Other Works* (London: Hogarth, 1955).

41. Freud, "Thoughts for the Times," 285.

42. Here I mean to invoke multiple resonances of the word *remote* as defined by *The Oxford English Dictionary*: "far," "distant," "removed," "different," "separate," "unfamiliar," "foreign," "alien," and so on.

43. Virilio, *Ground Zero*, 46.

44. Sigmund Freud, *Civilization and Its Discontents*, in *The Standard Edition of the Complete Psychological Works of Sigmund Freud*, trans. James Strachey, vol. 21, *The Future of an Illusion, Civilization and Its Discontents, and Other Works* (London: Hogarth, 1961), 92. Freud, unlike Marinetti (see later in the present chapter), is being ironic, of course. Gregory notes the "terrifying Olympian power released through the UAV's [unmanned aerial vehicle's] Hellfire missiles. 'Sometimes I felt like a God hurling thunderbolts from afar,' one pilot admits" ("From a View," 192).

45. "German Airmen Kill 97, Hurt 437 in London Raid" (*New York Times*, June 14, 1917), in Berg, *World War I*, 357, 361.

46. Douhet, *Command of the Air*, 196.

47. Douhet, 6, 19.

48. Douhet, 197. "To get an idea of the nature of future wars, one need only imagine what power of destruction that nation would possess whose bacteriologists should discover the means of spreading epidemics in the enemy's country and at the same time immunize its own people. Air power makes it possible not only to make high-explosive bombing raids over any sector of the enemy's territory, but also to ravage his whole country by chemical and bacteriological warfare." Douhet, 6–7.

49. Douhet, 146.

50. I follow Xabier Irujo in using the Basque spelling, Gernika.

51. Douhet, *Command of the Air*, 58.

52. Irujo, *Gernika*, vii.

53. Irujo, 68.

54. Irujo, 67.

55. Susan Sontag, "Fascinating Fascism" (1974), in *Under the Sign of Saturn* (New York: Farrar, Straus and Giroux, 1980), 79n.

56. Irujo, *Gernika*, 60.

57. On March 14, 1941, Mihail Sebastian noted in his journal, "Major bombing of London and Berlin on the same night." *Journal: 1935–1944*, trans. Patrick Camiller (Chicago: Ivan R. Dee, 2000), 330.

58. Douhet, *Command of the Air*, 61, 183. Italo Balbo (1896–1940) was Mussolini's marshal of the air force.

59. Douhet, 202.

60. Mitchell, *Winged Defense*, 29.

61. Douhet, *Command of the Air*, 61.

62. Hermann Rauschning, *Hitler Speaks: A Series of Political Conversations with Adolf Hitler on His Real Aims* (London: Thornton Butterworth, 1939), 13. In *On the Natural History of Destruction*, W. G. Sebald looks back on such scenes as they were eventually played out: "Scarcely anyone can now doubt that Air Marshal Göring would have wiped out London if his technical resources had allowed him to do so. Speer describes Hitler at a dinner in the Reich Chancellery in 1940 imagining the total destruction of the capital of the British Empire: 'have you ever seen a map of London? It is so densely built that one fire alone would be enough to

destroy the whole city, just as it did over two hundred years ago. Göring will start fires all over London, fires everywhere, with countless incendiary bombs of an entirely new type. Thousands of fires. They will unite in one huge blaze over the whole area. Göring has the right idea: high explosives don't work, but we can do it with incendiaries; we can destroy London completely. What will their firemen be able to do once it's really burning?'" W. G. Sebald, *On the Natural History of Destruction*, trans. Anthe Bell (Toronto: Vintage Canada, 2004), 103. The Nazi Blitz on London killed sixty thousand people and destroyed more than two million houses. Yuki Tanaka and Marilyn B. Young, *Bombing Civilians: A Twentieth-Century History* (New York: New Press, 2009), 2.

63. Friedrich Reck-Malleczewen, *Diary of a Man in Despair*, trans. Paul Rubens (London: Duckbacks, 2001), 159. The diary was kept in Bavaria during the Nazi years from 1936 to October 1944 (Reck-Malleczewen was murdered at Dachau on February 16, 1945).

64. With the phrase "excess of spirits," Wright, *Meditations in Green*, 125, is describing U.S. Air Force pilots in the Vietnam War. Also see Heinar Kipphardt, *In the Matter of J. Robert Oppenheimer: A Play Freely Adapted on the Basis of the Documents*, trans. Ruth Speirs (New York: Hill and Wang, 1964).

65. Mitchell, *Winged Defense*, 23, 189.

66. See Wohl, *Passion for Wings*, 140–45.

67. Wohl, 143. See also Claudia Salaris, "Aerial Imagery in Futurist Literature," in Mantura, Rosazza-Ferraris, and Velani, *Futurism in Flight*, 27–32.

68. Wohl, *Passion for Wings*, 142.

69. Wohl, 2. See David McCullough, *The Wright Brothers* (New York: Simon and Schuster, 2015), 155–78, for a vivid account of the Wright brothers' spectacular flight demonstrations in France.

70. F. T. Marinetti, "Let's Murder the Moonshine" (1909), trans. R. W. Flint and Arthur A. Coppotelli, in *Marinetti: Selected Writings* (New York: Farrar, Straus and Giroux, 1971), 52–53.

71. Edward V. Rickenbacker, *Fighting the Flying Circus* (New York: Frederick A. Stokes, 1919), 206.

72. Alan Bott, *Cavalry of the Clouds* (New York: Doubleday, Page, 1918), 154.

73. Bott, 161, 162.

74. William A. Bishop, *Winged Warfare* (New York: George H. Doran, 1918), 26.

75. Rickenbacker, *Fighting the Flying Circus*, 30, 162–63, 233–34. "Movement in a hostile trench was irresistible" (Bott, *Cavalry of the Clouds*, 161). See the male fantasies famously analyzed by Klaus Theweleit: "As if magnetically attracted, their eyes hunt out anything that moves. The more intense and agitated the movement, the better. When they spot such movement they narrow their eyes to slits (defense), sharpen their vision of it as a dead entity by training a spotlight on it (deanimation), then destroy it, to experience a strange satisfaction at the sight of this 'bloody mass.'" Theweleit, *Male Fantasies*, vol. 1, *Women, Floods, Bodies, History*, trans. Stephen Conway in collaboration with Erica Carter and Chris Turner (Minneapolis: University of Minnesota Press, 1987), 217.

76. James T. B. McCudden, *Flying Fury: Five Years in the Royal Flying Corps* (1918), ed. Stanley M. Ulanoff (n.p.: Bailey Brothers and Swinfen, 1973), 277.

77. Search with any of these keywords. For an account of what it is like to be on the receiving end of the A-10's munitions and the death by friendly fire in a "freak accident" of Canadian Olympic athlete and soldier Private Mark Graham, see Ryan Pagnacco, "Two Days in Panjwayi," in *Outside the Wire: The War in Afghanistan in the Words of Its Participants,* ed. Kevin Patterson and Jane Warren, foreword by Roméo Dallaire (Toronto: Random House Canada, 2007), 25–49.

78. Douhet, *Command of the Air,* 26.

79. David Stockton, "The Donald Undone: Tilting at the Swamp, Succumbing to Empire," Antiwar.com, December 8, 2018, https://original.antiwar.com/david_stockman/2018/12/07/the-donald-undone-tilting-at-the-swamp-succumbing-to-the-empire/. For harrowing accounts of cases of mistaken identity involving those with the same names on the SDN list, see Anand Gopal, *No Good Men among the Living: America, the Taliban, and the War through Afghan Eyes* (New York: Metropolitan Books, 2014); and Mohamedou Ould Slahi, *Guantánamo Diary,* ed. Larry Siems (New York: Little, Brown, 2015).

80. Gregory notes that "currently 185 personnel are required to support one Predator or Reaper Combat Air Patrol" ("From a View," 194–95). See David Buchanan in this volume on the question of corporate responsibility along the military "kill chain." He notes, "During Donald Trump's first week in office, a CV-22 that was launched from my base in Djibouti crashed in the Yemeni desert—killing a Navy SEAL—while flying in support of a raid that resulted in the death of this sailor, some enemy combatants, and a number of civilians, including children." See also Phil Klay's stunning "Ten Kliks South" in *Redeployment* (New York: Penguin, 2015), 271–88.

81. Gregory, "From a View," 188.

82. Sunshinepress, "Collateral Murder—Wikileaks—Iraq," YouTube video, 17:46, posted April 3, 2010, https://www.youtube.com/watch?v=5rXPrfnU3G0. See Finkel, *Good Soldiers,* 83–106, for an inside American eyewitness report on what happened.

83. Gregory, "From a View," 190, 203.

84. Robert D. Kaplan, "On the Ground in Afghanistan and Iraq," review of *The Fighters: Americans in Combat in Afghanistan and Iraq,* by C. J. Chivers, *New York Times,* August 14, 2018, https://www.nytimes.com/2018/08/14/books/review/cj-chivers-fighters.html.

CHAPTER 2

Warrior Woundings, Warrior Culture

An Ethos for Post-9/11 American War Culture

DAVID BUCHANAN

As the United States nears the completion of a second decade of constant war since 9/11, one of the most important questions that loom over critical assessments of contemporary war literature is whether anything new or different is happening in this body of writing.[1] These wars certainly seem different from our wars of the twentieth century, so it makes sense to hypothesize that the literature might be different as well and, therefore, reflect something back about the culture that has been sending military members off to fight for so long. Dominated by new technologies, extended to new geographies, and featuring new instruments that bring new weapons to bear on new enemies, post-9/11 war and its literature seem to be especially well positioned for such cultural analysis. As Ann-Katrine Nielsen points out in her essay in this volume, "distance becomes a central, multifaceted term in contemporary understandings of and debates on war."[2] Indeed, a number of literary scholars have posited a wide range of similar arguments regarding the literature that takes post-9/11 war as its subject, since its veterans experience war both from up close and from afar. Roy Scranton, Sam Sacks, Patrick Deer, and George Packer (to name but a few) have all chimed in about what does and does not stand out as exceptional in the last eighteen years of war literature.[3] Yet, as Scranton points out in his "Trauma Hero" piece published online by the *Los Angeles Review of Books* in 2015, there seems to be little change in contemporary war literature from previous generations regarding the fundamental shape and function of the narratives themselves.

In a 2014 piece for the *New York Times,* Michiko Kakutani rightly notes that "literary innovations associated with earlier wars have long since trickled down into the culture at large and been absorbed into our jangled, aesthetic DNA."[4] But it takes time for that trickle-down effect to appear in art, and—obviously—it takes even more time for scholarly assessment to follow. In *The Great War and Modern Memory* (not published until 1975), Paul Fussell outlines how the brutality of the First World War, as experienced and recorded by its closest observers, ushered in a corresponding change in popular war stories, from the traditions of romanticism to the ironies of modernism. In similar fashion, many scholars have traced the links between postmodernism and the Vietnam War.[5] Fredric Jameson, for one, called the Vietnam War "the first terrible postmodernist war."[6] No similarly compelling conclusions have emerged yet regarding post-9/11 war and American war literature.[7] Contemporary war literature, Kakutani asserts, continues to retain a "chamber music quality, using . . . fable-like allegories or keyhole views . . . to open small windows on these conflicts."[8] Scores of post-9/11 war novels and memoirs have appeared since Kakutani wrote that in 2014, but there still seems to exist a bit of scholarly impatience in war literature studies as we all wait for this generation's Hemingway, Heller, Herr, or O'Brien, an American war writer who can push the genre into new artistic waters and, in the process, reflect something back regarding American war culture and the nature of war's remoteness.

Jay Winter points out in his introduction to *Shadows of War: A Social History of Silence in the Twentieth Century* that some of the delay is due to "liturgical silences" that dominate any "framing of public understandings of war and violence, since these [tales] touch on the sacred, and on eternal themes of loss, mourning, sacrifice, and redemption."[9] As he sees it, silence is a cultural practice that, out of necessity, actively negotiates between memory and forgetting. He continues, "Silence, we hold, is a socially constructed space in which and about which subjects and words normally used in everyday life are not spoken. The circle around this space is described by groups of people who at one point in time deem it appropriate that there is a difference between the sayable and the unsayable, or the spoken and unspoken, and that such a distinction can and should be maintained and observed over time."[10] Linking stylistic innovation with a cultural condition may be a seductive goal for war literature studies, but as Winter astutely points out, it will likely take even longer when doing so requires penetrating the circles that are drawn around the sayable and unsayable. The silence extends even further when the combat résumé of the warrior-speaker is used as the ultimate determinant of where and how Winter's circles are drawn. In other words, these post-9/11 circles are particularly impenetrable.

As I see it, however, there exists a master narrative in post-9/11 war culture and its literature that is so at odds with the nature of post-9/11 war that the time has come to penetrate one liturgical space of silence in particular. This narrative—the one that dominates contemporary American war literature—primarily concerns itself with the woundings and healings delivered and received by a protagonist warrior. The master narrative, then, is presented as little more than an attempt to either explain combat to the inexperienced or catalog the human costs of war, costs that are typically limited to the warriors, their friends, and their families. Thanks to the bursts of patriotism and nationalism that followed 9/11 and endure today in American pop culture, the common post-9/11 war narrative effectively displaces the warrior's agency in the war-making machine, rendering him or her as the ultimate victim of a faceless, and therefore blameless, enemy. War culture in the United States, it would seem, is essentially a culture of victimhood, and its literature rarely expands beyond its value as a vehicle through which warriors either trumpet their grievances or assign blame. The result is a body of literature that tends to focus on the marginalized (and elite) status of wounded or unwounded combat warriors in novels that repetitively articulate warrior pain, suffering, and trauma.

Gazing at the Warrior

Literary warrior gazing is not necessarily new to the most recent wave of American war literature, but it can be linked, at least partially, to what Roy Scranton assesses in his "Trauma Hero" essay. There, Scranton suggests that American war fiction has long engaged in warrior scapegoating, a literary tradition preferred by readers of the most celebrated American literary voices (his examples are Hemingway and Tim O'Brien). Such a scapegoat mechanism results in a predictable narrative cycle, one that features a soon-to-be-wounded warrior who goes to war and is vicariously joined there by the audience. Scranton points out that this structure "serves a scapegoat function, discharging national bloodguilt by substituting the victim of trauma, the soldier, for the victim of violence, the enemy."[11] Scranton's point is a solid one, though his work is essentially an updated, albeit brief, application of Kenneth Burke's scapegoat mechanism to *American Sniper,* Kevin Powers's *The Yellow Birds,* and Phil Klay's short story "Redeployment."[12] American popular culture is all too eager to replicate combat experiences into first-person stories that function as titillating reportage, typically from or about Navy SEALs and other special operators. And war writers are all too eager to produce works of literature that deliver on the dictates of such a mechanism. As Burke outlined in various works throughout his career, the wounding of a vicarious victim serves as a purgative cure for the audience.[13] And in post-9/11 America, auditors and writers do not have to work too hard to find war zones. As Nick Turse points out in a piece for TomDispatch, in 2017 alone, U.S. Special Forces were deployed to 149 different countries around the world.[14] Stephanie Savell packages similar statistics into a stunning visual representation for *Smithsonian* magazine: as she reports, in January 2019, the U.S. military was operating in 40 percent of the world's nations.[15] No matter how one feels about the righteousness of those operations, the consumer of the typical story that emerges from this myriad array of war settings most certainly comes to it in need of a purge. So the audience's gaze naturally turns toward a wounded warrior who can, therein, easily become the convenient vessel that carries away all lingering guilt as the warrior-veteran seeks out a postwar cleanse of the stains and injuries of modern war.

As James Campbell points out in his 1999 essay "Combat Gnosticism: The Ideology of First World War Poetry Criticism," war literature and its criticism have long been entrenched in such an approach, one that grants the witness of direct combat the uppermost spot on a hierarchy of wartime epistemology. This combat gnosticism, Campbell argues, not only privileges one type of experience (combat) over all others but also silences dissent and voices from other war observers and participants.[16] Indeed, Samuel Hynes, in his magisterial 1997 book entitled *The Soldiers' Tale: Bearing Witness to Modern War,* made the case that very little else about war's experience matters to war historiography beyond first-person-narrated works penned by men (yes, always men) who "were there," men who felt "what it was really like to be there, where the actual killing was done."[17] It is time to open the lens of war literature studies considerably to, if nothing else, more honestly engage with the implications and limitations of such warrior deference. As Winter writes, "Today the collage of organised violence and the suffering it entails is much more complex, even dizzying in its shifting character. The tale of war can no longer be told primarily or exclusively within the unfolding saga of nationalism and the achievement of self-determination and national dignity."[18] To put it another way, considering the fluid and virtual status of the "there" of post-9/11 war, a more fluid and communal-based conception of the post-9/11 warrior should probably follow suit. It could also serve to limit the so-called military–civilian divide and act as an antidote to the valorization of violence that seems inherent in any representation of warrior behavior.

Still, the plight of the individual wounded warrior has a dominant hold on contemporary war literature, as contemporary war writing seems to be stuck on repeat as narrative after narrative examines the manner in which an American warrior goes to an easily identifiable war zone, is wounded or traumatized, and then achieves a postwounding redemption in a society that strives and strives—though it almost always fails—to reincorporate the wounded warrior into mainstream society.[19] Phil Klay's National Book Award–winning short-story collection *Redeployment*, Kevin Powers's novel *The Yellow Birds*, Ben Fountain's satirical *Billy Lynn's Long Halftime Walk*, and Brian Turner's memoir *My Life as a Foreign Country* (in addition to two poetry collections) are but four prominent examples of how important the combat-wounded and redeemed (or unredeemed) warrior still is in modern American war culture. This was, ostensibly, what drove Margaret MacMillan to attempt to "make sense of the warrior" and "to understand what makes a warrior" in a recent series of lectures for BBC4 Radio entitled "The Mark of Cain." As she asserts, we both "admire" and "fear" the warrior. She goes on, "It's said . . . that the next generation of fighter planes won't have pilots; they will not be needed any longer. But we'll still need, I think, the qualities that make good soldiers—the discipline, the commitment, the selflessness, the willingness to work with others—so that I can't see how a military can operate without those qualities whatever it is actually doing and whatever weapons it's actually using."[20] I could not agree more. However, the problem is that the warrior label—to include all the positive character traits Mac-Millan includes in her list—is not always so cleanly substituted for the "good soldier" label, since today's warrior, quite often, never gets anywhere near the war zone.

In the 2017 issue of *War, Literature, and the Arts,* Grace Miller examines how entrenched sentiment about warrior status among U.S. Air Force pilots has created a "real-life drone crisis of identity" for those who fly drones (or remotely piloted aircraft, as they are known in official military language). As Miller writes, these pilots' distance from the zone of destruction that their machines create causes them to doubt their roles as "fully embodied warriors," while they still suffer plenty, if not more, from the guilt and psychological stresses that face the traditional fighter pilot. Miller goes on to suggest that the remotely piloted aircraft "pilot's psychological state is the most embattled space of them all."[21] Miller applies Paul Virilio and Judith Butler to her analyses of George Brant's play *Grounded* and the 2014 movie *Good Kill* (starring Ethan Hawke), and she makes some excellent points about how the air force has worked very hard but has failed (unfairly, she implies) to validate the warrior bona fides of drone pilots:[22] "What Butler calls for, in light of her analysis, is a 'political dependency' that encourages all people, warfighters included, to see themselves as interconnected. Otherwise, the possibility of guilt will never become a factor in strategic, operational, or tactical planning. How the subject can go about imagining his or her interconnectedness with the other is anyone's guess when these wars are conducted from thousands of miles away."[23] Miller stops short of suggesting a solution to this identity crisis beyond arguing that this one category of military members deserves admission to the same old combat-experienced warrior club, the same club that dictates whose story of war matters the most later. Miller also dismisses Butler's suggestion as untenable, but even fighter pilots somehow manage to establish interconnectedness with their country and their fellow combatants, and even they maintain a definite distance from the destruction of war.

Without entering into debates over relative proximities to death, the comparative dangers of differing types of military vehicles, or the varying depths of trauma associated with different war experiences, it seems imperative to reconsider what we are really talking about when we talk about post-9/11 warriors. In fact, the increased distance between warriors and war, as Miller, Virilio, and Butler describe it, has reinforced the hierarchy of combat experience instead of leveling it. Hierarchies—like the one that keeps the combat-experienced warrior as the example on which a service-based military ethos is based—are extremely resilient. But they are vulnerable, too. As Kenneth Burke wrote in *A Rhetoric of Motives,* "hierarchy is inevitable," but "the crumbling of hierarchies is as true a fact about them as their formation."[24] I argue that the best and perhaps only way to affect Butler's political dependency and a corresponding change in America's war culture (and maybe in its literature) is by loosening the elitist clinch of the war's most sacred cow: the glorified combat (and wounded) warrior.

Where Are the Warriors?

Twenty-two days before Donald J. Trump was sworn in as the forty-fifth president of the United States, I said goodbye to my wife and boarded a plane for Djibouti, Africa. I am an officer in the air force, and my services were required in the Horn of Africa as part of the United States' still-growing war against the spread of global terrorism. It was my sixth deployment since 9/11 (I have since completed my seventh, in Bahrain), but when I left the continental United States in late 2016, I knew very little about the job I would be doing in Africa. What I did know was that the flight to get there was going to be a long one. Known as the Rotator, the flight itinerary was a regular one via a contract passenger carrier designed to efficiently and regularly distribute troops to and from bases overseas. There is more than one Rotator, but the one I was on departs the East Coast of the United States on a biweekly schedule. It bounces from U.S. bases in Europe to U.S. bases in Southwest Asia to U.S. bases in Africa, dropping off deploying troops before it turns around, picks up redeploying troops, and returns them home.

The Boeing 767 that I boarded that December night was a full one, and because of a number of delays we encountered along the way, it became my home for the next seventy hours. I caught up on a little sleep and a lot of reading. I started with Colson Whitehead's award-winning *Underground Railroad,* and then I moved on to Sherman Alexie's 2007 novel, *Flight,* a touching story about a time-traveling Native American teenager "from this or that tribe" who carries the unfortunate nickname of Zits.[25] No two books could have been more appropriate for my trip, and they have haunted me a bit ever since. On the last leg of my long trip—between Bahrain and Djibouti—I finished Alexie's novel. I put it down and looked around the dark cabin of what was, by then, a nearly empty plane. I remembered a line from *Catch-22*, from when Doc Daneeka reflects that climbing into a plane is akin to climbing back into the womb: "In an airplane," he muses, "there was absolutely no place in the world to go except to another part of the airplane."[26] I did not feel as imprisoned in my plane as Doc Daneeka did in his, but I did feel the same inertia. In my case, it was driven by a military career that began sixteen months before 9/11. The Rotator had stopped in Spain and then again in Italy and Bahrain, so only sixty people remained on the massive jet. They were all teenagers and twentysomethings—headphoned, sleeping—so I could not help but feel my age. I was one of two officers on board, so I also felt my rank. And, probably because of the two novels I had just read, I felt an undeniable urge to flee.

I was tired of this going-to-war drill; I wanted to step aside and let these youngsters get off the plane and go off to whatever jobs the military had ready for them. I wanted to stay behind and escape the momentum of forces that seemed to be beyond my control. Whitehead's and Alexie's novels were not only about war, but they were certainly about warriors, and they did what all war novels should do: they made the reader uneasy about his or her part in state-sponsored violence. Of course, some people would argue that I was not really going to war either. But uneasy I most certainly was—perhaps in a new way—about my part in our country's global military agenda, and these novels made me want to go home to my wife and my dog because something within them felt frustratingly familiar but distant at the same time. As I stepped off the plane and into the glare of a Djiboutian sun, I decided that it had become harder and harder to locate myself in the foreign projection of the U.S. military. But in the end, as I stood on that blazing-hot concrete ramp with the others, I resigned myself to the pull of institutionalized fear and power and hate that had long dictated the direction of my life. I felt small, powerless, and inconsequential.

I thought of Cora, the courageous protagonist of Whitehead's novel, and of the hopeful ending of Alexie's otherwise bleak novel. And then I thought of a line from a third novel, *The Things They Carried*, by Tim

O'Brien. In one of my favorite chapters, O'Brien's protagonist (also named Tim O'Brien) receives his draft notice for Vietnam, and so he runs away—sort of—to the U.S.–Canadian border, where he spends six quiet, life-defining days at a motel called the Tip Top Lodge. He is thinking of running from the draft and into Canada, but the proprietor, a man named Elroy Berdahl, "offer[s] exactly" what the narrator needs. Or, better yet, this old man offers the young draftee nothing more than, as O'Brien writes, "a silent, watchful presence." The two men work together, and they fish together, and in the end, the narrator returns home to accept his draft summons and go off to Vietnam. O'Brien closes the chapter with two sentences that rang in my head the day I landed in Djibouti: "I was a coward. I went to the war."[27]

Of course, Djibouti is not exactly part of an identifiable war zone, though poverty and paranoia make it feel like one. I have never experienced combat, at least not like O'Brien did in Vietnam, though I have flown over Iraq and Afghanistan as a pilot of a refueling tanker. Still, I have never really been scared for my life in any threat-based sense while I did manage to log over one thousand combat hours in my KC-10 refueling tanker. Things felt different in Djibouti, though. The job itself was boring and hot and tedious, but somehow it ended up feeling rewarding and important. For six months, I attended meetings and delivered briefings and negotiated contracts and prioritized activities and yelled at eighteen-year-olds for driving too fast on the graveled roads around our base. I emailed. I talked. I praised. I wrote citations for awards. I gave tours to various senior leaders from the State Department and the Department of Defense. I enforced standards of behavior, rank, and appearance. A friend said, "You spend your time telling people to stop freaking out or start freaking out." Yet I felt closer to any war than ever before, though I was still far, far from it. Moreover, I was safe. I did not witness death or destruction. I did not directly cause anyone else's death. I was not wounded or ever worried about being wounded. I worked; I went for a run every evening before I spoke with my wife on Facetime. When I told the men and women who worked for me that they were warriors, I meant it. I am not sure, however, that I believed it, and that bothered me. It still does.

The fact remains (for U.S. military members who have deployed in support of combat operations abroad since 9/11) that relatively few have experienced the facts of combat in any sense that Samuel Hynes would recognize. Yet my African deployment taught me some lessons about the nature of post-9/11 war, qualities that need to find their way into contemporary American war culture and the way we might conceive of a warrior ethos and a representative experience of war. With very few exceptions, no one at that small American base in that former French colony took an active part in war in any combat sense. But we still knew what O'Brien knew and struggled with, and we suffered what he suffered, varying only by degree and geography. The difference may not be distance, then; the difference may be a too-strict set of qualifications to earn a warrior status in post-9/11 war culture. Does one need to wound or be wounded to consider oneself a warrior? Without the wounding, I worry that we are allowed the chance to shirk what Primo Levi called a "proper quota of guilt."[28] Indeed, during Donald Trump's first week in office, a CV-22 that was launched from my base in Djibouti crashed in the Yemeni desert—killing a Navy SEAL—while flying in support of a raid that resulted in the death of this sailor, some enemy combatants, and a number of civilians, including children.[29] No one in my unit was involved in any way with this mission. We were "there," but we were silent and inconsequential; our "there" was still far from the site of death and destruction. We may not have recognized it then, but we still accessed the epistemology that came with being part of a military machine that exerts its influence on a global scale in such a manner. The mission made national news, and I overheard two men discussing the coverage at dinner one evening. "No one can say shit," one said, "except for the ones who were there." We all mourned the death of the Navy SEAL, but it occurred to me that our places at the bottom of the combat hierarchy rooted us in what Kenneth Burke termed a "hierarchical psychosis."[30] We were allowing the combat hierarchy to disqualify us and others from active commentary regarding individual agency in war. Thus, we insulated ourselves from further, critical engagement—Butler's political dependency—with strategic or doctrinal discussions regarding the wars we were there to support.

Were we *at* war? Were we involved in combat? I confidently say yes, but my own comfort, my wireless internet, and my physical distance from tangible threats and recognizable violence nag that answer. And I assert this with full awareness that I carried the label of what Vietnam troops famously called a REMF and troops in Iraq and Afghanistan called a FOBBIT.[31] In the end, though, the fact remains that the vast majority of U.S. military members in post-9/11 warfare are FOBBITs. We are all REMFs. As Elaine Scarry describes modern conflict in *The Body in Pain,* the "injuring" of modern war "disappears from view." Scarry continues, "The building-in of skill thus becomes in its most triumphant form, the building-out of consent. It is, of course, only at the 'firing' end of the weapon that human presence is eliminated: their presence at the receiving end is still very much required."[32] Who or what provides the silence and watchful presence that ultimately shapes America's warriors for their part in war, wherever those warriors may find themselves, whatever they may do when they get there? What thread of truth runs from other wars to ours? Am I allowed to even call these wars my own if I am not wounded by them? Scarry makes the point that modern war extends, now, to all of us who do not pull triggers or drop bombs or kick in doors; every aspect of military training is aimed at killing or unmaking the body of the enemy. It seems to me, however, that post-9/11 warriors may never accept such logic because of the modern hierarchy that has been reenergized since 9/11, one that reserves the warrior label for the chosen, wounding, and wounded few. I know Brian Turner, Sebastian Junger, and Kevin Powers saw destruction and death and faced hazards I did not, but I wonder whether a more democratic and realistic approach to the representation of war experience is one that refuses to privilege combat witness at all.

Now, as Donald Trump's presidency progresses and I hear the general approval of his policies and pronouncements from my peers, superiors, and subordinates, it becomes all too clear that, despite the hazards soldiers of differing generations meet and the deaths that our operations create, the individual agency of the U.S. soldier continues to exist in a liminal space of in-combat and not-in-combat. Is it possible that contemporary military members can use the epistemological freedom of their various places in the military to challenge the very hierarchy in which they operate? Now, as I read articles arguing the value of facts and news and fake news and alternative facts, another question seems relevant regarding the place of a REMF warrior in post-9/11 war. Does the nature of the experience of war's participants (willing or otherwise) change anything in the game of agency and blame that dictates how war stories are reported or how the image of the warrior is constructed? Of course it does, but maybe it should not. Is traumatic war experience really required for one to access, transmit, or understand the traumatic evils of war? Since the direct experience of combat and even death should probably be considered the exception for those millions who have deployed in support of U.S. military operations abroad since 9/11, an updated warrior ethos for a band of warriors who never get any closer to war than I have might deflect the forces of combat gnosticism, the trauma hero myth, and the traditional violence that is embedded in the term *warrior* itself.

In a 2011 interview with Patrick Smith, Tim O'Brien said this about post-9/11 war and war literature:

> The pool of doubters—or at least the number of people ambivalent about these current wars—is small, relative to what we saw during the Vietnam era. Many of the people now in uniform signed up to go to war. And *all* of them are volunteers. They weren't drafted, or yanked out of school, or hauled away from their families. They've enlisted and been deployed of their own volition, and they're of a certain type, clearly much different from the guys I served with in Vietnam. . . . As a consequence, I think the public will entertain fewer doubts about it all and will ask fewer questions. In the end, I fear, fewer Americans will address even the most fundamental issue when it comes to war: Is the killing and dying really worth it?[33]

Is the killing and dying really worth it? That is a question we should *all* ask and answer. I asked myself that same question during my deployment in Djibouti. And during the six months I was there, the answer was not always the same. But one thing does stay constant when I grapple with that question, even today. While art like O'Brien's and Whitehead's and Alexie's may never stop violence or war or deter the eagerness of war participants like me, it can still remind us all to question and doubt and challenge the way we shape a post-9/11 warrior who does or does not actually kill or die on our behalf.

Despite the volunteer status of the U.S. military member, I think it is possible to foster healthy ambivalence instead of the certainty O'Brien worries about in the foregoing quote, and this possibility exists mainly *because* of the liminal space that all military members occupy when we go to war. We know the trauma of combat without actually experiencing it because we share the guilt that follows us to and from our various war zones, and we do not (or should not) need a combat-experienced scapegoat to carry such burdens away for us. That is ultimately what O'Brien's novel *The Things They Carried* achieves as it dances back and forth across the blurry line of fiction and nonfiction. O'Brien saw combat in Vietnam, and a little of it does exist in his novel, but when he mentions those "little beads of truth" in his Smith interview, I know that he is not really even talking about combat and traumatic experience or the value of witness-based epistemology or his own warrior legacy.[34]

Interestingly enough, O'Brien included an introduction for a special Franklin Library first edition of his novel that says precisely that same thing (one wonders why the introduction has not been reprinted since). He writes,

> Shakespeare wasn't writing about kings—he wasn't telling "king stories"—and in this book I am not writing about the phenomenon of war. My concern is humanity. My subjects are courage, faith, loneliness, terror, humiliation, sorrow, longing, despair, holiness, pity. . . . Other stories in this book are about story-telling itself. How stories transform abstraction into emotion. How stories remind us of those fundamental, gene-deep truths we've always known but sometimes forget. How good stories never carry a moral, but how morality is always carried by a good story. How certain stories are true, and others aren't, and how the true stories are often invented while the false stories may have actually happened.[35]

That is a hard thing to accept for many war story readers. Joseph Heller once made a similar claim when he said, "*Catch-22* is not really about World War II."[36] The "physical details," he went on, "do come out of my own experiences," but he insisted the novel is really about the Korean War, Joseph McCarthy's political crusades, and the author's confessed "preoccupation with mortality."[37] So, as Frederick Kiley and Walter McDonald urge in their "casebook" to accompany the novel, *Catch-22* should be exempted from "wriggling among the great and varied corpus of prose fiction called, unfairly, 'war novels.'"[38] Heller satirized combat with the shenanigans of his combat-avoiding Yosarian, and O'Brien tried to remove his own experience (his warrior bona fides) through the metafictional structure of his narrative, but even

Heller and O'Brien have never managed to avoid wriggling under the combat-hungry gaze that auditors bring to the literature of war.

So yes, reshaping a popular conception of the warrior so the contemporary war story can move beyond hagiographic tracings of a warrior's wounding may be an impossible task, given the enduring power of the scapegoat mechanism. However, it *may* be possible to open up access to war's truths and lessons so that they come from all points of the war machine. Maybe then popular American war culture can find an antidote for, as O'Brien says, the "everyday, common-man rhetoric about supporting our soldiers because they're the greatest people on earth and can do no wrong."[39]

I will never see anything close to what O'Brien saw in Vietnam. I will also never know (thankfully) what it feels like to kill another human being on behalf of a scared and scarred nation. However, I do know what it means to be the symbolic carrier of a country's fear and antagonism, and I recognize the imperative for me to shoulder the moral burden that role entails. I know it without ever getting very close to war at all.

Native American Warrior Traditions and Contemporary War Culture

Brian Turner asks in *My Life as a Foreign Country,* "How does anyone leave a war behind them, no matter what war it is, and somehow walk into the rest of his life?"[40] It bothers me that the pity Turner requests in that question is often reserved only for men like him, who were "there," who dodged bullets and scanned the streets of Baghdad for improvised explosive devices or kicked in doors in Mosul.[41] As of early 2019, the United States is actively waging war in at least three distinct areas: East Africa and Yemen, Iraq/Syria, and Afghanistan. So there are hundreds of thousands of warriors involved in these efforts and in other places across the globe (not to mention those military members from other countries), while very few of them would fit what American culture and many corners of the military deem worthy of a warrior label. It still remains a fact, however, that warrior work includes more than combat and that it has changed vastly since Turner drove the streets of Baghdad and dodged one trauma-laden bullet after another.

Yet as I have suggested, the genre of contemporary war literature is almost entirely dominated by the presence or voice of the combat-wounded warrior and narratives that stand out as raw inscriptions of traumatic events driven home by the authenticity that attends such confessional, memoir-styled reportage. And this makes sense for good reason: the story of the typical, representative post-9/11 war veteran is probably a fairly boring one.[42] Perhaps, then, it is not surprising (though it is definitely ironic) that some big names in contemporary war literature, such as Sebastian Junger and Brian Turner, turn to Indigenous cultures in the United States to contend with the confusions facing post-9/11 warriors as they transition from at-war to not-at-war.

Such a move—consulting and partially appropriating Native American warrior traditions—can be a tricky one. In *Medicine Bags and Dog Tags*, Al Carroll considers the link between the "warrior/savage/mascot/military stereotypes" in modern American culture and goes so far as to ponder whether it might be time to abandon the deep connection that exists between U.S. military veteran traditions and tribal warrior societies.[43] Indeed, the term *warrior* is a poor substitute for the concept it represents in many Indigenous cultures. As Taiaiake Alfred and Lana Lowe outline in a report for the Ipperwash Inquiry in Canada, many Indigenous cultures in North and Central America include a warrior society in some form; however, there is a depth of meaning in the term *warrior* that eludes translation.[44] For example, for the Kanien'kehaka people, the word *rotiskenhrakete* literally means "carrying the burden of peace." For the Kuna of Central America, *napasapgued* means "one who protects or guards the land, or nature." For the Dakota, *akicita* is the word for "warrior," which is related to *akita*, meaning "to seek."[45] As Donald Mrozek points out, the term *warrior* should indicate "the emergence of a more complexly textured sense of the modern soldier, sailor, marine, and airman," since traditional contextual use of the term "tends toward extremes—almost toward the use of conflict as a mode of self-expression and self-identification." Mrozek concludes that if we insist on maintaining the concept of a warrior as an indispensable part of war (to include winning such a war), then the term should probably extend to all components of post-9/11 military members, including all jobs required by modern warfare, such as driving trucks and staring at computer screens.[46]

This is easier said than done, though, since the difficulties of fully interrogating (and defining) both desired and undesired elements of a post-9/11 warrior are rooted within the hierarchy that the United States (not just its military) uses to delineate the duties of its military members and the vast, largely invisible, legions of supporting civilian contractors. Also, glorifying a war-fighting hero has its obvious self-serving, recruiting, motivating, and memorializing purposes. So perhaps it makes sense that the ethos and culture that attract future warriors to the U.S. military have remained fairly static for centuries. It also takes no imagination, distasteful though it may be, to imagine why there persists a popular conception of warrior behavior that includes righteous aggression and undying stamina in eager service to unavoidable violence and sacrificial bloodletting. Unless the very concept of the warrior itself is significantly adjusted, we should probably expect such qualities to remain central to the dominant warrior ethos in American war culture.

In the memoir *My Life as a Foreign Country*, the warrior's return to the homeland is Brian Turner's primary concern. He makes it clear that there is no easy panacea for the returning warrior, wounded or otherwise. Rather, coming home from war, like going to war, is a process, one that rarely ends in a harmonious, recognizable place for a warrior within a community. That, Turner writes, is one "that takes years and years."[47] His memoir is a running contemplation of the events and memories that hurt him alongside those that, he hopes, will eventually heal him. And so it is fitting in tone and context that, in one of his final chapters, Turner closes the narrative arc by telling about a ritual cleansing, a rite he seeks out to hasten his reentry back into the years and years of postwar healing to come. He visits a sweat lodge on a small island off the coast of Rhode Island, an island once populated by the members of the Niantic Nation. This ritualized purge via the heat and pain of a traditional Niantic sweat lodge allows Turner to rediscover the warrior who deployed to Iraq in the first place. And this, this reconnection with aspects of a warrior ethos that Turner strove to keep in focus during his yearlong deployment to Iraq, is the most important element of his return and, essentially, the memoir. This ritual, this communal purge, allows Turner's memoir to end on a hopeful note. It also allows him to appropriate something about traditional native cultures that he finds missing in popular American war culture.

His final chapter begins, "Sgt. Turner is dead," and this statement is, I think, one to be read literally, not only in regard to his now-gone military rank and title but also in the sense that he is discarding something unhealthy, something that would taint an otherwise healthy re-entry.[48] It is easy to see how such a purge can be beneficial for Turner, and so the reader is left with a clear impression that there is a distinct mismatch between his prewar and postwar warrior self and ethos. In the quiet resolve of the final chapter that follows this purgative trip into the sweat lodge, Turner makes it clear that the being who survived Iraq had to die so that Brian Turner (an agent, not a victim) could live and reconnect with the sacred, a sanctity of the individual that he is able to locate in the physicality and pain of the lodge's heat. He writes, "I realize—heat draws the ocean from our bodies. It reduces us to mineral and bone. Desiccation. Heat demands that the desert reveal itself."[49] Thus, Turner's revitalization follows what Taiaiake Alfred calls the "warrior's way," a sometimes painful and always social ceremony that allows one to purify oneself in order to recommit to a continual, active, communally based warrior ethos.[50] And this is important: this ceremony allows Turner to *still* be a warrior when he emerges from the lodge and begin his healthy reintegration into American society, far from the army and far from war.

The journalist Sebastian Junger is probably best known for the works he produced after he was an imbedded reporter with a remote U.S. Army unit in the mountains of Afghanistan in 2007 and 2008. Since then, he has written and spoken extensively about his experiences and the experiences of the soldiers he lived with there, culminating in his 2010 book *War* and the follow-up documentary films *Restrepo* and *Korengal*. These works mainly focus on the wounded warriors who try to survive the action of war, showing us what happened to a small band of army troops in a remote Afghan region. Junger's latest book, *Tribe*, refocuses on the return of those soldiers to their homes in the United States. Why, he asks, does a country like Israel, "despite decades of intermittent war," experience lower rates of posttraumatic stress disorder among its military members than almost all modern countries? His answer is in the title. As Junger argues, modern American culture is one especially adept at exacerbating the problems that face a returning veteran and his or her attendant posttraumatic stress disorder because our lack of proximity to (our remoteness from) the war zone prevents the American public from creating, as Junger writes, a "shared public meaning of the war."[51]

Specifically, Junger blames our society's fractured sense of community and a dominant war apathy that deflects, at a societal level, any acceptance of a proper moral burden for the consequences that naturally follow war. In his preface, Junger writes that his book outlines "what we can learn from tribal societies about loyalty and belonging and the eternal human quest for meaning."[52] Matthew Crawford nicely summarizes Junger's thesis in his *New York Times* review of the book:

> Such is the misalignment of our culture and military service that someone who has fought is regarded as fundamentally damaged. The way we receive combat veterans returning home is by treating them as victims and putting them on disability. Victim status confers the only form of moral redemption we know, and we offer this freely—on the condition that a veteran submit to therapy. If the therapy is successful, he will come to accept the obsolescence of precisely those traits that made him a good fighter. With the help of a little medication they wither, like a limb that has been tied off to prevent an infection from spreading. Only then can the veteran hope to claim his prize, which is to become a well-adjusted consumer and cog in the corporate economy.[53]

Just as Turner's sweat lodge purged him of the stains of his combat traumas, Junger envisions a war culture that offers something similar for soldiers like the ones he knew in Afghanistan. Junger points to Apache and Dine cultures and the manner in which a number of Native American communities achieved purification for their warriors through ritual and communal sharing. As Junger writes, "The entire community participated in these rituals because every person in the tribe was assumed to have been affected by the war."[54] Inclusivity and communal sharing after war recast the traumatized and traumatizing warrior as, after his or her trip to war, once again responsible for taking care of others, for practicing self-discipline, and for providing leadership.

These are but two examples from contemporary war writing and what I see as a growing trend in war studies to turn to native cultures in the United States for guidance concerning how we help warriors become healthy and contributing members of society when they return. And for the most part, I think the impulse is justifiable and fruitful as long as it seeks out a fuller understanding and application of the term *warrior* itself. Such an effort definitely runs the risk of appropriation, but as N. Scott Momaday once said, "It is important to understand that the Native American has as much to offer American education as he has to gain. His long tenure in the land and his ancient wisdom are invaluable."[55] Momaday was, of course, talking about Native American studies and the humanities in general, but his words still apply to what Junger and Turner explore in their works. And as Momaday shows us through Abel—the wounded warrior of *House Made of Dawn*—the modern native veteran is not immune to the traumatic dislocation from self and community that war presents.

What is important to note about Abel, however, is that his community does not really change so that he can achieve his final self-cleanse following his war years, his prison years, and his years in Los Angeles, each one a purgatorial war zone in its own right. The healing of Momaday's postwar warrior cannot begin until he or she (as Abel does) *chooses* to (as opposed to being compelled or coerced to) abandon self-pity and take part in that community's normal rituals, rituals that exist and thrive because they remain outside the staining effects of war.[56] Abel joins the run of the dead at the end of the novel and thereby marks the end of his self-victimry (or wounded role) so that he can begin progressing toward an embodiment of the leadership-based (or warrior) ethic his grandfather Francisco modeled so well. When we leave Abel at the end of the novel, we are comforted by the hope that he will become, like Francisco, a sort of postwar warrior for his people.

Junger admits in *Tribe* that there is a problem with his oversimplified approach, his obvious cultural appropriation, and the ever-changing circumstances of wars and cultures. "Contemporary America is," Junger writes, "a secular society that obviously can't just borrow from Indian culture to heal its own wounds."[57] Likewise, Turner does not imply that every traumatized veteran can be healed by marching straight to the nearest sweat lodge. In many ways, then, perhaps the necessary ethic for a post-9/11 warrior (and the true value of learning from native cultures in the United States without appropriating them) is one that broadens the sign-carrying potential of the term itself. Might post-9/11 warriors be reimagined, in cultural and artistic practices, as responsible for communal caretaking, conflict resolution, and leadership instead of being treated as exceptional, sacrificial scapegoats?

Warriors like Francisco, Abel (in the end), Turner, and the soldiers Junger knew are exactly that; they are caretakers and negotiators, providers ready to endure in service to a community with patience and compromise. They all achieve their healthy returns from war when they reject victimhood. This sloughing off is easier said than done, though. As Junger admits, "Ex-combatants are incentivized to see themselves as victims rather than as perpetrators . . . whose victim status eclipses more accurate and meaningful understandings of violence."[58] Does it not make sense, then, to consider a healthier warrior ethos so that we may avoid underscoring difference or uniqueness and instead celebrate places that both deploying and redeploying military members share with the rest of the community?

Ethos Building

At the U.S. Air Force Academy, where I attended college and where I now teach, courses on leadership and character are, perhaps obviously, a large part of the educational curriculum. One of the nine institutional outcomes that the curriculum seeks to foster in Air Force Academy cadets is the concept of a warrior ethos. Or, as the academy defines the concept, embodying the "warrior ethos as airmen and citizens" means that one will be able to embody "the warrior spirit: tough mindedness, tireless motivation, an unceasing vigilance, a willingness to sacrifice one's life for the country, if necessary, and a commitment to be the world's premier air, space and cyberspace force."[59] This concept is further broken down into four categories: (1) understanding and examining the profession of arms through multiple perspectives; (2) exhibiting a level of integrity and moral courage despite adversity; (3) demonstrating physical courage and putting "the mission and others before one's self" with "grit" and a "hardiness of resistance to accept failure"; and (4) developing continually improving discipline and excellence according to communal customs, traditions, standards, and ceremonies.[60] I am, quite honestly, a fan of this warrior ethos outcome because it at least partially disavows the self-pity or difference-marking that is inherent in wounded warrior rhetoric. Stamina, courage, selflessness, resilience, discipline: these are worthy traits to foster in any human being.

In my classes, my students and I often consider the various duties of the warrior in the war literature we read, and it is easy to identify almost all of the characters as selfless and committed, combat experienced or not. As I see it, the best part of the academy's new warrior ethos outcome is the fact that it favors selfless societal caretaking and patient conflict resolution over national fantasies of aggression and vengeance. As a student once concluded, this ethos treats the gender-neutral warrior as a healthy part of society before, during, and after war. That same student wondered whether we should just call it a human ethos instead of a warrior ethos. Junger proposes that communities across the nation should have open-mic nights at community halls, Veterans of Foreign Wars posts, and high school gyms so veterans can share stories and so that communities can shoulder their fair share of war's moral burden. I am not so sure that would solve much, since Junger's *veteran* still seems to imply "combat veteran." Sharing stories is always a good idea, but as my students have shown me, it is through an opening of the very concept of the warrior that we might be able to come to terms with the health and survival of postwar veterans and the culture to which they return. Momaday writes in *The Way to Rainy Mountain* that, for his ancestors, "war was their sacred business. . . . But warfare for the Kiowas was pre-eminently a matter of disposition rather than survival, and they never understood the grim, unrelenting advance of the U.S. Calvary."[61] That disposition is what the wider war culture in America needs as war continues to move farther and farther away from the zone of war itself. In that conception, it remains possible, even, that the warriors of post-9/11 war culture could follow an ethos that is, just maybe, violence-free.

Notes

1. The term *war* is used here and elsewhere in this chapter to refer to any military operation or military effort endorsed by the United States since 9/11. The United States has not officially declared war against any country since 1942.

2. Interestingly enough, as Nielsen explains, in Denmark the 2010 Veteran Policy presented an official definition of *veteran,* one designed to "make the new veteran generation feel supported and acknowledged" by the nation state.

3. See Roy Scranton, "The Trauma Hero: From Wilfred Owen to *Redeployment* and 'American Sniper,'" *Los Angeles Review of Books,* January 25, 2015, https://lareviewofbooks.org/article/trauma-hero-wilfred-owen-redeployment-american-sniper/; Sam Sacks, "First-Person Shooters," *Harper's,* August 2015,

https://harpers.org/archive/2015/08/first-person-shooters-2/; Patrick Deer, "The Ends of War and the Limits of War Culture," *Social Text* 25, no. 2 (2007): 5–9; and George Packer, "Home Fires," *New Yorker,* April 7, 2014, 69–73.

4. Michiko Kakutani, "Human Costs of the Forever Wars, Enough to Fill a Bookshelf," *New York Times,* December 26, 2014, A1.

5. See Lucas Carpenter, "'It Don't Mean Nuthin': Vietnam War Fiction and Postmodernism," *College Literature* 30, no. 2 (Spring 2003): 30–50; in addition to Ty Hawkins, "Vietnam and Verisimilitude: Rethinking the Relationship between 'Postmodern War' and Naturalism," *War, Literature and the Arts* 24, no. 1–2 (2012), https://www.wlajournal.com/wlaarchive/24_1-2/Hawkins.pdf.

6. Fredric Jameson, *Postmodernism; or, The Cultural Logic of Late Capitalism* (Durham, N.C.: Duke University Press, 1991), 44.

7. This does not mean, however, that scholars have missed the opportunity. Ty Hawkins, for example, examines contemporary war literature as a sense-making exercise for veteran-authors in his essay "Modern War and American Literature: Ironic Realism, Satire, and Escape," in *Violence in Literature,* ed. Stacey Peebles (Ipswich, Mass.: Salem, 2014), 54–68.

8. Kakutani, "Human Costs," A1.

9. Jay Winter, "Thinking about Silence," in *Shadows of War: A Social History of Silence in the Twentieth Century,* ed. Efrat Ben-Ze'ev, Ruth Ginio, and Jay Winter (Cambridge: Cambridge University Press, 2010), 4.

10. Winter, 13.

11. Scranton, "Trauma Hero."

12. See David Buchanan, *Going Scapegoat: Post-9/11 War Literature, Language, and Culture* (Jefferson, N.C.: McFarland, 2016), for further analysis of the scapegoat function in contemporary war literature.

13. Burke developed his scapegoat mechanism across a body of work that spanned almost sixty years. His book *A Rhetoric of Motives* (New York: Prentice-Hall, 1950) contains some of his most detailed discussions of the mechanism's prevalence in literature. For secondary sources, see Elizabeth M. Weiser, "Burke and War: Rhetoricizing the Theory of Dramatism," *Rhetoric Review* 26, no. 3 (2007): 286–302. See also C. Allen Carter, *Kenneth Burke and the Scapegoat Process* (Norman: University of Oklahoma Press, 1996).

14. Nick Turse, "A Wider World of War," TomDispatch, December 14, 2017, http://www.tomdispatch.com/post/176363/tomgram%3A_nick_turse%2C_a_wider_world_of_war/.

15. Stephanie Savell, "This Map Shows Where in the World the U.S. Military Is Combatting Terrorism," *Smithsonian,* January 2019, https://www.smithsonianmag.com/history/map-shows-places-world-where-us-military-operates-180970997/.

16. James Campbell, "Combat Gnosticism: The Ideology of First World War Poetry Criticism," *New Literary History* 30, no. 1 (1999): 203–15.

17. Samuel Hynes, *The Soldier's Tale: Bearing Witness to Modern War* (New York: Penguin, 1997), 4, xvi.

18. Winter, "Thinking about Silence," 12.

19. Patrick Deer argues that contemporary war fiction "displays both a struggle to reconstruct damaged individual and collective memory and a skeptical view of any confident effort at postwar recovery" in "Beyond Recovery: Representing History and Memory in Iraq War Writing," *Modern Fiction Studies* 63, no. 3 (Summer 2017): 313. For a sociological examination of post-9/11 veterans as they negotiate the difficulties of redeployment, see Aaron Glantz, *The War Comes Home: Washington's Battle against America's Veterans* (Berkeley: University of California Press, 2009).

20. Margaret MacMillan, "Fearing and Loving: Making Sense of the Warrior," in "The Mark of Cain," Reith Lectures, July 3, 2018, BBC4 Radio, https://www.bbc.co.uk/programmes/b0b88hl4.

21. Grace E. Miller, "'Boom / [S]he Is Not': Drone Wars and the Vanishing Pilot," *War, Literature, and the Arts* 29, nos. 1–2 (2017): 2, 6, https://www.wlajournal.com/wlaarchive/29/miller.pdf.

22. The references are to Virilio's prescient 1989 book, *War and Cinema: The Logistics of Perception,* and Judith Butler's 2010 *Frames of War.*

23. Miller, "Boom / [S]he Is Not," 15.

24. Burke, *Rhetoric of Motives,* 141.

25. Sherman Alexie, *Flight* (New York: Black Cat, 2007), 4.

26. Joseph Heller, *Catch-22* (1955), 50th anniversary ed. (New York: Scribner, 1996), 42.

27. Tim O'Brien, *The Things They Carried* (Boston: Houghton Mifflin, 1990), 46, 58.

28. Primo Levi, *The Drowned and the Saved* (New York: Vintage Books, 1989*), 49.

29. See Cynthia McFadden, William M. Arkin, and Tim Uehlinger, "How the Trump Team's First Military Raid in Yemen Went Wrong," ABC News, October 2, 2017, https://www.nbcnews.com/news/us-news/how-trump-team-s-first-military-raid-went-wrong-n806246, for a brief discussion of the incident and various levels of civilian approval for such military operations.

30. Burke, *Rhetoric of Motives,* 281.

31. Both terms describe a military member who never leaves the safety of a secure military base. REMF was the acronym for "rear echelon mother fucker." FOBBIT combines FOB (forward operating base) with "Hobbit."

32. Elaine Scarry, *The Body in Pain: The Making and Unmaking of the World* (New York: Oxford University Press, 1985), 66, 152.

33. Tim O'Brien, "On War, Heroes, and the Power of Literature: A Conversation with Tim O'Brien," interview by Patrick A. Smith, in *Conversations with Tim O'Brien,* ed. Patrick A. Smith (Oxford: University Press of Mississippi, 2012), 190.

34. O'Brien, 194.

35. Tim O'Brien, "A Special Message for the First Edition from Tim O'Brien," foreword to *The Things They Carried* (Franklin Center, Penn.: Franklin Library, 1990).

36. Joseph Heller, "On Translating *Catch-22* into a Movie," in *A Catch-22 Casebook,* ed. Frederick Kiley and Walter McDonald (New York: Thomas Crowell, 1973), 357.

37. Joseph Heller, "Interview: Joseph Heller," interview by Sam Merrill, *Playboy* 22, no. 6 (June 1975): 68.

38. Frederick Kiley and Walter McDonald, preface to Kiley and McDonald, *Catch-22 Casebook,* v–vi.

39. O'Brien, "On War," 194.

40. Brian Turner, *My Life as a Foreign Country* (New York: Norton, 2014), 154.

41. For extensive analysis of the literary and civic value of pity and its relationship with self-pity, see David Punter, *The Literature of Pity* (Edinburgh: Edinburgh University Press, 2014); and Marina Berzins McCoy, *Wounded Heroes: Vulnerability as a Virtue in Ancient Greek Literature and Philosophy* (Oxford: Oxford University Press, 2013).

42. Only two novels come to mind that attempt to present the war stories of post-9/11 REMFs (David Abrams's *FOBBIT* and Helen Benedict's *Sand Queen*). Even then, both of these novels ultimately slide into a familiar shape by placing the noncombat troop in some form of identifiable combat through logistical or transportation-based accidents.

43. Al Carroll, *Medicine Bags and Dog Tags: American Indian Veterans from Colonial Times to the Second Iraq War* (Lincoln: University of Nebraska Press, 2008), 226.

44. The Ipperwash Inquiry examined events surrounding Dudley George's death in 1995 after the man was shot during a First Nations protest at Ipperwash Provincial Park in Ontario. For more information, see the official website at http://www.attorneygeneral.jus.gov.on.ca/inquiries/ipperwash.

45. Taiaiake Alfred and Lana Lowe, "Warrior Societies in Contemporary Indigenous Communities," Ipperwash Inquiry, 2007, 5, 6, http://www.attorney general.jus.gov.on.ca/inquiries/ipperwash/policy_part/research/pdf/Alfred_and _Lowe.pdf.

46. Donald J. Mrozek, "The Military, Sport, and Warrior Culture," in *The Columbia History of Post–World War II America,* ed. Mark C. Carnes (New York: Columbia University Press, 2007), 143.

47. Turner, *My Life,* 169.

48. Turner, 199.

49. Turner, 182.

50. Taiaiake Alfred, *Wasáse: Indigenous Pathways of Action and Freedom* (Toronto: University of Toronto Press, 2005), 11.

51. Sebastian Junger, *Tribe* (New York: Hachette, 2016), 96, 97.

52. Junger, xviii.

53. Matthew Crawford, "Sebastian Junger's *Tribe,*" *New York Times,* May 27, 2016, https://www.nytimes.com/2016/05/19/books/review-sebastian-jungers -tribe-examines-disbanded-brothers-returning-to-a-divided-country.html.

54. Junger, *Tribe,* 120.

55. N. Scott Momaday, "An Interview with N.(avarre) Scott Momaday," interview by Richard Mace, *St. John's University Humanities Review* 4, no. 1 (Spring 2006), http://facpub.stjohns.edu/~ganterg/sjureview/vol4-1/07Momaday -Mace.htm.

56. See also Bernard A. Hirsch, "Self-Hatred and Spiritual Corruption in *House Made of Dawn*," *Western American Literature* 17, no. 4 (Winter 1983): 307–20.

57. Junger, *Tribe*, 121.

58. Junger, 99.

59. "Outcomes," United States Air Force Academy, accessed January 29, 2020, https://www.usafa.edu/academics/outcomes/.

60. "Warrior Ethos as Airmen and Citizens," United States Air Force Academy, accessed January 29, 2020, https://www.usafa.edu/app/uploads/Warrior-Ethos -White-Paper-approved.pdf.

61. N. Scott Momaday, *House Made of Dawn* (1966; New York: Harper, 2010), 113.

CHAPTER 3

From Hermeneutics to Archives

Parasites and Predators in *Homeland*

JENS BORREBYE BJERING
AND ANDREAS IMMANUEL GRAAE

In his book on the history of American intelligence, journalist Thomas Powers describes how the challenges facing contemporary surveillance differ radically from those of the past: "Modern eavesdropping seldom mirrors the classic wiretap of yesteryear when FBI agents with earphones might record hundreds of hours of a Mafia chief chatting with his underboss in New York's Little Italy. The idea now is to see if *anyone* on the phone in New York or New Jersey sounds in any way like a Mafia chief. . . . If the first generation of targets numbered a hundred, let's say, and each of them had been talking to a hundred people in a second generation of targets, then even a third-generation search could easily sweep up a million people."[1] Of course, "sweep[ing] up a million people" would be no problem—at least not for the intelligence services—if this were all there was to it. Yet, as Richard A. Clarke, national security adviser to President Bill Clinton who also stayed on for a short while in the George W. Bush administration, describes it in his *Against All Enemies* (2004), turning vast amounts of information into actual "intelligence" means more than merely sweeping up as much intelligence as possible: "Intelligence involves analysis of raw reports, not merely their enumeration or weighing them by the pound. Analysis, in turn, involves finding independent means of corroborating the reports."[2] This quote refers specifically to the early days after 9/11, where the top echelons of U.S. government precisely demanded insight into raw, uncorroborated intelligence reports, and where this insight, according to James Baker, made the members of the administration "suffer from sensory overload."[3] Yet on a more general level, Clarke's point also relates to a new set of challenges produced by the changing cultures of remote warfare—more specifically, by the unprecedented possibilities of data harvesting and mass surveillance. When millions or billions of bits of data are swept up, how is rigorous organization or exhaustive interpretation of "raw intelligence" ever possible?

In the old days of Powers's old-school "Mafia chief," the interpretation of intelligence clearly fell under the rubric of *hermeneutics*, where, to use Fredric Jameson's definition, an "inert, objectal form is taken as a clue or a symptom for some vaster reality."[4] Of course, this "vaster reality" is never there in plain sight but must precisely be teased out from the words and the gestures as a sort of hidden sub- or supermessage that sometimes even runs counter to the explicit content of the locutions. For this reason, hermeneutics by its very nature involves a certain textual *parasitism* in which the interpreter both feeds off the text and destroys it at the same time, applying, to use Rita Felski's term, an "adversarial force" to the material to tease out its sub- or supermessage, while still relying on keeping the text "alive" to produce any result whatsoever.[5] Importantly, to interpret the relation between the "objectal form" and the reality for which it putatively stands, the agents or analysts must have some inkling of what is at stake, what they are listening for, what is relevant and what is not, and so on. They must, in short, have a certain knowledge about what Luc Boltanski, in a recent book on detective fiction, refers to as a "plane of reality" that "[reduces] uncertainty about the *whatness of what is*."[6] Without this basic knowledge, hermeneutics as such is a close to impossible task, since the interpretational frame of reference is absent; everything can be everything, all combinations and all interpretations of a given set of data are possible, and no definite meaning can ever be extracted from this chaotic flow of signifiers.

In a contemporary intelligence setting, where a "third-generation search could easily sweep up a million people," such a chaotic flow of signifiers is precisely what faces the analyst. Before even beginning to search for a "correct" interpretation of a given set of data—or at least an interpretation correct *enough* to turn raw reports into intelligence—an immense maze of potentially relevant pieces must be either included or discarded. This process of sorting out which nuggets of information should be included or excluded from the data set will naturally come before any actual process of interpretation, and it is therefore not a hermeneutic problem as such. But then what is it?

We suggest calling it a problem of the *archive*. As noted by Jacques Derrida in his *Archive Fever: A Freudian Impression*, the "principle of the archive is . . . a principle of consignation, that is, of gathering together."[7] Yet such a "gathering together" into an archive—which, naturally, is one of the overarching issues when it comes to surveillance in the name of national security—is, according to Derrida, never a peaceful or an orderly process: First, whoever builds an archive must act as an informational gatekeeper by allowing certain bits of data to enter the archive while barring others. Archiving is therefore an inherently violent or even predatory process, which promotes certain signifiers to relevance while demoting other signifiers to irrelevance.[8] Second—and even more importantly—all archives remain haunted by the practically infinite amount of information being excluded in this predatory process. Have relevant entries been missed in the selection process? Will one interpretation of the various elements of the archive become destabilized, or even false, if we include a vast number of new entries?

One of the main problems of the archive is thus that every archive demands a strict limitation of the number and nature of the entries, but this limitation comes back to haunt the archive as a suspicion that the archive is incomplete or that the terms of its selections are arbitrary or wrong. While this paradox, according to Derrida, is inherent to any archive, the information-harvesting capabilities of big data computing bring it to the fore, particularly when it comes to government surveillance: How "far" should the archive on a potential terrorist extend? Do you include his mother's online activity? His cousins'?[9] Under these specific issues linger more fundamental questions—namely, what is the correlation between archival choices and national security, and how does the modus operandi of national security change when new archival problems and practices occur?

This chapter investigates and analyzes how, over the course of its first four seasons, the television show *Homeland*—a series following the antiterror work of a young female CIA agent, Carrie Mathison (Claire Danes)—has evolved from being a show that problematizes the *interpretation* of an archive to a show that problematizes the archive *itself*, and how this development can be seen as a reaction to the new challenges faced by the intelligence community in the age of population-scale computerized surveillance. Specifically, the chapter focuses on how this overall development is indexed by a dramatic change in the protagonists' preferred technologies. While the earlier seasons of *Homeland* tended to focus on "bugs" (that is, hidden listening devices), in later seasons, the fictional agents have abandoned the bug and now use "drones" (that is, unmanned aerial vehicles) instead, thus essentially changing the show from being a sort of detective series to being a show about remote warfare. This aspect of *Homeland*'s evolution has not been given much attention in previous studies of the show—which have tended to focus on the program's relations to class, gender, and genre—although it stands at the very core of the show's (changing) visions of technology, terrorism, intelligence, and homeland security.[10]

This chapter does not focus on normative issues concerning remote warfare and its connection to a particular intelligence regime. Rather, it attempts to point out what we perceive to be the important dynamic between present-day intelligence gathering and drone warfare. As James Baker's quip about "sensory overload" demonstrates, this dynamic is not merely a matter of pointing out necessary causalities between intelligence and warfare but also about how we as humans relate affectively to certain situations. Documenting the evolution of the intelligence–warfare nexus in *Homeland* is therefore a matter not only of using a television show as an analytical stand-in for "real" intelligence gathering and warfare but also of using the medium of fictional narrative to discover how people and institutions act in crises, and—just as importantly—how we are *told* they act in crises. It is, in other words, not only a matter of how popular cultural imaginaries have been influencing our broader social imagination of remote warfare but also, and even more importantly, one of how the ideological subcurrents in these narratives have shaped—and are shaped by—very real politics.

Representing Danger

According to a 2010 article, "Intelligence and the Cinema," coauthored by a former CIA agent, many movies (and, presumably, also television shows) "tell viewers scarcely anything useful about intelligence" but are instead dominated by "gripping action and story line[s]," with the result that "the hard but vital intellectual work of analysis is underplayed at the expense of the more glamorous covert and counterintelligence work."[11] Be that as it may—and we have no grounds to doubt this assessment—the importance of a (fictional) movie or television show should perhaps not first and foremost be measured by the exactitude of its representations, but rather by the *impact* of its representations. And as documented by a number of scholars and journalists, serialized television narratives that dramatize topics such as military, intelligence, and police work have a strong impact on policy makers, the judiciary, and public opinion.[12] This impact, in turn, ends up translating into very real policies, precedents, and political preferences—and, as Brittany Hirth shows later in this book, into a public perception of remote warfare as particularly "clean."

As has been argued, *Homeland* specifically "refreshe[s] what ha[ve] become well-established conventions for representing the dangers of terrorism to America," thus taking over the mantle from the highly acclaimed television show *24,* with the latter finishing its run in 2010, a year before *Homeland* was first broadcast.[13] As noted by the editors of an issue of *Cinema Journal* focusing on *Homeland,* the program has since acquired significant cultural prominence as "the kind of program that anchors middle-class taste formations and cultural literacies while earning numerous accolades and drawing record-setting audiences for the cable network."[14] While most critics thus agree that *Homeland* does fall under the category of "quality television," its dramatization of intelligence work and warfare and its stance on the precarious balance between individual rights and national security have also been criticized for being overly accommodating to the workings of the American security state. James Castonguay, for instance, argues that the show "exploits post-9/11 insecurities, psychological trauma, and narrative complexity to produce ... propaganda for the Obama administration's 'overseas contingency operations' and its unprecedented domestic surveillance on the home front under the umbrella of an $80 billion US security state."[15] Also, Delphine Letort notes that the show has played a "significant role in the development of a post-9/11 culture of conspiracy, feeding on the paranoid mood fuelled by the unpredictability of terrorist actions and by the implementation of strong security policies aiming to prevent future attacks."[16]

While we tend to agree with the critical assessment of the show's ideological underpinnings in the post-9/11 American security state, it is important to realize that the image of national security, intelligence, and warfare conveyed by *Homeland* is by no means unequivocal, but instead changes dramatically over the seasons (a fact that also sets it apart from most other examples of "Terror TV," where the same narrative and topical formula seems to be employed from beginning to end). While seasons 1–3 of *Homeland* are concerned with more or less traditional puzzle solving, focusing on CIA agent Carrie Mathison's attempts to piece together disparate clues into a coherent and correct map of terrorist identities and actions, the later seasons are all about drones and remotely killing potential enemies before their plans materialize.

Decisively, these two different modes of waging the Global War on Terror in *Homeland* do not merely form a random sequence of topicalities; as we will argue, the transition from bugs to drones, from local(ized) surveillance to remote warfare, and from problems of hermeneutics to problems of the archive is presented by *Homeland* as the only solution to an epistemological impasse faced by the puzzle-solving Carrie Mathison in the early seasons of the show. As such, *Homeland* offers the viewer a fictional historicization of remote warfare, a sort of *how-we-got-here-and-why-it-was-necessary* narrative, which to a wide extent does serve the function of propaganda for American "overseas contingency operations." Embedded in the narrative logic of *Homeland* is thus a political need for these operations emerging from a larger history of state surveillance, which is explored further in the next chapter, by Nike Nivar Ortiz. So regarding the question of whether there is anything new or different going on here, raised by David Buchanan in the previous chapter, *Homeland*'s answer would be yes, there is clearly something new going on here.

Solving the Puzzle

When the first season of *Homeland* premiered in October 2011, the opening titles overlaid a dreamlike montage consisting of a number of grainy clips: a blonde girl sleeping; close-ups of eyes wide open and eyes shut, trembling in REM sleep; and strange images of this same girl playing trumpet, watching television, and wearing a bizarre *Donnie Darko*–style lion mask in a hedge maze. This gritty, somewhat surreal montage segues into a new montage of television footage featuring explosions, panicking people, military operations, and a line of presidents addressing different acts of terrorism: from Ronald Reagan's announcement of the Muammar al-Qaddafi attack in 1986 to Bill Clinton's and George H. W. Bush's statements on terror (the latter emphasizing the words "America, aggression, terrorism"), and then on to an upside-down President Barack Obama claiming that "we must and we will remain vigilant at home and abroad." Accompanying this montage is a medley of jazz improvisations and a chatter of voices, one of them particularly loud and clear: "It was right in front of my eyes. . . . Fuck! I missed something once before. I won't . . . I can't let that happen again."[17]

As the viewer starts getting into *Homeland,* they recognize the voice as belonging to Carrie Mathison, counterterrorist agent and main character in the show, but at the outset, the voice is as spectral and disembodied as the footage accompanying it. It is not so much the voice of a person as it is the voice of an institution, or perhaps even the voice of a *position:* the position of an intelligence community that has to make sense of millions of bits of footage, data, and conversation floating through the ether, similar to how television programs float to our televisions at home. It is, in other words, not so much the voice of an individual character as it is an echo of the structural and institutional problems that come with ubiquitous big-data surveillance and information flows that characterize late modern remote warfare. Yet as the development in *Homeland* well shows, this configuration has shifted significantly in the cultural and political imagination from a hermeneutic practice of *bugging* toward an archival practice of big-data surveillance with drones.

Even though the television in the opening titles might seem like a rather quaint reference in the age of streaming, it retains a *nowness* that any on-demand service lacks; television, as Fredric Jameson once noted, is defined by its "total flow," affording the medium an acuteness that *Homeland*'s opening montage uses both metaphorically (the flowing temporality of television and surveillance are comparable) and literally (intelligence services use cameras and monitors as technologies of surveillance).[18] As season 1 gets under way, the link between the flowing temporality of television and the temporality of surveillance only gets stronger. Throughout the season, Carrie is practically glued to the screen in her own living room, watching the private life of the

American war hero Sergeant Nick Brody (Damian Lewis), whom Carrie suspects has been turned by his former al-Qaeda captors and is now planning an attack as a one-man sleeper cell. In the hope of getting clues to support her suspicion, she secretly (and illegally) bugs every corner of his house with "eyes and ears," ready to monitor the most intimate details of his private life—including quarrels, awkward sex, and adultery. From the confines of her own living room, Carrie follows Brody's daily life while desperately trying to organize the constant stream of information into the correct configuration.

The information stream, then, seems to embody the "total flow" of an unstoppable real-time television transmission, which explains Carrie's manic desire to sit in front of the monitors in her living room in order not to miss anything.[19] Her fragmented words from the opening titles now get their full meaning as her 9/11 trauma is slowly revealed to the audience through a dialogue with her superior, Saul Berenson (Mandy Patinkin):

> CARRIE: I . . . I'm just making sure we don't get hit again.
> SAUL: Well, I'm glad someone's looking out for the country, Carrie.
> CARRIE: I'm serious. I missed something once before, I won't . . . I can't let that happen again.
> SAUL: It was ten years ago. Everyone missed something that day.
> CARRIE: Yeah, everyone's not me.

The shocking television images of a burning New York evidently haunt Carrie—as they have indeed haunted shifting U.S. governments—in her paranoid drive to see and know anything in the steady information flow that was activated by 9/11. Yet if the temporal axis of this transmission "flows," the spatial axis is clearly demarcated: the information she is so obsessed with streams from a specific number of bugs and cameras, placed in their stationary positions in the one specific house in which Brody and his family live. Like a detective waiting for the right clue to solve the riddle, Carrie is convinced that she has tapped into the relevant stream of data. The challenge is only to wait for the right pieces and then to identify and interpret them correctly—as when Carrie discovers more and more suspicious details of Brody's life— making the first seasons of *Homeland* into something close to a traditional detective show, albeit with quite a bit more at stake than in the classic whodunit.

The hermeneutic nature of Carrie's challenges in the first seasons—how to interpret the clues her surveillance gives her—is inextricable from the technology she uses to acquire the raw material for her interpretations: the hidden listening devices, the *bugs,* which, even more than the video footage, supply her with fresh data from the Brody household. As hinted in this chapter's introduction, there is something inherently parasitic in the very process of hermeneutics, in how the hermeneut squeezes a specific meaning out of a text that is not there on the text's surface, while still relying on the text to supply some sort of semantic input (or even an alibi). As such, there is a perfect metaphoric alignment between Carrie's epistemological strategy (hermeneutics) and the technologies with which she pursues it (bugs) in that both seem to rely on a significant measure of parasitism in order to function.

Furthermore, Carrie, as a true voyeur, also gets a significant amount of surplus *jouissance* (to use Lacan's famous term) out of following the Brody family at all hours. In one particular scene, for instance, she clearly feels excited and at the same time somewhat indisposed by watching Brody have sex with his wife—creating a certain jouissance that is mirrored in the viewer's own watching of Carrie's obsessive watching. Thus, the drive to know everything at any time—engendered by the regime of surveillance that characterizes the bug as epistemic figure—is established not only internally as part of the show but also performatively in the viewer of the show. This jouissance, however, is not merely parasitic in the sense of stealing nutrition, data, or enjoyment from the object of the parasite; it is also parasitic in the sense that Carrie slowly grows closer and closer to Brody in what might be termed a sort of *coevolution* of the two main protagonists toward a still closer symbiosis. This symbiosis, this total involvement in or *growing into* the subject of her surveillance, necessarily extends beyond the merely factual; she must pick up on his motivations and emotions, which is, of course, impossible without becoming emotionally involved herself. And having first become involved, she inevitably falls in love with Brody.

The love story ends up being one of the (if not *the*) most persistent themes in the early seasons, yet what is important here is not so much romantic love as it is the affective involvement of the hermeneut in what he or she interprets.[20] On multiple levels, Carrie's surveillance of Brody is driven by what we might call a *parasitic hermeneutics,* facilitated by bugs such as microphones, hidden cameras, and other secret devices and motivated by a need and a desire to subtract from him information and affects that she can subject to her interpretative gaze. In fact, those two different kinds of affect—on the one hand, romantic affection and, on the other hand, professionally affective engagement—constitute a highly significant dynamics, which is key to how the first seasons portray the necessity of intelligence and remote warfare in twenty-first century U.S. culture. In other words, Carrie's paranoid desire to see and know everything reflects the culture of fear and surveillance that has penetrated the American society after 9/11.

Breakdown

Carrie's manic obsession with surveilling Brody without missing anything is thus a result of a culture of emergency and necessity that was essentially created in the aftermath of the World Trade Center attacks of 9/11, when President George W. Bush called for radically enforced security and surveillance policies with the purpose of preventing future attacks. Naturally, this culture is the narrative motor of the show, which—besides taking a stand on the War on Terror—constantly produces epistemic situations that call on action. In the light of this epistemic premise, Carrie's manic obsession and total immersion in her paranoid world of surveilling and interpreting clues and signs are exacerbated by the fact that she suffers from bipolar disorder. While her mental illness could be read as merely an addition to the drama of the show, one could argue that it is more than that: that it is related to an increasing awareness that what we have called parasitic hermeneutics is no longer a tenable strategy. In short, the traditional cultures of careful puzzle-solving investigation are not any longer possible in the post-9/11 mass surveillance state of America—and Carrie's creeping paranoia becomes a symptom of this breakdown.

In one key scene, her mania has escalated so badly that she has been hospitalized. When her boss, Saul, visits her, she strongly argues against his working theory while also addressing her own shortcomings in a manic torrent of words and alliterations: "Well, it's wrong! Or . . . it's incomplete. . . . Walker is not even critical. He's just a part, a piece, a pixel, a pawn. He has no importance. There is a bigger pernicious plot. . . . We have to code it, collide it, collapse it, contain it."[21] The key words here are *incomplete* and *bigger,* both indicating that the local and stationary surveillance of one person is not and can never be enough in a globalized world where ideas, goods, and terrorists travel more or less freely. There are always more "part[s]," "piece[s]," and "pawn[s]" to add to the hermeneutic field, always an endless number of possible puzzle pieces that must be gathered and organized before any interpretation can take place. In order to "code" the signs, they thus have to be "collide[d]" or—as stated at the beginning of this chapter—they have to be "gathered together" into an archive. Slowly, then, we are moving toward a breakdown in the mode of surveillance that has hitherto dominated the show, facilitated by the inability of this mode's primary characteristics—the localized bug, the hermeneutic reading, the affective and deeply personalized man-to-(wo)man engagement—to lead to the "bigger pernicious plot." In short, we move from the problem of interpretation to the problem of gathering the correct, and the correct *number of,* signs into an archive, from the problem of *hermeneutics* to the problem of the *archive.*

The lack of clues is explicitly thematized in the same episode in which the foregoing breakdown takes place, when Carrie introduces Saul to her "archive" of clues on the Brody case. As is visible in the screenshot (Figure 3.1), Carrie uses an advanced system of color coding to assemble all of her gathered information into a wall montage: each color represents a certain phase of activities in the life of Abu Nazir (Navid Negahban), the terrorist leader whom she suspects has turned Brody to his radical Islamist cause. However, Carrie's image wall also shows a critical gap in chronology, a missing link, a lost piece of the puzzle, marked by the color yellow—"the fallow yellow," as she calls it. This "fallow yellow" serves as a visual index of a basic lack in her approach to the Brody case; her in-depth interpretation of signs and clues, no matter how clever and dedicated it is, can never be enough, since there will always be pieces missing from the puzzle, pieces that need to be gathered before interpretation can start properly.

Carrie's breakdown, then, is essentially a metaphor for the breakdown of the neatly delimited archive she has been building up throughout the season. With this breakdown—culminating in Carrie's taking

FIGURE 3.1. CIA-agent Carrie Mathison debates clues to the Brody case with her friend and boss, Saul Berenson, as laid out on a color-coded image wall. (*Homeland,* season 1, episode 11, "The Vest," December 2011, 41:54)

the consequences of her (apparent) misconceptions by getting a solid dose of electroshock therapy—the problem is no longer how to interpret the elements in a stable archive. Rather, the problem becomes the archive *itself,* which suddenly appears lacking, arbitrary, or even nonsensical because there is and always will be huge amounts of missing data. What is revealed, in other words, is the problem of the archive in the age of big-data surveillance, which threatens to collapse the archive with the sheer quantity of information. Such an archival breakdown, caused by the suspicion that the archive is lacking and that an arbitrarily huge number of entries could and must be added to it, is also described by Jacques Derrida as precisely an illness, as an "archive fever," which turns the archive into an "anarchive," threatening to make knowledge as such impossible.[22]

Franco Moretti—pioneer of digital humanities—asks in his seminal *Distant Reading,* "What will knowledge indeed mean, if our archive becomes ten times larger, or a hundred[?]"[23] This is the question that Carrie repeatedly asks herself and *Homeland* repeatedly asks the viewer during the first three seasons of the show.[24] Moretti's answer is straightforward: "Anarchy."[25] Yet anarchy is of course not an option when national security is at stake. Instead, as we will see, the answer literally comes from the skies.

The Drone Queen

When season 4 of *Homeland* premiered October 2014, the viewer immediately noticed a significant change: the opening sequence was different. Incorporated into the montage of grainy clips were now several bits of drone footage with thermal cameras and crosshairs aimed at crouching figures glowing white in dark, rocky landscapes. These landscapes then faded into the aforementioned hedge maze, which now featured a number of white figures running around bewildered and the propeller of a Predator drone ominously hovering in the distance. This new opening sequence indicates the show's newfound preoccupation—if not obsession—with drones, a change that is also visible in the camera work: suddenly, a notable number of scenes shot from an aerial perspective give the viewer a taste of the unimpeded overview and transparency of a drone-surveilled world, instead of horizontal shots that emulate the inherently limited vision of a human being. The drone thus seems to offer Carrie a solution to the problems of the previous seasons by giving her the opportunity to gaze unhindered at anyone or anything at any time. With the drone, her overview is no longer impeded by the limitations of a stationary bug or even by the rhythms of the human body. In season 1, she would sometimes fall asleep in front of the screens and loudspeakers, while in season 4 her surveillance is, strictly speaking, not *her* surveillance but rather the surveillance of a whole team of drone operators and analysts who work around the clock. Such expanded use of drones serves, as noted by Jonathan Crary, as a preeminent example of the "non-time" of today, with the drones watching "unblinkingly 24/7, indifferent to day, night, or weather."[26]

As the first episode of season 4 gets under way, we learn that Carrie has left her old job in the CIA and instead been appointed drone station chief in Afghanistan. The nature of her new task is demonstrated to the viewer with her authorization of an airstrike on a highly wanted Taliban leader, Haissam Haqqani (Numan Acar), who, based on an anonymous tip, is presumably hiding in a farmhouse. Despite Carrie's apparent unease with trusting anonymous intelligence blindly, she orders the drone pilots to fire, and in a long, dramatic scene Carrie, the staff, and the viewer watch the silent images of a farmhouse vanishing in a cloud of smoke. After this solemn piece of remote destruction, the scene takes a surprising turn when her staff presents her with a

FIGURE 3.2. After blowing up an Afghan wedding from a distance, Carrie is surprised by her staff presenting her with a special "Drone Queen" birthday cake. (*Homeland*, season 4, episode 1, "The Drone Queen," Showtime, October 2014, 5:56)

birthday cake on which "The Drone Queen" is inscribed in icing (Figure 3.2). For a viewer who has followed the first three seasons of the show, this scene is bizarre. First, the fact that Carrie—who, if anything, seemed like an unstable lone wolf who refused to take orders from anyone—is suddenly the official leader of a huge operation seems completely out of character. Second, and adding to this, the general mood of collegial conviviality and the fact that her subordinates seem to like her (underscored by them singing, "She's a jolly good fellow," while Carrie blows out the candles) also appear uncharacteristic. And third, and most importantly, the whole approach to her work seems radically different from in earlier seasons. Gone is the lonely, deeply immersed, affectively involved interpreter of signs and clues, and instead we see a new Carrie for whom killing by remote control has become everyday practice.

If the parasitic bug was the technological correlate of her former role as hermeneut, season 4 thus immediately seems to establish a new modus operandi. While Carrie arguably did not shy away from violence in the earlier seasons, it has always been a matter of last resort and up close and personal; however, in season 4 Carrie seems to take on a new role as cold-blooded assassin aided by the drone's predatory capabilities.

In order to, in the words of Grégoire Chamayou, "detect, deter, disrupt, detain, or destroy networks before they can harm innocents," Carrie, formerly a passionate parasite, has become Carrie the detached drone queen who wages remote warfare to kill every possible threat before it even materializes as a subject of analysis or interpretation, a transformation that not only represents a radical shift in the narrative logic of *Homeland* but also points to the changing politics of remote warfare taking place during 2011–14.[27]

Destroying the Archive

This practice of "detecting," "disrupting," "detaining," "destroying," and so on becomes increasingly evident the day after the strike, when Carrie, through the video feed of a Reaper drone, inspects the casualties and realizes the tragic result of her drone strike: while she cannot get the killing of the wanted terrorist confirmed, it becomes painfully clear that she has instead bombed an Afghan wedding. Among the lines of dead bodies, she spots a young man kneeling beside his dead sister, and the man also spots her: looking straight up at the drone, his fixed gaze catches Carrie's in a mixture of grief, blame, and disgust. Through this crosscutting between the eyes of the man and Carrie, an illusion of what appears to be real eye contact is established, thereby touching on the ambiguous experience that many real-life drone pilots have of watching their targets with, to use Derek Gregory's phrase, "voyeuristic intimacy," creating a paradoxical experience of remoteness and closeness at the same time (Figure 3.3).[28] Carrie seems to experience a moment of her well-known affective immersion in the subject of her work, emphasized by elegiac background music and a sonic fusion of the buzzing of cicadas on the ground in Afghanistan and the buzzing of computer screens in the control room. But it is nothing like her old obsessive involvement with Brody; there is an unbridgeable gulf between her and the man, the gulf of drone-driven remote warfare, and he is just one out of dozens of innocents who suffer from the attack, and one of thousands of victims more who suffer from drone warfare in general.

The scene therefore illustrates the paradoxical "voyeuristic intimacy" of remote warfare and the asymmetrical power relation between the hunter and the prey, a relation in which the predator—in this case the

FIGURE 3.3. Through the video feed of a Reaper drone, Carrie stares into the eyes of one of the victims of her aerial assault. (*Homeland,* season 4, episode 1, "The Drone Queen," Showtime, October 2014, 29:00)

drone queen Carrie—can choose to be intimate only when it benefits the situation, which it does in the case of the man.[29] Clearly, there is something about him—staged by the heavy zooming in on his intense gaze—that attracts her attention, creating a spectacular visual dynamics in the scene. Although this dynamic is, of course, far from true mutual eye contact, it nevertheless constructs something like a counterstare to Carrie's drone gaze, a construction that, apparently, gives the man "the right to look," as Nicholas Mirzoeff calls the autonomy and reciprocity that is necessary in order to acknowledge and see "the Other" at all.[30] Yet this staged mirroring of the two gazes is only a distant reminiscence of the old hermeneutics of bugging. As it turns out, the man, Aayan Ibrahim (Suraj Sharma), is the nephew of Haqqani, the terrorist Carrie is looking for. And when she realizes this, she takes advantage of his family relation by first seducing the man and then using him as a decoy to lead her to his uncle. Tracking him from the video feed of yet another drone, she watches as he meets up with the uncle, who quickly sees through the setup and ultimately kills him for recklessly leading the drone to him. After this, Carrie orders a drone strike even though her friend and ex-CIA director Saul Berenson has been taken hostage by the terrorists and would die too. In the chaos of war- and terrorism-ridden Afghanistan, nothing can thus be left standing—not even friends or former CIA bosses.

While on the surface it might seem that the show endorses this course of action, there is also a critical stance in the quite unflattering way it portrays Carrie's increasing callousness and her transition from bug queen to drone queen, a transition that has also affected her specific type of mania: previously, it took the form of a paranoid obsession with analyzing and interpreting a number of signs and clues within a specific hermeneutic field, while now it has turned into a predatory mania of extermination and destruction. If the hermeneutics of the bug involved Carrie as a parasitic investigator, dependent on keeping her source alive to continuously leech information, the predatory hunter–prey relation created by the drone marks a radically different regime of intelligence and warfare: everything has to die, even close friends. In short, the narrative logic of the show has tipped toward a far more militant culture of intelligence, surveillance, and remote warfare than the one that characterized the earlier seasons.

This transition from one regime to another is not random, nor is it merely an expression of how *Homeland* attempts to introduce cutting-edge elements and themes to its drama. Instead, the transition from bugs to drones is a very specific answer to the increasingly anarchic situation of the first three seasons of *Homeland*, a situation that was simply no longer sustainable, neither for Carrie personally nor from a more general homeland security perspective. There was simply too much data, too many threats, too many potential entries into the national security archive, for her method of close and highly immersed interpretation to remain feasible. What *Homeland* seems to tell us, then, is that no one, not even Carrie or the CIA, is able to keep a constant overview of the results of mass surveillance, and this structural impossibility is the source of brooding paranoia and Carrie's multiple manic, but ultimately fruitless, attempts over the first three seasons to regain control over the millions of nuggets of information.

For Carrie, the ultimate consequence of this anarchic situation is, as we have seen, several mental breakdowns. She thus fits into the narrative cycle of the soon-to-be-wounded warrior, introduced by Buchanan in the previous chapter. Yet while this narrative pattern, according to Buchanan, achieves a scapegoat function, substituting the victim of warrior trauma, in this case Carrie, with the victim of violence, Carrie's radical solution to her breakdowns comes in the end of season 1 not as victimization but with the electroshock: she wants to forget all about Brody, the terrorists, and all the other pieces swamping her puzzle. She wants, in other words, to close down her personal and ever-expanding archive of clues and pieces by literally short-circuiting it.

However, if the electroshock was merely a Band-Aid solution to Carrie's personal mania in season 1, the logic of termination is indeed extended and intensified to a much broader breakdown by the drones in season 4. Carrie—and by extension the fictional United States she works for—settles for the only remaining solution to this anarchic problem: when everything and everyone could potentially be part of a "bigger, pernicious plot," and when you realize that you cannot ever find the time or the resources to figure out all the connections, plots, and subplots, the next best thing to do is eradicate everything. In this logic, sacrificing forty wedding guests who might or might not have terrorist connections in the hunt for just *one* high-priority terrorist who happens to be on the "kill list" seems entirely justified—at least in the bipolar world of Carrie Mathison. One or more of the guests just might be or become terrorists, but the amount of data analysis it would take to establish guilt or innocence is so vast that any level of certainty in practice is beyond the possible; better to kill them all with a Hellfire missile than to let any of them walk away.

The ideological background behind this logic is, as stated before, not something that the series decides on unequivocally. Rather, it is a logic that mirrors the U.S. foreign politics of fighting an endless war on terror—established as a narrative necessity in order for the show to continue: it simply needs new terrorists to eliminate in order to proceed. Following this logic, the well-known, although specious, arguments often made by advocates of drone warfare about how the "surgical precision" of drone technology makes it possible to isolate targets and limit collateral damage—hence the public perception of remote warfare as "clean" (see Hirth's chapter in this volume)—are thus overshadowed by a contrary assumption: that is, the objection that drone strikes are counterproductive because they allow insurgents to recruit more volunteers in an endless repetition. Yet the show's solution to this problem seems to be an intensification of drone operations following the idea that, to use Chamayou's phrasing, drones can and will "win th[e] race and eliminate individuals at least as fast as new ones are recruited."[31]

The same logic applies to the rapidly growing archive of data provided by drone surveillance. When the archive of possible parts, pieces, and pixels threatens to extend to the entire globe, there can be no neatly ordered data set anymore, only anarchy and pure chaos. The only practical response to such chaos, or so *Homeland* seems to suggest, is remote-controlled destruction and violence that does not aim at restoring order to chaos through careful organization or interpretation. Rather, it aims at restoring order to chaos by eliminating all elements that make up this chaos. In order to achieve complete safety from any contingency or hidden threat, it is necessary not only to give up the hermeneutic practice that tries to make sense of a certain number of signs and clues but in fact to actively destroy the hermeneutic field. This is, essentially, a move from hermeneutics to *anti*hermeneutics, from a mania for reading signs to a mania for destroying signs. So, to repeat Franco Moretti's question, "What will knowledge indeed mean, if our archive becomes ten times larger, or a hundred[?]" He, as we have seen, answered, "Anarchy," and we can now add Carrie's and the fictional United States' answer: "Death by remote control."

In this chapter, we have attempted to offer the general outlines of *Homeland*'s path from bugs to drones—or, in more general terms, the show's path from a sort of *parasitic hermeneutics* to a *predatory antihermeneutics*. We have shown that this path is governed by an inner logic inextricable from the practice of mass surveillance, in which the sheer archive of what Richard A. Clarke calls "raw reports" grows to such ludicrous size that turning it into proper "intelligence" through careful analysis and interpretation is all but impossible—it simply "exceed[s] our human experiential capabilities," as Nike Nivar Ortiz will argue in the next chapter of this book. With Carrie's mental breakdowns as their metaphorical index, the first three seasons of *Homeland* move still closer to a sort of breaking point, beyond which the paranoia of having missed some vital piece of information among the millions or even billions of possible pieces of the puzzle is unbearable. As a consequence, the main issue gradually shifts from one of correct interpretation—as in traditional detective fiction—to one of the very

nature and extent of the archive itself, an issue that is ultimately resolved in season 4 with Carrie's transition from reader of signs to
destroyer of signs. Her transition, then, becomes a metaphor for the
rapidly changing cultures of military surveillance and remote warfare, going toward big-data-guided, targeted assassinations in which
the element of human interpretation is increasingly ailed.

While *Homeland*'s multiseason story arc is entirely fictional, the notion that contemporary mass-surveillance capabilities do not produce
any greatly enhanced feelings of safety but actually end up inducing a
radical paranoia is definitely not fictional. One example of such paranoia can be found in the top echelons of the Bush administration in
the months after 9/11, where, as journalist Mark Danner describes it,
a constant update on all sorts of incoming information contributed to
what reads as an almost hellish ambience of fear and desperation:

> Every day the President and other senior officials received the "threat
> matrix," a document that could be dozens of pages long listing "every
> threat directed at the United States" that had been sucked up during
> the last twenty-four hours by the vast electronic and human vacuum
> cleaner of information that was US intelligence: warnings of cata-
> strophic weapons, conventional attacks, planned attacks on allies,
> plots of every description and level of seriousness. "You simply could
> not sit where I did," George Tenet [director of the CIA] later wrote of
> the threat matrix, "and be anything other than scared to death about
> what it portended."[32]

As we know today, none of these threats ended up materializing, as
most of them were entirely ludicrous—yet the consequences of the Bush
administration's being subjected to them were not. Its direct complicity
in and green-lighting of torture can be seen as linked to the impression that "existential" dangers to the United States lurked around every corner and that radical measures had to be employed to meet those
dangers. While the administrations after Bush have officially discon-
tinued the torture regime, they have arguably found new and even
more insidious ways—including drone warfare and remote killings—of
coping with the feelings of paranoia and desperation produced by mass
surveillance. What *Homeland* does so well is to produce an analogous
feeling of paranoia and desperation in its main protagonist, Carrie, a

feeling that is arguably retransmitted to the viewers of the show as a "paranoiac mood that permeates cultural and political responses."[33] Thereby, the show implicitly argues, as do the supporters of former and current U.S. antiterror policies, that with the insights into various plots and plans against the United States given by mass surveillance, it is simply impossible and irresponsible *not* to do something radical right now in order to neutralize the threat before it grows into an actual attack.

Seen from this perspective, James Castonguay is indeed right in asserting that *Homeland* "exploits post-9/11 insecurities, psychological trauma, and narrative complexity to produce . . . propaganda for the Obama administration's 'overseas contingency operations.'"[34] But perhaps its "exploit[ation of] post-9/11 insecurities" could also be the source of a critical potential: in other words, one might read *Homeland* as way of saying that once a nation starts going down the path of mass surveillance of entire populations, it *inevitably* ends up in a situation of radical paranoia, a paranoia that can only be resolved through increasingly harsh and increasingly illegal security measures, be they torture or remote warfare.

Notes

1. Thomas Powers, *The Military Error: Baghdad and Beyond in America's War of Choice* (New York: New York Review of Books, 2008), 88–89.

2. Richard A. Clarke, *Against All Enemies: Inside America's War on Terror* (London: Free Press, 2004), 268.

3. James Baker cited in Jack Goldsmith, *The Terror Presidency: Law and Judgment inside the Bush Administration* (London: Norton, 2007), 72.

4. Fredric Jameson, *Postmodernism; or, The Cultural Logic of Late Capitalism* (London: Verso, 1991), 8.

5. Rita Felski, "Critique and the Hermeneutics of Suspicion," *M/C Journal* 15, no. 1 (2012): n.p.

6. Luc Boltanski, *Mysteries and Conspiracies: Detective Stories, Spy Novels and the Making of Modern Societies* (Oxford: Polity, 2014), 14.

7. Jacques Derrida, *Archive Fever: A Freudian Impression,* Religion and Postmodernism (Chicago: University of Chicago Press, 1996), 10.

8. "The gathering into itself of the One is never without violence," as Derrida notes (50).

9. As Torsten Arni Caleb Andreasen notes in "An Archaeology of Digital Knowledge: Imaginaries of the Digital Cultural Heritage Archive" (PhD thesis, University of Copenhagen, 2016), the obsession with archives and archival problems coincides with the "rise to prominence of digital storage around the

beginning of the millennium" (92), due, naturally, to the processes of filing, organization, and selection that staggering amounts of data must undergo in order for them to be useful to the user. For a discussion of the archival problems of persistent surveillance technologies, see also the next chapter, by Nike Nivar Ortiz.

10. See, for instance, Stephen Shapiro's study *"Homeland*'s Crisis of Middle-Class Transformation," *Cinema Journal* 54, no. 4 (2015): 152–59; and Emanuelle Wessels's critique of the show's neoliberal and postfeminist ideologies in Emanuelle Wessels, *"Homeland* and Neoliberalism: Text, Paratexts and Treatment of Affective Labor," *Feminist Media Studies* 16, no. 3 (2016): 511–26. Finally, for gender studies, feminism, and motherhood, see Lara Bradshaw, "Showtime's 'Female Problem': Cancer, Quality and Motherhood," *Journal of Consumer Culture* 13 (2013): 160–77; Lindsay Steenberg and Yvonne Tasker, "Pledge Allegiance: Gendered Surveillance, Crime Television, and *Homeland*," *Cinema Journal* 54, no. 4 (2015): 132–38; and Alex Bevan, "The National Body, Women, and Mental Health in *Homeland*," *Cinema Journal* 54, no. 4 (2015): 145–51.

11. John D. Stempel, Robert W. Pringle Jr., and Tom Stempel, "Intelligence and the Cinema," *International Journal of Intelligence and Counter Intelligence* 15, no. 1 (2010): 115, 124.

12. See, for instance, Steven Keslowitz, *The Tao of Jack Bauer: What Our Favorite Terrorist Buster Says about Life, Love, Torture, and Saving the World 24 Times in 24 Hours with No Lunch Break* (Bloomington: iUniverse, 2009), 29–33; and Kathleen Tierny, Christine Bevc, and Erica Kuligowski, "Metaphors Matter: Disaster Myths, Media Frames, and Their Consequences in Hurricane Katrina," *Annals of the American Academy of Political and Social Science* 604 (2006): 57–81.

13. Steenberg and Tasker, "Pledge Allegiance," 133. The show *24* arguably still represents the strongest case for the importance (and danger) of popular cultural representations of warfare and intelligence work. In his 2006 book *War by Other Means,* former assistant deputy attorney general John Yoo—the same John Yoo who wrote many of the legal defenses of the American torture program in the early days after 9/11—wrote, "What if, as the popular Fox television program *24* recently portrayed, a high-level terrorist leader is caught who knows the location of a nuclear weapon in an American city?" And the popularity of *24* among pro-torture hawks—a popularity that almost borders on fandom—is not exclusive to Yoo; in a 2007 primary debate, Tom Tancredo, Republican from Colorado, said, "We're wondering about whether waterboarding would be a—a bad thing to do? I'm looking for Jack Bauer [the rampantly torturing antihero of *24*] at that time, let me tell you." Alfred McCoy, *Torture and Impunity* (Madison: University of Wisconsin Press, 2012), 177. The *Los Angeles Times* called this debate a "Jack Bauer impersonation contest."

14. Diane Negra and Jorie Lagerwey, "Analyzing *Homeland*: Introduction," *Cinema Journal* 54, no. 4 (2015): 126.

15. James Castonguay, "Fictions of Terror: Complexity, Complicity and Insecurity in *Homeland*," *Cinema Journal* 54, no. 4 (2015): 139.

16. Delphine Letort, "Conspiracy Culture in *Homeland* (2011–2015)," *Media, War and Conflict* 10, no. 2 (2017): 152.

17. *Homeland,* season 1, title sequence, Showtime, December 2011.

18. Jameson, *Postmodernism,* 76.

19. A similar point has been made in relation to the television show *24* and how it functioned as a sort of model for the type of spectatorship that followed in the aftermath of 9/11 by Ina Rae Hark, "'Today Is the Longest Day of My Life': *24* as Mirror Narrative of 9/11," in *Film and Television after 9/11,* ed. Wheeler Winston Dixton (Carbondale: Southern Illinois University Press, 2004), 121–41. By introducing split screens as a way of letting the viewer simultaneously follow the action at different locations within the show, *24* mirrored the television news coverage of the tragedy of 9/11, establishing a kind of all-access aesthetics (Hark, 123).

20. This immersion-cum-love is a common trope in television shows on intelligence and warfare, with the most salient contemporary example being the series *The Americans,* where two Russian spies, planted in the United States as a married couple, slowly start to *become* Americans and to fall in love with the America(ns) they were supposed to spy on.

21. *Homeland,* season 1, episode 11, "The Vest," Showtime, December 2011.

22. Derrida, *Archive Fever,* 19, 51.

23. Franco Moretti, *Distant Reading* (London: Verso, 2013), 89.

24. Seasons 2 and 3 of *Homeland* essentially continue in the same track as season 1, with Carrie still relying on her hermeneutic method to unravel the conspiracies lurking under the surface—with frequent visits to the mental health clinic as a result. Even when reaching the turning point of season 2, where it turns out that she was right about Brody and the pieces thus seem to fall into place, suddenly new pieces interrupt her (an)archive in the final episode, where unknown forces blow up the CIA headquarters, framing Brody for the attack.

25. It is of course no coincidence that Moretti chooses this word to describe the breakdown of the traditional archive of canonized literature; when we extend the literary archive to include tons of new entries, we, following Derrida, end up with an *an*archive, an archive of anarchy.

26. Jonathan Crary, *24/7: Late Capitalism and the Ends of Sleep* (New York: Verso, 2013), 30, 32.

27. Grégoire Chamayou, "The Manhunt Doctrine," *Radical Philosophy* 169 (September/October 2011): 3.

28. Derek Gregory, "Drone Geographies," *Radical Philosophy* 183 (2014): 10. For an extensive investigation of the distanced and mediated intimacy of remote warfare and its relation to gaming, see Michael Richardson's chapter later in this book.

29. As Grégoire Chamayou notes, the predatory logic of the drone follows that of manhunting: "The art of modern tracking proceeds by means of a cartography of the prey's social networks that the 'hunter-analysts' piece together in order to succeed in tracing him back, through his friends or relatives, to his hideout." "Manhunt Doctrine," 2.

30. Nicholas Mirzoeff, *The Right to Look: A Counterhistory of Visuality* (Durham, N.C.: Duke University Press, 2011).

31. Grégoire Chamayou, *A Theory of the Drone* (New York: New Press, 2015), 71.

32. Mark Danner, "After September 11: Our State of Exception," *New York Review of Books,* October 13, 2011, http://www.nybooks.com/articles/2011/10/13/after-september-11-our-state-exception/.

33. Letort, "Conspiracy Culture in *Homeland,*" 153.

34. Castonguay, "Fictions of Terror," 139.

CHAPTER 4

Eye in the Sky

Persistent Surveillance Technology and the Age of Global War

NIKE NIVAR ORTIZ

> He is seen, but he does not see; he is the object of information, never a subject in communication.
>
> —Michel Foucault, *Discipline and Punish*

Emerging out of the remote warfare needs of the 2003 Iraq War, Persistent Surveillance Systems is now a private company that offers technologies and services capable of surveilling cities from ten thousand feet above. These technologies allow people to be tracked in space and time: with the click of a button, the operator is able to go back and forth in one-second increments, amassing an archive of everyday movements that can be mined for patterns of criminality. Hawkeye II, one of the most advanced systems this company sells, is a 192-megapixel, wide area surveillance camera that can watch over an area of sixty-four square kilometers.[1] Unlike expensive military drones, Hawkeye II can be attached to a small plane or blimp that circles the city largely unseen from the ground. The system helps to locate "suspicious" individuals as they move around the city: seeing where they go, whom they meet, and what spaces they occupy. With the commercial availability of remote warfare tools like those of Persistent Surveillance Systems, a civilian's day-to-day life becomes incidentally indexed as part of a perpetual manhunt for criminals lurking within the citizenry.

Persistent Surveillance Systems, and the persistent surveillance technologies and services it provides, has been around as a domestic product since 2004; it has been implemented on a trial basis in cities like Ciudad Juárez, Mexico; Baltimore, Maryland; Dayton, Ohio; and Compton, California. While the system has some arrests and cartel busts to its credit, it has not been institutionalized in any major way—through a partnership with the police department, for example. When the decision has been brought to the constituency whether their city should adopt this technology, there has been an uneasy tension between the concrete gains of total surveillance of the city and the abstract loss of having an "eye in the sky." The domestic institutionalization of this technology—beyond the short trials that have been carried out in Baltimore and Compton—looms on the horizon. There is increasing rhetoric from politicians that positions militarization as the solution to the high crime rates in urban centers. In August 2017 an executive order rolled back limits on a controversial program that provides local law enforcement agencies with surplus military gear such as armored vehicles, grenade launchers, high-caliber weapons, and camouflage uniforms.[2] Given the changing dynamics of the domestic sphere, we must consider how military-borne surveillance technologies gaining ground in the domestic sphere might affect our day-to-day lives in the twenty-first-century state. When military technology that was originally developed to battle enemy insurgents abroad becomes so easily translatable to the "friendly" domestic sphere, we must ask: What does it mean to be a civilian in the twenty-first century? How is it different from being an enemy of the state?

Charted within a larger history of sovereignty's optical and technological roots, persistent surveillance technologies arguably do not just affect the day-to-day lives of people but moreover reconfigure their social contract with the state. I argue that the availability of these technologies in the domestic sphere exposes the disconcerting conditions of life in the twenty-first century, in which foundational rights have been subjugated to the project of state security. At every turn, the increased militarization of the domestic sphere through remote warfare technologies encroaches on the space of the city and the rights of the citizen. This is part of a larger system of global war that has disarticulated the difference between zones of war and peace, leaving both friend and enemy under the totalizing gaze of the state. With this in mind, we must consider how the commercial availability of remote warfare tools will affect the personal liberties of the body politic as a whole, and our foundational power as a people. This discussion begins by understanding the terrible correlation between marginalization and criminalization; in other words, it is the most disenfranchised groups in our society that are the most vulnerable to these forms of state action. It is above their neighborhoods that these systems have been tested; it is their movements and interactions that are most likely to be coded as criminal.

Optics of Sovereignty

It is inarguable that the crime-solving potential of persistent surveillance technology is immense. However, its potential widespread implementation in cities across the United States raises questions about state power, citizenship, and the transformation of the intrinsic relationship between the two in the twenty-first century. As an all-seeing eye in the sky, persistent surveillance technology has a place in the long line of state technologies that perform sovereignty's optical function first embodied in the figure of the Leviathan-Behemoth monster that appears in the book of Job of the Old Testament. In *Leviathan*, Thomas Hobbes's foundational treatise on sovereignty and the social contract between a government and its peoples, appears a passage from the book of Job describing the namesake biblical eschatological monster; it reads, "He has no equal on earth; for he is made quite without fear. He looks down on all creatures, even the highest; he is king over all proud beasts."[3] In the biblical passage, and in Hobbes's reading of the text, the Leviathan emerges as a guard against the unknown, against what is feared, for "he has no equal on earth." The Leviathan is not just non-human; it is above the human, at a distance. As a tool of sovereign power that is imbued with a sovereign power in and of itself—the power of panoptic surveillance—the Leviathan bears a striking resemblance to today's sophisticated surveillance technologies. These technologies have been tasked with watching over cities, and like the Leviathan, they look down on all creatures, criminal and noncriminal alike.

In his 2015 book *Stasis: Civil War as a Political Paradigm*, Giorgio Agamben keenly draws out the visual and technological contours of sovereignty. He positions the Leviathan as "the effect of an optical contraption or a mask," which out of a multitude of people creates the illusion of a singular, all-powerful figure.[4] The significance of Agamben's intervention is twofold: first, he notes the coconstituency of the sovereign figure and the body politic, the "mutual Relation between Protection and Obedience" discussed by Hobbes in *Leviathan;* second, he grounds sovereign power in this total visualization of the body politic as a multitude.[5] For the sake of my discussion, sovereign power must be understood through the optical mechanisms that allow a singular political body to emerge, which via Agamben's reading can be figured in both a political and a technological sense. My discussion of persistent surveillance technology positions a landscape of contemporary sovereignty that hinges on the increasingly visual and technological sophistication of the Leviathan figure. These two functions of the Leviathan—as the behemoth monster rooted in the biblical tradition and as an optical device—set the stage for thinking about contemporary sovereignty through an archaeology of state technologies that has now come to militarize the domestic sphere.

I am aware of the critiques against the notion of an "all-seeing" view from above that I am positioning at the center of my discussion. Caren Kaplan, in her recent book *Aerial Aftermaths: Wartime from Above,* takes on the seduction of this God's-eye view, challenging notions of a total worldview that can be operationalized by the state. She writes that "aerial views from planes and satellites are presumed to 'see all,' but more often than not, the 'world picture' that they provide has failed to perceive any traces of what has been rendered impossible to know."[6] Her argument rightfully brings up the presence of the *un*seen and the *un*sensed, which necessarily escapes the view from above, and resists any notion of a "singular world, always already legible."[7] While at first blush this line of thinking seems incompatible with the type of sovereign power that I am locating in the case of persistent surveillance technology, the fundamental opacity that Kaplan rightfully notes factors into my discussion as well. My argument is not that state power has been perfected through this all-seeing, all-knowing eye in the sky; rather, it is that computational advances have precisely doubled down on *visible* evidence in order to calculate and predict criminality without much concern for other registers of knowledge. What these persistent surveillance systems "see" is what they have been coded to see, which includes human error and systemic prejudices against criminalized groups.

When I refer to the criminalized groups in our society who are most vulnerable to these state actions, I am calling attention to the fact that the urban centers where persistent surveillance technology has been deployed on a trial basis are also places with large nonwhite populations. The "total" and "objective" visualization that these systems enact is limited by prejudices regarding which behaviors, and geographical spaces, are considered criminal. Moreover, it is this recourse to the rhetoric of total vision, of a vision above the human, that works to absent the questions of state responsibility that I am raising; it bears noting that state responsibility and the dangers of state overreach seem to be less important when it comes to the city's "criminal" spaces. While Kaplan seeks to move away from a "linear continuum of the 'watching machine'" in her effort to understand the emergence of networked surveillance systems in the late twentieth and early twenty-first centuries, I think this technological evolution is important.[8] If thinkers like Paul Virilio, Grégoire Chamayou, and Kaplan herself have taken on the politics of this "watching machine," my intervention attempts to more closely think through the predictive capabilities that have been layered onto this view from above. The transformation of this relationship between the state and its people implicates not just the scope of surveillance but also the calculations in time and space that these networked surveillance machines can now readily perform. In other words, it is not just that the state is watching, but that their new computational technologies can track individuals in space and time and can calculate criminality based on opaque algorithms far removed from public consciousness. The preprogrammed narratives of criminality create virtual zones of enmity within our own borders that fracture the power of the people as a body politic.

Far from the total visibility that this "eye in the sky" purports, the most alarming aspect of this surveillance is that the people mapped by these systems are not afforded the traditional protection or visibility that the state owes to its citizens. They are data points that only become legible as people when they are suspected of suspicious behavior. In the logic of this technology, suspicious behavior is defined as being associated with a crime, a crime scene, or erratic behavior; the spaces and movements that "objectively" denote criminality are coded into the system by a human hand and are therefore susceptible to systemic prejudices that pervade in our society about which spaces, peoples, and movements are criminal. The criminality calculated by these systems can be thought of as retroactive, held within this archive as mere data until it is "interpreted" as criminal by the machine and prosecuted by the operator. Transgressions against the state remain invisible until the gatekeepers of this massive surveillance archive make them legible as "criminal."

In its original incarnation, persistent surveillance technology was developed by Ross McNutt to help the military detect improvised explosive devices (IEDs) in Fallujah from a safe distance. A *Radiolab* story from June 2015 is quick to inform the listener that persistent surveillance technology "is not just a military thing," insinuating that this story would otherwise not matter for the common listener. The hosts, Manoush Zomorodi and Alex Goldmark, suggest that this conversation is worth having because this technology is not just used on the enemy abroad but is also being used on "us." Throughout the program, reflection on this vague division of "us" versus "them" is largely absent, as is any consideration of why this discussion only matters now and not years ago when it was used against "them." The hosts begin by charting the technology's translation from Fallujah to Dayton, Ohio, a displacement that both journalists originally feel uneasy about. Mc-Nutt quickly makes sense of this displacement for the listeners, saying that American cities have "just as large of a problem as we do in Afghanistan and Iraq, only it is not IED's, it is crime."[9] For McNutt it is not only that there are equivalences between an active war zone and a U.S. city but also that there are equivalences between the external enemy and the internal criminal. It is these equivalences between crime and terror that McNutt says both legitimize and warrant the move of these technologies into the domestic sphere.

The sales pitch is quite seductive. For the price of a single police helicopter, McNutt promises a 30 to 40 percent decrease in crime; he claims that the implementation of this technology would mean an estimated $150 million saved per year. It is clear from a cost-benefit analysis standpoint that persistent surveillance technology would be a savior to state budgets around the country. Lower crime rates at a lower cost—what's not to like? Yet when the hosts see the technology at work, their attitude changes. When they see people being translated into pixels, Goldmark says, it "feels like we are a little less free"; he continues, "I feel like there is something being lost here but I can never put my finger on it. It's weird." It is not until Zomorodi and Goldmark are shown how the technology helped to bust a drug cartel in Ciudad Juárez that was responsible for the deaths of 1,500 people that the mood changes; a resigned Zomorodi says, "I guess that's how you have to take something like this down," pointing to some kind of imbalance in the fight between good and evil that has infiltrated our domestic sphere. She suggests that fighting a cartel network necessitates some complementary oppositional network of its own. The hosts, too, begin to see the equivalences between urban centers and war zones.[10]

It is important to note the resonance of a relatively far-off place like Ciudad Juárez, particularly in the context of a discussion about Dayton, Ohio. Although it goes unstated by the hosts, the specter of Ciudad Juárez seems to bridge the dissonance between external enemy and internal criminal that McNutt so readily deploys. Ciudad Juárez and its infamous cartels and murders serve as much-needed stable ground for the otherwise hazy and disorienting narrative spun around persistent surveillance technology. The crime networks south of the border—largely discussed in the press as threats to American lives, and by the Republican Party as a threat to American democracy—stands in for a global system of violence that is otherwise unthinkable for the normal civilian. It is not that the violence in Ciudad Juárez is overplayed or fictionalized, but that such a focus obscures larger narratives and longer histories that implicate the state as a perpetrator of the same violence it is denouncing.

When a contract with Persistent Surveillance Systems was brought to a vote in Dayton, the constituents in attendance were uncomfortably split. Twenty-five percent were very supportive, claiming that they had nothing to hide, while 15 percent found it to be a "grotesque invasion of privacy."[11] The rest of them, a significant 60 percent majority, had too many questions about the technology to pick a side—they were suspended between two sides, gesturing at a loss that was unarticulable but nonetheless affective. At the end of the public hearing in Dayton, state officials decided that it would take too much time and effort to answer the questions of this uncertain majority, and so they did not fund the implementation of the technology. This was by most measures a victory against the militarization of the domestic sphere, yet perhaps for all the wrong reasons. In this monumental conversation that would transform the lives of all the constituents, there was no discussion of the responsibility that the state has to its peoples, or the modes of accountability that would be foreclosed with technologies that necessarily function at a distance from the human. In short, the terms of the discussion were woefully insufficient in light of the magnitude of the potential ramifications.

Before Dayton, there were other trial runs done with persistent surveillance technology—in places like Baltimore and Compton. Yet for me Dayton stands as the most transparent and evocative case study. In Compton and other places, for instance, the trial runs were kept largely out of the public discussion. Sergeant Douglas Iketani from the Los Angeles County Sheriff's Department noted that his agency hid the trials to avoid public opposition: "A lot of people do have a problem with the eye in the sky, the Big Brother, so to mitigate those kinds of complaints we basically kept it pretty hush hush."[12] While war strategies and technologies are granted the highest of confidence levels, we must demand greater accountability when these technologies are utilized day to day in the domestic sphere. Whether deployed in Fallujah or Dayton, they continue to be remote warfare technologies. Dayton remains for me the clearest instance wherein the political confusion that structures the displacement of these technologies in the domestic sphere was the most palpable, even if the resolution left much to be desired. In other places, like Compton, the trial went largely unnoticed, and the implementation was discarded because of technological limitations instead of political limitations. In fact, the Los Angeles Sheriff's Department passed on Persistent Surveillance Systems in 2014 because, at the time, the system was not able to visualize faces well enough. As Conor Friedersdorf of the *Atlantic* notes, "It's hard to imagine that next technological barrier won't be broken soon."[13] From the vantage point of 2020, we can resolutely say that these barriers have indeed been broken.

Twenty-First-Century Technology

I am firmly positioning persistent surveillance technology as emblematic of twenty-first-century technology more broadly; as such, its modes of visualization and calculation are key to understanding the transformation of contemporary life in the twenty-first century under these technologies. In *Feed-Forward: On the Future of Twenty-First-Century Media*, Mark Hansen signals to a transformation of human experience in the twenty-first century contingent on the "complex entanglement of humans within networks of media technologies that operate predominantly, if not entirely, outside the scope of human modes of awareness"—such as consciousness, attention, and sense perception.[14] While Hansen largely grounds his discussion in the networks of big data and the massive social media archives that organize the twenty-first century, his intervention is applicable to the form and logic of persistent surveillance technology. Like the big-data networks he discusses, the network processes that make persistent surveillance technology successful operate largely outside our modes of cognition. The massive archives created through the constant surveillance of these crime-ridden cities easily exceed our human experiential capabilities while directly implicating us within them. These technologies are also largely undetectable from the ground, so that an individual's incorporation into this archive is imperceptible.

Beyond the incommensurability of data and the imperceptibility of the machine, there is a far more threatening capability of twenty-first-century technologies. Hansen argues that twenty-first-century media and technology represent "a shift from a past-directed recording platform to a data-driven anticipation of the future."[15] Persistent surveillance technology, and military surveillance technology more broadly, is invested in what I consider to be a form of *technological clairvoyance*. This is a function of the massive archives they collect, which, through carefully crafted algorithms, allow operators to map out potentialities unseen to the naked eye. The technology's aim of hyperefficient crime fighting *anticipates* criminality, coding certain spaces in the city as criminal, as well as certain stances and body movements; by extension, any individual who passes through these spaces or performs these movements—knowingly or not—is tainted with a spectral criminality. In this system, a data point can become a prophecy of a future crime, or of past wrongdoing that would otherwise be imperceptible to the human eye. With both the archive and the algorithm at a distance from the human, accountability over these prophecies lessens considerably.

The physical and cognitive distance between persistent surveillance technologies and the civilian on the ground bears further reflection here. First, try as they might, the general population will rarely be able to see these machines in action, for they operate at a sizable distance above the human; second, the excess visuality of their archives is beyond the limit of human cognition. Trained operators must rely on machines to reckon with the massive archives these systems routinely create, meaning that there is yet another level of mediation at work. In "Lines of Descent," Derek Gregory notes that operators must use machines that "filter out uneventful footage and distinguish 'normal' from 'abnormal' activity in a sort of militarized *rhythmanalysis* that is increasingly automated."[16] The distinction between "normal" and "abnormal" is not an objective demarcation; this taxonomy is dependent on information coded into the machine by human operators and influenced by their potential prejudices—be them personal or systemic. Part of the process of categorization, or criminalization, involves the use of programs that "quilt" images from multiple feeds in order to make sense of this effectively boundless archive. The totality of the archive used to make such decisions is inherently inaccessible to human cognition. As their imaging capabilities become more sophisticated, the horizon for these technologies would be to create a total archive of every civilian's life; in such a world, criminal and noncriminal alike would be reduced to images, their lives consumable by agents of the state but inaccessible to the people on the ground.

There is a key imbalance in the relationship between twenty-first-century technology and the larger society it is said to benefit. Hansen argues that there is a false pharmacological recompense at work in twenty-first-century technology—meaning that what is gained from these technologies is not congruous with what is lost in its implementation. Hansen builds on the work of Jacques Derrida in "Plato's Pharmacy," wherein Derrida considers the technology of writing as *pharmakon*, as both poison and cure.[17] I would venture to say that the threat of persistent surveillance technology is precisely its use as a writing technology: within its massive surveillance archives, the state finds written narratives of criminality that bolster discourses of security and cement the importance of law and order. Yet there is not enough attention given to the poison that this narrative hides; the opaque form of these criminal narratives exacerbates the poisonous effects of this technological prosthesis on personal liberties. Hansen notes that our long-standing prosthetic pharmacology "loses its prosthetic basis since the loss of our agency over our own behavioral data is recompensed by something that has no direct correlation with it"; in short, the loss and the recompense leveraged by these systems do not affect the same body.[18] It is important that we do not confuse the body politic—"we, the people"—with the body of the Leviathan; what is good for the state is not necessarily good for its people. With persistent surveillance systems—and twenty-first-century remote warfare technology more broadly—what the citizenry gains is not comparable to what it loses, even if that loss is hard to articulate, while the benefits are spectacularly quantifiable. The state only stands to gain in a world defined by these systems, whether it is a lower price tag for security measures or the ease of an all-encompassing network that enables cooperation between different branches of the federal government, and between the state and federal levels. Such a cost-benefit line of questioning obscures a more important discussion about the legal processes that are infringed on and the personal liberties that are eroded when the state can act on the individual without due process.

The commercial availability of persistent surveillance technology pushes us to rethink how the foundational political categories of friend and enemy function today. Carl Schmitt posits that the categories of friend and enemy are at the heart of the concept of the political; they are operational categories through which one can read the modern world order. Aligned with other foundational antithetical relationships like good and evil, friend and enemy can be superficially read as natural oppositional states. Yet Schmitt notes, "an enemy exists only when, at least potentially, one fighting collectivity of people confronts a similar collectivity"; this is to say that enmity has an origin—it is constructed at the point of an encounter with alterity. The enemy, writes Schmitt, is "the other, the stranger; and it is sufficient for his nature that he is, in a specially intense way, existentially something different and alien, so that in the extreme case, conflicts with him are possible."[19] In its mapping of the city, it is the borders between the citizen as friend and the criminal as enemy that persistent surveillance technology upholds. Via this technology, conflicts with the "other" that resides within the citizenry become not only possible but also computable—adding a veil of "objectivity" that is often attributed to sophisticated technologies at a remove from the human.

The promotional materials from Persistent Surveillance Systems boast that only "criminal bodies" are legible in this system.[20] In this logic, the body of the citizen seemingly recedes into the background as it becomes aligned with the power of the state, incorporated into the body of the sovereign and thus presumably guarded from its gaze. The do-gooder citizen is said to only benefit from this constant surveillance, as this Leviathan-like structure boasts that it protects the citizen from the enemy that lurks in the crowd. True to its philosophical roots, sovereign power still acts on individuals from above, the algorithm beyond human comprehension, at a distance; as an emblem for the future of sovereignty in the twenty-first century, this protection now comes via a commercial technology available on the commercial market. The militarization of the public sphere is perhaps most imperceptible when it happens through the neoliberal market.

Horizons of Global War

In a world defined by persistent surveillance, everything is computable and calculable. However, this is not a new anxiety of the twenty-first century; the discomfort of the mapped and surveilled city, and the intangible loss suffered by its inhabitants, is a well-documented symptom of modern life. Charles Baudelaire's essay "The Painter of Modern Life" explores these anxieties through the figure of the flaneur, who is said to be a "passionate lover of crowds and incognitos."[21] Baudelaire describes the flaneur as follows:

> The crowd is his element. . . . His passion and his profession are to become one flesh with the crowd. For the perfect flâneur, for the passionate spectator, it is an immerse joy to set up house in the heart of the multitude, amid the ebb and flow of movement, in the midst of the fugitive and the infinite. To be away from home and yet feel oneself everywhere at home; to see the world, to be at the center of the world, and yet to be hidden from the world. . . . The spectator is a prince who everywhere rejoices in his incognito.[22]

The surveilled crowds of Dayton, Compton, and Ciudad Juárez would be a nightmare for the flaneur. For it is precisely this experience of being lost in the crowd that is foreclosed with persistent surveillance technology. To be unknown is no longer possible when a multitude of cameras watch you from ten thousand feet, tracking every step, every second of your walk throughout the city. If the flaneur is most at home in the *unhomely* crowd, it is because the unknown is a space of refuge from the proliferating eyes of the modern world; these eyes aim to encroach on every possible intimacy and personal liberty. This is also to say that the eye in the sky encroaches on the right of the individual to exist outside the body of the Leviathan and taints the possibility of relating to the other in the crowd outside the logic and language of the state. If only these machines can tell us who in the crowd is a friend or enemy, then the multitude loses its appeal and subversive power.

The logic of the manhunt that has come to organize contemporary warfare becomes operative here. As Grégoire Chamayou argues in "The Manhunt Doctrine," warfare today functions through the "logic of the manhunt," which he defines as a predator–prey relationship that breaks with the rules of conventional warfare and does away with clear battlefronts and face-to-face combat.[23] This has led to an age in which wars mimic police action—think of a "war on terror" waged against individuals instead of states, and with no formal declaration needed by Congress; conversely, it has also led to police action that mimics aspects of formal wars—with police forces utilizing sophisticated drone technologies developed for fighting insurgents abroad. These are the markings of the age of global war: war without boundaries, be they geographic, technological, or political. In this new paradigm of war, Chamayou affirms, "the first task no longer involves immobilizing the enemy but instead requires identifying and locating him."[24] Surveillance systems gain incredible importance as the state seeks to visualize what lurks in the crowd in order to categorize it as friend or enemy. Yet even before their implementation, there is already a discourse about the criminality of certain crowds. In the domestic sphere, which is treated as a zone of war, the rights of the twenty-first-century civilian are in decline: in the home, legislation like the U.S. Patriot Act of 2001 infringes on their private communications regardless of culpability; in the streets, persistent surveillance technologies are able to turn their movements into a language of criminality. At every turn, the right of the individual to exist apart from the sanctity of the state is disarticulated through the surveillance of spaces that once proved too opaque for the gaze of the Leviathan.

At stake in this totalizing gaze of persistent surveillance technology is the potential of the city to serve as a place of refuge and commonality. In a 1996 lecture titled "On Cosmopolitanism," Jacques Derrida positions the city as a key site for upholding the integrity of the subject outside the language of the state. Derrida asks, "Could the city, equipped with new rights and greater sovereignty, open up new horizons of possibility previously undreamt of by international state law?"[25] This emboldened city would be a city for the people, and it is a direct response to a long history of violence perpetrated by the state against its own people. The horizon Derrida imagines is seemingly foreclosed in a world defined by persistent surveillance technology. As the state hovers above through this technological avatar, the city as a space of escape, separate from the agenda of the state, is lost. In these surveilled spaces, the individual is reduced to a spectacle readied for state consumption and susceptible to its narratives of criminality.

This massive system of surveillance has immense biopolitical ramifications that affect not just our being in the world but also our *being together* in the world; it affects both how we inhabit the city and how we come to view ourselves in relation to (or separate from) the other in the crowd. While ideologically these technologies are said to work to secure everyone they surveil, in practice they work to breed suspicion of the other. In the case of the urban centers that have become the focus of these technologies, this boils down to an added suspicion of groups that have already been marginalized by personal or systemic prejudices. As Shoshana Amielle Magnet argues in *When Biometrics Fail: Gender, Race, and the Technology of Identity*, these technologies rely on "rigid and essentialized understandings of race and gender" that work to control and classify already vulnerable and marginalized groups.[26] In her book *Dark Matters*, Simone Browne goes a step further, arguing that contemporary surveillance is informed by a long history of policing black lives; she states that its form and logic are built on the "constitutive genealogies" of transatlantic slavery.[27] While people like McNutt boast that these technologies work to remedy human error and bias, it is naive to believe that these deeply imbedded societal prejudices and unresolved violent histories would not be coded into the system, consciously or not.

Michel Foucault's work on the relationship between state power and visuality is key to this discussion. In *Discipline and Punish* Foucault writes, "Our society is one not of spectacle, but of surveillance. . . . It is not that the beautiful totality of the individual is amputated, repressed, altered by our social order, it is rather that the individual is carefully fabricated in it, according to a whole technique of forces and bodies."[28]

While I do not argue against the totality and reach of surveillance technologies, the type of imaging of the city that occurs with persistent
surveillance technology suggests that it is becoming more and more
difficult to mark a clear boundary between surveillance and spectacle
in the twenty-first century. This totalizing surveillance structure reduces the civilian to a mere image easily interpolated into the spectacular archives of state power. For me, these surveillance archives are
spectacular not just in size, but also because they are instrumental in
performing a spectacle of sovereign power. The civilian living in a
world defined by twenty-first-century surveillance technologies lives
perpetually under threat of being exposed as a criminal by an ever-
present, but largely inaccessible, eye in the sky. In this totalizing
structure, surveillance and spectacle go hand in hand.

Foucault sharply notes that in the modern order reified in Jeremy
Bentham's panopticon "visibility is a trap," harking to the material
structure of control at work.[29] However, the world of persistent surveillance technology is not panoptic; it is synoptic. Thus, in what we may
call the "synopticon" order of the twenty-first century, this trap has
been virtualized and extended into the city. In *Political Spaces and
Global War,* Carlo Galli explores the move from the panopticon order
of the modern era to a synopticon order "that seems to be the visibility
of all on behalf of all"; however, this is a false pharmacology, to evoke
the language of Hansen.[30] The synopticon order hides an imbalance
of power and a confusion of political geographies with no clear boundaries between friend and enemy or zones of war and peace. More than
the eye in the sky standing in for the guard in the tower, and the city
functioning as a mass of prison cells, this virtualization of the panopticon structure utilizes massive surveillance archives to "read" the
crowd and calculate criminality in a seemingly open city. In the synopticon order of the age of global war, and its constitutive persistent
surveillance systems, the high visibility of the civilian lessens the need
for material forms of control. The interaction between individuals in
Bentham's panopticon is quite limited, with each individual securely
confined to a cell and divided by sidewalls that hinder contact with the
other inmates.[31] Such a structure lends itself to Foucault's exaltation of
surveillance over spectacle. However, in the case of persistent surveillance technology, the separation of individuals is done in a less material, yet no less effective, manner. It is not cell walls but rather the

potential criminality of those around them that inhibits any productive collectivity that would challenge state overreach.

In this progression from panopticon to synopticon, the vantage point of the surveillance apparatus remains intact as it continues to watch over a fractured body politic. Foucault writes that "the crowd, a compact mass, a locus of multiple exchanges, individualities merging together, a collective effect, is abolished and replaced by a collection of separated individualities."[32] Yet beyond the fracturing of a collectivity, the synopticon order enacts a boundary between civilians that evokes the language of war, the split between friend and enemy that Carl Schmitt locates at the heart of the concept of the political. Thus what is at stake in the move from the panopticon order of the modern age to the synopticon order of the age of global war is not an epistemic break but an evolution of the power of the state through the capabilities of sophisticated technologies. It is not that the panopticon order is no longer relevant for the working of the twenty-first century but that technologies of war have heightened and virtualized its modes of control.

These new technologies transform the domestic sphere into an imperceptible war zone wherein individuals can no longer come together as a crowd, as a body politic, without the fear of what lurks above and within. As Carlo Galli notes, "The image of the world, or better, the world reduced to image is not itself removed from the reality of power."[33] This is to say that while these technologies are now presented as commercial tools, given their totalizing surveillance, they a priori serve the interest of the state. They provide a view from above that reifies systems of control. The fractures enacted within the body politic by persistent surveillance technologies, even a decidedly commercial technology that can be implemented by institution and individual alike, serve the purposes of the state above all else; this is a clear mark of a neoliberal world order that hinges the power of the state to the might of the economy. What this system does above all else is disperse the multitude. For all the assurances that Ross McNutt gives that only suspicious individuals are visualized by the system, this constant surveillance—even when not directed at a singular figure, as it often is—visualizes something far worse: the suspension of the affordances of citizenship, and the erosion of the contract between a state and its peoples that grants power and accountability over both.

False Positives

The interconnectedness of state power and the free market implicates a global system beyond the United States, whose military technologies readily infiltrate spaces beyond U.S. borders. While I have focused thus far on the application of persistent surveillance technology in the context of the United States and its direct sphere of influence, it is important to sketch out the global reach of these intelligent surveillance systems as a mark of life in the twenty-first century, or "the age of global war," as thinkers like Carlo Galli have termed it. Thus far I have argued that persistent surveillance technology's move from the outside in has made it possible for the U.S. government to visualize Dayton in the same way as Fallujah—already a global perspective but one inherently defined by U.S. intervention. I would like to extend this discussion beyond the United States and beyond the realm of crime and terror, thereby sketching out a broader system of global war that the rise of these technologies has buoyed. This is a horizon of global war that knows no geographical or political boundaries and that collapses the difference between city center and war zone.

Esther Hovers's *False Positives* project takes as a point of departure the imbrication of intelligent surveillance systems in urban spaces, exploring both the human experience of being in such spaces and the distinction between normative and criminal behavior that such surveillance systems operate on. Hovers worked with intelligent surveillance experts to pinpoint eight different "compositions" of humans in urban spaces that are said to indicate criminal intent; through these anomalies, algorithms are built to detect deviant behavior.[34] These anomalous signs become the rules of archival consignment for a twenty-first-century system of surveillance that, like persistent surveillance technology, is largely above the human. Like the inhabitants of Dayton, the people surveilled in the Brussels business district are reduced to signs denoting culpability. Hovers's project was set in this district, using computer-generated analyses of the types of movements recorded in that area. Her aim in *False Positives* was to challenge viewers "to act as an intelligent surveillance system" and, in doing so, to push them "to question the behavior of the different people within the photographs."[35] What emerges from the juxtaposition of these different forms (photographs and hand-drawn diagrams) and perspectives (human and machine) is an understanding of the twenty-first-century subject as always in relation to larger systems that not only image them but moreover do so in a language outside their comprehension.

The fact that this project took place in the Brussels business district speaks to the *glocality* of the contemporary world. As Carlo Galli notes, global war can also be characterized as "glocal war," by which he means a system in which "a single point is in immediate contact with the whole—the world-system."[36] It is worth mentioning that Brussels is not alone in its use of this type of "smart" camera: Washington, Boston, Chicago, Amsterdam, and other cities have implemented smart surveillance technology. It is no longer possible to talk of discrete spaces or local conflicts. Just as persistent surveillance technologies were operational in both Fallujah and Dayton, the separation of those locations as discrete political spaces is disarticulated; in such cases it becomes not just possible but necessary to talk about the *glocal,* about moments where a single point or event exposes the world system and makes visible obscured networks of power.

Hovers's work, by articulating these surveillance systems across different forms—and in forms other than their "natural" technological state—attempts to make legible twenty-first-century modes of seeing that would otherwise be inscrutable to humans. In essence, she creates a "key" to read urban landscapes in a way that approximates the type of readings done by persistent surveillance systems. The project challenges the structural opacity of these systems that enable certain readings and foreclose others in the space of law. Hovers's scenarios offer a glimpse into an otherwise impenetrable archive of state surveillance akin to the archives wielded by the operators of Persistent Surveillance Systems or the drone operators of the U.S. military. The project also intimates an understanding of the twenty-first-century subject as image, visualized and suspended within the state's sophisticated technologies of control. The time frames Hovers includes with each photograph indicate the time spent waiting for a contrast to arise between deviant and normal behavior; this, for me, signals to a type of subject in suspension, waiting for this algorithm to read their movements in the city and to categorize these movements as "normal" or "deviant."

The name of Hovers's project, *False Positives,* bears further reflection. A false positive is a test that incorrectly indicates the presence of some condition or attribute, the false presence of deviance in a normal movement, for example. There are two types of false-positive errors: one that falsely infers the existence of something that is not there and one that falsely infers the absence of something that is there. Both errors, of false presence and of false absence, speak to the questions Hovers's project evokes about the articulation of the categories of normalcy and deviance, and more broadly about the politics that can take root in such a totalizing structure. These questions underpin my overall discussion: What does it mean to be a citizen in the twenty-first century? How is it different from being an enemy of the state? Twenty-first-century surveillance technologies, here and abroad, work to transform the relationship between citizens and the state by working to dismantle spaces wherein the individual might be sheltered from the eye of the Leviathan. Driven by the fast evolution, cost effectiveness, and commercial availability of persistent surveillance technology, these technologies are positioned to become emblems not just of twenty-first-century warfare but of daily life in the twenty-first century more broadly.

The globalization of these technologies should be considered as yet another chapter in the ongoing post-9/11 militarization of the domestic sphere, which thinkers like Allen Feldman have termed "public safety wars." Feldman writes that, unlike the classic global and guerrilla wars of the twentieth century, public safety wars "are not wars of utopia, but wars of dystopia that assume that 'perfected' liberal democracies are threatened by an invisible, infiltrating menace."[37] While these technologies are said to protect the public at large, they work by casting a veil of suspicion on those who are different or take part in "abnormal" behavior. The act of defining and coding what normal and abnormal behavior is in itself already betrays and alienates part of the public it is said to be protecting. These already vulnerable groups—low-income communities, people of color, immigrants, and so on—become further marginalized and criminalized for the security of the community at large.

As the Dayton hearings showed, the social divisions that fuel persistent surveillance technology turn the body politic against itself. A city watched over by an eye in the sky, parsing the crowd for signs of enmity, is a city in civil strife or stasis. Giorgio Agamben notes that stasis "constitutes a zone of indifference between the un-political space of the family and the political space of the city"; thus "civil war functions as a threshold of politicization and de-politicization, through which the house is exceeded in the city and the city is depoliticized in the family."[38] Stasis, as a zone of both politicization and depoliticization, of both inactivity and civil strife, sheds light on the workings of contemporary sovereignty in a technologically ordered world that disarticulates the spaces that the categories of friend and enemy traditionally inhabit. The use of military technology in our cities transforms the city into a space of war; it is a thinly veiled instance of a state waging war against its own people. When remote warfare technologies become normalized in the domestic sphere, the realm of peace will no longer be thinkable. With these technologies of global war, the neoliberal state can easily wage informal war against internal criminal and external enemy alike.

Notes

1. Persistent Surveillance Systems, accessed July 20, 2019, https://www.pss-1.com.

2. Sadie Gurman, "Trump Clears the Way for Local Police to Obtain Military Gear," Associated Press, August 28, 2017, https://apnews.com/f6896860cb5d4eccbcdb49665ca0ed9b.

3. Job 41:33–34 (King James Version).

4. Giorgio Agamben, *Stasis: Civil War as a Political Paradigm*, trans. Nicholas Heron (Stanford, Calif.: Stanford University Press, 2015), 15.

5. Thomas Hobbes, *Leviathan*, ed. Richard Tuck (Cambridge: Cambridge University Press, 1996), 396.

6. Caren Kaplan, *Aerial Aftermaths: Wartime from Above* (Durham, N.C.: Duke University Press, 2018), 28.

7. Kaplan, 2.

8. Kaplan, 29.

9. Manoush Zomorodi and Alex Goldmark, "Eye in the Sky," in *Radiolab*, WNYC Radio, June 18, 2015, http://www.radiolab.org/story/eye-sky/.

10. Zomorodi and Goldmark.

11. Zomorodi and Goldmark.

12. Conor Friedersdorf, "Eyes over Compton: How Police Spied on a Whole City," *Atlantic*, April 21, 2014, https://www.theatlantic.com/national/archive/2014/04/sheriffs-deputy-compares-drone-surveillance-of-compton-to-big-brother/360954/.

13. Friedersdorf.

14. Mark Hansen, *Feed-Forward: On the Future of Twenty-First-Century Media* (Chicago: University of Chicago Press, 2015), 5.

15. Hansen, 4.

16. Derek Gregory, "Lines of Descent," openDemocracy, November 8, 2011, https://www.opendemocracy.net/en/lines-of-descent/.

17. Jacques Derrida, "Plato's Pharmacy," in *Dissemination,* trans. Barbara Johnson (Chicago: University of Chicago Press, 1981).

18. Hansen, *Feed-Forward,* 221.

19. Carl Schmitt, *The Concept of the Political,* trans. George Schwab (Chicago: University of Chicago Press, 2007), 28, 27.

20. In the *Radiolab* interview, McNutt says that operators are trained to only zoom down to a certain level, protecting the privacy of innocent individuals. Zomorodi and Goldmark, "Eye in the Sky."

21. Charles Baudelaire, "The Painter of Modern Life," in *The Painter of Modern Life, and Other Essays,* trans. Jonathan Mayne (London: Phaidon, 1964), 5.

22. Baudelaire, 9.

23. Grégoire Chamayou, "The Manhunt Doctrine," *Radical Philosophy* 169 (2011): 2.

24. Chamayou, 2.

25. Jacques Derrida, "On Cosmopolitanism," in *On Cosmopolitanism and Forgiveness* (London: Routledge, 2001), 7–8.

26. Shoshana Amielle Magnet, *When Biometrics Fail: Gender, Race, and the Technology of Identity* (Durham, N.C.: Duke University Press, 2011), 20.

27. Simone Brown, *Dark Matters: On the Surveillance of Blackness* (Durham, N.C.: Duke University Press, 2015), 13.

28. Michel Foucault, *Discipline and Punish: The Birth of the Prison,* trans. Alan Sheridan (New York: Vintage Books, 1995), 217.

29. Foucault, 200.

30. Carlo Galli, *Political Spaces and Global War,* trans. Elisabeth Fay (Minneapolis: University of Minnesota Press, 2010), 112.

31. Foucault, *Discipline and Punish,* 200.

32. Foucault, 201.

33. Galli, *Political Spaces,* 112.

34. Esther Hovers, *False Positives,* 2017, https://estherhovers.com/False-Positives-1.

35. Hovers.

36. Galli, *Political Spaces,* 162.

37. Allen Feldman, "Securocratic Wars of Public Safety," *Interventions: International Journal of Postcolonial Studies* 6, no. 3 (2001): 334.

38. Agamben, *Stasis,* 16.

PART II

INTIMACIES

CHAPTER 5

Of Games and Drones

Mediating Traumatic Affect
in the Age of Remote Warfare

MICHAEL RICHARDSON

Drone warfare is often simplistically conflated with video gaming. Activists describe a "PlayStation mentality" behind drone killings that encourages swift recourse to violence, and news media frequently evoke video games in the context of drone operations.[1] In his ethnographic study of drone crews in the U.S. military, Hugh Gusterson shows how they are often culturally marginalized, seen as gamers rather than real pilots, safely ensconced in bases in the United States rather than operating out of traditional theaters of war.[2] This kind of killing at a distance has often been figured as far easier than killing in immediate proximity, yet drone pilots are quitting faster than they can be trained, despite the increasing centrality of the role of Predators, Reapers, and other unmanned aerial vehicles in U.S. defense strategy.[3] Military culture is one contributing factor, particularly the contempt and derision expressed by those whose bodies come into harm's way and the problem of assessing and awarding valor, yet the experience of drone killing itself is also a component.[4] While the extent of posttraumatic stress disorder among drone pilots and sensor operators remains contested, there is little doubt that such roles are not without significant psychological, social, and familial costs.[5] As former drone sensor operator Brandon Bryant, visual culture scholar Caren Kaplan, and others point out, the advanced visualization, targeting, and control systems in modern drones make the killing of enemies and civilians an intimate act that is at once similar to and utterly unlike gaming.[6]

Research into drone warfare operations and their consequences for pilots, such as the widely read reports of the Stimson Center's Task Force on US Drone Policy, has thoroughly debunked the mythology of a video game mentality that lends itself to reflexive violence.[7] Yet the aesthetic and cultural associations between drone warfare and video games continue to possess a cultural currency that blurs popular understanding and muddies the ground for debate about the costs and consequences of drone warfare for the United States and other enthusiastic adherents. The surface similarities between killing by drone and gaming—the view through a screen, the controllers that drive the interfaces, the pressing of a button to fire—obscure the crucial differences and disjunctures that sever the sutures binding drone warfare and video games. While David Grossman's classic military study *On Killing* argues that a soldier's resistance to killing declines in linear relation to his or her distance from the opponent, the processes of mediation inherent to drone warfare undo that distancing effect.[8] By situating the drone crew thousands of miles away geographically yet intimately close through mediating technologies, drones "take the straight line in Grossman's graph and twist it into a Mobius strip where beginning and end, although still separate, cross."[9] At issue here is the fact that "physical distance no longer necessarily implies perceptual distance."[10] Brought into perceptual proximity with those who will be killed, drone crews experience those deaths as an unbearable intimacy, as Tim Jelfs shows in his contribution to this volume. This intensity is bound up with the bodily quality of mediation itself, as the sustained physical engagement with the screens, interfaces, and interactive demands of operating drones brings the pilot and sensor operator into a complex, intimate, and lively relationship with the act of killing at an intimate distance.

This chapter addresses the processes of mediation within intimately distant acts of killing, their entanglement with video games, and the ways in which traumatic affects generate, circulate, and manifest in gaming responses to drone warfare. It asks how gaming as a genre might uncover the more complex forces at work in the relationship between gaming and drone warfare. Critiquing drone warfare from within the genre of cultural production synonymous with its mythologies, the serious games analyzed in this chapter—*Killbox* and *Unmanned*—address the entanglement of games and drones in aesthetic form and tease out the nuanced mediations and traumatic affects inherent to remote war.[11] While the violence of drone warfare is visited almost exclusively on those who live with them flying overhead, my focus here is primarily on drone crews, technological mediations, and traumatic affects. I engage in this bracketing reluctantly, cautiously, and provisionally—as Annika Brunck points out in this volume, the very underpinning of remote warfare is the production and maintenance of spatial, cultural, and psychological remoteness. Yet my hope is that repeating that separation here makes a worthy contribution to the larger project of unraveling the notion that drone war is video game war. This task matters because the persistence of this mythology prevents us from seeing drone warfare's traumatic violence clearly, whether on targeted people and populations or on those who operate drones, participants in war who struggle within the notions of warrior and wounding explored by David Buchanan elsewhere in this volume. At the same time, the mythology of video game war stops us from recognizing the cultural consequences of its seemingly inevitable rise to a starring role in contemporary militaries around the globe and, first and foremost, in the United States.

A Brief Primer on War and Games

The long history of entanglement between war and games is a well-trodden scholarly path, so what follows is a brief and necessarily incomplete foray.

From the two-thousand-year-old Chinese go to adaptations of chess in nineteenth-century Germany, games have provided strategic training through the simulation of battlefield situations. After World War I, new board games "took frequent inspiration from their military precursors, as commercial designers and military personnel frequently exchanged notes and jobs (Dunnigan, 2000; Perla, 1990)."[12] With the emergence of video games in the 1960s, this imbrication of gaming and war at once accelerated and tightened. Not only were games—like almost all computing—dependent on material technologies with military origins, many early game creators had worked for the U.S. military or conducted military-funded research. In the early 1980s, the military occasionally financed the development of games, but it also began to import games from the arcade to its training facilities. As

Nina B. Huntemann and Matthew Thomas Payne write in their introduction to *Joystick Soldiers: The Politics of Play in Military Video Games,*
the Pentagon soon shifted "from being a more hands-off backer of
game technologies into a considerably more active game producer with
the emergence of the military-entertainment complex."[13] Central to
this evolution was its increased control over game creation and industry partners, but so too was the increased emphasis on exploiting the
entertainment industry to normalize militarism in the United States
and fuse it with the very notion of patriotism.

Unsurprisingly, perhaps, the "publication of military-themed
video games has increased since 2001, with a significant portion of
these games focusing on terrorist/counter-terrorist conflict."[14] As
such, games have been active participants in refiguring post-9/11 militarism in the West, as Payne argues in *Playing War: Military Video
Games after 9/11.*[15] For Frédérick Gagnon, this is exemplified in the
Call of Duty series, which "resonates with and reinforces a tabloid
imaginary of post-9/11 geopolitics when it tells players that 'we' are
constantly on the brink of war with international actors such as Arab
terrorists and Russia, who will not hesitate to invade 'our' countries and
attack 'us' with nuclear weapons."[16] Yet as Carrie Andersen argues, later
games in the series display an anxiety about the role of the soldier as
they imagine future wars in which autonomous, weaponized drones
dominate battlefields.[17] Such unease is rare. Video games are much
more likely to align with the fusion of militarism and popular culture
that James Der Derian describes as the "military-industrial-media-
entertainment network."[18] This deliberately expansive conception links
together everything from the active participation of the Pentagon in the
production of movies to the embedding of reporters in military units to
air force flyovers of football games. For Der Derian, however, video
games are an important site of analysis because of their pervasiveness
across the spectrum of the military-entertainment complex.

One of the clearest—and most critiqued—instances of this is the
Pentagon-produced *America's Army* series of games, which simultaneously functions as a recruitment, training, and propaganda tool. The
America's Army games are freely available and arguably the most successful, cost-effective recruitment tool in U.S. military history. According to the official website, players of the sixth and most recent game in
the series, *America's Army: Proving Ground,* "take on the role of an 11B

Infantryman as part of a Long Range Combined Arms–Recon (LRCA-R) unit, a full spectrum capable team that embarks on special operations missions behind enemy lines." It promises "small unit tactical maneuvers and training that echoes true-to-life Army scenarios."[19] Developed and published by the U.S. Army, the game series has received dozens of industry awards and positive reviews by players and the gaming media, but more significantly, its four major releases and Xbox, mobile phone, and arcade versions are widely downloaded and played. It is regarded as a remarkable recruitment success by the U.S. Army but also held up as a totemic example of creeping militarism in cultural life.

In this light, scholars have subjected *America's Army* to considerable critique. Drawing on several years of ethnographic research with the game's developers, Robertson Allen argues that the games reflect "a militarized logic of biopolitical governance that aims to more efficiently streamline the apparatuses of war, to enable potential soldiers, recruited soldiers, and traumatized soldiers to become more 'battle ready.'"[20] While only a small percentage go on to enlist, any player who "comes to more readily accept the status quo of army norms, priorities, and ways of thinking about the world counts as a success as well."[21] David Neiborg argues that the series "is a powerful example of the U.S.'s ability to successfully wield soft, and thus sweet power by tapping into and affecting popular culture by becoming culturally popular."[22] In his detailed review of the academic literature on the game, Marcus Schulzke argues that much of this criticism rests on normative claims about civic–military relations and fails to consider the benefits of the game for military training, particularly around ethics.[23]

Yet regardless of any specific positive consequences of these games, what interests me in the context of drone warfare is the work they do to embed militarism in U.S. culture both discursively and affectively. This is crucial because the various studies of *America's Army* make clear that there is a sharp disparity between its affective texture and that of war itself. As Neiborg points out, the game's success depends on its sophisticated mix of gameplay, propaganda, and education delivered through a fully realized first-person-shooter gaming experience.[24] Immersive gameplay pulls the player into a carefully crafted experience of war geared toward recruitment. Its affectivity coalesces around shared success via cooperative missions and the buildup, modulation, and release of intensities through firefights. Its aesthetics, missions, and weaponry provide a kind of sanitized yet decidedly masculine realism: "true-to-life" with "real weapons used by the US Army" yet stripped of the fatigue, boredom, death, pain, trauma, and visceral corporeality of war itself. The dominant experiential mode is what Payne calls ludic war, or "the pleasurable experience of playing military-themed video games alone or with others."[25] Here, the purified intensities and regular rhythms of the first-person military shooter shape the formation of war as an affective atmosphere.

Affective atmosphere is the term used by the critical geographer Ben Anderson to describe collective experiences of feeling that are not reducible to the specific experience of any individual.[26] Affective atmospheres are produced through shared experiences that entangle the feeling states and collective experiences of multiple subjects in varying contexts. The term provides a way of accounting for the complex undercurrents of shared feeling and experience that cannot simply be described in representational terms. Affective atmospheres are how we feel with, within, and alongside things, contexts, and events, rather than how we feel *about* them. In the context of war, they are the ambiguous, hard-to-pin-down qualities that contribute to the orientation toward and experience of war—both the thing itself and in its culturally mediated forms, such as video games. In military shooters, for example, the most self-consciously "real" instances of video war gaming, there is a disjuncture between representation, gaming affect, and experience. This disjuncture is to be expected, of course, but it signals the necessity of thinking beyond representation and aesthetics in considering the relations between drones and games—particularly so when the experiential dynamics of drone operation are examined more closely.

Mediations in the Ground Control Station

For drone operators, most experiences of the battlespace are of a kind of vigilant boredom. Shifts often last twelve hours, the screens filled with sparsely populated landscape, or a vacant compound, or an empty road. Trapped inside a trailer some eight feet wide and thirty feet long, the pilot, sensor operator, and intelligence analyst pass long hours attuned to monitors that display very little of interest. "It's dark, mostly

FIGURE 5.1. Inside an MQ-9 Reaper training mission from a ground control station on Holloman Air Force Base, New Mexico. (U.S. Air Force photo by Airman 1st Class Michael Shoemaker/Released)

boring, quiet, while suffocating the soul, body, and mind," writes former sensor operator Brandon Bryant.[27] Video and data feeds are also monitored by analysts located elsewhere who comb footage, intercepts, and images for information and enemies, but in the ground control station the space is intimate: three bodies, padded seats, and a host of screens and control interfaces (Figure 5.1). Engaging comfortably with these technologies suits a particular mind-set and is often described with references to gaming. As one older drone squadron commander tells Peter W. Singer, the younger operators "will sit there and watch all four of their screens at once, monitoring everything from the map to the weapons to fuel, while also peeking over at the pilot beside them's screen, to see what he is looking at. That comes from all those games."[28] And, again in a mode similar to that of online gaming environments, communication with those not in the room occurs via a set of chat-rooms, displayed on screens located between the pilot and sensor operator. Operating Predators is "an endless loop of watching: scanning roads, circling compounds, tracking suspicious activity." For the crew, time often passes "in a haze of banal images of rooftops, walled courtyards, or traffic-snarled intersections."[29] Yet there are distinct departures from the experience of gaming and the atmosphere of forced attention that pervades the ground-control station, the crew's bodies attuned to the images and words crawling across their screens in an open-ended fashion that bears only a passing similarity to the attentional dynamics of video games.

Attention in video games is structured and directed through affective design, which James Ash defines as "the process of attempting to indirectly generate particular kinds of affects or responses through the material and aesthetic design of products in order to capture and hold users' attention."[30] At this level of interactivity, structure, and affective design, drone video feeds can be differentiated from video games in a number of ways: games are discontinuous and marked by level restarts, pausing, and so on, whereas video feeds are continuous; games tend to simplify landscapes and populations, rendering most other figures into enemies, while drone feeds reveal watched landscapes to be far more populated and difficult to decode; and where games present simplified rules of engagement, war zones are subject to a complex raft of laws, codes, and procedures regarding killing.[31] There is thus a complex layering of meanings, affects, connotations, and tendencies that crowd the notion of the video game war and the experiential realities of operating weaponized drones. While the presence in the ground control station of multiple screens, control and communication interfaces, information feeds, and various icons recalls certain aesthetic and interactive qualities of gaming, the lack of narrative structure, design, and constraint in drone warfare necessitates a more consciously evoked attention, produced via routines of engagement (checking instruments, reviewing logs, eyes shifting from screen to screen) that aim to cut through the dulling effects of boredom.

Yet the atmosphere within the ground control station can swiftly shift to a razor edge of intensity: a "kill list" target goes on the move, a pattern of behavior triggers an alarm, or U.S. forces come under fire. Then "the chatrooms and radio wavelengths can spring to life with messages bouncing back and forth between nodes in the network," the crew flung from alert stagnation to heightened engagement.[32] Yet within the matrix of decision-making, the crew itself possesses only limited agency, as the very technologies of remote warfare enable intervention within operations by geographically distant officers, including generals and lawyers. Potential missile strikes are thus thickets of

competing pressures, interests, and perspectives, which continually interrupt the rapidly intensifying experience of the operators themselves. For the drone crews, these periods of impending violence are
opportunities to transform the tension of watchful hours, days, or even
weeks into the raw stuff of war fighting. "It was exhilarating when we
were actually doing something," writes Bryant, "when we were studying our very human targets."[33]

This exhilaration can become an anxious desire to *fire,* a feeling captured powerfully in the accounts of pilots like Matt Martin, or in the
scant transcripts made public, such as that of a lethal operation gone
wrong that opens both Grégoire Chamayou's *Drone Theory* and Andrew Cockburn's *Kill Chain*.[34] In these textual accounts, lacking any
sense of the visuality or mediation essential to the events, the crews
seem to read the scenes they surveil with an intensity geared toward
pulling the trigger. On the page, verbatim transcripts show the direct communication between the crews and other stakeholders but
elide everything else. This renders invisible the mediations, imagery,
rhythms, and atmospheres that are so essential to this form of killing.
Such transcripts cannot capture how, when the order is given, drone
crews "often report a sense that everything is in slow motion as they
pray that a child does not step into the picture or that the target does
not step out of range."[35] So much coheres on these glacial seconds: button pressed and missile launched, the endless attention to what the
drone sees, and the wrangling of commanders.

Within the narrow confines of the ground control station, these
crews are caught in what Jan Slaby, Rainer Mülhoff, and Philipp
Wüschner call an affective arrangement: the constellation of bodies,
actions, perceptions, gestures, mediations, screens, controllers, movements, and flows of video, data, and time that shape the bodily and relational dynamics of drone crew experiences.[36] Yet they are also folded
into the wider assemblage of the military drone network, one with an
array of technological, discursive, institutional, and affective dynamics of its own.[37] In the remainder of this chapter, I want to uncover some
ways that games might operate as critiques of drone warfare, both in
an overt, rhetorical sense and as interventions into the processes of
mediation and affect at work in both games and military drones. Working within very different ludic, aesthetic, and affective registers, the serious games *Killbox* and *Unmanned* deploy the very cultural genre in

question to problematize the popular imagining of drone warfare as analogous to video games. In doing so, they bring to the fore the complex, multifaceted, and often obscured relationship between mediation and trauma in the context of drone warfare. Attuned to the traumatic affects and violent sensations embedded within the mediations inherent to drone warfare, these games offer a way into thinking about the relationship between drones and games that disentangles them at the level of mediation itself. Deviating from much of the critical commentary on the mythology of the video game war, which applies empirical research methodologies to the conduct of war itself, my analysis of these two games shows how drones and games might be further disentangled on the terrain of culture production and meaning making. This disentangling is a crucial element in broadening and deepening debates about drone warfare itself—and better enabling the aesthetic and cultural work necessary to illuminate its costs and consequences to wider publics.

Gaming the Killbox

While the first autonomous aerial vehicles that earned the moniker "drones" were used as target practice in the First World War, the precursors to the contemporary drone can be found in the Vietnam War—a war that was, not at all coincidentally, the first to deploy computing technologies on a large scale. It was, as Ian Shaw writes, "a technologically intensive conflict fought with sophisticated electronic prosthetics, from remote sensors that listened to enemy movements to jet-powered Firebee drones that screamed through the skies."[38] This technowar was a war directed via abstractions, a set of managerial frames, systems, and geometries that transformed bodies, terrain, and slaughter into numbers. Yet "rather than illuminating the world with the bright light of statistical clarity, cybernetic warfare blinded its practitioners."[39] Despite the failure of military planning in Vietnam, the Pentagon's obsession with dominating the electronic battlefield and with autonomous vehicles was just beginning. Initially, hunting and killing were viewed as distinct functions: drones were designed for surveillance, while remote- and computer-controlled missiles were the key weapons.[40] That changed with the Predator, first deployed in 1994 as part of the NATO air campaign over Bosnia. Both there and later over Kosovo, the Predator was primarily a targeting tool: monitoring the battlefield, it beamed unprecedented images back to commanders who would then call in air strikes on Serbian forces or fortifications. After 9/11, "the United States began undertaking targeted killings by drones, deploying the MQ-1B Predator and MQ-9 Reaper, armed with precision-guided munitions, to match their adversaries' flexible tactics."[41] These weaponized drones dangled the tantalizing promise of extending precise warfare capabilities into previously inaccessible geographies without risking soldiers' deaths, but in doing so they also intensified the networked mediation of warfare on which the cultural imagining and rhetoric of video game war depend.

Of course, mediation and war have long been bedfellows. Figurines were moved across maps to represent troop movements in the surveying and planning of war, geographies became coordinates to plot artillery fire, the sighting cameras on bombers or the radars on naval vessels were used to track skies and seas, and the heads-up displays of fighter jets augmented the human field of view. But digital technologies have made mediation near ubiquitous: battlefield computers, GPS trackers, improvised explosive device–defusing robots, and hand-launched drones, to name just a few. Sarah Kember and Joanna Zylinska argue that mediation is "a key trope for understanding and articulating our being, becoming with, the technological world, our emergence and ways of intra-acting with it, as well as the acts and processes of temporarily stabilizing the world into media, agents, relations, and networks."[42] Military mediation works on soldiers and officers in just this way, reducing the complex battle environment into discretely manageable components that are nonetheless lively and material. Recognizing these military mediations as processes rather than static objects is crucial. It is not so much that *media* play a vital role in contemporary technowar, but that *processes of mediation* underpin the transformation of the world into the electronically enclosed battlespace necessary for what the U.S. military calls full-spectrum dominance, or "the control of terrestrial, maritime, atmospheric, and extraterrestrial spaces by a sophisticated war machine."[43] At the level of infrastructure, this militarized drive for greater control is made possible by networked architectures that mirror in more secure form and sometimes even overlap with those of the civilian internet: optical fiber cables, server farms, satellites, and much more. At the level of interface and aesthetics, the popular imagining of technological warfare is fueled by films and video games that purport to depict a kind of aesthetic realism, aided and abetted by the entanglements between the entertainment industry and military institutions in the United States. Operating in both affective and representational registers, this confluence of the war and culture has a particular intensity in gaming precisely because games themselves are so often concerned with producing an intensive yet aestheticized experience of violence and war.[44]

Killbox, created by Joseph DeLappe and Scotland-based artists and game developers Malath Abbas, Tom Demajo, and Albert Elwin of Biome Collective, intervenes in precisely this complex knot of aesthetics, mediation, violence, and gaming. Available for download on the popular gaming platform Steam, exhibited at galleries and festivals, including the Victoria and Albert Museum in London, and chosen as an official selection at A MAZE Berlin, IndieCade, and the Scottish British Academy of Film and Television Arts Awards, *Killbox* deploys the video game genre as a mode of interactive new media art. It places its players in two very different roles: that of a drone pilot who launches missiles within the tight constraints of the military machine and that of a villager whose community is the target of a lethal strike. The term *kill box* is military in origin: it refers to a geographic zone that is both scalable and circumstantial, and in which aerial forces are preauthorized to engage targets. "Within a given cube," writes Chamayou, "one may fire at will."[45] As the game's creators point out, these activated spatial coordinates "legalise drone missile strikes in countries with which there is no official war."[46] While a "kill box is a temporary zone of slaughter," it is also one that comes into being in and through media.[47] *Killbox* critically examines the mediation of warfare, but it also places in tension the radically different experiences of those who fly drones and those who live under them.

The game is structured around two experiences of the same missile strike. After launching the game, you are given the choice "either to play as a Waziri villager in Pakistan living under the audible threat of a drone circling unseen above—or that of a remotely based drone pilot targeting the same location from afar."[48] Choosing the pilot places you in a context of great power but with little freedom of action or movement; choosing the villager places you powerlessly on the ground but able to move freely within the game space. Because both

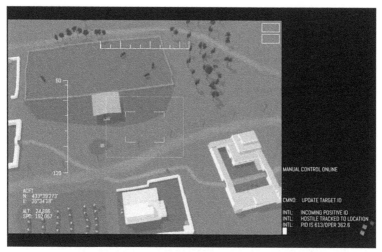

FIGURE 5.2. View from the drone operator gameplay mode. (Screenshot from *Killbox*, by Joseph DeLappe and Biome Collective, 2015)

experiences inescapably culminate in a missile strike, player actions and choices have no narrative impact. Violence is presented as the inevitable and unavoidable outcome of the drone mission: sooner or later, the game suggests, a missile will be launched and people will die. As the pilot, you are instructed on what to do from moment to moment: logging into the system, connecting to the drone apparatus, panning and zooming the camera, locking onto a target, launching the missile, and watching it speed toward the village below. Finally, you launch the second missile of a "double-tap" strike and confirm your kills. The emphasis throughout is on conformity: there is no possibility of deviating without quitting the game entirely. The process of killing is technical: a series of keystrokes, coolly executed. What the camera sees is flattened and distant, positioning the pilot as disconnected from the events below (Figure 5.2).

Playing as the villager is an inverse experience. The perspective is first person and the village unfolds as a three-dimensional environment composed of gray polygon buildings, green fields, and gardens populated by other villagers, each represented by a brightly colored ball that floats just above the ground (Figure 5.3). Unlike the pilot, who encounters a restricted environment, the villager can look and

FIGURE 5.3. View from the villager gameplay mode after the drone strike. (Screenshot from *Killbox,* by Joseph DeLappe and Biome Collective, 2015)

move at will. As a game space, the village itself is simple—buildings cannot be entered and interactions with other villagers consist only of bumping into them—but the capacity for movement sets up a very different relationship to the arriving drone strike. As time passes, the low buzz of the drone overhead sharpens into a rising whine as the missile speeds through the air. This diegetic sound mimics the telltale whir described by those who do live under drones and (at least for this player) produces a palpable anxiety. Playing as the villager, the weight of the pending explosion accumulates in tension with the whimsical, disarming quality of the scenes of daily life. The strike itself shatters the village lifeworld: the ground shakes, black smoke billows. While replaying the game as the pilot simply repeats the same regimented processes, doing so as the villager makes possible a series of different relations to the village and to the strike—except, of course, escape from its inevitability. The strike can happen outside visual range altogether or in the near distance, prompting a race to the cratered hole where two villagers used to stand. Or, if you know where the strike will land, you can wait at ground zero and bear the brunt of the explosion only to "survive" trapped within the wreckage, able only to spin the point of view.

Both playing experiences continually call attention to the genre status of *Killbox,* asserting its standing as a game. In the pilot level, the village is seen through the heads-up display that mimics that of the Predator drone itself, but which is also familiar to players of flight simulators—a genre of game that has an intimate relationship to the military via training programs and shared visualities. By contrast, the villager perspective recalls the first-person positioning of adventure or shooter games yet without any capacity for lethality or resistance to the pending violent attack, while the simplistic graphics, smooth movements, and environment interactions are reminiscent of classic platform games. Most pointedly, the rendering of the villagers themselves as brightly colored balls is, in the words of the creators, "representative of the 'data points' used by information visualizations on drone strikes" and intended to give "these statistical representations life through movement and a sense of context—people in a place doing things."[49] Just as the visuality, or technoculturally mediated vision, of twentieth-century warfare was defined by its imbrication with the cinematic, so the scopic regime of drone wars is coconstitutively enmeshed with that of the network.[50] As Derek Gregory points out in an influential article, "The hierarchies of the network are flat and fluid, its spaces complex and compound, and the missions are executed on-screen through video feeds and chat rooms (displays show as many as 30 different chats at a time) that bring a series of personnel with different skills in different locations into the same zone."[51]

This flatness and fluidity combine with the liveness of video and sensor feeds to produce what J. David Bolter and Richard Grusin call hypermediacy, or that which "makes us aware of the medium or media (and in sometimes subtle and sometimes obvious ways) reminds us of our desires for immediacy."[52] Hypermediacy predominates in *Killbox* as both perspectives call attention to their mediated quality, to the complex processes through which war is waged on bodies and bodies are datafied. While the networked mediations critiqued in *Killbox* bring the temporally concurrent battlefield live to distant locations, they also call attention to the centrality of mediation itself—and to the extent to which what has been remediated within that mediation is the visuality of video games: exerting remote control across a distributed network, reading and responding to real-time data flows, decoding movements and their meanings from an eye in the sky. Its aesthetics render the "lives" of the villagers solely within the ambit of drone warfare, reducing them to faceless data points that are, through the act of playing, given a kind of liveliness that grants an affective force to the destructive arrival of the missile. Despite the occlusion of bodies as flesh and blood—particularly the bodies of the villagers but also that of the faceless, unseen pilot—the missile strike shatters the lifeworld of the village, shuddering the ground and leaching all color from the scene. Once the game has been played once (and perhaps even before), the inevitable arrival of the missile shapes the affective experience: the certainty of violence haunts the gameplay, pulling attention toward the future. Playing as the villager, all action becomes geared toward a future that will only ever arrive with destruction in its wake. This pervasive atmosphere of *waiting for ruin* brings alive that distinctive trauma of life under drone warfare: ever present and yet indefinitely deferred.

Thus while *Killbox* reproduces the traumas of drone warfare in a representational sense, it does so even more potently as an affective force rendered intensive through the conjunction of gameplay and aesthetics. Trauma resides not only in the aftermath of the violence itself but also in the disjunction between the two experiences and in the absence of effective agency for both pilot and villager. *Killbox* thus works to decouple games and drones from within the confines of the video game genre itself without abandoning the need to better understand the divergences and convergences in the processes of mediation constitutive of both drones and games.

Unmanned by Drone Warfare

Created by Italian provocateurs Molleindustria in 2012, *Unmanned* is a browser-based game that allows players to experience a day in the life of an American drone sensor operator. Like other web games produced by the left-wing collective, *Unmanned* is designed to critique the relationships among alienation, state or corporate power, and cultural activities such as gaming. A more multilayered game than *Killbox*, *Unmanned* received positive critical attention, won Best Game at the 2012 IndieCade awards, and has been presented at a number of galleries and festivals.[53] Bookended by the protagonist's waking from dreaming and drifting off to sleep, the narrative moves through a series of scenes in the sensor operator's day: shaving, commuting to his station in the Nevada desert, monitoring a target, breaking for a cigarette, launching a lethal strike, playing video games at home with his son. Each scene bleeds everyday life into the actions and experiences of drone warfare, such that dialogue and gameplay move uneasily between talk of doctors' visits or an aging parent, the militarized language of tracking and acquiring targets, and the careful circling around potential traumas. In this volume, David Buchanan notes that "very few" of today's warriors "would fit what American culture and many corners of the military deem worthy of a warrior label." *Unmanned* contributes to a necessary redefinition of what it means to fight war—and what the costs of doing so might be.

Unmanned's graphic aesthetics are highly stylized, referencing the early history of platform and war games. This cartoonish imagery is usually presented in a split-screen format, with one panel for dialogue and the other containing interactive tasks, such as keeping the cursor on a potential enemy combatant or shooting Nazis in a game-within-the-game deliberately reminiscent of the popular *Call of Duty* series. Gameplay involves simple point-and-click actions with the mouse but often requires multitasking between dialogue choices and other actions. Working through each scene, players may acquire twelve different ironically named medals: Oneiric Achievement, Outstanding Introspection, Excellence in Shaving, Legion of Karaoke Commendation, Driving Operations Award, Gallantry in Action, Meritorious Surveillance, Husband Good Conduct, Valorous Flirting in Combat, Death from Above Merit, Distinguished Gaming Services, and Honorable Dad Unit. "Winning" these medals means performing the role of a good soldier in various contexts, which also means refusing, suppressing, or silencing trauma and dissent—not least the disjuncture of war fighting and domestic living operating in the same space and time. In a certain sense, then, "winning" the game actually means adopting the least critical stance toward drone warfare, as the mocking title for each of the medals suggests. But earning each of the medals is not actually tied to progress within the game, making it possible to play against the grain and reject the good-soldier identity while still completing the narrative.

Structuring the gameplay and imagery around the split-screen format embeds an unsettling quality in *Unmanned* (Figure 5.4). A face is almost always present on the screen—most often the player-protagonist, but also his copilot, Jane, or his son—but tends to remain impassive,

FIGURE 5.4. Internal monologue choices during shaving minigame. (Screenshot from *Unmanned,* by Molleindustria and No Media Kings, 2012)

its movements minimally expressive. This rendering of faces in stasis mutes their capacity for affective expression, at least in the terms outlined by Silvan Tomkins.[54] For Tomkins, the face is the primary site of affect—it is where his discrete affects of shame, disgust, fear, and others are most powerfully manifest. So too is the face that which signals the arrival of affect before it is cognitively processed; eyes, for instance, already widening in fear before the mind makes sense of sensation and decodes what the body is feeling.

Yet the blank expressions of *Unmanned* have an affective potency. Encountered within the intense context of drone warfare and in conjunction with dialogue and gameplay that tends toward silence and delimiting excesses of feeling, the minimal movement of these faces marks not an absence of affect but its congealing. Faces within the game are not simply stoic or affectless but rather caught within a set of traumatic relations that make the expression of feeling and worldly engagement difficult, if not impossible, as any kind of meaningful actuality. Instead, the eyes of the player shuttle back and forth, attention split between faces and action, action and dialogue, faces and words—caught between states, never quite cohesive, never quite settling. While the gameplay itself is hardly challenging, this continual partiality of attention generates an uneasy, discomforting atmosphere. It captures the disjunctive and dislocating experience of remote-control war, the blurring of spaces and bodies between the domestic and the military.

In this sense, *Unmanned* can be understood as an affect machine: what the game seeks to generate is a rupture or break in the experiential relationships among the daily activities of drone warfare, the expected performances of soldier/father/husband, and the larger networked architecture of the military itself. The game does more than narrate a story loaded with symbolism. It both generates *and* interrogates traumatic affect, encounters with trauma that are *traumatically affecting* yet not necessarily *traumatizing*. As Meera Atkinson and I have argued, traumatic affect describes "the mode, substance and dynamics of relation through which trauma is experienced, transmitted, conveyed, and represented."[55] As such, it offers a way of understanding the traumatic that is not reducible to the strictures of psychological discourse but instead accounts for the fluid, mutable, and varied forms in which trauma is so encountered, particularly as a cultural phenomenon produced in and through mediation. Conceiving of trauma in affective terms means placing emphasis on the forms and intensities of relation that it engenders and constrains, whether encountering death and disappearance on social media or in video games such as *Unmanned*.[56] Rather than focusing on specific symptoms as such, reading for traumatic affect places the emphasis on the force of disruptive effects of trauma on the interplay of bodies, contexts, and objects across time—and, crucially, through processes of mediation. This is of particular significance in thinking about trauma in remote warfare because it allows for conceiving of how trauma might be produced and even shared across geographical distances and through networked technologies and media. Understood in this way, *Unmanned* brings the gaming body into an affective relation with the traumatic through the interactive work of gameplay with its physical and perceptual engagement of the body in media.

Unlike typical video games, which emphasize the rapid movements and sudden violence of war, *Unmanned* attends to the body in the minor moments of living. In one early scene, the player slowly shaves—move too swiftly and the protagonist's face is cut and no medal earned. Later, the player must control the speed at which a cigarette is smoked, lifting it to the lips and sucking in—yet the speed does not matter and the sequence simply entails the forced passage of time, such that the player must attend to time's passing through the minor action of smoking. These and other small gestures are what compose the everyday;

their emphasis in the game sits uncomfortably with the context of net-worked war fighting. After smoking the cigarette outside the trailer that houses the ground control station, the protagonist is asked to launch a missile at an identified target. This order can be ignored, yet doing so does nothing to the narrative; it is simply one less medal earned. Rather than focusing on violence, *Unmanned* is attuned to the long hours of drone warfare: the boredom, the precise ways in which it is not at all like a game.

This is particularly evident in the series of games-within-the-game through which the player progresses. Each of these subverts tropes of various video game genres. In the opening dream sequence, for exam-ple, you must avoid angry villagers until the player avatar transforms into a drone, moving through an open, two-dimensional space remi-niscent of *The Legend of Zelda* and other top-down console games. Later, you are given the dull task of keeping the protagonist's car driv-ing down a long, straight road. Surveilling and killing an enemy tar-get while operating the drone sensors lacks intensity in the gameplay: the task itself involves slow mouse movements and a single click. None of these tasks can be "won" in any traditional sense—achievements are earned or not, but progress itself is not at stake. There are no "lives" to be lost.

For much of the game, there are no moments of speed or muscle re-action in these sequences, nothing familiar to players of the first-person shooter or real-time strategy games associated with the Play-Station mentality. The exception to this is the final pair of games, which you play on a console with your son in the penultimate scene. These are the only moments that involve tricky gameplay as you shoot first terrorists and then Nazis while engaging in dialogue with your son. While somewhat didactic in its attention to the potentially negative ef-fects of violent video games, this sequence also makes for a stark con-trast. These games are nothing like those that otherwise compose the protagonist's day, including the "game" in which a target is acquired and killed. Instead, each of the other minigames emphasizes the muted quality of the drone warfare experience, its grinding tedium. In doing so, they take aim at those popular mythologies of the video game war, but they also emphasize the traumatic atmosphere in which drone crews operate. Each game offers the potential for doing the "wrong" thing—launching the missile early, driving the car off the road, and so on—in a way that might be construed as psychological breakdown, or the failure to be the good soldier. Set against the protagonist's experience of the war, these games work to highlight the tensions, contradictions, and anxieties of moving between war and family life on a daily basis.

Bringing this tension into the minutiae of daily life gives the large arc of the game—progress through the day, structured by dialogue choices—a contrasting weight. Much of the gameplay involves choosing what to say in response to the protagonist's own thoughts or to the words of others. Within each scene, these choices produce different responses and conversation branches that can in turn lead to more medals. However, breaking with the "correct" response has no real consequence—there is no way to fail the game, nor is there anything that might definitively count as success as such. Thus, dialogue choices are primarily about shaping the experience of the narrative rather than its outcomes. Doing the "right" thing demonstrates the difficult line that drone crews need to walk, accepting the necessity of suppressing emotion and engaging in deliberate performance of certain roles—the good husband, the stoic soldier, the gently flirtatious comrade. Responding in an overtly sexual manner to the pilot Jane or belligerently on the phone call with the protagonist's wife shifts the affective engagement with the game into uncomfortable territory, yet it makes manifest the circulation of traumatic affect. Such choices show the protagonist out of kilter and on the brink of traumatic rupture. As a player, pursuing these other options—lashing out, resisting, critiquing—provides a mechanism of pushing back against the discursive-affective formation of the military. Yet doing so has no substantive narrative consequences: neither conformity nor resistance affects the protagonist's agency or changes the militarized environment through which he moves.

Where *Killbox* primarily intervenes in the cultural imagining of video game war at the level of shared visuality and networked experience across the larger drone assemblage, *Unmanned* radically subverts the dynamics of the supposed PlayStation mentality of killing. Yet it does so without rendering the relation between games and drones irrelevant or meaningless. Rather, it positions that very relation as a site of traumatic affectivity: just as drone warfare cannot be reduced to mere video game war, so too games cannot be elided from the culture and operation of drone warfare itself. *Unmanned* suggests that the very

notion of the PlayStation mentality is part of the problem for participants *in* drone warfare: even they can find it difficult to unknot the
discursive knotting of drones and games. The forceful presence of the
language, motifs, and tropes of gaming does damage because it elides
or makes difficult to describe the all too traumatic affectivity of drone
warfare. The protagonist of *Unmanned* cannot begin to make sense of
his own trauma in part because he cannot grasp it without becoming
caught in the discursive logic of gaming. *Unmanned,* in short, makes
visible the cost of the video game mythology and in doing so makes
clear what is at stake in its perpetuation for those most intimately engaged in waging drone warfare.

This mythology of the video game war is powerful precisely because
of its grounding in the modes, forms, and aesthetics of mediation on
which drone warfare depends. It draws on a long history of moral panic
about new forms of media and the blame they receive for all manner
of social, cultural, and political ills. Widespread suspicion of new media
technologies—witness the current anxieties about young people and
social media—makes for fertile rhetorical ground for activists rightly
eager to critique drone warfare, and the similarities in aesthetic and
interface between video games and the flying of militarized drones
produces a kind of discursive greenhouse effect. Drone operators have
done themselves few favors in this regard. Chamayou, for example, re-
provingly quotes these three comments about the experience of killing via remote control:

> Oh, it's a gamer's delight.

> Almost like playing the computer game Civilization, in which you di-
> rect units and armies in battle.

> It's like a video game. It can get a little bloodthirsty. But it's fucking
> cool.[57]

On the one hand, there is an obligation to take such comments at face
value. On the other, these and other such remarks might well signal
the difficulty of accounting for the experiences of drone warfare in an
environment that lacks the cultural language to do so. Yet the easy

conflation of games and drones in the execution of state violence does much to obscure the more complex dynamics at play in drone warfare and in the networked processes of mediation that underpin its operations. This is what makes both *Killbox* and *Unmanned* fascinating interventions into the emergent culture around drone warfare. Each in different ways attends to the tensions and paradoxes in the affective and discursive formations by which this new mode of war is made known to wider publics—and through which it is experienced by the participants themselves. Just as drones can be deployed for much more than war and games for much more than pleasurable violence, so too are the relations between them far more complex than popular imagining suggests. Technologically mediated yet frequently immersed in traumatic affect, the relations that compose this assemblage of games and drones make clear the necessity of dismantling the trope of the PlayStation war without somehow transforming drone crews into victims or eliding the significant relations and resonances between games and drones. There are, after all, uncounted thousands across the world for whom drone warfare is anything but a game, and so disentangling the mythology while continuing to interrogate their aesthetic, affective, and mediated relations is a crucial task.

Notes

1. Chris Cole, Mary Dobbing, and Amy Hailwood, *Convenient Killing: Armed Drones and the "Playstation" Mentality* (Oxford: Fellowship of Reconciliation, 2010), https://dronewarsuk.files.wordpress.com/2010/10/conv-killing -final.pdf.

2. Hugh Gusterson, *Drone: Remote Control Warfare* (Cambridge, Mass.: MIT Press, 2016).

3. Pratap Chatterjee, "Are Pilots Deserting Washington's Remote-Control War?," Huffington Post, March 5, 2015, https://www.huffingtonpost.com/pratap -chatterjee/are-pilots-deserting-washingtons-remote-war_b_6808634.html; Dave Grossman, *On Killing: The Psychological Cost of Learning to Kill in War and Society,* rev. ed. (New York: Back Bay Books, 2009).

4. Gusterson, *Drone,* 29–58.

5. Wayne Chappelle et al., "An Analysis of Post-traumatic Stress Symptoms in United States Air Force Drone Operators," *Journal of Anxiety Disorders* 28, no. 5 (June 2014): 480–87.

6. Brandon Bryant, "Letter from a Sensor Operator," in *Life in the Age of Drone Warfare,* ed. Lisa Parks and Caren Kaplan (Durham, N.C.: Duke University Press, 2017), 315–23; Caren Kaplan, "Drone-o-Rama: Troubling the

Temporal and Spatial Logics of Distance Warfare," in Parks and Kaplan, *Life in the Age,* 161–94.

7. John P. Abizaid and Rosa Brooks, *Recommendations and Report of the Task Force on US Drone Policy,* 2nd ed. (Washington, D.C.: Stimson Center, April 2015).

8. Grossman, *On Killing.*

9. Gusterson, *Drone,* 72.

10. Grégoire Chamayou, *Drone Theory,* trans. Janet Lloyd (London: Penguin, 2015), 116.

11. *Killbox* (Joseph DeLappe and Biome Collective, 2015); *Unmanned* (Molleindustria and Jim Munroe, 2012).

12. Sebastian Deterding, "Living Room Wars: Remediation, Boardgames, and the Early History of Video Wargaming," in *Joystick Soldiers: The Politics of Play in Military Video Games,* ed. Nina B. Huntemann and Matthew Thomas Payne (New York: Routledge, 2010), 21.

13. Nina B. Huntemann and Matthew Thomas Payne, introduction to Huntemann and Payne, *Joystick Soldiers,* 5.

14. Huntemann and Payne, introduction, 10.

15. Matthew Thomas Payne, *Playing War: Military Video Games after 9/11* (New York: New York University Press, 2016).

16. Frédérick Gagnon, "'Invading Your Hearts and Minds': *Call of Duty®* and the (Re)writing of Militarism in U.S. Digital Games and Popular Culture," *European Journal of American Studies* 5, no. 3 (June 27, 2010): 28.

17. Carrie Andersen, "Games of Drones: The Uneasy Future of the Soldier-Hero in *Call of Duty: Black Ops II," Surveillance and Society* 12, no. 3 (2014): 360–76.

18. James Der Derian, *Virtuous War: Mapping the Military-Industrial-Media-Entertainment Network* (New York: Routledge, 2009).

19. "AA Proving Grounds," U.S. Army, 2016, https://www.americasarmy.com /aapg.

20. Robertson Allen, "Software and Soldier Life Cycles of Recruitment, Training, and Rehabilitation in the Post-9/11 Era," in *The War of My Generation: Youth Culture and the War on Terror,* ed. David Kieran (New Brunswick, N.J.: Rutgers University Press, 2015), 163.

21. Robertson Allen, *America's Digital Army: Games at Work and War* (Lincoln: University of Nebraska Press, 2017), 6.

22. David Nieborg, "Empower Yourself, Defend Freedom! Playing Games during Times of War," in *Digital Material: Tracing New Media in Everyday Life and Technology,* ed. Marianne van den Boomen (Amsterdam: Amsterdam University Press, 2009), 58.

23. Marcus Schulzke, "Rethinking Military Gaming: America's Army and Its Critics," *Games and Culture* 8, no. 2 (March 1, 2013): 59–76.

24. David Neiborg, "Training Recruits and Conditioning Youth: The Soft Power of Military Games," in Huntemann and Payne, *Joystick Soldiers,* 53–66.

25. Payne, *Playing War,* 11.

26. Ben Anderson, "Affective Atmospheres," *Emotion, Space and Society* 2, no. 2 (2009): 77–81.

27. Bryant, "Letter from a Sensor Operator," 315.

28. P. W. Singer, *Wired for War: The Robotics Revolution and Conflict in the 21st Century* (New York: Penguin Books, 2009), 366.

29. Matthew Power quoted in Gusterson, *Drone,* 34.

30. James Ash, "Attention, Videogames and the Retentional Economies of Affective Amplification," *Theory, Culture and Society* 29, no. 6 (November 1, 2012): 4.

31. Derek Gregory, "From a View to a Kill: Drones and Late Modern War," *Theory, Culture and Society* 28, nos. 7–8 (December 1, 2011): 198.

32. Gusterson, *Drone,* 36.

33. Bryant, "Letter from a Sensor Operator," 317.

34. Matt J. Martin, *Predator: The Remote-Control Air War over Iraq and Afghanistan: A Pilot's Story* (Minneapolis: Zenith, 2010); Chamayou, *Drone Theory*; Andrew Cockburn, *Kill Chain: Drones and the Rise of High-Tech Assassins* (New York: Verso, 2015).

35. Gusterson, *Drone,* 39.

36. Jan Slaby, Rainer Mühlhoff, and Philipp Wüschner, "Affective Arrangements," *Emotion Review,* published ahead of print, 2017, 1–10, https://doi.org /10.1177/1754073917722214.

37. Michael Richardson, "Drone's-Eye View: Affect Witnessing and Technicities of Perception," in *Image Testimonies: Witnessing in Times of Social Media,* ed. Kerstin Schankweiler and Verena Straub (New York: Routledge, 2018).

38. Ian G. R. Shaw, *Predator Empire: Drone Warfare and Full Spectrum Dominance* (Minneapolis: University of Minnesota Press, 2016), 71.

39. Shaw, 79.

40. Shaw, 105.

41. John Kaag and Sarah Kreps, *Drone Warfare: War and Conflict in the Modern World* (Cambridge: Polity, 2014), 5.

42. Sarah Kember and Joanna Zylinska, *Life after New Media: Mediation as a Vital Process* (Cambridge, Mass.: MIT Press, 2012), xv.

43. Shaw, *Predator Empire,* 111.

44. Payne, *Playing War.*

45. Chamayou, *Drone Theory,* 55.

46. Malath Abbas et al., "Killbox," in *Proceedings of the 2016 CHI Conference Extended Abstracts on Human Factors in Computing Systems,* CHI EA '16 (New York: ACM, 2016), 3812.

47. Chamayou, *Drone Theory,* 55.

48. Abbas et al., "Killbox," 3813.

49. Abbas et al., 3814.

50. Paul Virilio, *War and Cinema: The Logistics of Perception* (New York: Verso, 1989).

51. Gregory, "From a View to a Kill," 195.

52. J. David Bolter and Richard Grusin, *Remediation: Understanding New Media* (Cambridge, Mass.: MIT Press, 1999), 34.

53. Jeffrey Matulef, "IndieCade 2012 Winners Announced, Unmanned Takes the Top Prize," Eurogamer, October 12, 2012, http://www.eurogamer.net /articles/2012-10-12-indiecade-2012-winners-announced-unmanned-takes-the -top-prize.

54. Eve Kosofsky Sedgwick and Adam Frank, "Shame in the Cybernetic Fold: Reading Silvan Tomkins," in *Shame and Its Sisters: A Silvan Tomkins Reader,* ed. Eve Kosofsky Sedgwick and Adam Frank (Durham, N.C.: Duke University Press, 1995), 1–28.

55. Meera Atkinson and Michael Richardson, "At the Nexus: An Introduction," in *Traumatic Affect,* ed. Meera Atkinson and Michael Richardson (Cambridge: Cambridge Scholars, 2013), 12.

56. Michael Richardson, "Radical Absence: Encountering Traumatic Affect in Digitally Mediated Disappearance," *Cultural Studies* 32, no. 1 (January 2, 2018): 63–80.

57. Chamayou, *Drone Theory,* 107.

CHAPTER 6

Over There?

War Writing, Lethal Technology, and Democracy in America

TIM JELFS

What does literature—or literary criticism, for that matter—have to offer a volume on remote warfare? The answer may depend on what counts as a literary text and on what counts as war writing. Consider the narrative in which Officer Darren Wilson of the Ferguson Police Department related how, on the morning of August 9, 2014, he had been called to attend to a "sick infant" in the Northwinds apartment complex. It was a "pretty laid-back call," handled without assistance from other officers.[1] During the call (an ambulance arrived, the infant and her mother were transported to hospital), Wilson heard over his portable radio, or "walky," that a "stealing [was] in progress from the local market on West Florissant," that "a suspect was wearing a black shirt and that a box of Cigarillos was stolen."[2] Two other officers were dispatched to deal with that call, but it was Wilson himself, some minutes after leaving the Northwinds complex, who would come across "two men walking down the middle of the street."[3] Their names were Michael Brown and Dorian Johnson. After their encounter with Wilson and all that Wilson brought with him—not least his car, a "Chevy Tahoe police vehicle fully marked with a light bar," and his gun, "Sig Sauer a P229 .40 caliber"—Brown lay dead.[4]

The text quoted is from the transcript of Wilson's ultimately exculpatory grand jury testimony. Given the impact of Brown's death in igniting the Black Lives Matter movement, it is a document of interest as far as the recent history of race relations in the United States goes. But it is striking how this transcript also pulls into focus two other topics relevant to this collection: the agency of objects (like the gun that killed Brown) and the militarization of U.S. policing.[5] Using Wilson's testimony as its starting and ending point, this chapter both reflects on the relationship between those two topics and shows that what contemporary literary criticism has to offer this volume is its attentiveness to the interplay between humans and lethal technologies like the Sig Sauer Wilson describes himself carrying. For, given the influence of a field of study known as actor-network theory (ANT) on the "material turn" in literary studies, literary scholars are now well equipped to analyze representations of interactions between humans and the technologies we have devised for killing one another. And a focus on those interactions, as we will see, is characteristic not only of Wilson's testimony but also of numerous passages in modern American war writing.

In what follows, then, I incorporate an ANT-influenced analysis of passages from American war writers including Mark Twain, George Oppen, James Salter, and Tim O'Brien, and I propose that such an analysis yields two important insights on the concept of remote war. The first is that the relationship between humans and the lethal technologies with which they have waged war may not, in fact, be characterized merely by an ever-increasing sense of remoteness, but by a dialectic of the remote and the intimate in which unexpected intimacies repeatedly assert themselves even as technology enables us to deliver violence on one another from ever-greater distances. The second is that such war writing problematizes how we think about both remote warfare and citizen-to-citizen and citizen-to-state interactions within the United States itself, especially in relation to approaches to policing in the twenty-first century. In this context, the war writing this chapter examines takes on enhanced significance because it does not speak of anything so remote-seeming as war alone, instead raising the possibility that a dialectic of the remote and the intimate mediated by lethal technology has been typical of democratic life in the United States for some time. In this way, war writing reminds us that it is not just humans who act in the networks and associations that war calls into being, and, paradoxically, that those networks do not always render us as remote from one another as we might assume. Once we are able to see *that*, it should become clearer that Wilson's testimony itself constitutes a form of war writing that is telling a tale far older than the most recent developments in the history of policing in the United States.

Wilson's Testimony and Actor-Network Theory

The tale Wilson told in his grand jury testimony is certainly one of things, not just people. There are the cigarillos Brown stole, but also Wilson's car, gun, and other accoutrements, which Wilson inventoried in detail under questioning from Assistant Prosecutor Kathi Alizadeh: "Full department uniform, light duty boots, dark navy blue pants, my issue duty belt," on the last of which, Wilson explained, "magazine pouches sit right here, my weapon is on my right hip . . . an asp that sits kind of behind me and kind of to the right and then a set of handcuffs, another set of handcuffs, my OC spray or mace is on this side and then my radio and that's it."[6] Such objects play a role in the drama that the text goes on to narrate. Here is Wilson's description of how he used his patrol car in the encounter with Brown and Johnson: "I then placed my car in reverse and backed up and I backed up just past them and then angled my vehicle, the back of my vehicle to kind of cut them off kind to keep them somewhat contained [*sic*]."[7] Wilson then relates how he and his things grew entangled with Brown and the cigarillos: "I then opened my door again and used my door to push him backwards." He explains how the things on his belt became the objects of a frantic carousel of thoughts, in which he "considered" using first his mace, then his asp, then a flashlight, and finally a gun in order to extricate himself from the tangle of things and bodies: "So the only other option I thought I had was my gun. I drew my gun, I turned."[8]

We know the sequel, but may wonder whether it was Wilson alone doing the considering and acting here. After all, the emergence of ANT has placed considerable pressure on long-held assumptions about human agency. The "I" of Wilson's testimony sounds authoritative enough, the linguistic and ontological agent that backs up cars and opens doors, an "I" that thinks and draws and turns. But since the 1990s, actor-network theorists have recast "agency" as distributed across networks of the human and nonhuman. The distinction between subject and object, between the agentic "I" and the objects that such subjects act upon and work with, fails to grasp the full truth of any state of affairs, social relation, or ontological or scientific fact, according to ANT. In the words of Bruno Latour, whose work has been central to the development of ANT, "An 'actor' in ANT is a semiotic definition—an actant—, that is something that acts or to which activity is granted by others. It implies *no* special motivation of *human individual* actors, nor of humans in general. An actant can literally be anything provided it is granted to be the source of action."[9]

Who or what, then, is *not* a source of action here? Wilson and the men he confronted were surrounded by objects, including the mace, asp, flashlight, gun, and car that he describes with such care. Do those things have no agency? Should we "grant" them no "activity"? At the very least, they are part of a network of the human and nonhuman important enough to have been worth tracing in front of a grand jury with some degree of care. This is what Wilson, under questioning from Alizadeh, did. "Let us suppose now that someone comes to find you with an association of humans and nonhumans, an association whose exact composition is not yet known to anyone, but about which a series of trials makes it possible to say that its members act," Latour has proposed.[10] Wilson and Alizadeh themselves were putting an association of the human and nonhuman on trial (that tangle of body and objects Wilson describes) in an effort to absolve Wilson of a crime by showing just how central to the death of Brown the particular interplay of things about Wilson's person was. As her critics have pointed out, Alizadeh's interest certainly appears less than prosecutorial as far as Wilson was concerned; the tale she and Wilson tell is one of tragic inevitability, in which everything might have been different if only every *thing* had not been disposed and functioned just the way it did. In this case, it may not be "agency" that the coauthors of this text are attempting to distribute across the network of people and things that they describe so much as moral and legal responsibility. But the impression they sought to convey was, in essence, that it was neither Wilson alone nor his gun alone that killed Brown, but the interaction of all the different "actants" in the association that they so carefully describe.[11]

To this some might object that "actor-network theory" sounds like little more than a new name for old thoughts. Think of Chekhov's gun: hung on the wall in the first act, doomed to go off in the last, it hardly has "agency" of its own, to the extent that it was placed there by its author, the granter of its activity.[12] On this view, Alizadeh's interest in what hung on Wilson's belt was just a case of so much mise-en-scène, a necessary precursor to a narrative effect. But narrative texts and their relations to the realities they purport to depict are, according to actor-network theorists, rather less problematic than they may appear. In Latour's telling, ANT was originally an attempt to turn semiotic insights developed in the 1960s and 1970s not merely to literary texts but to social and scientific facts, thus enabling what he calls a "semiotics of things."[13] This semiotics, which renders the social interplay of the human and nonhuman as interpretable as literary texts, hardly excludes literary or textual representations. As Latour puts it, "This move [toward a semiotics of things] can be said either to elevate things to the dignity of texts or to elevate texts to the ontological status of things. . . . The new hybrid status gives *to all entities* both the action, variety and circulating existence recognized in the study of textual characters *and* the reality, solidity, externality that was recognized in things."[14]

By this logic, Wilson's text is itself also a thing, an actant in a larger network, and its author and coauthor are themselves actants in wider social contexts. ANT simply invites us to use what Latour calls its "empty methodological frame" to trace such networks wherever they may lead. That, in short, is what I do in the remainder of this chapter, not in an effort to establish the veracity or otherwise of Wilson's testimony but to embed that testimony and its depiction of a violent association of the human and nonhuman in a series of broader literary, historical, and social contexts that will hopefully shed light on the questions of whether technology really renders war more "remote," and whether war itself may be less remote to the everyday life of the United States than is sometimes assumed. "No net exists independently of the very act of tracing it, and no tracing is done by an actor exterior to the net," writes Latour.[15] This chapter itself is in one sense no more than a tracing of "a net," in which some of the semiotic filaments found in Wilson's testimony lead to other, more obviously fictional texts, which in turn lead to a consideration of larger social and historical facts. To illustrate the point: the objects Wilson describes surrounding him before his encounter with Brown and Johnson might for some recall the attention the opening title sequence of James William Guercio's *Electra Glide in Blue* (1973) lavishes on the gear of the motorcycle cop John Wintergreen (Robert Blake) as he readies himself to go on shift. Suited, booted, and tooled up, Wintergreen is made what he is, an agent of the state, by the tools of his trade.[16] But Wilson's description of himself and his gear might also lead us to a more recent literary iteration of the image of the armored police officer, such as that in *American Rust* (2009), Philipp Meyer's novel about a Pennsylvania steel town in postindustrial decline: "In addition to his assault rifle, which had such a short barrel it might have been a submachine gun, he had a load-bearing vest with several extra magazines for the rifle, a baton, some other equipment Isaac didn't recognize. He could have been a military contractor just out of Iraq."[17]

Alongside these fictional texts, Wilson and his things already begin to look as if they might be part of a much larger network of humans, things, and representations of their associations closely related to the militarization of policing that has taken place in the United States since the 1960s. While this shows how ANT-influenced analyses can trace paths across different kinds of texts and different sets of social facts, it is also important to bear in mind that they can lead in and out of different historical moments. Indeed, this is inherent to the methodology. As Latour writes, "The first advantage of thinking in terms of networks is that we get rid of 'the tyranny of distance' or proximity. Elements which are close when disconnected may be infinitely remote when their connections are analyzed; conversely, elements which would appear as infinitely distant may be close when their connections are brought back into the picture."[18] This paradox of remoteness and proximity informs both the methodology of what follows and its argument, as the remainder of this chapter examines texts remote from one another historically but whose content is connected by the representation of networks or associations of the human and nonhuman that are similar to those seen in Wilson's testimony. Examining literary representations of such networks, we will see how American war writers have grappled with combat's progression beyond mano-a-mano fighting to meditate on the role that technologically advanced weaponry plays in modern conflict, structuring as it does one's relation to the enemy. What becomes clear is that this way of looking at such interactions often appears to transform some writers of war into what we might think of as actor-network theorists *avant la lettre,* as their texts limn some of the complexities of what it means for war to be waged not just by and between humans but by, between, and among things too.

Remote War in Literature: From Mark Twain to the Age of the Drone

The thought that warfare has been rendered remoter by virtue of its reliance on technology has found repeated expression in modern literary culture, and war writers have often articulated that thought by depicting associations of the human and the lethal technologies with which war is fought. At the end of Mark Twain's *A Connecticut Yankee in King Arthur's Court* (1899), the eponymous Hank acts in concert with the modern technology he has brought back to medieval England to lay waste to thirty thousand knights. Having just proclaimed a republic, Hank ends up ensconced in Merlin's Cave with his helpmate Clarence and "fifty-two fresh, bright, well-educated, clean-minded British boys."[19] Besieged by counterrevolutionary forces, he dynamites the front ranks of the enemy forces, turning them into "a whirling tempest of rags and fragments," before his network of anachronistic and asymmetric technologies assists in electrocuting, Gatling gunning, and drowning the remnants: "Within ten short minutes after we had opened fire, armed resistance was totally annihilated, the campaign was ended, we fifty-four were masters of England! Twenty-five thousand men lay dead around us."[20] Hand-to-hand combat proves unnecessary in this scenario, with Hank's technology rendering the death count difficult to confirm: "We could not *count* the dead, because they did not exist as individuals, but merely as homogenous protoplasm, with alloys of irons and buttons."[21] As early as the turn of the nineteenth century, Twain appears to suggest, "technowar" had already arrived at a grotesque reductio ad absurdum, in which the Walter Scott–inspired legacies of chivalry he recalled from his southern adolescence ran up hard against the realities of technologically advanced weaponry; the end result was the literal fusion of human and nonhuman, protoplasm mixed with pieces of metal.[22]

Following two world wars and the advent of the atom bomb, the Irish playwright George Bernard Shaw meditated on the relationship between technological change in the waging of war and the counterintuitive persistence of war in ways similar to Twain. Shaw noted, for example, the

list of previous discoveries, dating back to B.C., which have developed the technique of killing from the single combats of the Trojan war, fought man to man, to artillery operations and air raids in which the combatants are hundreds of miles apart on the ground or thousands of feet up in the air dropping bombs and flying away at a speed of ten miles per second, never seeing one another nor the mischief they do. At every development it is complained that war is no longer justifiable as a test of heroic personal qualities, and demonstrated that it has become too ruinous to be tolerated as an institution.[23]

Shaw appears to be writing in the same vein as Twain here, fleshing out the thought that a chivalric ethos has been lost to the degree that technology has enhanced man's destructive capabilities, while those same technologies render war as such less and less conscionable. And yet, as Shaw observed, war "persist[s] none the less."[24] The poet George Oppen, who fought with the 103rd Infantry Division at the Battle of the Bulge, relayed how he had experienced this modern reliance on technology as a distancing from the human: "Fought / No man / But the fragments of metal," read some particularly dazed and staggered-seeming lines of Oppen's.[25]

Yet post–Second World War war writing hardly confines itself to meditations on a technologically determined remoteness alone. There was a certain Cold War discourse that saw the species-threatening potential of atomic weaponry as calling forth new and perhaps counterintuitive intimacies in ways that bring to mind Latour's paradox of remoteness and proximity. Hence Oppen's poetic insistence in "Time of the Missile" that "we are endangered / Totally at last." Being endangered "totally" suggested its own intimacies, even as the whole world found itself networked for destruction by a new actant in human history. One of the best-known literary illustrations of the point is John Hersey's *Hiroshima* (1946). Indeed, it is remarkable to consider just how soon after the bombings of Hiroshima and Nagasaki Hersey was able to challenge the racialized tropes of the Japanese that had circulated during the war. Taking as his model Thornton Wilder's novel *The Bridge of San Luis Rey* (1927), Hersey sought to show not just the interconnectedness of six survivors of the bombing but also the common humanity of the Japanese victims and his American readership. The remote Other, it transpired, was not so different from us after all. They were doctors, a factory clerk, a tailor's widow, a Methodist pastor, a (German) Jesuit priest.[26]

Just how uncomfortably close the bomb could bring people was illustrated in the 1955 *This Is Your Life* episode that reunited one of the survivors Hersey wrote about, the Reverend Kiyoshi Tanimoto, with Air Force Lieutenant Robert Lewis, copilot of the *Enola Gay*.[27] A visibly nervous Lewis explained that the pilots of the *Enola Gay* had witnessed what they had done, because curiosity had led them to turn back to find out. Contrary to George Bernard Shaw's expectations, then, Lewis had seen the "mischief" he had done and lived not only to see but to clasp hands with a survivor of it. Such cultural responses to atomic weaponry usefully complicate one-dimensional understandings of remote war. Modern lethal technology does not just render humans remote from one another, they suggest. Rather, it mediates more complex networks of relations in which unexpected intimacies repeatedly (re)assert themselves. These networks themselves illustrate Latour's observations about the relation between remoteness and proximity, even as they emphasize just how influential in those networks nonhuman actants like the bomb are.

The sheer power of the bomb makes it sui generis as far as lethal technologies go. But smaller-scale iterations of the complex relations of the human and the nonhuman, and the remote and the intimate, can be found elsewhere in the archives of modern American war writing. They feature, for example, in James Salter's *The Hunters* (1956) and Tim O'Brien's *The Things They Carried* (1990). Salter's novel is a lyrical depiction of fighter-pilot combat during the Korean War, in which Salter flew F-86s. It was a form of warfare in which certain chivalric vestiges clung on, it appears: "We're in a child's dream and a man's heaven, living a medieval life under sanitary conditions, flying the last shreds of something irreplaceable, I don't know what, in a sport too kingly even for kings," remarks one of the fighter pilots.[28] And yet modern machinery makes a series of technologically enhanced metamorphoses possible: "When the sleekness of his ship and the completeness of his equipment so enveloped him . . . to a person as near as a wingman or far as a mechanic watching him climb out of sight, he inherited the beauty of his machine."[29] Again, not just the medieval and the modern, but the human and nonhuman become one in the miracle of the manned fighter jet, until the human is obscured altogether: "Toward the final test and winnowing they flew together, and though a man on the ground could neither see nor hear them, they were up, specks of metal moving through a prehistoric sky."[30] Salter's "specks of metal" echo Oppen's invocation of the "fragments of metal" that he fought in the Second World War. To all intents and purposes, that is what Salter's language makes of the fighter pilot; at most, perhaps, he is there to help deliver the fragments of metal that were waging this pre–drone age war.

The sense of remoteness and solitude that obtains as just one actant in the lethal network that Salter describes is striking:

> You lived and died alone, especially in fighters. . . . You slipped into the hollow cockpit and strapped and plugged yourself into the machine. The canopy ground shut and sealed you off. Your oxygen, your very breath, you carried with you into the chilled vacuum, in a steel bottle. If you wanted to speak, you used the radio. You were as isolated as a deep-sea diver, only you went up, into nothing, instead of down. You were accompanied. They flew with you in heraldic patterns and fought alongside you, sometimes skillfully, always at least two ships together, but they were really of no help. You were alone. At the end, there was no one you could touch.[31]

And yet, for all this human loneliness, there are also peculiar intimacies in the metal-flecked skies that Salter describes. The main action of *The Hunters* advances toward a decisive battle between Captain Cleve Connell and the enemy MiG pilot who commands the most respect from the U.S. airmen. Identifiable only by the black stripes on his aircraft, that pilot is given an all-American nickname—Casey Jones, after the legendary railroad engineer. Suitably ambivalent terms frame the psychological complexities that render the enemy Other anything but other for Cleve: "For the first time [he] felt the possession of hard knowledge, the thrill and disappointment of finding an enemy to be human. Alone now, retreating . . . he could almost feel the presence, dark and strong, of his chosen enemy, more than that, his friend. He had never seen him."[32] Salter's prose is riven with contradictions that both delimit the extent of the fighter pilot's solitude and make a friend of the unseen enemy (a human, not just a thing, here). In the novel's closing sentences, the reader learns that Cleve's own death is remote, yet intimate, that he dies alone and yet not alone, even while the language Salter uses to describe his end simultaneously insists on the enduring merger of man and machine: "For Cleve, the war had ended in those final minutes of solitude he had always dreaded. . . . They had overcome him in the end, tenaciously, scissoring past him, taking him down. Their heavy shots had splashed into him, and they had followed all the way, firing as they did, with that contagious passion peculiar to hunters."[33] The intimacy of hunter and prey is a peculiar and atavistic one, even amid the technologically advanced war machines of Salter's novel, but it remains unclear what the object pronoun "him" refers to here. Is it Cleve or his plane? Where does the human actant end and the nonhuman one begin?

Compare those chapters of Tim O'Brien's *The Things They Carried* in which the narrator recalls how he killed and responded to having killed a Vietnamese adversary. This is war fought, and wrought, not in the air but at ground level, in which face-to-face intimacy with a de-humanized enemy is still perfectly possible. Technology mediates engagements and encounters just as surely as in Salter's skies above the Yalu River. The human and the nonhuman form networks of agency qualitatively distinct from those in Salter's novel, however, in which one feels that it is still at some level the pilot doing whatever piloting of metal needs to be done. Can the same be said of O'Brien's narrative? "I had already pulled the pin on the grenade. . . . It was entirely automatic," O'Brien's narrator recalls of how he responded to coming face-to-face with the enemy.[34] O'Brien's description suggests that it may not even have been him, O'Brien, acting in this instance, or if he was acting, he was not acting alone: "The grenade was to make him go away—just evaporate—and I leaned back and felt my mind go empty and then felt it fill up again. I had already thrown the grenade before telling myself to throw it."[35] No calculation is necessary; the grenade does what it was there for, framed by its narrator as part of a network of barely conscious agency. In intimate close-quarter combat, conflict is not entirely mano a mano; lethal objects inevitably intervene in the process, even down at ground level, and in a passage like this, it is hard to argue that they do not evince something like agency.

Such examples suggest that one of the uses of such literary accounts, many of them written by veterans, might be to exert pressure on the idea that technology only makes war more remote. For in such war writing, associations of the human and nonhuman repeatedly provide the mediating grounds not for mere reflections on war's remoteness but for a negotiation between the remote and the intimate. The writing of Hersey, Salter, and O'Brien, after all, shows how intimate even supposedly remote *enemies* remain in a technologically advanced stage of history, offering statements of their essential semblance. The chapter immediately preceding the one in *The Things They Carried* in which O'Brien's narrator relates the killing just described is called "The Man I Killed." In it, O'Brien's narrator states, "Now and then, when I'm reading a newspaper or just sitting alone in a room, I'll look up and see the young man coming out of the morning fog. . . . He'll pass within a few yards of me and suddenly smile."[36] The reason the young man had to be killed has been stated plainly enough by Kiowa, the narrator's comrade-in-arms: "Tim, it's a *war*. The guy wasn't Heidi—he had a weapon, right?"[37] His "having" a weapon, and the narrator having his grenades, was not just what separated them from one another but what brought them together and holds them together, long after the war has ended, actants in the same enduring network. "*Mon frère, mon semblable,*" these texts seem unexpectedly to say to and of the enemy Other, who is just another node in the intricate network of modern war.

Even today, in the age of the drone, enemies achieve similar intimacies, the discourse on remoteness surrounding drone warfare notwithstanding. "The pilots sit in dimly lit, air-conditioned trailers, each staring at glowing video and data screens and toggling a joystick that controls an armed drone flying somewhere in the world," reads one typical lede from a 2015 *Los Angeles Times* story, describing the trailers of Creech Air Force Base in Nevada from which drone pilots operate.[38] More nuanced reflections complicate the journalistic emphasis placed on the air-conditioned, sanitized spaces from which drones are operated. The poet and literary critic Andrea Brady, for example, has argued that drones have the power to transform space, recasting swaths of territory as spaces of incarceration. "Just like you lock people in prison, they are locked in a room," she quotes a Waziri explaining people's existence under constant drone overflight.[39] The work that drone pilots carry out in their own air-conditioned rooms is itself subject to forms of spatial transformation too, shattering the appearance of remoteness: "Many operators speak of the space between themselves and the object as miniscule—18 inches, or the distance from face to screen. As Col. Pete Gersten told a reporter, 'You're 8000 miles away. What's the big deal? But it's not 8000 miles away. It's 18 inches away.'"[40]

The colonel's words speak to the complexities of seeing that obtain in the context of drone warfare and the potential intimacies that even the remotest targets might acquire. Events like the 2010 Uruzgan massacre, in which twenty-seven Afghan civilians were killed after Predator drone operators misidentified them, suggest one problem with drones might be that their operators are unable to see their enemy or their arms, for all the cutting-edge technology they use. Reading the transcript of the attack, one discovers a drone sensor operator reflecting on whether a figure visible onscreen *after* a helicopter attack had been called in is that of a "child" or an "adolescent." "No way to tell from here," reads the transcript.[41] At the same time, the fear that, as one *Military Medicine* report puts it, "there are drone operators who perceive the deployment of weapons and exposure to live video feed of combat (i.e., destruction/death of enemy combatants and ground forces) as highly stressful events" suggests that seeing may be just as problematic as not seeing in the age of the drone.[42] As Brady puts it, "intimacy with the object," by which she means drones' human targets, "is an operational risk of drone surveillance" precisely because killing may be made harder if some counterintuitive trace of the human (the capacity to see another person and recognize him or her as such) endures in the spatially diffuse associations of the human and nonhuman that drone warfare calls into being.[43] In this sense, war itself may today remain much *less* remote than we often assume. "A bayonet," an old slogan of the anti-imperialist left used to state, "is a weapon with a worker on each end." Technology has changed, but the human nodes of the networks of lethal violence that make war possible remain human and mutually enmeshed in the same dialectic of the intimate and the remote that has long characterized warfare.

Over There?

Tracing this networked corpus of thematically linked war writing may not seem all that intimately related to the starting point of this essay, Darren Wilson's account of the killing of Michael Brown. The network of texts appears to have led us far from where we began. But one reason for that is that, since the end of the Civil War, warfare itself has often appeared remote to American life, something that usually happened "over there," in the words of George M. Cohan's patriotic First

World War–era song—or "In the snow of far-off Northern lands / And in sunny tropic scenes," as the "hymn" of the U.S. Marine Corps has it. On this view, the attacks on Pearl Harbor and the 9/11 attacks were stunning exceptions to a sense of national impregnability voiced by a young Abraham Lincoln as early as 1838: "Shall we expect some trans-atlantic military giant, to step the Ocean, and crush us at a blow? Never!—All the armies of Europe, Asia and Africa combined . . . could not by force, take a drink from the Ohio, or make a track on the Blue Ridge, in a trial of a thousand years."[44] There have been moments when it has been politic for elites not to stress that relative impregnability, emphasizing instead the nation's vulnerability to foreign attack. If the atomic age validated such fears, the same may or may not have been true of the kind of propaganda that circulated during the two world wars. From the First World War–era depiction of a bestial, slathering Prussian militarism clambering ashore in America, the smoldering ru-ins of Europe silhouetted in the background (Figure 6.1), to the asser-tions drawn in Frank Capra's *Why We Fight* series of movies for the Department of War that the United States was in danger of being invaded and overrun by German Nazi forces attacking through Latin America, the U.S. government has periodically attempted to shake Americans out of any sense of residual invulnerability that may have clung to them in modern times.[45] Lincoln's belief in his Lyceum Address was that the republic could only be harmed by Americans themselves; more recently politicians have emphasized vulnerability to foreign threats, frequently using that vulnerability to justify mili-tary action far from the homeland. "We will fight them over there so we do not have to face them in the United States of America," Presi-dent George W. Bush explained of the nation's enemies in the Middle East in 2007, more than half a decade after the United States found itself under attack on 9/11.[46]

The normative remoteness of war is in turn part of what makes the grand jury testimony with which this chapter began so troubling. For Wilson's testimony speaks to one of the peculiarities of democratic life in America—namely, the fact that interactions between citizens and between citizens and the state are frequently mediated by the same lethal weaponry one encounters in so much war writing. Another way to put this is to say that contemporary life in the United States

FIGURE 6.1. "Destroy This Mad Brute" enlistment poster.

exhibits surprisingly pre-, post-, or simply undemocratic tinges. The state of nature, Thomas Hobbes observed, was a war of all against all (*bellum omnia contra omnes*); and so, sometimes, does U.S. life appear, even in the twenty-first century. While some statistics show that violent crime is dropping overall, mass shootings and the politics of the Second Amendment mandate that serious public energy is still wasted on the question of whether guns or people kill people. As any actor-network theorist would tell you, and as some of the writing of war discussed earlier in this chapter shows, it is networks of the human and nonhuman that kill people. How such networks might scar everyday life in the United States can be seen in Douglas Fairbairn's *Shoot* (1974), a novel contemporaneous with cinematic examinations of the relationship between the counterculture and well-armed political reaction like *Easy Rider* (1969), *Joe* (1970), *Dirty Harry* (1971), and the aforementioned *Electra Glide in Blue*. Published just a few years before the dramatic reorientation and radicalization of the National Rifle Association inaugurated the Second Amendment politics so familiar today, Fairbairn's novel is another node in the network of representations of the association of humans and their lethal technologies that we have already seen are characteristic of war writing. On its release, the book was billed as a commentary on what happens when veterans of the nation's foreign wars return home with a passion for the weapons used in those wars. "When you've seen action in Korea or Vietnam, you can get a thing about guns. For some men the war is never over," declared the paperback edition's back cover.

The novel opens with its narrator, Rex Jeannette, relating a hunting trip he took with four friends, on which they come across another group of men "standing over on the opposite bank" of a river:

> They looked more or less the same as us—were dressed in camouflage the same as us and seemed to be about the same age as us. They didn't wave or anything when they saw us, so we didn't either. They just stood there looking across the river at us, and for a couple of minutes we just stood there looking back at them. Then, all of a sudden, without any warning, and I swear to God without the slightest provocation from us, one of them raises his rifle and fired at us, hitting Pete Rinaldi in the head.[47]

The repeated emphasis on the resemblances between the two groups of men makes clear from the outset of the novel what often only slowly unfolds in other kinds of war writing: that the enemy is indeed less of a remote Other than he often seems. By beginning with the likeness of the men to one another, a mirrored, fraternal resemblance in which every atom belonging to one group as good belongs to the other, Fairbairn shows how weapons could mediate citizen-to-citizen encounters in the late twentieth-century United States. American *semblables* gaze across a river at one another and someone shoots: while the violence that erupts from the measured contemplation of sameness is in some sense surprising, it becomes less so once we read how guns proliferate through the pages of the novel as potentially agentic figures. Rex Jeannette and several of his buddies collect guns (or do the guns collect them?). Rex has a "Kentucky pistol, a Colt 1860 .44, a Harper's Ferry Model 1806 flintlock and the Model 1855 .58 Dragoon pistol, a Wells Fargo, a .58 buffalo gun, and a lot of other very fine stuff."[48] Lou is more technologically cutting-edge, for he possesses "an impressive collection of automatic weapons, which was his pride and joy, and the envy of every gun buff in the state," including "not only . . . the Schmeisser MP40 but the earlier MP38, a Sten, both the Soviet PPShM1941 and the PPS1943, and the American M3 and M3A1."[49] This is just a small selection of the novel's arsenal of Chekhovian armaments, bound to go off after the rifle shot in the novel's opening page has already initiated the action of the drama.

For the avoidance of doubt, precisely *whom* all these guns are to be used on is articulated by the widow of the man whom Jeanette's group of hunters end up killing in the shootout with which the novel begins. Her husband's death in a "hunting accident" has done nothing to dissuade her from the virtues of armed citizenship, she avers: "Ed told me that if ever sometime he wasn't there and I had to defend myself, the first effing nigger or hippie or junkie that comes through that door I'm to blow his effing head off, and that's what I'm going to do."[50] However, in the shootout with which the novel begins, and in the much more heavily armed one with which it ends, all the men who die are—with but one exception—white. None of them is a hippie or junkie. This is significant because the final battle—in which Lou's collection of weaponry, along with the armory of the local national guard and the hardware that Rex's gang's antagonists bring back to the river, features heavily—reads something like a series of friendly fire incidents writ large. The peaceful democratic home life of the United States has been poisoned, Fairbairn appears to propose, by the new American imperialism of the Cold War era; now war, which once was remote, has been brought home by these troubled veterans and combined with the reactionary politics of a counter-counterculture to produce something like a second civil war. And the victims of that war, at least as it is depicted in the two framing gunfights of Fairbairn's novel, are white men.

But the premise that war has ever really been remote as far as the United States and its democracy are concerned is itself dubious. For one way of reading Fairbairn's *Shoot* is as exposing the enduring truth that political ideals sit in peculiar relation to the lived realities of American life as far as many of the North American continent's populations go. "Free?" D. H. Lawrence asks in *Studies in Classic American Literature*. "Why, I have never been in any country where the individual has such an abject fear of his fellow countrymen. Because, as I say, they are free to lynch the moment he shows he is not one of them."[51] *Shoot* might be read as showing one of the results of those fears—namely, that an overarmed white citizenry ran the risk of lynching not its habitual nonwhite victims but itself. For Fairbairn gives the only noticeably nonwhite character in the novel, Ogilvie Trumbull, the kind of treatment described by Leslie Fiedler in his seminal essay, "Come Back to the Raft Ag'in, Huck Honey!" (1948). Trumbull is the finest fighter of them all, in the eyes of Rex, his buddies' relentless racism notwithstanding, and in a last stand that they take together, Rex gives voice to the same "outrageous" dream that Fiedler identified decades ago: that desire, encapsulated in the pairings of white and nonwhite male protagonists at the heart of much canonical American literature, for the white man to find what Fiedler called "acceptance at the breast he has most utterly offended."[52] In *Shoot,* that desire is expressed in Rex's insistence that he has "never felt closer to a man in [his] whole life" than he does to Trumbull as they fight together, Ogilvie dies, and Rex ends up half man, half thing, a grotesque testament to the adage that it is fragments of metal that one fights in war: "So I have a plate in my head and my face is destroyed and my body is all torn up and full of fragments that they can't seem to dig out, and I'm fed by a tube they stick in my arm."[53]

By the end of this war-at-home novel, Rex himself is an association of the human and nonhuman, the racialized Other is as intimate as it is possible to be, and the narrator's *semblables* assume the form of either lethal enemies or fallen corpses.

The key point here is that while *Shoot* problematizes the idea that war is remote from the U.S. homeland, it does so in problematic ways. It warns that the Hobbesian *bellum omnia contra omnes* implied by the networks of lethal violence that widespread gun ownership makes possible lies far closer to the surface of U.S. civilian life than one might think. At the same time, Fairbairn's novel casts both irruptions of the state of nature and the presence in everyday life of military-grade weaponry such as that collected by Lou as imported from foreign wars. This is a familiar enough thesis. For many American supporters of gun control today, mass shootings in high schools, nightclubs, and other public spaces represent a gross deviation from a democratic norm brought about by the modern politics of the Second Amendment, not a "boomerang" effect of the waging of foreign wars.[54] Roxanne Dunbar-Ortiz has recently shown, however, that neither of these interpretations factors in just how long the homeland of what is now the United States has been a battlefield for many populations. The contemporary politics of the Second Amendment, Dunbar-Ortiz argues, occludes gun ownership's deep historical roots in settler colonialism, the conquest of Indigenous lands, and the obligations white settlers had to police slave patrols.[55] The thesis that war is remote to the North American continent thus makes sense only when considering large-scale geopolitical conflicts since the end of the Civil War and obscures not only the wars of conquest and expansion that took place before that conflict but also the sense that still obtained for marginalized populations in the era in which Fairbairn published his novel that "white America" itself was an occupying army. That was certainly how the Black Panthers had seen the matter in the 1960s and why they had argued that black Americans had every right to arm and defend themselves.[56] What Fairbairn presents as a new aberration in citizen-to-citizen encounters imported in foreign wars had, on this view, long characterized encounters between the state and other political subjects, whether de jure citizens of the United States or not. They had been subject for centuries to inclusion in the same lethal networks of the human and nonhuman that I have traced through modern war writing.

Ferguson, Missouri, August 9, 2014

The foregoing, I hope, illuminates Wilson's grand jury testimony in interesting ways. Amid the uproar that followed Wilson's killing of Brown, images emerged from Ferguson that did nothing to disavow the proposition that the occupying armies of "white America" were still very much in place. The militarization of policing that has been a feature of recent decades appeared to confirm that the logic of the battlefield persisted in an urban environment in which a majority-white police force patrolled a majority-black neighborhood. And there certainly is, we can now see, the same warlike dialectic of the intimate and the remote mediated by lethal technology in the official narrative of the fatal interactions between Wilson and Brown as recurs throughout the war writing examined in this chapter. It is there in the peculiar intensity with which the prosecuting attorney focused attention on the things that Wilson carried about his person before the killing of Brown. It is there too in the pressing intimacy of bodies and objects that Wilson delineates as he narrates his story of how Brown reached for Wilson's gun in the cramped confines of his patrol car. And it is also there in the sense of vulnerable solitude that Wilson's account of a lone cop in his car attempts to convey. ("You lived and died alone, especially in fighters," wrote Salter. "You were as isolated as a deep-sea diver.") And were you the hunter or the hunted? The latter, Wilson implies, and by something other than men. For describing Brown's final moments, Wilson portrays the physical intimacy that obtained during the clinch in the car irretrievably reversed once he has managed to discharge his pistol. The unarmed Brown is transformed, distant now to the point of being wholly Other: "The only way I can describe it, it [*sic*] looks like a demon, that's how angry he looked."[57] The object pronoun "it" speaks volumes; one thinks of the depiction of the slathering, dehumanized enemy threatening the homeland in the First World War propaganda referred to earlier (Figure 6.1).

And yet, as I hope I have made clear, it would be wrong merely to conclude that Wilson's testimony can be read as a species of war writing, a dispatch from occupied territory, as a result of relatively recent events alone. It is true that recent developments in the politics and jurisprudence of the Second Amendment, recent developments in foreign policy, and recent developments in the militarization of policing have all facilitated domestic networks of lethal violence that have long characterized war zones "over there." And it is right, I think, to decry the consequences of the fact that in a demos in which more or less everyone has an uninfringeable right to be lethally armed, what is paradigmatic of war is also potentially paradigmatic of interactions between U.S. citizens and between those citizens and representatives of the state. For those interactions will always risk being tempered by whatever complex effects networks of mutual suspicion, fear, defensiveness, and lethal technology are liable to set off. The result is the normalization of dead Americans as part of the common run of American life and the periodic exposure of a battlefield of a nation littered with the corpses of citizens and their children, including Brown. But focusing too much on recent developments risks misunderstanding the depth and nature of some of the roots of the United States' present impasse. For the problem with any "boomerang" thesis that sees the transfer of war, normatively remote, back to the homeland as the consequence of recent military adventurism alone is that it rehearses the errors of Fairbairn's Vietnam-era *Shoot*. For too many Americans, there is, in fact, nothing recent about the process that leaves them at the mercy of whatever lethal networks and objects happen to sustain the regnant status quo. Thus, neither war nor tyranny needs to "come home" from "over there" because neither war nor tyranny ever conclusively went away. In this sense, the network of texts and social and historical facts that this chapter has traced suggests that if Wilson's testimony is a war story, it is all the more chilling for being one so deeply in, and not against, the American grain.

Notes

1. *State of Missouri v. Darren Wilson*, Grand Jury, vol. 5, September 16, 2014, 201, https://www.documentcloud.org/documents/1371222-wilson-testimony.html.
2. *Wilson*, 202.
3. *Wilson*, 207.
4. *Wilson*, 204, 205.
5. For scholarship on the militarization of policing and its juridico-legal support in the United States and effects on populations of color, respectively, see Radley Balko, *Rise of the Warrior Cop: The Militarization of America's Police Forces* (New York: Public Affairs, 2013); and Michelle Alexander, *The New Jim Crow: Mass Incarceration in the Age of Colorblindness* (New York: New Press, 2012), 63–77.

6. *Wilson*, 203–4.

7. *Wilson*, 209.

8. *Wilson*, 214.

9. Bruno Latour, "On Actor-Network Theory: A Few Clarifications," *Soziale Welt* 47, no. 4 (1996): 373.

10. Bruno Latour, *Politics of Nature* (Cambridge, Mass.: Harvard University Press, 2004), 75.

11. For Latour's own brief analysis of the relationship between humans and guns, see his *Pandora's Hope: Essays on the Reality of Science Studies* (Cambridge, Mass.: Harvard University Press, 1999), 180.

12. See Donald Rayfield, *Anton Chekhov: A Life* (Evanston, Ill.: Northwestern University Press, 1998), 203.

13. Latour, "On Actor-Network Theory," 375.

14. Latour, 375.

15. Latour, 378.

16. James William Guercio, dir., *Electra Glide in Blue* (United States: United Artists, 1973). The opening title sequence is available at https://www.artofthe title.com/title/electra-glide-in-blue/.

17. Philipp Meyer, *American Rust* (London: Simon and Schuster, 2009), 59.

18. Latour, "On Actor-Network Theory," 371.

19. Mark Twain, *A Connecticut Yankee in King Arthur's Court*, ed. Justin Kaplan (1971; repr., Harmondsworth, U.K.: Penguin, 1976), 391.

20. Twain, 395, 404–5.

21. Twain, 394, 396, emphasis added.

22. For Twain's critique of Scott, see *Life on the Mississippi* (Oxford: World's Classics, 1990), 270–71, 303–5.

23. George Bernard Shaw, preface to *Geneva, Cymbeline Refinished, and Good King Charles* (London: Constable, 1946), 11.

24. Shaw, 12.

25. George Oppen, "Of Hours," in *Collected Poems* (New York: New Directions, 1975), 211.

26. John Hersey, *Hiroshima* (Harmondsworth, U.K.: Penguin, 1946), vii.

27. *This Is Your Life*, "Kiyoshi Tanimoto," aired May 11, 1955, https://www .dailymotion.com/video/xl3jx5.

28. James Salter, *The Hunters* (New York: Vintage, 1999), 116.

29. Salter, 49.

30. Salter, 211.

31. Salter, 193.

32. Salter, 178.

33. Salter, 233.

34. Tim O'Brien, *The Things They Carried* (London: Flamingo, 1991), 130.

35. O'Brien, 130.

36. O'Brien, 131.

37. O'Brien, 123.

38. W. J. Hennigan, "Drone Pilots Go to War in the Nevada Desert, Staring at Video Screens," *Los Angeles Times,* June 17, 2015, http://www.latimes.com/nation/la-na-drone-pilots-20150617-story.html.

39. Andrea Brady, "Drone Poetics," *New Formations* 89 (2017): 117–18.

40. Brady, 130.

41. "Transcripts of U.S. Drone Attack," *Los Angeles Times,* April 8, 2011, 72, 7, http://documents.latimes.com/transcript-of-drone-attack/.

42. Wayne L. Chappelle et al., "Symptoms of Psychological Distress and Post-traumatic Stress Disorder in United States Air Force 'Drone Operators,'" *Military Medicine* 179, no. 8 (2014): 67.

43. Brady, "Drone Poetics," 133.

44. Abraham Lincoln, "The Perpetuation of Our Political Institutions (Address before the Young Men's Lyceum of Springfield, January 27, 1838)," *Journal of the Abraham Lincoln Association* 6, no. 1 (1984): 6–7.

45. H. R. Hopps, "Destroy This Mad Brute—Enlist U.S. Army," poster, 1917–18; Frank Capra and Anatole Litvak. dirs., *Why We Fight: War Comes to America* (U.S. Army Pictorial Services, 1945).

46. George W. Bush, "Remarks at the Veterans of Foreign Wars National Convention in Kansas City, Missouri," August 22, 2007, American Presidency Project, http://www.presidency.ucsb.edu/ws/?pid=75710.

47. Douglas Fairbairn, *Shoot* (London: Pan, 1978), 5.

48. Fairbairn, 29.

49. Fairbairn, 19.

50. Fairbairn, 38–39.

51. D. H. Lawrence, "The Spirit of Place," in *The Cambridge Edition of the Works of D. H. Lawrence,* vol. 2, *Studies in Classic American Literature,* ed. Ezra Greenspan, Lindeth Vasey, and John Worthen (Cambridge: Cambridge University Press, 2003), 15.

52. Leslie Fiedler, "Come Back to the Raft Ag'in, Huck Honey!," in *The Devil Gets His Due: The Uncollected Essays of Leslie Fiedler,* ed. Samuele F. S. Pardini (Berkeley: Counterpoint, 2008), 53.

53. Fairbairn, *Shoot,* 141–42.

54. On the "boomerang" effect by means of which human capital, military-grade weaponry, and tactical training return from overseas missions to the domestic scene, see Christopher J. Coyne and Abigail R. Hall, *Tyranny Comes Home: The Domestic Fate of U.S. Militarism* (Stanford, Calif.: Stanford University Press, 2018).

55. Roxanne Dunbar-Ortiz, *Loaded: A Disarming History of the Second Amendment* (San Francisco: City Lights, 2018), 11–27.

56. See, for example, "A Letter to Black Students," *Black Panther,* November 23, 1967, 6.

57. Wilson, 225.

CHAPTER 7

"Wanted Dead or Alive"

The Hunt for Osama bin Laden

ANNIKA BRUNCK

When White House communications director Dan Pfeiffer tweeted on May 1, 2011, at 9:45 p.m. about plans for "POTUS to address the nation tonight at 10:30 p.m. Eastern Time," many newsmakers in Washington and beyond immediately speculated whether President Barack Obama's statement could be related in any way to Osama bin Laden and his whereabouts, while Twitter and other social media sites were equally abuzz with rumors.[1] At 10:25 p.m., Keith Urbahn, who then worked as chief of staff for former secretary of defense Donald Rumsfeld, tweeted, "So I'm told by a reputable person they have killed Osama Bin Laden. Hot damn."[2] By 10:45 p.m., the major television news channels ABC, CBS, and NBC had interrupted their regular programming to report on this breaking news. The rumors continued to spread, predominantly on social media sites like Twitter and Facebook. At the height of the frenzy, Facebook recorded more than a dozen posts per second that contained the words "bin Laden."[3] News websites like the ones of the Huffington Post and the *New York Post* featured banners and headlines announcing that bin Laden had been killed in a successful secret mission.[4] People anxiously awaited the president's official statement, which kept being postponed.

Finally, at 11:35 p.m., President Obama addressed the nation from the East Room of the White House. He confirmed to the American public and audiences all over the world that "the United States has conducted an operation that killed [O]sama bin Laden, the leader of Al Qaida and a terrorist who's responsible for the murder of thousands of innocent men, women, and children."[5] As the news spread, celebrations broke out across the United States: At the baseball game between the New York Mets and the Philadelphia Phillies, the audience began an incessant chant of "USA! USA! USA!" while sharing the news on smartphones with their seat neighbors. WWE wrestling star John Cena announced the death of Osama bin Laden to a frantic audience at the end of one of his matches, declaring, "I feel damned proud to be an American," as people erupted into roaring applause.[6] More crowds gathered in New York City, Washington, and other big cities across the nation as people poured into the streets, waving American flags, singing "The Star-Spangled Banner" and other patriotic songs, cheering, and generally celebrating through the night. The man who had organized and financed the infamous "terrorist" attacks on September 11, 2001, was finally dead—"Justice has been done," Obama confirmed.[7]

Public reactions in the wake of the news that Osama bin Laden had been found and killed indicate that the American public perceived these events as an important moment in the decade-long War on Terror. Elizabeth Harris, a journalist for the *New York Times*, reported on initial reactions to the news and interviewed people in the crowds in New York City regarding their opinion about bin Laden's death. Stacey Betsalel, for example, told Harris that the killing of bin Laden would warn "terrorists worldwide" that "they will be caught and they will have to pay for their actions. You can't mess with the United States for very long and get away with it."[8] But not all Americans responded with ecstatic joy to the news. Harris also interviewed a 9/11 survivor who told the journalist, "If this means there is one less death in the future, then I'm glad for that. . . . But I just can't find it in me to be glad one more person is dead, even if it is Osama Bin Laden."[9] He added later that "whatever the justice of this, it won't bring back the people they lost," clearly expressing a more skeptical view about the event and its supposed meaning.[10] Yet while people differed over how they evaluated the killing of bin Laden almost ten years after the 9/11 attacks, they generally agreed that it constituted a significant event.

As these examples show, bin Laden (and the hunt for him) maintained a central position in discourses on the War on Terror and America's fight against terrorism even more than a decade after the attacks of 9/11. In what follows, I therefore want to analyze the role that narratives of finding and capturing bin Laden played in discourses on remote warfare generally and the War on Terror in particular. To be clear, I understand the War on Terror initiated by the George W. Bush administration in response to the 9/11 attacks as a case of remote warfare. The term most frequently refers to the aspect of highly technologized warfare. Indeed, the U.S.-led wars in Afghanistan and Iraq, as well as operations in Pakistan, Yemen, and elsewhere, saw an increased use of equipment and techniques associated with remote warfare, especially the development and deployment of armed drones.[11]

However, in my understanding of the term, the notion of remote warfare also encapsulates ideas about spatial, cultural, and psychological remoteness. *Spatial remoteness* refers to geographical space, meaning that the conflict takes place in a location far away from the host country, but also to a bodily, physical remoteness where the soldiers engaged in remote warfare wage war from a distance. *Cultural remoteness*, in turn, expresses the notion that one country wages war on a nation or region of the world about whose cultures it knows very little. Moreover, the home country does not deem it particularly necessary to acquire knowledge and understanding about those it is fighting; indeed, since it could foster empathy and awareness, it is often seen as counterproductive to the war effort. Ultimately, cultural remoteness is expressed in processes of Othering—that is, constructions of the warring nation as different and inherently, innately *not* like the home country.[12] Similar to what Ann-Katrine S. Nielsen calls "existential remoteness" in her contribution to this volume, *psychological remoteness* describes the sense of emotional detachment that results from spatial and cultural remoteness as people living in the home country feel neither connected to nor responsible for war and violence bestowed upon the enemy. They ignore or even outright deny the humanity of the enemy.

While these theoretical ruminations suggest a neat separation between these different aspects of remote warfare, it is important to bear in mind that, in practice, they cannot be as clearly divided and rather overlap, intertwine, and trigger each other. In my view, then, the War on Terror waged by the Bush (and later Obama) administration constitutes remote warfare: apart from the technological aspect mentioned earlier, the War on Terror took (and continues to take) place in and against nations far away from America in terms of space, but also with regard to the American cultural imaginary. Countries like

Afghanistan, Iraq, and Pakistan are not only geographically remote; the majority of Americans also neither know much about the peoples and their cultures nor care much about learning more. Cultural ties between the United States and these countries are not central to American mainstream life, thus furthering cultural remoteness.

These dynamics can be problematic when it comes to securing and maintaining public support for the War on Terror since its remoteness requires additional justifications to the populace that the war is not only necessary and just but also winnable. I argue in the rest of the chapter that narratives about bin Laden as evil mastermind initially worked to bridge the remoteness inherent in the War on Terror, thus preserving public support for the campaign by making the war appear as not remote but near and affecting American everyday lives. However, as the years went on and bin Laden remained elusive, this discursive strategy no longer worked. Instead of overcoming the remoteness inherent in the War on Terror, references to bin Laden actually made the remoteness of the military campaign visible and open for criticism and depicted the war as no longer winnable and just. Ultimately, things changed once more after the successful killing of bin Laden in 2011, as it briefly collapsed the paradigm of remote warfare only to, paradoxically, reaffirm it afterward as dominant framework for the War on Terror.

Coming from the field of cultural studies, I take a constructionist approach and am therefore not so much interested in who bin Laden "really" was or how he was "really" killed. Rather, I am interested in *discursive constructions* of the man behind the 9/11 attacks, as well as narratives about the hunt for him. These discursive constructions of bin Laden are inherently flexible and shift as cultural, historical, and political contexts change, thus giving us insight into how the American public responded to the War on Terror and issues of remote warfare at the time. Similarly, I also understand labels such as "evil" and "terrorist" as discursive constructions whose meanings are context dependent and shaped by historical and ideological forces. All of these discursive constructions can be exploited for specific purposes by those in power at a particular historical moment—or, alternatively, function as sites of resistance and vehicle to question the status quo.

In the next section, I turn to framings of bin Laden in the aftermath of the 9/11 attacks as exceptionally evil and the role these constructions played in justifying the beginning of the War on Terror. The Bush administration made the need to find bin Laden a central trope in its justifications for invading Afghanistan in order to bridge the remote aspects of this war and present it as just, winnable, and necessary instead. I then analyze in the second section how, as the War on Terror went on, the figure of bin Laden became a symbol for American failure in the military campaign and, contrary to its functions in the first phase of the war, worked to accentuate and comment on the remoteness of the War on Terror. In the third section, I discuss how this development culminated in the eventual assassination of bin Laden in 2011, which caused the paradigm of remote warfare to first disintegrate before, in a paradoxical move, reestablishing it. I also examine popular reactions to the CIA Twitter campaign to commemorate the mission to kill bin Laden five years later in response to the remote warfare of the War on Terror.

Bridging the Remoteness of Warfare in Afghanistan

After the attacks of 9/11, the Bush administration quickly decided it would respond by initiating a "war against terrorism," a phrase that President Bush already employed in the evening of that fateful day.[13] He then expanded on this notion during a highly anticipated address to Congress on September 20, explaining that "our war on terror begins with Al Qaida, but it does not end there. It will not end until every terrorist group of global reach has been found, stopped, and defeated."[14] The first installment of this military campaign to root out "terrorism" was Afghanistan, the country harboring bin Laden, but it was clear from the start that the War on Terror would not be limited to it, meaning that more wars were to follow in the future.

From its inception, the war in Afghanistan was led as a type of remote warfare encompassing the concept's technological, spatial, cultural, and psychological dimensions. Regarding the technological aspect, the war in Afghanistan became one of the first military conflicts to increasingly rely on remote warfare technology, particularly drones. As James DeShaw Rae has pointed out, after 9/11 "the United States greatly accelerated its drones program, building bases around the world, diversifying the types of drones in production, and affixing some with greater weapons capabilities."[15] For the war in Afghanistan, this also meant that drones were no longer purely used for surveillance and reconnaissance but became an effective means to target and kill "terrorists" as well.[16]

But the war in Afghanistan was "remote" beyond its technological characteristics. At the beginning of the War on Terror, the space in which the war was set to take place was practically unknown to the majority of Americans. Closely tied to this was the fact that not only was the Middle East unfamiliar territory, its peoples and their cultures were equally enigmatic.[17] The spatial and cultural remoteness of the War on Terror became visible when various television news channels began broadcasting shows and documentaries aimed at explaining to audiences where the Middle East was located, which countries and cultures it contained, and what kinds of relationships the United States maintained with them.

For instance, ABC News aired a documentary with Peter Jennings on October 11, one month after the attacks, called "Minefield: The United States and the Muslim World."[18] In it, he explained to viewers the geography of the Middle East and introduced them to the different countries in it, pointing out how they related to the United States. He also warned of the dangers inherent in Islam and painted the Muslim communities in the region as angry, frustrated, and often jealous of "the West," here meaning the United States, and its achievements and power. Overall, the documentary is notable for its pedagogical style, suggesting that it was meant to educate audiences about the region in which the first installments of the War on Terror were about to take place. Other channels, such as CNN and NBC, followed suit with similar programming.

Documentaries of this kind functioned as texts that bridged the spatial and cultural remoteness of the War on Terror, particularly the impending invasion of Afghanistan. In ABC's documentary, for example, Jennings could be seen walking through the studio, which had been turned into a map of the Middle East, while he narrated. As Sandra Silberstein has argued, "Jennings, the U.S. newscaster, literally walked through the 'Muslim world,' physically dominating it as he spoke," thus presenting the Middle East as a region physically controlled and inhabited by the United States.[19] What is more, he transcended the geographical remoteness of the region and not only visualized it (the studio-as-map even took the region's topography into account) but quite literally brought it home to those Americans who were watching the show and seeing the region in close proximity, some of them for the first time.

Likewise, the portrayal of Middle Eastern Muslims in American culture, politics, and news media after 9/11 tapped into already well-established stereotypes about Islam and its believers, particularly the trope of the "Muslim terrorist" with fanatical hatred for "the West," which already existed in American mainstream society.[20] Broadcasts like Jennings's documentary could confidently claim that "the Islamists turned their attention against Western targets because it's very easy to mobilize and to recruit true soldiers against American interests."[21] Statements of this kind activated these already circulating stereotypes about Muslims and presented audiences with a clearly identifiable Other, imparting knowledge claims about the region in question as well as the people living in it. This effectively counteracted feelings of cultural remoteness by presenting an easily recognizable and understandable enemy in the War on Terror.

These dynamics of bridging the remoteness of the War on Terror in Afghanistan were significantly aided by the specter of bin Laden, who was systematically vilified as an exceptionally "evil terrorist mastermind," a discursive strategy on which the Bush administration relied from the beginning. On September 26, for instance, Bush outright condemned bin Laden as "an evil man," continuing that "this is a man who hates. This is a man who's declared war on innocent people. This is a man who doesn't mind destroying women and children. This is man who hates freedom. This is an evil man."[22] When a reporter asked whether bin Laden had any political objectives, the president vehemently denied this, instead arguing that "he has got evil goals. And it's hard to think in conventional terms about a man so dominated by evil."[23] This particular focus on bin Laden's "evilness," cast in almost mythical proportions, as the main reason for 9/11 served a tangible political objective: it blocked any other explanations or interpretations of the events in nonbellicose terms and prevented any further questioning of the political course taken by the Bush administration. It also systematically denied that bin Laden and al-Qaeda harbored legitimate political objectives and rather explained the attacks as stemming from the perpetrators' evilness while simultaneously positioning the United States as innocent victim.[24]

The presidential rhetoric also made it clear that the hunt for bin Laden could (and would) only end when the man had been found and, by implication, killed by the United States. No alternative scenario would be considered as constituting "justice" for 9/11. Thus, when a reporter asked the president whether he wanted bin Laden dead, Bush infamously responded, "I want him held—I want justice. There's an old poster out West, as I recall, that said, 'Wanted: Dead or Alive.'"[25] A few minutes later, that same reporter repeated the question for clarification, and the president reiterated his assertion, saying, "When I was a kid, I remember that they used to put out there, in the Old West, a wanted poster. It said, 'Wanted: Dead or Alive.' All I want—and America wants him brought to justice. That's what we want."[26] As these examples show, Bush explicitly tied the notion of justice to bin Laden's death by tapping into central national myths and grand narratives.[27] Indeed, as Rachel Hall has argued, this kind of rhetoric "articulated the perceived boundary violation of the terrorist attacks to the American myth of innocence lost," suggesting that it could only be restored by killing bin Laden.[28]

Bin Laden's exceptional "evilness" and the need to punish him for it thus became the primary justification for invading Afghanistan on October 7, 2001, as the first installment of a war against "terrorism." On October 9, for instance, Bush stated that "the action that is presently being taken in Afghanistan is not at all directed against the people of Afghanistan; it is not at all directed against Islam; it is far rather directed against Usama bin Laden and the very ruthless regime behind him."[29] Similarly, on October 11, the president told reporters that "he [bin Laden] thought he had hijacked a country [Afghanistan]. . . . And it became a safe haven for bin Laden and the Al Qaida organization. It's no longer a safe haven, that's for sure, because of our military activity."[30] In this manner, the war in Afghanistan was legitimized by declaring it necessary to capture bin Laden while simultaneously assuring the American public that the war was practically won already. The figure of bin Laden thus played an important role in justifying the War on Terror because it enabled proponents of the military campaign to bridge its remoteness in ways that kept the American public engaged and supportive of the war effort. It also worked to convince the majority of Americans that the war was legitimate, necessary, and winnable.

The U.S. president was not the only discursive actor to evoke the figure of bin Laden to argue for the need to go to war in Afghanistan. In Jennings's documentary, for example, the image of bin Laden and translated sound bites of his speeches and statements appeared repeatedly. At another point in the program, Jennings stated that "for Osama bin Laden Afghanistan may have been the only place left to go. The roughness of the terrain and the weakness of the government made it a place where he could operate freely."[31] The ABC documentary also featured in its opening sequence an expert asserting that "even if we got to Osama bin Laden tomorrow, you gonna have dozens of hundreds of Osama bin Ladens all over the . . . world."[32] His voice provided the commentary while the camera panned over a long list of headshots of wanted Middle Eastern "terrorists," suggesting that bin Laden was the representative of a more endemic threat facing the United States. Claims like these not only familiarized audiences with bin Laden's image but also discursively tied him to Afghanistan as well as Muslim cultures in the Middle East, making the war as well as the enemy more tangible and less abstract. Moreover, they worked to connect the United States to these remote parts of the world, constructing them as appropriate avenues for American intervention. By bridging the remoteness of the region in terms of spatial, cultural, and emotional ties, U.S. (military) involvement became "logical" and necessary.

Similarly, the October 8, 2001, front page of the *New York Times* reacted to the invasion of Afghanistan not only by running articles on the beginning of the military campaign itself but also by including pieces on bin Laden's reaction to it. John Burns, for example, wrote a front-page article entitled "Bin Laden Taunts U.S. and Praises Hijackers," summarizing the content of a new video released by "the man accused of orchestrating the [9/11] attacks" and stressing that "Mr. bin Laden, looking as untroubled as if he were on a camping trip, used the occasion to vent his hatred of America."[33] This indicated to readers that bin Laden was the central figure in the War on Terror since he had organized the 9/11 attacks and that "his hatred of America" was the main catalyst for the war, endowing him with disproportionate power and influence. It also evoked constructions of bin Laden as exceptionally evil and driven by his irrational hatred for the United States, further justifying the need to wage a war on terror.

Burns connected bin Laden to both 9/11 and the invasion of Afghanistan from the very beginning, opening his piece by writing that "within hours of the first American bombs dropping on Afghanistan, the world's most wanted man, Osama bin Laden, appeared in a videotape broadcast worldwide in which he taunted the United States and celebrated the Sept. 11 terrorist attacks."[34] In this single sentence, Burns evoked American military might ("bombs dropping"), framed it explicitly as a response to "the Sept. 11 terrorist attacks," and linked bin Laden to both 9/11 and the war in Afghanistan. The article invited readers to personalize the events through the figure of bin Laden, thus making the war more concrete and less remote while also diverting attention away from the victims of the American bombings. Moreover, Burns subtly coded the conflict as legitimate by suggesting that capturing bin Laden, after all "the world's most wanted man," was the main objective and as such a legitimate military goal. At the same time, this phrasing suggested that bin Laden was extremely powerful because he, a single man, could challenge and defy the United States.

These effects were further enhanced through visual means. The newspaper printed not only a picture of Bush on its front page but also one of bin Laden in his familiar camouflage military outfit and turban, as well as a photo of a U.S. bomb being wheeled into a launching position. Taken together, these pictures visualized the conflict as one between George W. Bush and Osama bin Laden and invited readers to individualize the warring parties, thus bridging the remote nature of the war. Readers, already accustomed to vilifications of bin Laden, could subconsciously read Bush as representing the good and innocent United States while understanding bin Laden as an embodiment of evil that needed to be eradicated. In conjunction with the photo of American weaponry, the pictures not only showed the superiority of the American military, with its skills in remote warfare, but also insinuated that the war was easily winnable. This message was further underscored by the newspaper as it quoted Bush as addressing "all the men and women in our military . . . : Your mission is defined, your objectives are clear, your goal is just."[35] The presidential statement framed the war as necessary, fair, and enjoying broad public support while hinting at constructions of the enemy, personified in the image of bin Laden, as the exact opposite.

Overall, then, references to bin Laden in word and image worked to counterbalance the spatial remoteness of the War on Terror because they clearly signaled to audiences who the enemy was and where he was to be found. Moreover, by visualizing the Muslim Other through bin Laden himself, it covered up appearances of cultural difference and made both the space in which the war was taking place and the enemy it had been declared on seem recognizable and understandable. This made it easier for readers and viewers to have an emotional response to the War on Terror initiated in Afghanistan because of its individualized and personalized nature, obscuring feelings of psychological remoteness. As a result, audiences were invested in the war and its outcome, a discursive move that effectively bridged the remoteness of the War on Terror. Likewise, the insistence on American moral and technological superiority constructed the War on Terror as legitimate and easily winnable, thus further ensuring broad public support.

However, these discursive constructions could not be maintained indefinitely, in part because they were predicated on the United States eventually capturing bin Laden. In the next section, I analyze how this rhetorical strategy slowly began to unravel as the War on Terror progressed, revealing the remoteness of the war, before eventually collapsing entirely when Navy SEALs killed bin Laden in a carefully orchestrated raid in 2011.

Making Visible the Remoteness of the War on Terror

Using the figure of an exceptionally evil Osama bin Laden to bridge the remote characteristics of the War on Terror in not only a spatial but also a cultural and psychological sense proved a successful discursive strategy at the beginning of the military campaign, ensuring public support for the invasion of Afghanistan and subsequent military engagement in the Middle East. But the continued success of the narrative, which posited that bin Laden had to be captured in order to obtain justice for the 9/11 attacks, hinged on the U.S. military actually catching bin Laden in order to demonstrate American (military) superiority. Thus when, after a few years of combat in Afghanistan and Iraq, bin Laden remained unfound yet clearly alive (as the regular video messages broadcast on international television indicated), the narrative began to lose its power and influence, accentuating the remote nature of the War on Terror and opening up spaces to criticize the conduct of the war via references to bin Laden.

In many ways, then, the Bush administration's tough rhetoric on finding (and killing) bin Laden backfired. As the years passed, it became apparent that even though the U.S. military had superior warfare technology and higher numbers of well-trained soldiers with excellent equipment, all these advantages still did not enable it to capture bin Laden. The missions in Afghanistan and especially Iraq turned out to be extremely costly operations in terms of both personnel and material. Studies estimate the costs for the wars in Afghanistan and Iraq at more than US$4 trillion.[36] The Department of Defense states that during these wars, more than 2,200 U.S. soldiers died in Afghanistan and more than 4,400 service members died in the war in Iraq.[37] As these numbers show, the United States paid a heavy price for the War on Terror while bin Laden remained as elusive as before.

Voices critical of how the War on Terror was going as well as the Bush administration's inability to locate and capture bin Laden could be heard increasingly loudly and openly. This criticism addressed the remote aspects of the War on Terror and often used the figure of bin Laden to represent American failure in the war as well as to signify its remoteness, now made visible and perceived as problematic. Criticism of the spatial remoteness of the War on Terror was expressed in part via discussions of bin Laden's whereabouts. Mary Anne Weaver, for instance, writing in the *New York Times Magazine* four years after the 9/11 attacks, imagined bin Laden either in the caves of Tora Bora, Afghanistan, or somewhere in Pakistan. She then described the caves as a practically impenetrable maze and the perfect hiding spot for bin Laden, at one point quoting an official as saying that the caves in Tora Bora "are rugged, formidable and isolated. . . . If you know them, you can come and go with ease. But if you don't, they're a labyrinth that you can't penetrate."[38] Here, bin Laden's presumed hiding spot was depicted as unmapped territory, reminding readers not only that the man was still alive and free but also that the War on Terror, ostensibly waged to capture him, was taking place in a confusing, dangerous space far away from the United States. Moreover, the military's failure to provide enough ground forces to capture bin Laden was described by one official as "the gravest error of the war," an evaluation Weaver clearly shared.[39] This suggests that the unknown location of bin Laden was understood as embodying the general spatial remoteness of the War on Terror and often used as a vehicle to criticize its conduct.

Similarly, criticism of the now visible cultural remoteness of the war made use of the fact that bin Laden remained uncaptured. Mark Danner, for instance, wrote a piece entitled "Taking Stock of the Forever War" in the same edition of the *New York Times Magazine* as Weaver's article. In his article, he assessed the progress and success of the ongoing War on Terror, lamenting that "four years after the collapse of the towers, evil is still with us and so is terrorism."[40] Danner also detailed bin Laden's aims and objectives, his ideology, and his ideas about warfare and terrorism, effectively characterizing bin Laden and his followers as "Islamic terrorist" Others attacking the United States, albeit with a list of political goals. Notably, whereas references to bin Laden in the early phase of the War on Terror had functioned as a way to bridge its remoteness, they now fulfilled the opposite purpose as they made the war's remoteness visible instead of hiding it. This dynamic speaks to the constructed nature of discourses on remote warfare, as well as the fact that these discursive constructions respond to changing contexts and historical moments, reminding us that meanings are inherently unstable.

In his article, Danner then reflected on this changed perception of the War on Terror as remote, criticizing that "we stubbornly insisted on fighting a war of the imagination, an ideological struggle that we defined not by frankly appraising the real enemy before us but by focusing on the mirror of our own obsessions."[41] Danner suggested that instead of focusing on "the real enemy," meaning bin Laden and al-Qaeda, and accepting their remote nature, the American cultural imaginary had projected its "own obsessions," fears, and anxieties onto them, thus bridging the cultural remoteness of the War on Terror and embroiling the nation in an unwinnable war. Importantly, in his own analysis, Danner, by giving references to bin Laden a new meaning, contributed to a reframing of the war as disastrous because of its remoteness.

The psychological effect of having bin Laden still remain free after years of war was equally reflected in contemporary commentary. Sheryl Stolberg, writing for the *New York Times* in September 2008, for example, quoted a State Department official as acknowledging that "if somebody had told us shortly after 9/11 that we still wouldn't have captured or killed bin Laden, there would have been real shock."[42] More-over, Stolberg recounted to readers that the Democratic Party was intending to capitalize on the Bush administration's failure to capture bin Laden in the upcoming elections, clearly viewing it as a central political fiasco of the outgoing administration. The inability to locate bin Laden after all these years made the remoteness of the War on Terror visible and signaled the failure and futility of the military campaign. Articles like the one written by Stolberg highlighted people's emotional response to the situation, thus foregrounding the public's general psychological remoteness to both the war and the campaign to find bin Laden. Moreover, it functioned as a focal point for criticism of the Bush administration's handling of the war and approach to foreign policy generally.

Ultimately, references to the failure to find and capture bin Laden suggested that, contrary to earlier claims, the war was no longer winnable or, rather, that it had never been winnable in the first place. In his piece, Danner, for instance, commented that "the failure to find the weapons of mass destruction, and the collapse of the rationale for the war, left terribly exposed precisely what bin Laden had targeted as the critical American vulnerability: the will to fight."[43] Here, Danner argued that the United States had fallen into bin Laden's trap by becoming enmeshed in the quagmire of a war against "terrorism" that was no longer justified and in which it could no longer triumph.

Indeed, the Bush administration appeared to be aware of the symbolic power inherent in the image of a free bin Laden and soon began to downplay his importance for the War on Terror. Famously, President Bush declared during a press conference on March 13, 2002, "I am truly not that concerned about him [bin Laden]," suggesting that the man was no longer central to the war efforts in Afghanistan. In that press conference, the president dismissed questions by reporters focusing on bin Laden's whereabouts by stating, "The idea of focusing on one person is—really indicates to me people don't understand the scope of the mission."[44] At this point, the Bush administration had already convinced all five major television networks in the United States to severely limit their coverage of bin Laden videos, ostensibly because they might contain hidden messages to al-Qaeda cells.[45] Presidential rhetoric and acts of these kinds were meant to remove bin Laden from his central position in discourses on the War on Terror by silencing his voice and making his image disappear—ultimately, the aim was to marginalize bin Laden from the War on Terror because his figure had become a way to criticize the administration and its handling of the military campaign, making its remoteness visible and eroding public support for it.

Breaking *and* Affirming the Paradigm of Remote Warfare

When the Obama administration eventually came to power in 2009, the figure of bin Laden was no longer central to discourses on the War on Terror. Mark Hughes, a contributor for *Forbes,* summarized the situation aptly when he wrote, "For a decade we have been at war, a war supposedly launched to find and punish Osama bin Laden and al-Qaeda for the attacks of September 11, 2001. We searched and tried to capture or kill bin Laden, until it proved hard enough that it became easier to pretend he didn't matter after all. . . . For several years, he was like a ghost, seemingly forgotten, as the war turned in a new direction and we began to face the ugly revelations about torture and mass civilian casualties."[46] Indeed, in some ways President Obama exploited the fact that the figure of bin Laden had been made remote to discourses on the War on Terror by using this silence and discursive absence to plan and execute Operation Neptune Spear, the SEAL mission that found and killed bin Laden.

While the exact order of events of Operation Neptune Spear remains contested as different versions about it circulate, what nevertheless seems to be clear is that a group of highly trained SEALs flew into Abbottabad, Pakistan, and raided the bin Laden compound during the night of May 1 to May 2, 2011 (local time).[47] They killed five people living in the compound, including one of bin Laden's sons and Osama bin Laden himself. After the successful completion of the mission, the SEALs took custody of bin Laden's body, destroyed all sensitive material in the one helicopter that had crashed when landing in the compound, and flew out, body in tow, in the other helicopter. After bin Laden's identity was confirmed, the body was buried at sea, presumably in accordance with Muslim religious rituals.

In my view, Operation Neptune Spear *collapsed* the paradigm of remote warfare that had so far governed the execution of the War on

Terror, as well as the discourses about it. This becomes apparent when considering the technological side of the concept. Notably, while commentators agree that remote warfare technologies, above all drones, were indispensable in finding bin Laden's secret hideout, the actual mission itself was planned and executed in terms of more conventional warfare and combat.[48] It relied on elite human soldiers who were supplied with advanced technology, even though other high-technology solutions were available. Bowden, for instance, explained that this "option allowed the possibility of taking bin Laden alive and, probably more important, . . . if bin Laden was killed in a ground assault, his death could be proved."[49] But the choice to rely on human soldiers also enabled the Obama administration to tap into powerful cultural narratives about fairness and honor in war and fighting in order to frame the mission and endow it with political capital. Thus, the fact that conventional warfare was given precedence over remote warfare in the actual killing of bin Laden effectively collapsed the latter paradigm by suggesting that remote warfare was impractical, even useless, because it did not meet the needs of the situation.

Similarly, Operation Neptune Spear broke down the spatial remoteness in the hunt for bin Laden. The mission essentially constituted a projection of power into a geographically remote area and an autonomous, sovereign nation, signaling to enemies and allies alike that borders and questions of national sovereignty did not matter to the United States when it came to killing bin Laden. Indeed, American aviation technology had enabled the soldiers to travel a vast amount of geographical space in a short amount of time while remaining undetected, demonstrating that they could appear at will in any spot on the globe, overcoming spatial remoteness with ease. Moreover, the SEALs shot bin Laden at close range in his home, nullifying his bodily remoteness. This culminated in the soldiers taking control over bin Laden's dead body, another move that demonstrated American superiority and domination of previously unknown and remote spaces and people.

In that same manner, the raid to capture (and kill) bin Laden broke down any remnants of cultural remoteness. Operation Neptune Spear also projected American power by expressing complete disregard—without fear of retribution—for another nation and culture when the SEALs entered Pakistani territory. What is more, the SEALs' killing of bin Laden also signified the domination and destruction of the Muslim

Other and the terrorist Other in American culture. Lastly, the successful killing of bin Laden shattered feelings of psychological remoteness. As I discussed in the introduction of this chapter, when the news about bin Laden's death became public, spontaneous celebrations broke out in the streets of America. For many people, this information was tangible, describing an understandable action and its causal outcome. It constituted a clearly defined and measurable success in the otherwise desolate War on Terror and tapped into deep-seated cultural narratives, allowing people to indulge in feelings of patriotism and nationalism, as the responses and comments of people quoted at the beginning of this chapter make clear.

But even though the killing of Osama bin Laden, the personification of terrorism against the United States, had been touted as the definite marker of success and vindication for 9/11 and the act had shattered the paradigm of remote warfare, the aftermath was different. Rather, afterward, President Obama, in a powerful move, used the killing of bin Laden to *affirm* remote warfare as the main ideological frame for the War on Terror. In his remarks on May 1, 2011, the president noted,

> For over two decades, bin Laden has been Al Qaida's leader and symbol and has continued to plot attacks against our country and our friends and allies. The death of bin Laden marks the most significant achievement to date in our Nation's effort to defeat Al Qaida.
>
> Yet his death does not mark the end of our effort. There's no doubt that Al Qaida will continue to pursue attacks against us. We must—and we will—remain vigilant at home and abroad.[50]

The president's comments revealed the paradoxical political situation: On the one hand, the killing of bin Laden was widely understood to mark an endpoint, given the central role bin Laden had played in discourses on remote warfare and terrorism in the United States. Yet, on the other hand, the War on Terror would continue unabashedly, thus exposing the diminished importance of bin Laden and ratifying the paradigm of remote warfare as the dominant approach in American foreign policy.

After the initial celebrations over the success of Operation Neptune Spear, the realization that the death of the man once wanted "dead or alive" did not significantly change the course of the War on Terror and its exploitation of remote warfare gradually took hold in American society. This becomes particularly evident when considering the forceful reactions some years later to the CIA Twitter campaign meant to celebrate and commemorate the five-year anniversary of Operation Neptune Spear. On May 1, 2016, the CIA announced on Twitter, "To mark the 5th anniversary of the Usama Bin Ladin operation in Abbottabad we will tweet the raid as if it were happening today."[51] In the hours that followed, the CIA faithfully tweeted the major milestones of Operation Neptune Spear, eventually announcing at 9:39 p.m., "Usama Bin Ladin found on third floor and killed."[52] The PR stunt finished at 1:01 a.m. on May 2, 2016, with the information that "@POTUS receives confirmation of high probability of positive identification of Usama Bin Ladin," followed by the assertion, "Daring #UBLRaid was an IC team effort & in close collaboration with our military partners."[53] The hashtag #UBLRaid was a trending topic that day on Twitter, indicating that the narrative of how the United States finally hunted down and killed the man responsible for 9/11 still stirred up emotions five years later.

The majority reaction, however, was far from positive. Many Twitter users responded to the CIA tweets in a markedly critical fashion. Some posted screenshots of themselves reporting the CIA tweets as violating Twitter's rules of conduct; others tweeted back openly critical or sarcastic comments meant to highlight their rejection of the CIA's tweet series.[54] Famously, *The Daily Show* wrote, "If you live tweet the Bay of Pigs invasion, call us. Otherwise, stop it."[55] Others uploaded various Internet memes and GIFs that showed famous stars or characters from popular television series like *The Office* making excessively shocked and dramatic faces. Posting these exaggerated, clearly performed reactions became another way to mock the tweet series and to criticize what was overwhelmingly perceived as inappropriate gloating by the intelligence community, particularly because it was clear that bin Laden's death five years earlier had not actually ended the War on Terror in any way.

Five years after Operation Neptune Spear, it was evident that even though the killing of bin Laden had been constructed as the main objective of the War on Terror and a symbol for revenge and justice for 9/11, in reality, his death had not significantly changed the course of the War on Terror or challenged the paradigm of remote warfare. Instead, the CIA tweet series brought to the fore the fact that years had passed while geopolitical realities had remained the same, revealing that the United States was engaged in a potentially endless remote war against terrorism globally. As Mark Hughes noted,

> All of that tension and aggression, all of that killing and warfare, all of those revelations about the United States engaging in torture and se-cret prisons and rejection of international law and Geneva Conventions, it was all supposed to be building to this moment. bin Laden's death was supposed to be worth all of it, the justification for what had come before, and in his death the nation had expected some resolution and fulfillment. . . . But the next morning, bin Laden was gone but the rest was still here. The war was still here, the debates were still here, the tor-ture and Geneva Conventions were still here, and the sense that there was never going to be a definitive end to any of it was still here.[56]

Ultimately, the success of Operation Neptune Spear had not only af-firmed the paradigm of remote warfare as a dominant, powerful way to conduct the increasingly expanding War on Terror but also paved the way for remote warfare without end, extended indefinitely in time and space. Indeed, given that more recent military engagements in re-mote places like Syria or Djibouti have barely received any public and media attention, it appears that remote warfare has become the new standard for warfare in the twenty-first century.

Notes

1. Dan Pfeiffer (@pfeiffer44), Twitter, May 1, 2011, https://twitter.com/Obama WhiteHouse/status/64877330794946560?ref_src=twsrc%5Etfw&ref_url=https %3A%2F%2Fwww.poynter.org%2F2015%2Ftoday-in-media-history-in-2011 -twitter-broke-the-news-of-osama-bin-ladens-death%2F340913%2F; Brian Stel-ter, "How the Bin Laden Announcement Leaked Out," *New York Times,* May 1, 2011, https://mediadecoder.blogs.nytimes.com/2011/05/01/how-the-osama -announcement-leaked-out/.

2. Keith Urbahn (@keithurbahn), Twitter, May 1, 2011, https://twitter.com /keithurbahn/status/64877790624886784?lang=de.

3. Stelter, "How the Bin Laden Announcement."

4. Stelter.

5. Barack Obama, "Remarks on the Death of Al Qaida Terrorist Organiza-tion Leader Usama bin Laden," May 1, 2011, American Presidency Project, https://www.presidency.ucsb.edu/node/289988.

6. 25perez, "WWE John Cena Announces Osama Bin Laden Death at WWE Extreme Rules in Tampa 5-1-2011," YouTube video, 2:14, posted May 2, 2011, https://www.youtube.com/watch?v=WfkCEffFENo.

7. Obama, "Remarks on the Death."

8. Elizabeth A. Harris, "Amid Cheers, a Message: 'They Will Be Caught,'" *New York Times*, May 2, 2011, https://www.nytimes.com/2011/05/02/nyregion/amid-cheers-a-message-they-will-be-caught.html.

9. Harris.

10. Harris.

11. Grégoire Chamayou, *A Theory of the Drone*, trans. Janet Lloyd (New York: New Press, 2013), 32; James DeShaw Rae, *Analyzing the Drone Debates: Targeted Killing, Remote Warfare, and Military Technology* (New York: Palgrave Macmillan, 2014), 9; Heather Ashley Hayes, *Violent Subjects and Rhetorical Cartography in the Age of the Terror Wars* (London: Palgrave Macmillan, 2016), 82.

12. Recent developments indicate that the U.S. military has begun to insist on the importance of understanding the culture of the enemy in order to successfully wage war. See particularly Laleh Khalili, *Time in the Shadows: Confinement in Counterinsurgencies* (Stanford, Calif.: Stanford University Press, 2013); and Derek Gregory, "'The Rush to the Intimate': Counterinsurgency and the Cultural Turn in Late Modern War," *Radical Philosophy* 150 (Spring 2008): 1–46. It is important to note, however, that this development does not automatically preclude processes of Othering the enemy based on perceived cultural differences and can, in fact, actually underscore them when, for example, field manuals consistently stress that the enemy's culture and value system are "different" from (and, by implication, "inferior" to) the American ones.

13. George W. Bush, "Address to the Nation on the Terrorist Attacks," September 11, 2001, American Presidency Project, https://www.presidency.ucsb.edu/node/216451.

14. George W. Bush, "Address before a Joint Session of the Congress on the United States Response to the Terrorist Attacks of September 11," September 20, 2001, American Presidency Project, https://www.presidency.ucsb.edu/node/213749.

15. Rae, *Analyzing the Drone Debates*, 9.

16. Rae, 9.

17. Sandra Silberstein, *War of Words: Language, Politics and 9/11* (London: Routledge, 2002), 149.

18. Charles Atencio, "Minefield: The United States and the Muslim World," narr. Peter Jennings, aired October 11, 2001, ABC News, YouTube video, 43:36, posted January 4, 2013, https://www.youtube.com/watch?v=l5XxaMOOP9I.

19. Silberstein, *War of Words*, 150.

20. See, e.g., Douglas Little, *American Orientalism: The United States and the Middle East since 1945*, 3rd ed. (Chapel Hill: University of North Carolina Press, 2008); Sunaina Maira, "Dissenting Citizenship: South Asian Muslim Youth in the United States after 9/11," in *Youth Cultures in the Age of Global Media*, ed.

David Buckingham, Sara Bragg, and Mary Jane Kehily (Houndmills, U.K.: Palgrave Macmillan, 2014), 104–18; Melani McAlister, *Epic Encounters: Culture, Media, and U.S. Interests in the Middle East since 1945*, 2nd ed. (Berkeley: University of California Press, 2005); and Leti Volpp, "The Citizen and the Terrorist," *UCLA Law Review* 49 (January 2002): 1575–1600.

21. Atencio, "Minefield."

22. George W. Bush, "Remarks prior to Discussions with Muslim Community Leaders and an Exchange with Reporters," September 26, 2001, American Presidency Project, https://www.presidency.ucsb.edu/node/214419.

23. Bush.

24. For a similar argument, see also Richard Jackson, *Writing the War on Terrorism: Language, Politics and Counter-terrorism* (Manchester: Manchester University Press, 2005); and Silberstein, *War of Words*.

25. George W. Bush, "Remarks to Employees in the Pentagon and an Exchange with Reporters in Arlington, Virginia," September 17, 2001, American Presidency Project, https://www.presidency.ucsb.edu/node/211537.

26. Bush.

27. Richard Slotkin, *Gunfighter Nation: The Myth of the Frontier in Twentieth-Century America* (Norman: University of Oklahoma Press, 1998), 3–4.

28. Rachel Hall, *Wanted: The Outlaw in American Visual Culture* (Charlottesville: University of Virginia Press, 2009), 22.

29. George W. Bush, "Remarks following Discussions with Chancellor Gerhard Schroeder of Germany and an Exchange with Reporters," October 9, 2001, American Presidency Project, https://www.presidency.ucsb.edu/node/212503.

30. George W. Bush, "The President's News Conference," October 11, 2001, American Presidency Project, https://www.presidency.ucsb.edu/node/216279.

31. Atencio, "Minefield."

32. Atencio.

33. John F. Burns, "Bin Laden Taunts U.S. and Praises Hijackers," *New York Times*, October 8, 2001, https://www.nytimes.com/2001/10/08/world/a-nation-challenged-the-wanted-man-bin-laden-taunts-us-and-praises-hijackers.html.

34. Burns.

35. Patrick E. Tyler, "U.S. and Britain Strike Afghanistan, Aiming at Bases and Terrorist Camps; Bush Warns 'Taliban Will Pay a Price,'" *New York Times*, October 8, 2001, https://www.nytimes.com/2001/10/08/world/nation-challenged-attack-us-britain-strike-afghanistan-aiming-bases-terrorist.html.

36. The Watson Institute for International and Public Affairs at Brown University published a report in September 2016, estimating the total cost for the wars in Afghanistan, Iran, Pakistan, Syria, and Homeland Security at US$7.79 trillion for the period 2001–16. See Neta C. Crawford, "Budgetary Costs of Wars through 2016: $4.79 Trillion and Counting. Summary of Costs of the US Wars in Iraq, Syria, Afghanistan and Pakistan and Homeland Security," accessed March 22, 2020, https://watson.brown.edu/costsofwar/files/cow/imce

/papers/2016/Costs%20of%20War%20through%202016%20FINAL%20final
%20v2.pdf.

37. "U.S. Casualty Status," U.S. Department of Defense, last modified August 4, 2017, https://www.defense.gov/casualty.pdf.

38. Mary Anne Weaver, "Lost at Tora Bora," *New York Times Magazine,* September 11, 2005, https://www.nytimes.com/2005/09/11/magazine/lost-at-tora
-bora.html.

39. Weaver.

40. Mark Danner, "Taking Stock of the Forever War," *New York Times Magazine,* September 11, 2005, https://www.nytimes.com/2005/09/11/magazine/taking
-stock-of-the-forever-war.html.

41. Danner.

42. Sheryl Gay Stolberg, "New Significance for bin Laden Hunt," *New York Times,* September 12, 2008, https://www.nytimes.com/2008/09/12/us/politics
/12web-stolberg.html.

43. Danner, "Taking Stock."

44. George W. Bush, "The President's News Conference," March 13, 2002, American Presidency Project, https://www.presidency.ucsb.edu/node/212036.

45. See, e.g., Julian Borger and Patrick Barkham, "US Television to Censor Videos from bin Laden," *Guardian,* October 12, 2001, https://www.theguardian.com
/media/2001/oct/12/september112001.broadcasting.

46. Mark Hughes, "'Zero Dark Thirty' Review: A Film to Define a Decade," *Forbes,* December 18, 2012, https://www.forbes.com/sites/markhughes/2012/12/18
/zero-dark-thirty/#f59601762e58.

47. See, e.g., Chuck Pfarrer, *SEAL Target Geronimo* (New York: St. Martin's, 2011); and Matt Bissonnette, *No Easy Day* (Boston: Dutton Penguin, 2012). In 2015, respected journalist Seymour Hersh published an alternate account in the *London Review of Books,* arguing that Pakistan knew about bin Laden's compound and closely monitored it, only giving his location up when U.S. financial aid started to decline.

48. See, e.g., Brian Glyn Williams, *Predators: The CIA's Drone War on al Qaeda* (Washington, D.C.: Potomac Books, 2013); and Mark Bowden, "The Killing Machines: How to Think about Drones," *Atlantic,* September, 2013, https://
www.theatlantic.com/magazine/archive/2013/09/the-killing-machines-how-to
-think-about-drones/309434/.

49. Bowden, "Killing Machines."

50. Obama, "Remarks on the Death."

51. CIA (@CIA), Twitter, May 1, 2016, https://twitter.com/CIA/status/7268
24007220125696?ref_src=twsrc%5Etfw&ref_url=https%3A%2F%2Fstorify
.com%2Fdfoxfarrington%2Fcia-tweets-timeline-of-bin-laden-raid. The complete tweet series is archived here: dfoxfarrington, "CIA Tweets Timeline of bin Laden Raid," Browse, accessed August 4, 2017, storify.com/dfoxfarrington/cia
-tweets-timeline-of-bin-laden-raid.

52. CIA (@CIA), Twitter, May 1, 2016, https://twitter.com/CIA/status/7268585 00219924480?ref_src=twsrc%5Etfw&ref_url=https%3A%2F%2Fstorify.com%2 Fdfoxfarrington%2Fcia-tweets-timeline-of-bin-laden-raid.

53. CIA (@CIA).

54. See, e.g., normal person here (@garbagekate), Twitter, May 1, 2016, https:// twitter.com/garbagekate/status/726848361467273216; and Any Mai (@MaiAndy), Twitter, May 1, 2016, https://twitter.com/MaiAndy/status/726861945689792512 ?ref_src=twsrc%5Etfw&ref_url=https%3A%2F%2Fwww.theguardian.com%2F world%2F2016%2Fmay%2F02%2Fcia-live-tweets-osama-bin-laden-raid -anniversary.

55. Daily Show (@TheDailyShow), Twitter, May 1, 2016, https://twitter.com /TheDailyShow/status/726944736552972288?ref_src=twsrc%5Etfw&ref_url =https%3A%2F%2Fwww.theguardian.com%2Fworld%2F2016%2Fmay%2F02 %2Fcia-live-tweets-osama-bin-laden-raid-anniversary.

56. Hughes, "'Zero Dark Thirty' Review."

CHAPTER 8

Home, Away, Home

Remoteness and Intimacy in Contemporary
Danish Veteran Literature

ANN-KATRINE S. NIELSEN

Throughout the 1990s and 2000s, Danish foreign policy has been increasingly (re)militarized. A new Danish stance on the use of military
means and the concomitant participation in international coalitional
warfare have resulted in the emergence of the Danish veteran as a novel
political and sociocultural figure.[1] Reading the veteran as an embodied link to and a metonymic figure of distant warfare, this chapter explores how the veteran inevitably brings Danish society into intimate
contact with the "new" remote wars in, for example, Iraq and Afghanistan.[2] By considering the perspective of the Danish veteran, I aim
to present a more complex notion of remoteness in contemporary
warfare, (re)inscribing intimacy and contact and expanding the analytical focus from the technologies, geographies, and mediascapes of
contemporary war to include the corporal-affective resonances of
remote warfare.

Today, in most Western nations, including Denmark, the act of going to war does not imply an actual march to a locally or even region-
ally situated front line. Contemporary wars are mobilized through air
bases and by commercial airlines transporting the troops to the remote
areas of the Middle East and South Asia where a majority of contemporary Western wars are fought. Additionally, since mass conscrip-
tion is abolished or rendered redundant in most Western countries,
the major part of the privileged civilian populations of the Western
and Northern Hemispheres "get to choose whether or not to pay attention when war is waged elsewhere."[3] Thus, *distance* becomes a central,

multifaceted term in contemporary understandings of and debates on war. *Geographical, technological,* and *existential* remoteness characterize contemporary Western warfare: at present, wars are waged on distant territories, with long-range weapons and drones, and out of mind and touch with the civilian populations on the Western home fronts (see also Annika Brunck's parameters of remoteness in this volume).

The notions of "distance" and "remoteness" in contemporary warfare have, however, predominantly been considered through the lens of (weapons) technology, drones, strategy, and the (ethics of) preemptive strikes.[4] The resulting Americanized, techno-fixated, and future-oriented discourse tends to subdue other aspects and experiences of present warfare at a distance. As Michael Hardt and Antonio Negri write, "The image of a future soldierless war seems to block consideration of the real soldiers who still conduct war today."[5] As such, the incessant articulation of "remote warfare" risks drowning out the actuality and relevance of soldiers' very corpo-*real* experiences of remote warfare. Moreover, when consistently conceptualizing war as a remote and faraway "bodyless" business, we might enhance a sense of existential decoupling of the wars among Western citizens. Thus, we miss the crucial intimacies, the interlacing, and multiple contact surfaces not only between soldier and war but also between war zone and home front, shaping and affecting our political, psychological, embodied, and prosaic everyday lives.[6]

The analysis of two literary works on the Danish veteran, the novel *Mikael* (2014) by author, Afghanistan reporter, and former partner of a veteran Dy Plambeck and the collection of poems *Så efterlades alt flæskende* (2014) by Iraq veteran Mikkel Brixvold, suggests a refocusing on the vulnerable, situated, and affectively entangled human body of remote warfare.[7] The chapter introduces the notions of dis/connectivity, palimpsests, and hauntings in order to probe, respectively, the kinetic, spatial, and temporal experiences of contemporary veterancy. As such, selected from a limited but growing body of Danish veteran-informed art and literature, these two texts forge an encounter with the war as something other and more than a remote (media) spectacle. Rather, they raise the specter of war in a haunting gesture not only affecting the returned veteran but also, in a more general sense, troubling the reader and a Danish civil society hesitantly adjusting to a new role as a belligerent nation state. Hence, the two texts are of interest to the analysis of remote warfare as they allow us to see how the (post)war experience cannot be contained by or bound in the individual veteran body but perpetually seeps and leaks through to create intimate and affective entanglements between remote war, veteran, civilian reader, and society. However, before I engage in this textual analysis, I will set up a framework of remote warfare, war bodies, and modern Danish war history.

Remote Warfare: Globalization, Media, and Bodies

Ever since the constitution of the modern nation-state, wars have been intimately associated with the upholding of national borders and territory. As anthropologist Thomas Hylland Eriksen writes, "Wars are fought by the military, whose mission it is to protect the external borders of the country. A nation-state thus has a clearly defined inside and outside."[8] However, as several globalization theorists have pointed out, the deterritorialization processes of globalization increasingly challenge this assumption. In a globalized world characterized by intensified movement and exchange, as well as feelings of national vulnerability, contemporary warfare is a deterritorialized, complex, and international affair.[9] Today multilateral coalitions and organizations (for example, NATO) often wage wars against non–territorially defined enemies (for example, the War on Terror or that against the Islamic State of Iraq and the Levant). Hence, "security . . . is being decoupled from a statist territoriality."[10] Moreover, as mentioned earlier, the Western waging of wars has by and large been displaced or transferred from the Anglo-European nation-states of the Northern Hemisphere to the southern regions of the globe.[11] In this regard, it is instructive that the Danish War Museum calls the permanent exhibition on the war in Afghanistan "A Distant War." The exhibition describes a young soldier's journey from his Danish home to "distant Afghanistan": going to war is a journey across borders, continents, and cultures.[12]

Contemporary remote warfare, however, has not been entirely decoupled from the Western nation-states. Through ubiquitous media representations, contemporary wars have become representationally more accessible than ever at home. Anthropologists Mads Daugbjerg and Birgitte Refslund Sørensen contend, "Consequences of war and violence are never further away than a TV newsroom or a swipe of your smartphone. In that sense, and even for those who consider themselves uninvolved, the 'distant wars' have become ever present."[13] Thus, globalization and media scholars have shown how global media networks facilitate a distant, ambiguous witnessing and continually inscribe certain information, images, and logics of the remote war zones into the national home and public.[14] As such, the majority of Western populations experience the remote wars primarily as media consumers and spectators. Caren Kaplan characterizes this as a "postcolonial way of life," "living through war that one never knows directly, that one cannot experience viscerally, but that is inalterably structuring of [sic] everyday life."[15] Hence, while remote warfare continually shapes our everyday lives—often without being noticed—for most civilians, these wars are mediated and remote occurrences that seemingly do not have any direct or urgent relation to their lives. Again, from a civilian Western perspective, contemporary wars unfolding as scenes on a screen are technologically, geographically, and *existentially* remote.

In spite of this pervasive sense of remoteness among a Western media audience, contemporary wars do, of course, take place in very devastating, concrete, and tangible ways. As sociologist Kevin McSorley reminds us, "The reality of war is not just politics by any other means but politics incarnate, politics written on and experienced through the thinking, feeling bodies of men and women."[16] The assertion of this chapter is that the literary texts of contemporary Danish veterancy may help the reader make sense of these wars as something other than remote, visually consumed media spectacles. Thus, the veteran figure signals an unsettling presence of the remote wars in Danish society as such. This approach investigates the veteran experience of living in the fissures, joints, distances, and intimacies of remote warfare and stresses the prosaic, carnal, and social continuities of war, as well as its sustained affective impacts on individuals and familial and social structures. Hence, the chapter focuses on remote warfare as a deeply ingrained sensory, intimate, and bodily experience by applying an affect theoretical framework.

Affect may briefly be described as "*forces of encounter*": a transformation, an alteration of intensities and relations in and between bodies caused by an encounter between body and world.[17] The so-called affective turn marks contemporary social sciences and humanities through an interest in corporeal transformations, intensities, and "*in-between-ness*: in the capacities to act and be acted upon."[18] McSorley suggests the need for an affect theoretical approach to and a "corporeal turn" in war studies in the anthology *War and the Body* (2013): "While this will include the examination of specific modes of embodying force and practices of 'warfighting,' the analysis extends both temporally and spatially to consider the bodily preparations for, and the corporeal aftermaths of, war. . . . Indeed, an analytic focus upon the body tends to render any clear demarcation of discrete war zones and times problematic, emphasising instead the enactment and reproduction of war through affective dispositions, corporeal careers, embodied suffering and somatic memories that endure across time and space."[19] As such, a focus on the corporal experiences of remote warfare urges us to include pre- and postdispositions of "war bodies" and to redirect the analytical focus from battlefield to home, from deployment to homecoming, from soldier to veteran. Furthermore, the affect theoretical framework allows us to ask, "What unspoken legacies of war do we carry silently as embodied narratives that shape the lives that we live?"—not only on the part of the war veteran but also more generally on the part of the Danish public.[20]

When investigating the war veteran through this affective framework, we can no longer understand the war and its impacts as past experiences contained within the mind or psyche of the autonomous veteran, who might subsequently freely choose whether to communicate or overcome these experiences. Affect theory is characterized by a focus on bodily material, socioemotional, and trans-subjective environments and encounters. It substitutes the notion of an autonomous, self-contained self for a constitutively open and entangled subject. Thus, we have to abandon the normative focus on subjective transition and reintegration observable in some veteran research (see, for example, the opening editorial of the *Journal of Veterans Studies*).[21] Instead, we may conceive of the war as an affective encounter resonating not only in the veteran body but across the civilian bodies and the national home through the entanglements of (post)war assemblages. The notion of the assemblage is a Deleuze-Guattarian concept used to "think about the relationships between bodies and the flows of affect through space and time."[22] As such, it helps us conceptualize how the war might affectively haunt and reverberate across geographical boundaries and temporal distances, affecting and entangling, for example, military and civilian bodies, war zones and home fronts, literature, publics, and art. Such entanglement comes to the fore, for example, when considering how the emerging veteran figure in a Danish context is constituted by the geographic remoteness of contemporary warfare while at the same time acting as an embodied link to and a haunting metonymy of the remote wars within the Danish public.

The Danish Veteran: A Brief History of War

"The veteran" is a novel presence in the Danish public, political, and cultural imagination. As military historians Niels Bo Poulsen and Jakob Brink Rasmussen state, "It is instructive that the word 'veteran' was virtually absent from public discourse . . . and only came into use as a term for Danish soldiers returning from abroad during the 2000s."[23] The modern Danish history of war can at least partially explain this absence of the Danish veteran.

In 1864, Prussian and Austrian troops defeated the Danish army. As a result, many lives and a substantial part of Danish territory were lost. While some of this territory was given back to the Danish state after a referendum in 1920, a major part remained (and remains) German. Since this nationally diminishing and devastating defeat, Danish foreign policy has been focused on adapting to the alternating power relations of international politics.[24] During the First World War Denmark managed to stay neutral, and during the Second World War German forces occupied the country without major military resistance.[25] Positioned as an international small state, Denmark played a reserved role in international military affairs throughout the twentieth century. Danish soldiers were regularly part of UN peacekeeping missions in, for example, Congo, Cyprus, and Namibia. However, the Danish army was not engaged in any belligerent missions or actual combat for decades. As Poulsen and Rasmussen contend, a "virtual absence of war" for more than a century meant that Denmark "ceased to produce war veterans, at least if we limit the definition to soldiers officially sent to war by the government under the Danish flag."[26]

However, this situation and pacifist attitude started to slowly shift around the end of the Cold War. This happened as a result of multiple national and foreign political changes, such as the annulment of the Soviet military threat and a domestic redistribution of power in matters of foreign policy. As such, during the 1990s and 2000s, Danish foreign policy was increasingly militarized. In the predominantly pacifist small state, a new political majority endorsing the use of military force as a political tool had formed. The seriousness of this new political stance was for the first time tested with the participation in the UN missions in the disintegrating Yugoslavia during the 1990s.[27] However, since 9/11 and the election of a new liberal-conservative, pro-American government in November 2001, Danish military and foreign policies have been closely tied to the American line of action. The deployment of Danish troops has as of late almost become a matter of habit and has resulted in, for example, lengthy participation in the wars in Afghanistan (2002–14) and Iraq (2003–7). The missions in Afghanistan were widely supported in the Danish parliament and by the public—even when Danish forces took over responsibility in the dangerous Helmand province and thus suffered almost forty casualties. The Danish participation in the Iraq War was expectedly controversial. The Danish military engagement was nevertheless maintained until 2007. Subsequently, Danish forces have been involved in missions of various kinds in, for example, Libya, Mali, and the fight against the Islamic State in Iraq and the Levant. The Danish political transition from a pacifist small state to a belligerent nation-state and a loyal coalition partner of the United States has been astoundingly quick and effective. Today it is no longer a question of *whether* to engage the Danish military abroad but *how*.[28]

The thorough (re)militarization of Danish foreign policies has also brought about domestic sociocultural and political changes. Birgitte Refslund Sørensen has shown how a range of new rituals, monuments, and policies has been launched in order to venerate Danish soldiers and establish a new warring national identity.[29] Additionally, the war veteran has since the late 2000s become a debated public figure. The Danish definition of *veteran* states, "By a veteran we understand any person who—individually or as part of a unit—has been deployed in at least one international operation. This person may continue to be employed by the Danish Defense or other state authorities but may also have transferred to the civilian educational system, job market or other."[30] Hence, in contrast to the U.S. definition, for example, a

Danish veteran may still be employed as a professional soldier. As such, the definition applies to all 31,852 Danes deployed between 1992 and 2016.[31] This number is a rather significant portion of a population of approximately 5.8 million people. However, as mentioned, it was not until the late 2000s—almost twenty years after the beginning of the missions in the Balkans and approximately a decade into the Afghanistan war—that the Danish veterans attained national public attention. The tardy emergence of the Danish veterans issue can be ascribed a number of reasons: the long-lived pacifist tradition of Danish foreign politics outlined earlier; the 2006 takeover in Helmand and the formation and maturation of a new "warrior generation" that had seen extensive combat; the persistent work and lobbying of grassroots organizations such as De Blå Baretter (the Blue Berets); and the award-winning series of articles on the physical and psychological injuries of war in the national newspaper *Jyllands-Posten* in 2010.[32]

The article series in particular spurred a national focus on the physical and mental scars of the veterans and the failings of the Danish welfare state to care for them. A media discourse on the scarred veteran formed during the late 2000s. In order to accommodate the needs of the wounded veterans and respond to the intense media debate, the government presented the first Danish Veteran Policy in the fall of 2010. It contains the previously cited official veteran definition and various initiatives to make the new veteran generation feel supported and acknowledged, as well as initiatives meant to compensate for the nation's failure to care for the returned Balkan veterans. Poulsen and Rasmussen conclude, "That Denmark suddenly adopted a veteran's policy was fostered by the new missions in the Balkans, Afghanistan and Iraq. These missions created a whole new generation of more vocal war veterans, just as the wars they participated in represented a new type of military engagement for Denmark."[33] Other examples of recent national initiatives to acknowledge Danish veterans are the annual National Flag Flying Day for Deployed Personnel on September 5 (since 2009), the inauguration of "the Monument of Denmark's international contribution since 1948" (2011), and the establishment of a national Veteran's Centre (2011) administering veterans services, surveys, and research. Thus, as a result of the perpetual production of veteran bodies, experiences, and subjects throughout the 1990s and 2000s, a series of domestic political actions have been set in motion.

Alongside this expanding range of public and political initiatives, a novel focus on the veteran as a cultural figure has presented itself. A range of cultural practices and contemporary artworks such as You-Tube vlogs, ballets, literature, (auto)biographies, pop music, and theater plays about, with, or by veterans examines the relationship between home fronts and war zones from the perspective of the Danish war veteran. These works of art and cultural practices investigate a new Danish reality marked by remote, coalitional, and mediatized warfare through the prism of the veteran. Thus, they probe what it is like to live as a body formed by the distances, connections, and impacts of contemporary wars. As such, a consistent interest in the soldier or veteran experience characterizes contemporary Danish art on the remote wars.[34] Danish literary critic Klaus Rothstein laments this artistic interest in the "experientiality" of war, as he perceives it to be at the cost of a critical investigation into the political landscapes and decisions behind the Danish remilitarization.[35] However, instead of working along the lines of such dichotomous notions of "private" and "political," "experiential" and "critical," we may analyze how the intimate, corporal renderings of the veteran experience in Danish veteran literature become the grounds on which an affectively engaging encounter between the remote wars and a literary public are forged.

Thus, in the following, I turn to the two aforementioned literary works. Both works represent novel aesthetic attempts at describing the new Danish warring reality. *Så efterlades alt flæskende* is the first published poetry collection by a Danish Iraq veteran. The poetry collection addresses a deployment to and homecoming from Iraq, interspersed by fragmented memories of childhood and a troubled adolescence. The poems render the recalcitrance, irritation, anger, ennui, and casual sex of homecoming in a fragmented way and an aggressive lyrical style. The narrative in the novel *Mikael* outlines the development of a romantic relationship between the two protagonists, the soldier Mikael and the war reporter Becky. Set in Afghanistan, Sardinia, and Copenhagen, the novel investigates global intimacies of warfare and the difficulties of accessing and understanding the war experience, the soldier, the beloved other, and the self. One could categorize both works as "war narratives": they deal aesthetically with war experiences. However, as neither of them ends when the soldier returns home, I see fit to treat them as *works of veterancy,* dealing distinctively with the aftermath of war. Hence, both texts describe a homecoming process characterized by friction, alienation, and frustration through the prism of the veteran body. As literary scholar Kate McLoughlin points out, literary criticism is prone to assign the literary veteran a place on the margins of analysis and academic interest.[36] However, attending to the veteran might help us grasp contemporary remote warfare in a new way. In the following section, I will analyze how the texts describe the homecoming process as a kinetic experience of dis/connectivity. This renders the veteran as a figure in between war and home, unsettling dichotomies and tangling up war zone and home front.[37]

Going Home? The Kinetic Experiences of Homecoming

Airports, departure lounges, and airstrips are common inventory items in the Danish veteran experience: in spite of delays and cancellations, they forge the material and infrastructural premises of the connections and movements between the war and the home. We tend to perceive this movement in terms of a physical journey through space, which, because of technological developments, more or less smoothly lets the veteran arrive at the final destination: here, home. Thus, a dichotomous structure dividing home and away, peace and war, here and there, and a concomitant home/away/home narrative of *Bildung,* growth, and adulthood would seem to structure the experience of going to war.[38]

However, a swift physical journey through space from war to home, from camp to hometown, does not solely comprise the kinetic experience of returning from the remote war. One of Brixvold's poems, for example, addresses the slowness of time when awaiting a flight home from the war zone:

> waiting
> for our flight number shows
> on the military departure screen DAYS
> may
> go by[39]

The excerpt simmers with the bodily affective buildup of boredom and frustration boiling over in the capital letters of "DAYS." The veteran is caught in the frustrating logics of global aerial movements and block-age, connections and decoupling. Moreover, when finally arriving home, a corporal, emotional, and existential experience of unsettle-ment continually undoes the flag-adorned homecoming. Thus, the veteran Mikael, longing to go back to Afghanistan, narrates the final words in Plambeck's novel: "Sometimes everything around me feels like a giant vacuum. I cannot sense any life. I do not feel any substance in houses, furniture, traffic, bird song or rain. It does not exist. There is only my wish to go back to Afghanistan. A wish which overshadows anything else."[40] Here, Plambeck describes the return home as an expe-rience of existential emptiness and isolation through a corporal sensation of vacuum and touch. Mikael is out of touch with the meaningfulness of war *and* the intimacy of the home (a well-known trope in war litera-ture; see, for example, Tim O'Brien's *The Things They Carried* [1990], Ben Fountain's *Billy Lynn's Long Halftime Walk* [2012], and Phil Klay's *Redeployment* [2014]).[41] Birgitte Refslund Sørensen has made a similar observation among her interlocutors: "As many veteran interlocutors expressed it, Denmark and everyday life in civilian surroundings loses an intimate sense of home and reappears as an anxiety-provoking terrain or one devoid of purpose and meaningfulness. What is publicly referred to as homecoming many veterans experience as a displacement in to an unsettling environment."[42] As such, the following analysis could be made along the lines of McLoughlin's assertion that liter-ary veterans "question certain notions about personal and social iden-tity: that we live our lives in sequential order, that we remain the same person over time, that mutual respect is the best basis for our relations with others."[43] The war experience seems to have developed not a ma-ture Danish citizen who adds indispensable knowledge and experience to Danish society but rather a veteran longing for war and deprived of a sense of existential meaningfulness. However, in the literary excerpts, the recalcitrant corporal and affective dimensions of the homecom-ing experience are remarkable: a *sensation* of anxiety, frustration, annoyance, vacuum, and disconnection hinders the veteran from ex-periencing the homecoming as a true, encompassing *reconnection* and return. Thus, staying with the affective framework and the con-cern with the corporal discomfort of veterancy, I suggest that instead of turning to the common theme of social identity, we pursue the aes-thetically emphasized sensorial disconnect between veteran and home.

I will describe these ambiguous homecomings through the concept of dis/connectivity coined by sociologists Sven Opitz and Ute Tellmann. Opitz and Tellmann apply this term in order to clarify how global movement is never simply about flows, connections, and links but also implies blockages, disconnections, and ruptures of movement. When analyzing the global flow and retention of money and refugees through offshore zones, dis/connectivity comes to assign a perpetual "making and unmaking of connectivity: between money, law, subjects, spaces, obligations, and accountability."[44] Thus, dis/connectivity affords us the analytical possibility of nuancing the often overlapping and complex sensations of connectivity *and* disconnectivity, movement *and* blockage, of the veteran experience. How does it feel to be a body caught in the flows and ruptures of contemporary warfare determined by international relations and geopolitics?

By means of the turning of the verse and the ruptures of the stanza, Brixvold often works with a rather tangible and literal insistence on such dis/connectivity in his poems. Considering the ambiguities and turns of poetic verses, we may consider poetry as a clear-cut genre for inscribing the dis/connections of remote warfare: oscillating between connectivity and disruption, flow and fragment, the form embodies the kinetic experience of contemporary veterancy. For example, by omitting the description of the homecoming event itself and employing the gaps and fractures of poetry, Brixvold underscores the disconnection experienced by the soldier-become-veteran when abruptly finding himself at home:

> Suddenly one day
> on the way home in the stairwell
> my clothes are strangely radically
> civilized[45]

An alienating and unsettling decoupling and disconnection of clothes, places, and function characterizes the beginning of this stanza: home is a sudden interference and rupture in the flows, meanings, routines, and everyday life of war. Thus, home is no longer a place intimately known but a space devoid of meaning, safety, and familiarity. In another poem, Brixvold once again employs the dis/connections of the verses to examine the dis/connections of remote, globalized warfare

stretched between the Iraqi military camp, Falluja, and Varde, a small
rural village in Denmark:

in from red comes
boy eloped from re-educational stay
who speaks a language they understand
in Falluja and
Varde says he wants to go home where is that
exactly
we ask[46]

Because of the lack of grammatical guidance and the ambivalent verse
structure of the poem, we can read the stanza in two ways. We may
understand the final question—where is home?—to be directed either
at the eloped boy (an interpreter, a runaway Danish boy in Iraq, a
being of global dis/connectivity?) or, since it is common to nickname soldiers after their hometown in the Danish Defense, at a soldier nicknamed Varde. If the latter is the case, asking where the soldier's
home is seems redundant: it must obviously be in Varde. However,
because of the war experience, "Varde" has lost its situating homeliness
and has become nothing more than a random military nickname. As
such, the poem points to the dis/connectivity of globalized veterancy by introducing a nominal confusion and an existential home-
lessness. Furthermore, when confounding the Danish soldier and
the Arabic(-Danish)-speaking boy, the poem also makes unexpected,
unsettling connections of remote warfare visible. Distinctions between us/them and friend/enemy thus become muddled.

The confounding of the intimacies and distances of remote warfare in the two literary works is further enhanced by the consistent
reversal of home and war zone. Plambeck employs several spatial
metaphors—for example, comparing the war to a house, a dangerous
yet well-known home: "Mikael said that the war was a house in which
all the rooms were leading you to the place where you would be killed.
To avoid this you had to organize the rooms in the right way."[47] A subtle reversal of the intimacies of the home and the strangeness of the
war inscribes an uncanny cancellation of the home–away dichotomy:
"When you have been here, Mikael said, you will never truly return
home."[48] Through such spatial metaphors, the war is consistently linked

to and inscribed in the intimate spaces of the body and the home, which in turn become infected by the resonances, routines, and materiality of remote warfare. This is in Plambeck's novel most effectively exemplified by desert sand cutting into intimate space and skin: "There were traces of sand after Mikael in the hallway and in the bathroom, tiny grains of sand next to the sink, fine sand, which cut into my fingers as I pressed them against it."[49]

So exactly where is "home"—in the well-known faraway war zone, in the disturbingly intimate Danish home, here or there? The ambiguities and uncanny reversals of home front and war zone render a veteran figure occupying the interstices and dis/connectivities of remote warfare, marked by an experience of corporal dislocation and affective unsettlement. As such, a fundamentally frustrated kinetic experience characterizes the recalcitrant homecoming in these two literary works: affective dis/connectivity and corporal displacement render the homecomings as incomplete and the veteran as a figure in between. This "in-betweenness" becomes an unsettling experience not only for the veteran but also for the reader when further considering how the remote warscapes infiltrate the Danish home.

Palimpsestic Landscapes: The Spatial Experiences of Remoteness

The rendering of spatiality in the two texts enhances the sense of an incomplete homecoming and the veteran's in-betweenness: a spatial multiplicity or superimposition of the warscapes on the landscapes of the home can be observed. Plambeck writes: "When we came back to my apartment Mikael kept his jacket and shoes on in the hallway, he didn't turn on the lights but went into the living room, out to the bathroom, into the bedroom and the kitchen. He opened the kitchen door and looked down the back stairs. He didn't turn on the lights in the kitchen until he had closed the door."[50] The everyday action of returning home and entering an apartment becomes the scene of an elaborate security scan and military search where the veteran body involuntarily performs and repeats seemingly misplaced actions and patterns of movement. This type of episode has become a reappearing scene in cultural representations of the veteran experience and is often described in temporal terms as a flashback, a symptom of posttraumatic stress disorder.[51] However, in the following, I propose to view the logics of such episodes in spatial terms through the prism of the palimpsest. This may shift the focus from a psychopathological examination of the individual veteran psyche to a broader investigation of how the logics of palimpsestic spatiality affectively inscribe the remote wars into the Danish home and literary public.[52]

Andreas Huyssen describes such spatial multiplicity in terms of the palimpsest.[53] The word *palimpsest* originally designated a manuscript showing traces of two different texts: an original, incompletely erased text and the text with which it has been overwritten.[54] Huyssen, however, proposes reading the cityscape of Berlin as a palimpsest where layers of past, present, and future are continually interwoven.

Similarly, a palimpsestic spatiality comes to the fore in the two texts that are the focus of this chapter when the logics of the past and the war landscape reappear in the present of the safe Danish home. Thus, a military routinized but now displaced, scanning for dangers in the landscapes and architectures of the home, occurs in both of the works:

do not turn the lights on honey light
equals death we can
see in the dark
unlock the door and not before
we are inside
are we safe[55]

Such misplaced actions point us to how the veteran reads space as a "double text," a palimpsestic landscape where the war always resides just underneath the surface. Thus, as a result of the corporal memory of the disciplined veteran body, the remote warscapes may always—like an incompletely erased text—intrude and interfere in the reading of the second, present "text": home. Hence, as war experiences, routines, and landscapes permeate the veteran body, they may suddenly confiscate and erode the assumed temporal and spatial unity and autonomy of the subject, the now, and the home. Thus, these veteran experiences call into question the linearity of time and the autonomy of places and subjects. They point to the entanglement of different times and landscapes. The texts once again render the homecoming of the veteran as incomplete. It is at constant risk of being undermined by a palimpsestic spatiality forging disorienting connections between home and war, Danish apartment buildings and Middle Eastern warscapes. However, this is not solely a disturbing and disorienting experience for the veteran body; as we shall see, it also opens up the possibility of entangling the civilian reader.

Plambeck provides another example of palimpsestic spatiality in her novel. When a pack of cigarettes is stolen from Mikael, he is transformed into a hunting, running, sweating combat soldier taking down his prey, the cigarette thief. The corporal manuscripts of war are superimposed on the prosaic situation in the streets of Copenhagen: "They ran for a long time, blood pumped through his body, sweat appeared on his forehead and under his arms. . . . He shouted at him. His voice resounded between the concrete walls. He stopped and looked up. People were leaning out over their balconies and looking at him. There were people looking at him from behind as well. He stood there for a moment and looked at the people who were looking down upon him. Then he felt that he was cold."[56] Through such scenes of palimpsestic spatiality, Plambeck's novel may be said to touch on what Grégoire Chamayou terms the "contemporary doctrine of hunting warfare," where the logics of conventional warfare are replaced by a merging of military and police logics in a global, targeted manhunt.[57] A reflection on the random targeting of civilians by the always alert, anxious military machine may be spurred in the reader by (dis)placing the hunt to the peaceful streets of the Danish capital and distorting the proportions and reactions of the hunter. The troubling veteran behavior thus becomes a synecdoche of the logics of contemporary "manhunting" warfare as such. It is, however, the corporeality of the excerpt that once again stands out. The literary presentation of corporal processes opens a possibility for the reader to move in close to the hunting veteran body: blood is pumping, sweat is running, and skin is suddenly chilled. When his own resounding echo and the curious gazing residents in an apartment building confront Mikael with the obscurity of his actions, he feels cold.

The final thermal sensation underlines the discomfort of the palimpsestic spatiality. When the logics of the remote warscape reappear in the landscapes of the home, unsettling connections and intimacies are revealed. Distance is revoked through such disorienting spatial experiences in a chilling way. I contend that such palimpsestic discomfort not only applies to the individual veteran's misreading of the situation but also in a broader sense renders the disturbing presence of the remote wars at home. As the pounding heart, the cold sweat, and the chill on the surface of the skin invite a corporal identification with the veteran experience, the text enables a disturbing affective entanglement in the remote wars. As such, the text creates a space for the civilian reader to encounter the embodied, affectively intense war experiences resonating across space and time, borders and distances. Caren Kaplan suggests, "Even when war is presumed to be at a far distance . . . it may still be *felt* or perceived throughout everyday life."[58] The literary text provides an opportunity for such a felt encounter with the remote wars to crystallize. The readers enter this space in different ways and with different backgrounds and, thus, have different reactions to the encounter with the veteran experience; veterans may identify with Mikael, war opponents may pathologize Mikael, other civilians may sympathize with Mikael or be surprised, bored, annoyed, or sad when reading the scene. As Sara Ahmed writes, the "contact is shaped by past histories of contact, unavailable in the present."[59] However, the text works to form an encounter of experiential, bodily resonance, unsettling our prosaic perception of and presumptions about time and space. Thus, the literary work forms part of a (post)war assemblage where the affectively disturbing and unsettling resonances of the war are potentially transmitted across the entangled bodies of war and home, words and flesh, veteran and civilian reader. In the following, turning to the temporality of veterancy, we shall see how this may be understood as a haunting presence of the remote wars in the Danish home.

Haunting: The Temporal Experiences of Veterancy

Kate McLoughlin writes, "Veterancy is a temporal condition."[60] While it is certainly true that *past* actions wholly form the veteran identity, it also becomes clear when examining the veteran experience in the two literary works studied in this chapter that the temporality of veterancy never follows the straight line of conventional time.

For instance, we may observe how in both texts a chronological narrative structure is repeatedly interrupted and fragmented. In *Mikael*, the narrative of the female first-person narrator Becky is intermittently interrupted by the voice of Mikael, the veteran, who through fragments of perceptions, memories, or reflections renders his experiences of war. Thus, while Becky is the creator of narrative cohesion, progress, and linearity in the novel, the veteran voice repeatedly severs the narrative progress of the novel to dwell on reflections and sensations of remote warfare. A similar tension between linear progression and fragmentation may be observed in *Så efterlades alt flæskende.* While adhering to a basic chronology of deployment and subsequent homecoming for the better part of the text, with frequent chronologically ordered "flashbacks" to a childhood and a troubled adolescence, all sense of linear time and narrativity is dissolved toward the end of the poetry collection, where an aggressive, redundant, and lustful ejaculation of words takes over. In a rhythmically spiraling text, the annulment of temporal linearity and progress implies the cyclic, repetitious pattern of war, violence, and trauma:

> until nothing
> is new but forever
> ancient repetitions and
> then
> dies
> even
> time for a while I
> am not old
> enough to feel this
> old . . .[61]

In the poem, even time is temporarily extinguished. As such, the veteran is never in (the right) time but perpetually out of sync.[62] He is caught in the repetitive, transgressive temporality of warfare past—a temporality of haunting.

In the psychoanalytic-Deleuzian-hauntological framework established by sociologist Grace Cho, haunting conveys an unstable, fluid, transgressive temporality in which it is revealed not only "how the past is in the present" but also how affects, silenced memories, and traumas may be transmitted and circulate between entangled bodies.[63] I suggest that the two literary texts examined here can be said to open a space of haunting, a space where not only the veteran but also the reader may become entangled in and haunted by the resonating corpo-*realities* of remote wars.

In both texts, an encounter with a dead civilian child becomes an instance of haunting. In *Mikael,* this traumatic encounter is retrospectively shared by the veteran with—and through—Becky, who once again becomes the narrating, cohesive force: "There was a voice inside of him, who wanted to tell of his experiences, but when he tried to say something out loud it disappeared. Yet he had been able to tell it to me."[64] A complex splitting and embedding of voices is observable here; the veteran's silence is revoked by an unfamiliar "inner" voice, which is embedded in the narration of the listening-writing woman, Becky, whose narrative is again embedded in the text of the novel processed by a (most likely civilian) reader. As such, the haunting feel of a dead Afghan girl in Mikael's arms is transmitted by an array of voices and across a range of bodies entangled in and by the literary work: a (post)war assemblage transmitting an affective unsettling encounter between bodies and pasts is forged. The text invites the reader to feel the "weight of the head as it fell against him when he lifted her out of the wheelbarrow."[65] A space of affectively resonating and haunting encounters with the war is established.

In Brixvold's poetry, we can observe a similar haunting encounter with a dead civilian girl. However, here, the rendering of the episode is broken off by the (un)ending silence of the stanza:

we probably waited
2 seconds too long
hammer heavy judgementhourtime then
he shot her then
we shot him and then[66]

The last "and then" is never completed. The stanza is interrupted as the traumatic event where a civilian girl is held captive in a car and shot by an Iraqi man transgresses the possibility of articulation and leaves nothing but a silent trace of violence and death in the poem: and then . . . In spite of this unresolved silence, a haunting "knowledge" of the fatality and tragedy of the situation may in the context of the literary work's raw lyric treatment of war be transmitted across space and time to the reader. Thus, while the stanza does not explicitly communicate the details of war, but gives up in the face of human tragedy, the reader is still left with "an affective sense that *something* happened," something deeply devastating.[67] The (un)ending silence of the stanza may be read as echoing with unarticulated gunshots, screams, and the shattering of car windows.

Hence, through the rendering of embedded voices, muted voices, and echoing silences, both of the literary works aims to transmit an encounter with the violent realities of remote warfare. Brixvold further engages such affectively disturbing, entangling silences in a poem that lyrically revolts against false media representations and the military censoring of the realities of war. He mockingly writes,

> will you join
> our song will you
> sing in unison with us sing us
> a song about lies and
> nonviolence let us hear us nonscream let
> us let us let us let us let's
> not and pretend
> that everything's all good let us let[68]

As the "let us" anaphor gradually dissolves all linguistic meaning (in the media critical context this becomes a symbolic parallel to the repeated platitudes and the meaninglessness of the renderings of war in contemporary media coverage), an enigmatic *nonscream* stands out. The call to "hear us nonscream" is oxymoronic, as it undermines itself. Even though *scream* is not always considered an onomatopoeic word, it almost inevitably procures the resounding echoes of screaming voices in the auditory memory of the reader and poses the question of *who* actually screams while we are nonscreaming. As the poem forges an auditory, corporally engaging, and affectively entangling encounter between reader, ear, text, veteran voice, vacuum, and war, it thus also implicitly, silently summons the muted screams of remote warfare. The voices of victims may be said to form a silent/silenced yet haunting part of the (post)war assemblages of remote warfare. Hence, through the double negation of "nonviolence" and "nonscreams," the actual violence and screams of war victims are haunting the text, the veteran, and, as such, potentially the reader. Thus, the text presents an intangible but troubling rendering of the Danish complicity in the violence, death, and traumas of war. The poetic oxymoron resounding in the text disturbs immediate linguistic decoding and thus unsettles the reader, allowing for a haunting encounter with the "silent" screams of the war zone.

Of course, one may easily read over, dismiss, or reject this encounter. It requires work and engagement to allow ourselves to be haunted, to perceive the absent presences of remote screams of war at the margins of linguistic meaning and in the gaps of narrative linearity. However, according to Jacques Derrida, such haunting is necessary since "no ethics, no politics, whether revolutionary or not, seems possible and thinkable and *just* that does not recognize in its principle the respect for those others who are no longer or for those others who are not yet *there*, presently living, whether they are already dead or not yet born."[69] If listened to, the haunted voices and haunting silences forge an intimately felt "knowledge" of the consequences of war, which revokes notions of distance and remoteness. Such an intimate encounter with war is highly unsettling in a nation-state still adjusting to its new role as a belligerent agent on a global scale. As the literary works examined here confound distance and intimacy and form part of a haunting assemblage of (post)war voices, art, bodies, ghosts, silences, and veterans, they challenge and renegotiate an abstract sense of the "remoteness" of contemporary warfare in the Danish public—and implicitly, the inaudibleness of screams across geographical and discursive borders. This is also the political potential of the two texts. The affective entanglements, the corporal engagements, and the hauntings of the literary encounter with the veteran text do not allow for the reader to "stand by" on the outside of the (post)war assemblage but instead continually endeavor to inscribe and underline a felt compliance in global histories of war and pain.

Notes

1. See Birgitte Refslund Sørensen, "Veterans' Homecomings: Secrecy and Postdeployment Social Becoming," *Current Anthropology* 56, no. 12 (2015): 231–40; and Niels Bo Poulsen and Jakob Brink Rasmussen, "The Long Road towards an Official Danish Veterans Policy, 1848–2010," *Contemporary Military Challenges* 19, no. 2 (2017): 89–105.

2. Literary scholar Kate McLoughlin terms the veteran a synecdoche. See Kate McLoughlin, *Veteran Poetics: British Literature in the Age of Mass Warfare, 1790–2015* (Cambridge: Cambridge University Press, 2018), 1. However, because of the chapter's focus on intimacy, corporeality, and touch, I prefer *metonymy*.

3. Caren Kaplan, "Sensing Distance: The Time and Space of Contemporary War," *Social Text Online,* June 17, 2013, https://socialtextjournal.org/periscope_article/sensing-distance-the-time-and-space-of-contemporary-war/.

4. In, e.g., Peter Singer, *Wired for War* (New York: Penguin, 2009); Tyler Wall and Torin Monahan, "Surveillance and Violence from Afar: The Politics of Drones and Liminal Security-Scapes," *Theoretical Criminology* 15, no. 3 (2011): 239–54; Grégoire Chamayou, *A Theory of the Drone* (New York: New Press, 2015); Anders Henriksen and Jens Ringsmose, "Drone Warfare and Morality in Riskless War," *Global Affairs* 1, no. 3 (2015): 285–91; Martin Schulzke, "The Morality of Remote Warfare: Against the Asymmetry Objection to Remote Weaponry," *Political Studies* 64, no. 1 (2016): 90–105; Lisa Parks and Caren Kaplan, *Life in the Age of Drone Warfare* (Durham, N.C.: Duke University Press, 2017); and Brunck, this volume.

5. Michael Hardt and Antonio Negri, *Multitude: War and Democracy in the Age of Empire* (New York: Penguin, 2004), 46.

6. For work on prosaic processes of militarization of the home front, see also Cynthia Enloe, *Maneuvers* (Berkeley: University of California Press, 2000); Catherine A. Lutz, *Homefront: A Military City and the American Twentieth Century* (Boston: Beacon, 2001); Mary Favret, *War at a Distance: Romanticism and the Making of Modern Wartime* (Princeton, N.J.: Princeton University Press, 2009); Grace M. Cho, *Haunting the Korean Diaspora: Shame, Secrecy and the Forgotten War* (Minneapolis: University of Minnesota Press, 2008); and Victor Seidler, "Bodies, Masculinities and Complex Inheritances," in *War and the Body: Militarisation, Practice and Experience,* ed. Kevin McSorley (London: Routledge, 2013), 225–29.

7. The English version of the untranslatable Danish title of Brixvold's work is tentatively "Then everything is left assailing/attacking/pork-like/fleshing." Neither of the two texts has been published in English.

8. Thomas Hylland Eriksen, *Globalization: The Key Concepts* (Oxford: Berg, 2007), 15.

9. For deterritorialization and conflict, see also Eriksen, *Globalization;* Kaplan, "Sensing Distance"; David Held and Anthony G. McGrew, *Globalization/Anti-globalization: Beyond the Great Divide,* 2nd ed. (Cambridge: Polity, 2007); Mette Mortensen, "Den digitale slagmark: Danske soldaters krigsvideoer fra Afghanistan," *Kosmorama,* no. 241 (2008): 25–35; John Tomlinson, *Globalization and Culture* (Cambridge: Polity, 1999).

10. Held and McGrew, *Globalization/Anti-globalization,* 53

11. Held and McGrew, 47.

12. "Den fjerne krig," Danish War Museum, accessed June 8, 2018, https://natmus.dk/museer-og-slotte/krigsmuseet/udstillinger/den-fjerne-krig/.

13. Mads Daugbjerg and Birgitte Refslund Sørensen, "Becoming a Warring Nation: The Danish 'Military Moment' and Its Repercussions," *Critical Military Studies* 3, no. 1 (2017): 2.

14. See Mortensen, "Den digitale slagmark"; Kaplan, "Sensing Distance"; and Judith Butler, *Frames of War* (New York: Verso, 2009).

15. Kaplan, "Sensing Distance."

16. Kevin McSorley, "War and the Body," in McSorley, *War and the Body,* 1.

17. Gregory J. Seigworth and Melissa Gregg, "An Inventory of Shimmers," in *The Affect Theory Reader,* ed. Gregory J. Seigworth and Melissa Gregg (Durham, N.C.: Duke University Press, 2010), 2; Camilla Møhring Reestorff, "Den affektive intensivering af Danmark," *Passage,* no. 76 (2016): 98–99. See also Brian Massumi, *Parables for the Virtual* (Durham, N.C.: Duke University Press, 2002); Sara Ahmed, *The Cultural Politics of Emotion* (Edinburgh: Edinburgh University Press, 2014); and Britta Timm Knudsen and Carsten Stage, *Global Media, Biopolitics and Affect* (New York: Routledge, 2015).

18. Seigworth and Gregg, "Inventory of Shimmers," 1.

19. McSorley, "War and the Body," 2.

20. Seidler, "Bodies, Masculinities and Complex Inheritances," 225.

21. Mariana Grohowski, "Letter from the Editor," *Journal of Veterans Studies* 1, no. 1 (2016): i–viii.

22. Jette Kofoed and Jessica Ringrose, "Travelling and Sticky Affects: Exploring Teens and Sexualized Cyberbullying through a Butlerian-Deleuzian-Guattarian Lens," *Discourse: Studies in the Cultural Politics of Education* 33, no. 1 (2012): 9.

23. Poulsen and Rasmussen, "Long Road," 97.

24. Kristian Søby Kristensen, "Indledning: Demokrati, politik og strategi i den militære aktivisme," in *Danmark i krig: Demokrati, politik og strategi i den militære aktivisme,* ed. Kristian Søby Kristensen (Copenhagen: Jurist-og Økonomiforbundets Forlag, 2013), 17.

25. Sixteen Danes, however, were killed on April 9, 1940, when the German military crossed the Danish border. I do not mean to dismiss or ignore this Danish military resistance, the civilian resistance during the German occupation of Denmark (1940–45), or the subsequent Danish contributions to international UN peacekeeping missions throughout the latter half of the twentieth century. However, I do mean to stress that a radical shift in foreign policy was initiated during the 1990s as Denmark transformed itself into a belligerent nation-state for the first time in more than a century.

26. Poulsen and Rasmussen, "Long Road," 92.

27. Denmark also participated in the first Gulf War with the corvette *Olfert Fischer.* However, the corvette was politically restricted from working in and, in fact, from entering the actual war zone. See Bo Lidegaard, *Danmark i krig* (Aarhus: Aarhus Universitetsforlag, 2018), 5.

28. Rosanna Farbøl, *Koldkrigere, medløbere og røde lejesvende—Kampen om historien* (Copenhagen: Gads forlag, 2017), 122. The chapter's outline of Danish foreign policy and warfare furthermore draws on work within history, anthropology, and political science in Lidegaard, *Danmark i krig*; Daugbjerg and Sørensen, "Becoming a Warring Nation"; and Anders Wivel, "Danmarks militære aktivisme," Peter Viggo Jakobsen, "Hvorfor er danskerne så krigsglade og tolerante over for tab?," and Kristian Søby Kristensen, "Indledning: Demokrati, politik og strategi i den militære aktivisme," all in *Danmark i krig: Demokrati, politik og strategi i den militære aktivisme,* ed. Kristian Søby Kristensen (Copenhagen: Jurist-og Økonomiforbundets Forlag, 2013).

29. See Sørensen, "Veterans' Homecomings"; Birgitte Refslund Sørensen, "Public Commemorations of Danish Soldiers: Monuments, Memorials, and Tombstones," *Critical Military Studies,* published ahead of print, 2016, http://dx.doi.org/10.1080/23337486.2016.1184417; and Birgitte Refslund Sørensen and Thomas Pedersen, "Hjemkomstparader for danske soldater," *Slagmark,* no. 63 (2012): 31–46.

30. Regeringen [Danish Government], *Anerkendelse og støtte: Veteranpolitik* (Copenhagen: Forsvarsministeriet, 2010), 5 (my translation).

31. "Fakta," Veterancentret [National Veterans' Centre], accessed July 24, 2018, http://veteran.forsvaret.dk/Omos/sporgsmal/Pages/default.aspx.

32. For more on the "warrior generation," see Thomas Randrup Pedersen, "Soldierly Becomings: A Grunt Ethnography of Denmark's New 'Warrior Generation'" (PhD diss., Department of Anthropology, Faculty of Social Sciences, University of Copenhagen, 2017); for De Blå Baretter, see Lars Reinhardt Møller, *Veteraner—en kamp i civil* (Copenhagen: Lindhardt and Ringhof, 2018).

33. Poulsen and Rasmussen, "Long Road," 102.

34. See, e.g., Solveig Gade, "The War, the Body, and the Nation," *TDR: The Drama Review* 60, no. 2 (2016): 32–47; and Birgit Eriksson, "Are We Really There and in Contact? Staging First-Hand Witnesses of Contemporary Danish Warfare?," *Peripeti,* no. 27/28 (2017): 30–40.

35. Klaus Rothstein, *Soldatens år: Afghanistan-krigen i dansk litteratur og kultur* (Copenhagen: Tiderne skifter, 2014).

36. McLoughlin, *Veteran Poetics,* 2

37. Throughout the analysis, I use *his/he.* As is the case in the two texts, most Danish veterans are male. However, it falls on another analysis to consider this gender aspect of Danish veterancy.

38. See McLoughlin, *Veteran Poetics,* 28–62.

39. Mikkel Brixvold, *Så efterlades alt flæskende* (Copenhagen: Lindhardt and Ringhof, 2014), 43. I have translated all quotes from *Mikael* and *Så efterlades alt flæskende.* Lyrical language characterizes both works, and thus the translations do not do justice to the literary and aesthetic qualities of the books.

40. Dy Plambeck, *Mikael* (Copenhagen: Gyldendal, 2014), 266.

41. Tim O'Brien, *The Things They Carried* (London: Fourth Estate, 2015); Ben Fountain, *Billy Lynn's Long Halftime Walk* (Edinburgh: Canongate Books, 2016); Phil Klay, *Redeployment* (Edinburgh: Canongate Books, 2015).

42. Sørensen, "Veterans' Homecomings," 231.

43. McLoughlin, *Veteran Poetics,* 23.

44. Sven Opitz and Ute Tellmann, "Global Territories: Zones of Economic and Legal Dis/connectivity," *Distinktion: Journal of Social Theory* 13, no. 3 (2012): 267.

45. Brixvold, *Så efterlades alt flæskende,* 45.

46. Brixvold, 36.

47. Plambeck, *Mikael,* 225.

48. Plambeck, 46.

49. Plambeck, 228.

50. Plambeck, 237.

51. "PTSD: Information om sygdom og behandling til veteraner og pårørende," Veterancentret, accessed July 29, 2018, http://veteran.forsvaret.dk/Omos/publikation/Documents/PTSD-folder-web.pdf.

52. The concern of the chapter is with how the remote wars may come to haunt the reader and literary public through the literary texts. Though I am writing of traumatic incidents, I have no interest in diagnosing either the literary veteran or the writer as traumatized or suffering from various mental dysfunctions. Neither of the texts uses diagnoses or medical language to describe the veteran.

53. Andreas Huyssen, *Present Pasts: Urban Palimpsests and the Politics of Memory* (Stanford, Calif.: Stanford University Press, 2003), 49–71.

54. Sarah Dillon, "Reinscribing De Quincey's Palimpsest: The Significance of the Palimpsest in Contemporary Literary and Cultural Studies," *Textual Practice* 19, no. 3 (2005): 243–63.

55. Brixvold, *Så efterlades alt flæskende,* 45.

56. Plambeck, *Mikael,* 240–41.

57. Chamayou, *Theory of the Drone,* 33.

58. Kaplan, "Sensing Distance," emphasis added.

59. Ahmed, *The Cultural Politics of Emotion,* 7.

60. McLoughlin, *Veteran Poetics,* 28.

61. Brixvold, *Så efterlades alt flæskende,* 60.

62. McLoughlin, *Veteran Poetics,* 37.

63. Cho, *Haunting the Korean Diaspora,* 29.

64. Plambeck, *Mikael,* 254–55.

65. Plambeck, 255.

66. Brixvold, *Så efterlades alt flæskende,* 19.

67. Cho, *Haunting the Korean Diaspora,* 181.

68. Brixvold, *Så efterlades alt flæskende,* 42.

69. Jacques Derrida, *Spectres of Marx* (New York: Routledge, 2006), xviii.

PART III

RECONFIGURATIONS

CHAPTER 9

Necrospace, Media, and Remote War

Ethnographic Notes from Lebanon and Pakistan, 2006–2008

SYED IRFAN ASHRAF AND KRISTIN SHAMAS

This chapter takes as its starting point the prevalence of death within geographic locations subjected to remote warfare. It argues that killing from a distance is quite intimate, as the perpetrator perceives itself in relationship with an enemy "other"—a subjectively assessed body located within a particular space.[1] In this supposedly distant relationship, details of another human's spatialization (its objective and subjective geographic characteristics), and the signs and connotations of its embodiment, come together to form the meanings of its death. We utilize critical perspectives on communication (construction of shared meanings) to examine two case studies of remote warfare in which this meaning-making nexus around space, bodies, and death was necropolitical (carried out under a rule of death). As Achille Mbembe asserts, necropolitics seek absolute power over who is allowed to live in this world and who can be "justifiably" killed.[2] Arguably, not all remote warfare is necropolitical. Some instances orient toward only a particular conflict or enemy; war is defined in its use value, as a necessity to resolve *this* conflict. Yet in the two case studies—aerial bombardment and cluster munitions in Lebanon (2006–8), and drone warfare in Pakistan (2008)—remote warfare was imposed to maintain an imperial regime over which human bodies can be continually killed with impunity.

Related to Lebanon and Pakistan, we draw on our observations of remote warfare to explain how contemporary necropolitics create necrospaces—geographic spaces in which residents are allowably killed.[3]

We argue that necropolitics extend the new global economy of war, partly via ways in which inhabitants living in necrospaces try to resist subjugation. This resistance is carried out through the meanings residents make around death, their communication strategies related to it, and their engagements with necropolitical forms and practices of media, all of which have lingering structural and cultural effects.[4] Such mediatization (adaptation of social processes to media processes) of resistance contributes to ongoing war, as it re-creates and projects violent translocal meanings about geographically positioned dead bodies.

During our ethnographic fieldwork for this study, each of us identified processes of necrospatialization, a macabre development in which meanings and materialities of bodies, spaces, and death produce places of "justifiable" killing whose meanings extend beyond the geographic site of conflict. Humans perceive space as signs and symbols that require cognitive interpretation; therefore space is polysemic—that is, open to multiple meanings.[5] As "objective" physical landscapes produce "places"—uniquely situated space, or space with meaning—they are encoded and decoded by humans embedded in social circumstances and constellations of discourses (narratives, arguments, and representations).[6] From this perspective, necrospatialization is a form of relational place-making, a socially structuring process in which humans co-utter and "iteratively create and recreate . . . experienced geography."[7] For example, at the northwestern border of Pakistan, signified as the "lawless" zone of the Federally Administered Tribal Areas (FATA), isolated mountainous terrain becomes geographically meaningful as a place of hiddenness, violence, remote death, and fear.[8] Contemporary media practices, particularly by "legacy" (old guard, elite) media institutions and corporations, not only extend the FATA's unique colonial history; their focus on the aesthetics of war normalizes the FATA's status as an ungoverned space, which works to justify militarization and killing. Both the material and semiotic attributes of landscapes are coconstituted with violent events; a drone strike produces physical destruction and death, while it also reproduces necropolitical relationships and discourses within the geographic necrospace and beyond, through mediated representation, including commercial and alternative journalism.

Geographically displaced, necropolitics operate from multiple sites, including from established centers of power devised from imperial systems.[9] Necropolitics function via diverse ways that states and other strewn actors subjugate certain people—through policies, corporate decisions, economic relationships and trade, foreign aid, institutions, media representation, and so on.[10] Necropolitics operate at levels super and sub to institutional and juridical systems of governmentality, including within global politics and representations that work to validate foreign states violating the sovereignty of other states—in this case, Lebanon and Pakistan.[11] Necropolitical dynamics sometimes cooperate, sometimes collide, and can operate in conjunction with state power or against it. Situated within multiple trajectories and relationships, necrospatialization provides a potent site to translocally contest, signify, or reproduce ongoing war.

Both of our case studies involve an asymmetrical conflict between decentralized, networked Islamic groups and territorialized, non-Muslim-majority nation-states. In the context of the so-called War on Terror, necrospatialization operates as a form of ethnoterritorialism, an attempt to partition space and give it meaning according to ethnic categories and practices. Discursive and material, ethnoterritorial ideas and practices of embodied ethnicity vie to order living spaces and make them the site of various social and political projects.[12] Because ethnoterritorial logics "set in place" other ethnic logics, such as ideas of ethnic cleansing, necrospatialization is both a means and a product of sowing human differentiation and division.[13] We describe necrospatialization within asymmetrical, postcolonial power relationships that linger via macropolitical structures (global press organizations) and micropolitical techniques (journalistic practices).[14] We also point out how necropolitical structures and practices afford sites of resistance, which in turn perpetuate necropolitics.

As a resource to the economy of ongoing war, necrospace contains value not as a host of livelihoods or agricultural or industrial production. The potential value of necrospace is located in its own destruction. Reposed in the new economy of ongoing war, necrospace provides surplus value in its capacity to justify not only *this* conflict but also other, "similar" conflicts. Such retrogressive value of worth-in-destruction permeates intersubjective relationships within the geographic space and, through media, beyond. The two case studies add to the literature on necropolitics; they highlight how necrospaces are indeterminate, but at the same time, they are so retrogressive that even resistance perpetuates logics of death. Notably, in comparing processes of necrospatialization and resistance between the two case studies of remote warfare—aerial bombardment in Lebanon and a drone strike in the FATA region between Pakistan and Afghanistan—we detected nothing novel about the necrospatializing capacity of drones. Both situations of remote warfare exhibited similar necrospatializing currents of news flows, as well as locally situated modes of mediated necropolitical response.

The remainder of the chapter is divided into two sections. The first section provides ethnographic accounts of two cases studies: the summer 2006 conflict between the Lebanese Shi'a Party of God, or Hizballah, and Israel (written by Kristin Shamas); and a 2008 drone strike in the tribal belt of northwestern Pakistan (written by Syed Irfan Ashraf). Juxtaposition highlights how necrospaces are not isolated; they work in combination to justify ongoing war. The first case study emphasizes necrospatialization as discursive, examining how it operates at the level of representation and argument to affect material structure; the second case study focuses on necrospatialization at the levels of material structure and embodied practice driven by discourse. Together, the two case studies illustrate how necrocultures situate locally within trajectories of fraught imperial histories yet are maintained translocally, including within internationally connected media practices and structures. The final section offers analysis of the two case studies, explaining translocal media as a means not only to represent conflict but also to structure and conduct conflict.[15] It argues that, through such mediatization of conflict, necrospatialization (re)produces imperial notions and policies of geographically based human disposability.

Necrospatializing (Parts of) Lebanon, 2006

In July and August 2006, I (Kristin) "watched" from the United States as much of Lebanon incurred major destruction and loss of human life. The summer 2006 war between Israel and the Lebanese Shi'a organization Hizballah began on July 12, 2006, after a cross-border attack by the military arm of Hizballah on the Israeli Defense Forces (IDF). In this operation, Hizballah captured two Israeli soldiers to barter in ongoing, routine prisoner swaps, and at least three other IDF soldiers that followed across the Lebanese border were killed.[16] Within hours, the Israeli military conducted air and artillery strikes not only against the Shi'a political party's positions but also against Lebanon's civilian infrastructure. As Hizballah continued artillery attacks into northern Israel, Israel added an air and sea blockade of Lebanon and a full-scale land invasion of south Lebanon. In the course of the massively destructive conflict, direct damage to Lebanese infrastructure, by the lowest estimates, amounted to US$1 billion. This figure does not include indirect damages or the severe diminishment of the Lebanese agricultural sector over the next ten years due to unexploded ordnance— millions of cluster munitions dropped in southern Lebanon, mostly after the August 14 ceasefire.[17] During the thirty-four days of the war, more than one thousand civilians were killed, forty-three of them Israelis.

The summer 2006 war was a mediated event of "substantial significance throughout the world."[18] In addition to global news coverage, including legacy U.S. and European high-profile news sources, a prolific Lebanese blogosphere emerged that focused on the conflict. As bloggers in Lebanon, Israel, and beyond shared information, opinions, and alternative views of events, the conflict became "the most blogged about war in history."[19] Unprecedented patterns of information produced a global mediasphere of perspectives from victims, witnesses, scholars, and activists. Many blog posts were remediated (presented in other media forms) within global legacy news. As explained shortly, on-the-ground perspectives interrupted the discursive and material necrospatialization of Lebanon.

My initial experience of the war was from the United States as I monitored global media and alternative news sources, including blogs. From November 2006 until April 2008, I intermittently resided in Beirut and traveled to southern Lebanon regularly. For much of the first year, during the drive from Beirut to south Lebanon, I passed through rubble-filled and crater-marked areas of south Beirut and took precarious detours along gravel roads. Unexploded ordnance in southern Lebanon affected the spatial experiences of daily life, as areas had to be avoided and international landmine-clearing teams exploded found ordnance. This section is drawn from my experience of media coverage of the conflict, secondary textual analyses of media coverage, and interviews I conducted in Lebanon after the conflict.

Like previous conflicts in Lebanon, the summer 2006 war was spatially sectarianized; it geographically played out on the basis of what sects (ethnoreligious groups based on religion and ancestry) lived in what areas of the country. The Shi'a spaces incurred the most bombardments and fatalities in the conflict, correlating to Shi'a Hizballah's position as the primary antagonist. Many villages in southern Lebanon were decimated, a majority of them formally and informally associated with Hizballah. Israel also targeted southern Beirut, a primarily Shi'a area, bombing densely populated areas and reducing multiple apartment and other buildings to rubble.

Space constructs boundaries or borders between sects in Lebanon—that is, between Lebanese Druze, Jews, Maronites, Melkite, Orthodox, Protestants, Shi'a, Sunni, and so on—and vice versa: sectarianism constructs social and physical space, as demonstrated by the Green Line separating Christian and Muslim areas of Beirut during the 1975–90 civil war.[20] Post–civil war, contemporary southern Lebanon (which borders Syria and Israel) and southern Beirut (located in the latitudinal center of Lebanon, on the country's Mediterranean coast) are predominantly Shi'a spaces. These Shi'a areas resemble what Giorgio Agamben calls a "space of exception," a space that exists in a precarious relationship to law.[21] All of Lebanon constituted a space of exception during the 1975–90 civil war. Afterward, many Shi'a areas remained precarious as a result of ongoing militarized conflict with Israel, as well as through the ambiguous state status of refugee-descended Palestinian populations living in Shi'a areas.

At least since the 1918–22 creation of the border between Palestine and Lebanon, Zionists have pushed for the inclusion of southern Lebanon in an Israeli state. Motivations include the "historical" status of southern Lebanon as part of Eretz Israel, as well as water resources and strategic transportation routes.[22] Militarized occupation and conflict work with this imperialist cartography: the Israeli military has been active in southern Lebanon since the Palestine Liberation Organization moved in from Jordan after the 1967 Arab-Israeli War. Between 1982 and 2000, the IDF conducted a full-scale militarized occupation of southern Lebanon, which created a monitored, secure border between south Lebanon and Lebanon north of the Litani River. After Israeli withdrawal in May 2000, a sectarianized Lebanese state stalled in its redevelopment and extension of services into the south of the country, which facilitated Hizballah's increased presence and management of the area.

Similarly, southern Beirut has been structured through conflict and sectarianism. After the 1975–90 civil war, Beirut's urban spaces include Christian enclaves to the north and Shi'a enclaves and Palestinian camps to the south. Over the decades, Shi'a displaced from southern Lebanon by Israeli incursions have continued to move into southern Beirut; increasingly dense overpopulation strains state governance and authority, a structural void filled by Hizballah.[23]

Historically situated, spaces of exception lend themselves to the controlling technologies of necropower and its productive logics of death.[24] The 2006 conflict between Israel and Hizballah rapidly escalated and instantaneously garnered 24/7 global media coverage. Western legacy news represented Shi'a-controlled southern Lebanon and southern Beirut as spaces in which the inhabitants could be justifiably killed.[25] Legacy media relied on preexisting journalistic shortcuts to depict Hizballah as a "shadowy," "faceless evil" rather than explaining the party's complexities within Lebanese society.[26] Western news outlets asserted that Israeli actions were justified; U.S. photojournalism depicted Hizballah as aggressors and Israelis as defenders.[27] Traditional global media relied on already existing, culturally congruent stereotypes and militarized tropes (for example, "smart, strategic warfare") and explanations from Israeli military commanders to report on the conflict.[28]

Key to the process of necrospatializing areas of Lebanon was to cast bodies as disposable just for being resident. As Derek Gregory describes, the 2006 Hizballah–Israeli conflict involved "the death of the civilian," as first Shi'a and then all Lebanese were positioned by Israeli spokespeople as complicit with Hizballah fighters and thus "justifiable" targets.[29] Near Qana, a village in southern Lebanon, on July 30, 2006, sixteen Lebanese Shi'a children were among tens of civilians killed in an airstrike on a building in which they were sheltering. Israeli spokespeople stated the building was targeted because it was next to an arms cache or it was a "hiding place for terrorists."[30] In other instances, Israel asserted that the population was hiding military hardware or

Hizballah fighters among the population, in schools, in UN shelters, among aid workers, and in humanitarian convoys.

As a strategy oriented to audiences beyond the geographic site of conflict, the construction of justifiable targets varies according to differing historical and imperial relationships. From the first day of conflict, Israeli spokespeople put in place a discursive framework that threatened to necrospatialize all of Lebanon beyond just Shi'a areas. Israeli military spokespeople warned they would "turn Lebanon's clock back 20 years . . . if the Lebanese government did not manage to rein in Hizballah."[31] Israel's Ministry of Foreign Affairs attributed responsibility to the Lebanese state for Hizballah's militarized hostilities against Israel from Lebanese territory.[32] In line with bellicose statements toward Lebanon from Israeli prime minister Ehud Olmert, all of Lebanon outside Hizballah/Shi'a areas was treated as "fair game" by the IDF for bombing and artillery.[33]

To resignify all of Lebanon—population and infrastructure—as a justifiable target, Israeli forces utilized a retrogressive discursive framework different from the frames employed to necrospatialize Shi'a areas. The Israeli military worked through war to induce state failure in Lebanon, and through discourse to position Lebanon as a "failed state" in the hands of a rogue militia backed by a terroristic Iranian regime. During the conflict, the Israeli military manufactured a scale of displacement and death and a blockade of resources that would render the Lebanese state institutionally and structurally incapable of dealing with the conditions of violence. Israel engaged in a complete sea blockade of Lebanon and a restricted air blockade. Fuel tankers remained docked in Cyprus, preventing a new supply of fuel to Lebanon for a month. Hospitals, already strained with high numbers of injuries, lacked fuel for generators. Thousands of displaced people inhabited parks or deserted buildings.

Concurrently, global legacy news represented Lebanon as a weak or "failed" state known for its cyclical history of violence. Imperial consternation about the capacity of Lebanese for independent sovereignty goes back to the 1920 transition of Lebanon from an Ottoman-controlled district to one mandated by the French. Subsequently, "failed state" narratives have informed journalistic and development discourses about the country, including recent journalistic "shortcuts" that evoke the 1975–90 civil war to provide salience and meaning to contemporary events.[34] This was the case in summer 2006. Besides highlighting the presence of Islamic "terrorists" in Lebanon, Western legacy media positioned the conflict as a proxy war between Iran and Israel or the United States, with the weakened or "failed state" of Lebanon subservient to Hizballah or Syria and Iran.[35] As constituents of a failed state incapable of controlling a resident terrorist militia, civilian populations and the spaces they inhabit were positioned as legitimate targets. Strategies to create a state crisis and justify targeting a population were based in local experience and history yet translocally dispersed through the representational power of legacy media.

However, contemporary mediatized conflicts comprise media flows that are not "top-down" but also "bottom-up."[36] From the start of the 2006 war, an unprecedented number of grassroots bloggers writing about the conflict worked to interrupt dominant military and journalistic narratives and bring on-the-ground perspectives to Western legacy news coverage. Rapid grassroots media-oriented responses to necrospatialization emerged from Lebanon's particular history. Since the 1975–90 civil war, much Lebanese cultural production (novels, films, and other art) has indicted international media misrepresentations and oversimplifications for having perpetuated conflict and international tolerance for the long Lebanese civil war.[37] In interviews I conducted between 2006 and 2008, Lebanese bloggers reported that their primary motivation for blogging during the 2006 conflict was that, again, war in Lebanon was being misrepresented and underexplained.

A day after the start of the war, bloggers called for those in the United States and the rest of the West to counter traditional news bias by "talking to people" and circulating other information.[38] Blogger Z. in Quebec posted a letter to his blog from an expatriate in Beirut that stated, "I want to reiterate that we need your help in disseminating this information and hopefully getting it to the press. The news you are receiving is skewed."[39] Such comments articulated a media praxis against necrospatialization focused specifically on political power outside Lebanon. Bloggers made available broader currents of information and analysis; they described Lebanon's complex social and political makeup, they dialogued about historic relations between Israel and various Lebanese groups. For instance, the Wizard of Beirut provided a detailed explanation of the geography and conflict surrounding Shebaa farms, pointing out that continued Israeli occupation of the hamlet provided Hizballah an excuse to attack Israel.[40] Bloggers critiqued dominant Western accounts of conflict and rebutted official Israeli assertions of precise instrumentality and minimal damage: "55+ dead, 21+ children. Must be those precision smart bombs that Condy Rice rushed to Israel."[41] Bloggers further denaturalized the myth of "clean warfare" by compiling and highlighting evidence suggesting the use of illegal forms of weaponry by Israel, including white phosphorous.[42]

Bloggers and other activists utilized interactive communication technologies to disseminate multimedia evidence of damage to civilian areas and citizen casualties.[43] Tears for Lebanon linked to Flickr to circulate photographs of damaged buildings and victims of cluster bombs.[44] Scholars produced a map of areas hit in the strikes for website Al Mashriq and linked it to Google Earth; bloggers circulated links to the map on the website.[45] After the bombing near Qana on July 30, in which the IDF attempted to characterize the civilians killed, including children, as Hizballah allies and thus as justifiable targets, bloggers intensified their efforts to contest Israeli explanations.[46] A photo collage of injured and dead children circulated, and bloggers posted photos of demonstrations against the war in Lebanon, including protest signs addressed to Western audiences.[47]

Legacy media outlets such as Fox News, CNN, BBC, the *New York Times,* and the *San Francisco Chronicle* remediated blogs on their platforms.[48] Lebanese bloggers broke a story on the Israeli shelling of oil storage tanks on Lebanon's southern coast and the environmental crisis that ensued. The blogs that broke these stories formed the coverage of the events by legacy news media when they finally reported on the Mediterranean oil spill. As the world witnessed the cost of the war for the people and environment of Lebanon, news reports briefly replaced the necrospatializing nomenclature of "clean, smart war" with discourses on the humanitarian cost of the war for Lebanon. In particular, after the July 30 Israeli bombing of children and civilians near Qana, reports in the United States and Europe framed Lebanese and Lebanon as victims and the Israeli response as disproportionate.[49] International opinion shifted, to varying degrees, against Israeli air strikes and military operations. On July 31, Israel announced that it would pause air strikes for forty-eight hours.[50] A permanent ceasefire to the conflict followed on August 14.

In interviews, bloggers described their media activism as an attempt to replace the absence of reporting on Israeli aggression in global news narratives with presence; they sought to document the sea blockade, the food and petrol shortages, and the inability of civilians to vacate. More generally, they sought to convey the war's brutality. Some Western commentators described the images of death in blogs and Arab satellite news as reflecting a "bloodthirsty" Arab penchant for death.[51] Yet various bloggers described their necropolitical praxis of showing dead bodies in contexts related to historical U.S.–Arab relations. They discussed how sanitized images of war support imperialist discourses. One blogger described photos of dead victims on his blog as a direct response to "a U.S.-sponsored war. If people in the U.S. don't want to see these images, then tell your government not to sponsor wars on Arab people."[52] Bloggers emphasized that pictures of the dead were circulated to *explain* the experience of violence. As one blogger stated, "If they don't see what U.S. bombs do, then they will continue to give Israel bombs."[53] Another used images of the dead not just as a call for political action to end this particular war but also as a necessary comment on the capacity of humans to inflict suffering on other humans: "Only if we know how truly capable of ugliness we are, we can move forward."[54]

New forms of media technology provide a potential site of resistance to necrospatialization, as historically situated hegemonic struggles are waged to make meaning of and signify death. Yet, through new media and remediation, necrologics are not only contested, they are reproduced. The next section describes how death functions at both discursive and material levels within necrospatialization, providing an ethnographic case study of embodied journalism and necropolitical activism as it happened on the ground.

A Stateless Life in Pakistan's Tribal Belt

The Federally Administered Tribal Areas (FATA), a buffer zone between Pakistan and Afghanistan, is home to six million Pashtuns whose representation is the site of the politicization of difference. For example, the FATA's local identity as *illaqa ghair,* an "alien land," was a marker of ethnoterritorial difference developed by the British at the start of their colonial regime in the area during the second half of the nineteenth century. Before that, independent Pashtun tribes lived in this region under their Indigenous cultural code, called Riwaj. The roles and responsibilities that unified these scattered tribes were collectively defined.[55] Chagha (the call) was a local summon for raising Badraga and Lashker. Badraga is a group of local volunteers organized from villages and tribes. Lashker, on the other hand, is a tribal militia of volunteers. The use of such conflict-resolution mechanisms created in-group solidarity against out-group aggression, helping these tribes to not only resolve intratribal conflicts but also, through Riwaj, to keep their ethnonational identity as Pashtuns intact. However, they were unable to sustain these Indigenous sociocultural practices and processes in the face of a rivalry between the British Empire and Russia in the nineteenth century.

In order to establish strategic control over trade routes leading to Russia in the north, the British colonial regime of the United India not only imposed three wars on neighboring Afghanistan, it also marked the Pashtun-dominated geographic fringes of the United India as a bulwark of colonial cartography. As a first line of spatial defense, the FATA was carved out in 1893, and another administrative boundary, that of the North-West Frontier Province, was drawn in 1901. Peshawar was made the capital city of the province. In this politics of differentiation, the British treatment of the tribal Pashtuns tied the latter's political identity with colonial interests. Ethnopolitical differentiation was reinforced through the imposition of the Frontier Crimes Regulation, which stripped tribal Pashtuns of their juridical and political rights. Sitting in Peshawar, the Office of the Governor ruled the neighboring FATA on behalf of Delhi, the capital of the United India. Reducing Pashtuns to ethnoterritorial bodies helped the British turn the FATA into an appendage of imperialism, a militarized bulwark against Russia, an extrajuridical status that Agamben calls a "state of exception."[56]

This exclusion of the stateless tribal people continued after the British left the subcontinent in 1947, the year Pakistan and India became two independent countries. Reinforcing the colonial marginalization of the FATA's ungoverned space, the new rulers of Pakistan began to use the FATA's tribal people and their land as a foreign policy tool. Tribal Lashkirs were sent to fight in Kashmir against India in 1948, against India on the Lahore front in 1965, and against the Soviets in Afghanistan in the U.S.-funded Afghan war in 1979.[57] Having their ethnoterritorialized bodies used as part of the national security strategy made life a zero-sum game for the tribal Pashtuns of the FATA. Their backwardness was deemed indispensable for the good of the country. In Pakistan, for example, veterans of the Afghan war were officially called "good Taliban" (Taliban means "seminary students"). In 1998, the much-celebrated Taliban even fought alongside Pakistani troops against India in the Kargil War. In the post-9/11 context, however, this politics of differentiation saw a new shift, turning the FATA into a bedrock of global terrorism, a buffer state that "can be interpreted as classic territorial exceptions—states by virtue of not being other states."[58] The FATA's status as a space of exception, subject to the use of the state's necropolitical technologies and violence, intensified after 2001 when the United States launched the so-called War on Terror. Pakistan participated in the war apparently to eliminate al-Qaeda's sanctuaries in Afghanistan.

Although Pakistan became a frontline U.S. ally, the United States held Pakistan responsible for not doing enough to stop al-Qaeda from crossing from Afghanistan into the FATA. The Western media also blamed Pakistan for playing a "double game," and the Pakistani mainstream national press declared al-Qaeda an "elusive" entity to track.[59] Yet Pakistan's alliance with the United States continued. What followed was the start of high-tech drone strikes in 2004 in the FATA by the U.S. military, a wave of death and destruction whose lack of discrimination was attributed to the supposedly ambiguous nature of al-Qaeda. Carried out secretly with the consent of Pakistani authorities, these strikes reinforced the historically situated politics of differentiation and the FATA as a "state of exception." From 2004 to 2018, a total of 430 U.S. drone strikes were carried out in the FATA, killing between 2,515 and 4,026 people, including militants and civilians.[60] Hence, the "uneven geo-legalities of war, state discrimination, and exception make drone warfare a reality in certain spaces and not others."[61] The War on Terror aligned the interests of U.S. imperialism, the Taliban, the global media, and the Pakistani state in reinforcing the tribal peoples' ethnoterritorialized status. This is explained in the next section in reference to the FATA's village of Damadola.

Damadola, Deaths, and Drones

Damadola is a small, hilly village of scattered houses in the FATA. In 2006, around ninety people were killed in this border site during a U.S. drone strike, including eighty students, mostly children aged four to fifteen years. The high-profile attack was carried out on a religious seminary to target al-Qaeda's second in command, Ayman al-Zawahiri.[62] However, the target was too elusive to be hit. Working as a Peshawar-based reporter with a national television channel, I often visited the FATA from 2006 to 2010 and kept a notebook in which I recorded observations. I published around fifty articles in national and international media based on these observations. Although I did not visit the site of this particular drone strike for my reporting, I have noted details of many drone strikes similar to this one, in which the nature of targets was unclear and media reporting misleading.

For example, the *New York Times* published the iconic Associated Press picture of the first Damadola strike, accompanied by the story of a journalist of Pakistani origin entitled "Pakistan Says It Killed 80 Militants in Attack on Islamic School." The picture went viral and was reprinted in different international media networks with the Associated Press caption that was published in the *New York Times* story. The caption said, "Tribesmen attended the funeral for up to 80 people killed when the Pakistani military launched an airstrike on a religious school near the Afghan border." In the wide-range camera view of the photo, around twenty-five shroud-draped dead bodies of madrassa (school) students are shown arranged in cots, lying in rows close to the targeted site. Surrounded by hundreds of local onlookers, the bodies are the center of a public spectacle. This necroevent was apparently organized to invoke local solidarity and to highlight the tragedy in national and international media. As was known locally and outside the conflict zone, this tragedy was caused by the U.S. strike in pursuit of an elusive target. However, when the *New York Times* published the picture, it attributed the strike to Pakistani military, which also took responsibility, as mentioned in the caption: "A military spokesman said the bombed building was housing militants who had used the site as a terror-training facility."[63]

The reporting of elusive targets misled in that it kept hidden the dreadful culture of distant warfare in the FATA, where imperialist militarization was promoted by bombing local territories and people. More notably, it also raised the market value of local journalists whose ability to access the war zone made them a dependable local source of crucial information on drone strikes. Through my notes on a second drone strike on Damadola, and through quotes from an eyewitness account of the event by a local Pashtun journalist associated with a popular international news media organization, I want to demonstrate how local reporters provide an on-the-ground, embodied perspective on how life is subjected to the rule of death, in this case at the site of journalistic professionalism and practice. By comparing two accounts of the same event, based on real-time notes and postevent media coverage, I explain the way necrocultures are transformed into discursive media practices, a reflexive exercise in which local reporters reinforce elements of fear by using terrorism as fodder for their stories, weaving a narrative that is meant for market consumption only.

On May 14, 2008, a drone strike hitting an elusive target on a dark, cloudy summer night invited local journalists' attention to Damadola. Sitting in my Peshawar office, I received a journalist friend's phone call. "A drone has struck again," said Riffat Orakzai, a BBC correspondent. We later found out that around eighteen people were killed in the strike, including foreign militants.[64] Those who follow counterterrorism operations in Pakistan know that this distant drone warfare carried meanings larger than the sum of its on-the-ground destruction: Pakistani military rules this theater during the daytime, the Taliban come out at night, and U.S. drones rule the skies 24/7. This militarization defines the global value of local journalism. The plans, reputations, and economic livelihood of the Pashtun reporters depend on their insight into the theater of war. Reporting for local, national, and global media, they must be aware of every strike to sell news and offer analysis of the on-the-ground situation. Orakzai's telephone call to me suggested the significance of the drone attack and his eagerness to visit the site for possible clues to the high-value, elusive target.

The timing of the strike was notable. In 2008, the Pakistani state was engaged in secret peace talks with al-Qaeda-inspired rival Taliban groups, called in Pakistan the "bad Taliban."[65] Local reporters looked at the FATA, fearing that the U.S. drone strike might sabotage the peace process. The fresh attack raised eyebrows in Pakistan. The Taliban had cordoned off the site within minutes after the strike, indicating the killing of a highly ranked target.[66] Orakzai's informer, a tribal reporter, had talked to a Taliban group that agreed to take Peshawar-based reporters to the site of the strike in order for them to record anger against the U.S. aggression. These factors made the coverage worth risking travel into the FATA.

We, a group of seven reporters riding in two cars, left for Damadola in the early morning. Upon entering the FATA, there is an uncanny sense of insecurity; it is a spine-chilling ride amid towering mountains. Traveling on alternative routes, the group made a brief stopover in a thatched restaurant, where the residents cautioned the reporters about the hazards of going deep inside the war zone. Passing through imposing beige mountains on both sides of the barren road, signs of terror added to the uncomfortable warmth of the day. Burned vehicles marked the Taliban's attack on a military convoy, revealing the Pakistani military's apparent challenge in policing its border with Afghanistan. Roadside houses made of mud and stones looked abandoned, constituting a mark of fear reinforced by an eerie silence in the surrounding area. We were later told that unscheduled spells of curfew had literally imprisoned people inside their houses. It took us two hours to reach Nawagai, an entry point into Bajaur, a fort-size garrison structure at the middle of a mile-long mountain pass. Constructed at a corridor whose opposite side was blocked by majestic hills at the foot of which is a dry riverbed, this ghost site was part of an old colonial structure located at a safe distance from the road. As we waited for our turn to cross the checkpoint, a chain hooked to a barrier, worried truck drivers with heavy loads of supplies were being quizzed by about ten security officials.

Committed to reaching our destination, our party of journalists came down the steep pass, entered a drainage channel carved out by flood water, and entered Bajaur Agency by traveling a mile into the dry channel. Hiring a local taxi driver, who skillfully drove through a web of alternative routes, we reached our destination only to find a few armed Taliban interrogating the local informer who had invited the Peshawar-based journalists. Calling all journalists "state agents," the Taliban group threatened to kill the visitors. However, timely intervention by a friendly Taliban group settled the issue. Taking reporters to the site of the drone strike, the friendly Taliban group asked the head of the aggrieved family to appear on camera. Villagers in the hundreds thronged the site, yet they were all tight-lipped. In his BBC website report, Orakzai explained the situation: "Taliban militants appear to be in complete control of two Bajaur sub-districts, Mamund and Salarzai, and people seem to be reluctant to express their opinions freely. . . . So there is no way of knowing who was killed in the attack, and whether any foreign al-Qaeda militants were among the dead. . . . There were hundreds of people as well as armed militants at the scene of the missile strike. They were unanimous in their condemnation of NATO troops for carrying out the attack. . . . They seemed to have been told not to discuss these matters with the press."[67]

Talking to reporters, the aggrieved family expressed anger at the loss of three of their members and vowed to take revenge. This encouraged the surrounding Taliban to incite people to raise a collective call for revenge. The Taliban chanted "Allaho Akbar" ("God is great," an Islamic incantation), which drew the focus of the visiting reporters. Ironically, the caption to the picture of the site of devastation released by the international British news agency Reuters, published outside Pakistan, did not mention the armed Taliban standing in the first row. The caption reads, "Tribesmen chant anti-U.S. slogans after a missile attack in Damadola village of the Bajaur tribal region in Pakistan May 15, 2008."[68] This caption portrays the show of strength in a local context, calling the protesters "tribesmen." It is a misrepresentation that risks signifying the conflict with a local "tribal" character, rather than signifying it as a systematic, sophisticated global conflict that involves the Taliban, the Pakistani military, and the United States.[69]

This media representation of the congested site provided gruesome evidence, a graphic scene that helped the Taliban incite local revenge and demonstrate strength before the visiting journalists. The roof of the two-story concrete structure bore a gaping hole and the surrounding veranda was ripped apart beyond repair. Everything was burned black yet still standing. The stench of burnt human flesh hung in the damp air, making it difficult for us to stand inside the structure. Outside the partly gutted house, which was built in the mountain's basin at the edge of a crop field, six burned bodies were arranged on thatched sheets in the courtyard. The bodies, which, contrary to the Islamic tradition of burying the dead as soon as possible, were displayed on wooden cots, attracted visitors and provided a novel photo opportunity for the visiting reporters. The shrill voice of a tall, lean, and thick-bearded local cleric animated the scene. His sermon, delivered in a piercing voice, was the only rhetorical force to break the spell of this macabre display, a call to fight back and a challenge to the United States.

Looking at the audience and then at the journalists' cameras, the cleric's flailing hands reinforced the rhetorical value of his vengeful words. "We follow one God and that is Allah," and "we face one enemy and that is America." Every time the cleric repeated the words *God* and *enemy*, his index finger went up, directed at the clear, blue sky. The Taliban, talking to the visiting reporters later, stated that the drone strikes were an effort to derail the Taliban's "peace talks" with the Pakistani state.[70] This understanding of the war brought the Taliban and the Pakistani state to the same page, making the War on Terror as contradictory as the historical process of creating stateless ethnoterritorialized bodies.

Media practices are key to reinforcing theatrics of contemporary militarization in the FATA. During the entire ride back, a BBC reporter repeatedly asked me to scan the sky for drone predators. Despite my assurances that no drone was in sight, my colleagues were apparently tense and frightened, indicating an awareness that one's mere presence in the space made a person vulnerable to the terror of the drones. This fear, albeit genuine, contained a professional value. In reporting for their respective media outlets, the local reporters reflected this fear in their stories. The reflexive write-up of one of my colleagues, for instance, exemplified this fear in the following BBC report from 2008: "It wasn't the mountain terrain, or the fact that we were driving along a completely deserted track. It was the fear of another NATO strike. One of my colleagues from Dawn News was sitting next to the window. While the militants engaged us in conversation, I quietly urged him to keep scanning the sky for a NATO drone."[71] This is a pattern of media coverage whose commercial value depends on its own discursive contribution to necropower. In the next section, we consider how necropolitics reduce some humans to ethnoterritorial bodies in order to reinforce imperialism through a mediatized politics of differentiation.

Necrospatialization

As seen in the two case studies, a historically constituted territorial "space of exception" provides the framework for necrospatialization.

The juridical and political insignificance of people in these territories is reinforced through a combination of violent destruction within and political discourse about their territorialized space. Violence, discourse, and space are coconstituted. For example, the sky served as a symbolic reference in the sermon of the Taliban cleric to identify two sovereignties, the divine order and the U.S. imperial order. Spatial actions (drone strikes) create on-the-ground repercussions (including discourse), giving necropower an organic, locally specific nature and structure. This groundedness of spatialized necropower—its embeddedness within local specificities and history as it retrogressively produces a space's value-in-destruction—is key to understanding the longevity of the conflicts discussed, cycles of violence in which militants are killed yet militancy increases with each strike. It is also key to understanding how necropower functions to produce ongoing war, with no end in sight.

In conflict, control over the meanings of local death constitutes a form of power; thus there is a "deliberateness" to the representation of death that corresponds to media logics, practices, and structures.[72] As commercial media consumption is driven by audience fear, reporters of conflict increase media value by reinforcing a presence of violence; risk adds value to the reporter's experience, while violence produces reports that appeal to a commercial, global media structure like the BBC. Yet, besides increasing media value, conflicts mediated by legacy media reinvent ethnoterritorial bodies according to fear and rebrand places as continually "terror spewing." In both the case studies, rather than explain historical power relations and systemic violence, legacy media spectacularized conflict according to a localized palette, recreating southern Lebanon and the FATA as historically situated "spaces of exception." For example, the people and spaces in the FATA were globally signified by the Taliban's calls for revenge, rather than by local realities of widespread fear and oppression. In both case studies, violence was portrayed as a local shortcoming, a lack of official control over historically situated "savage" affairs in that space—over a "terrorist" militia, a "failed state," or a "tribal" desire for revenge.

In the case studies, necrospatialization relied on an imperial process of differentiation, a mediatized construction of a spatialized "other." As Dag Tuastad describes, "new barbarism"—localized depictions of "barbarism versus civilization" by legacy media and Western spokespeople—work to justify continued U.S. or Western military and political intervention against Muslim networks.[73] Lebanese bloggers usurped this mantle of necropolitical spectacle—barbarism versus civilization—and turned it on Israel and its allies, forcing the world to witness dead civilian bodies, illegal forms of warfare, and reckless environmental destruction.[74] Yet, arguably, these forms of media resistance reproject and reproduce necrologics and necroculture. As the material realities of death are consumed by the spectacle—such as in the Taliban's arranging dead bodies to evoke local responses for the media, despite the fact that this arrangement prevented the postdeath rituals mandated by religious doctrine—necropolitical media practices extend logics of war and revenge, which creates an enduring case for militarization and remote warfare, and so the cycle continues.

As our studies jointly depict, necrospatialization perpetuates conflict through an interplay of geosocial dynamics, media users, and media technologies and structures.[75] Selective media representation reinforces necropolitics; it empowers warring parties, such as by reinforcing the Taliban's social control in and around the FATA. A drone strike might lead to deadlock between the United States and Pakistan, but occasional confrontation with the United States helps secure the power of Pakistani military elites as a force with which the rest of the world must reckon. Similarly, Lebanon is vulnerable to future conflict because of Hizballah's continued development of extrastate communication and military apparatuses in Lebanon, a process that has intensified in the aftermath of the 2006 war. These case studies show necrospatialization to be an ongoing structuration of death, place, and media in interrelation.

Like Mbembe, who considers necropower within the neoliberal interests of the state, we situate necrospace and the disposability of some territorialized bodies as serving neoliberal interests through the ongoing War on Terror.[76] In the global necrocapitalism of perpetual war, discourses on space as worthy of destruction, and its inhabitants as justifiable targets, are resources. The *necro-* in *necrospatialization* focuses on the dead, ethnoterritorialized body as the site of a "politicization of difference which drives cultures of securitization and global governance and their accompanied militarization."[77] Necropolitical media perpetuates material violence through the spatially situated retrogressive culture that it projects, which in turn restructures necropolitical media.

Debates about the social and political novelty of drones often refer to Mbembe and other critics of necropolitics who consider the power of death in regions of imperialist domination. Such debates are enriching in many ways but reductive in that they give primacy to war technology, organized narratives of religious extremists, and centralized power structures (state or imperialism), as they overlook the necropolitical interplay between on-the-ground, retrogressive realities and translocal media as colonial structures that intersect with market economies. As a tool in necrospatialization, drones are not unique. Like other forms of remote warfare, they help perpetuate conflict by providing for legacy media and journalism a necrospectacle of localized death and resistance that reprojects and extends logics of ethnoterritorial conflict (the West versus Islam) beyond a single location, mode of war, or device. Through necrospatialization, modalities of power not only diminish the sovereignty of postcolonial "troubled" borderlands, such as the southern Lebanese boundary with Israel, and the Pakistani tribal belt that borders Afghanistan; they produce total war, a war without end.

Notes

1. Michael Jackson, *The Politics of Storytelling: Violence, Transgression, and Intersubjectivity,* vol. 3 (Copenhagen: Museum Tusculanum, 2002).

2. Achille Mbembe, "Necropolitics," trans. Libby Meintjes, *Public Culture* 15, no. 1 (2003): 11–12.

3. M. W. Wright, "Necropolitics, Narcopolitics, and Femicide: Gendered Violence on the Mexico-US Border," *Signs* 36 (2011): 707–31.

4. Noam Lesham, "Over Our Dead Bodies: Placing Necropolitical Activism," *Political Geography* 45 (2015): 34–44.

5. Paul C. Adams and André Jansson, "Communication Geography: A Bridge between Disciplines," *Communication Theory* 22, no. 3 (2012): 299–318.

6. Theresa Ann Donofrio, "Ground Zero and Place-Making Authority: The Conservative Metaphors in 9/11 Families' 'Take Back the Memorial' Rhetoric," *Western Journal of Communication* 74, no. 2 (2010): 150–69.

7. Joseph Pierce, Deborah G. Martin, and James T. Murphy, "Relational Place-Making: The Networked Politics of Place," *Transactions of the Institute of British Geographers* 36, no. 1 (2011): 54.

8. In 2018, FATA was officially merged with Khyber Pakhtunkhwa (KP), one of the total four provinces of Pakistan previously called North West Frontier

Province (NWFP). We will, however, retain the nomenclature FATA and NWFP in this chapter because of our focus on the region's colonial history.

9. Thomas Blom Hansen and Finn Stepputat, "Sovereignty Revisited," *Annual Review of Anthropology* 35 (2006): 295–315.

10. Giorgio Agamben, *Homo Sacer: Sovereign Power and Bare Life,* trans. Daniel Heller-Roazen (Stanford, Calif.: Stanford University Press, 1998).

11. Hansen and Stepputat, "Sovereignty Revisited."

12. Adam Moore, "Ethno-territoriality and Ethnic Conflict," *Geographical Review* 106, no. 1 (2016): 92–108.

13. Veena Das, "The Spatialization of Violence: Case Study of a 'Communal Riot,'" in *Unravelling the Nation: Sectarian Conflict and India's Secular Identity,* ed. Kaushik Basu and Sanjay Subrahmanyam (New York: Penguin, 1996), 97.

14. Susan Stryker, Paisley Currah, and Lisa Jean Moore, "Introduction: Trans-, Trans, or Transgender?," *WSQ: Women's Studies Quarterly* 36, no. 3 (2008): 14.

15. Simon Cottle, *Mediatized Conflict: Understanding Media and Conflicts in the Contemporary World* (Berkshire, U.K.: McGraw-Hill Education, 2006).

16. The Israeli Winograd Commission later reported that Israeli prime minister Ehud Olmert and defense minister Amir Peretz planned destructive operations against Lebanon at least four months in advance of the July war on the assumption of a future "kidnapping" by Hizballah, as Israel held high-profile Hizballah prisoners to swap. Conal Urquhart, "Israel Planned for Lebanon War Months in Advance, PM Says," *Guardian,* March 9, 2007, https://www.theguardian.com/world/2007/mar/09/syria.israelandthepalestinians.

17. Ragy Darwish, Nadim Farajalla, and Rania Masri, "The 2006 War and Its Inter-temporal Economic Impact on Agriculture in Lebanon," *Disasters* 33 (2009): 629–44.

18. Leslie A. Rill and Corey B. Davis, "Testing the Second Level of Agenda Setting: Effects of News Frames on Reader-Assigned Attributes of Hezbollah and Israel in the 2006 War in Lebanon," *Journalism and Mass Communication Quarterly* 85, no. 3 (2008): 612.

19. Will Ward, "Uneasy Bedfellows: Bloggers and Mainstream Media Report the Lebanon Conflict," *Arab Media and Society,* no. 1 (Spring 2007): 5, http://arabmediasociety.sqgd.co.uk/?article=17.

20. Daniel Meier, "Borders, Boundaries, and Identity Building in Lebanon: An Introduction," *Mediterranean Politics* 18, no. 3 (2013): 352–57.

21. Agamben, *Homo Sacer,* 122.

22. Asher Kaufman, "Between Palestine and Lebanon: Seven Shi'i Villages as a Case Study of Boundaries, Identities, and Conflict," *Middle East Journal* 60, no. 4 (2006): 685–706.

23. Imad Salamey and Frederic Pearson, "Hezbollah: A Proletarian Party with an Islamic Manifesto—A Sociopolitical Analysis of Islamist Populism in Lebanon and the Middle East," *Small Wars and Insurgencies* 18, no. 3 (2007): 416–38.

24. Mbembe, "Necropolitics."

25. Ivor Gaber, Emily Seymour, and Lisa Thomas, "Is the BBC Biased? The Corporation and the Coverage of the 2006 Israeli-Hezbollah War," *Journalism*

10 (2009): 239–59; Dov Shinar, "Why Not More Peace Journalism? The Coverage of the 2006 Lebanon War in the Canadian and Israeli Media," in *Peace Journalism in Times of War,* ed. Susan Dente Ross and Majid Tehranian, vol. 13, *Peace and Policy* (New Brunswick, N.J.: Transaction, 2017), 7.

26. V. Firmo-Fontan and D. Murray, "The International Media and the Lebanese Hezbollah in the Wake of the September 11th Attacks: Reporting or Supporting a Third Party?," in *The Emotion and the Truth: Studies in Mass Communication and Conflict,* ed. M. Aguirre and F. Ferrandiz (Bilbao: University of Duesto and Humanitarian Net, 2010); Katy Parry, "A Visual Framing Analysis of British Press Photography during the 2006 Israel-Lebanon Conflict," *Media, War and Conflict* 3, no. 1 (2010): 67–85.

27. Brooke Mascagni, "Evoking Fear and Suffering in Photojournalism: The 2006 Israeli-Hizbullah War" (paper presented at the Annual Meeting of Western Political Science Association, University of California, Santa Barbara, 2008).

28. Jad Melki, "The Interplay of Politics, Economics and Culture in News Framing the Middle East Wars," *Media, War and Conflict* 7, no. 2 (2014): 165–86; L. Pintak, "The Fog of Cable: A Critique of U.S. TV's Lebanon War," *Columbia Journalism Review,* July 21, 2006; Mahdi Yaghoobi, "A Critical Discourse Analysis of the Selected Iranian and American Printed Media on the Representations of the Hizbullah-Israeli War," *Journal of Intercultural Communication* 21 (2009), http://www.immi.se/intercultural/nr21/yaghoobi.htm.

29. Derek Gregory, "The Death of the Civilian?," *Environment and Planning D: Society and Space* 24 (2006): 633–38.

30. Marvin Kalb and Carol Saivetz, "The Israeli-Hezbollah War of 2006: The Media as a Weapon in an Asymmetrical Conflict," *Harvard International Journal of Press/Politics* 12, no. 3 (2007): 43–66; "Buried in Rubble, Mother Saved Lives in Qana," NBC News, August 3, 2006, http://www.nbcnews.com/id/14167 395/ns/world_news-mideast_n_africa/t/buried-rubble-mother-saved-lives -qana/#.Wm99yUtJlLo.

31. Elise Labott, "Israel Authorizes 'Severe' Response to Abductions," CNN .com, July 12, 2006, http://www.cnn.com/world/meast/07/12/mideast/.

32. Israel Ministry of Foreign Affairs, "Special Cabinet Communique— Hizbullah Attack," July 12, 2006, http://www.mfa.gov.il/MFA/Government /Communiques/2006/Special%20Cabinet%20Communique%20-%20Hizbullah %20attack%2012-Jul-2006.

33. Peter Bouckaert and Nadim Houry, "Fatal Strikes: Israel's Indiscriminate Attacks against Civilians in Lebanon," *Human Rights Watch,* August 3, 2006, https://www.hrw.org/report/2006/08/02/fatal-strikes/israels-indiscriminate -attacks-against-civilians-lebanon.

34. Nikolas Kosmatopoulos, "Toward an Anthropology of 'State Failure': Lebanon's Leviathan and Peace Expertise," *Social Analysis* 55, no. 3 (2011): 115–42; J. H. Van Melle, "Locked in Time? The Hariri Assassination and the Making of a Usable Past for Lebanon" (MA thesis, Bowling Green State University, 2009).

35. Con Coughlin, "Israeli Crisis Is a Smokescreen for Iran's Nuclear Ambitions," *The Telegraph,* July 16, 2016; Lea Mandelzis and Samuel Peleg, "War

Journalism as Media Manipulation: Seesawing between the Second Lebanon War and the Iranian Nuclear Threat," in Ross and Tehranian, *Peace Journalism,* 79.

36. Asimina Michailidou and Hans-Jorg Trenz, "Mediatized Transnational Conflicts: Online Media and the Politicisation of the European Union in Times of Crisis," in *The Dynamics of Mediatized Conflicts* (New York: Peter Lang, 2015), 232–50.

37. Sune Haugbolle, *War and Memory in Lebanon* (New York: Cambridge University Press, 2010).

38. Renee Codsi, "Letter from Beirut: Return to the Dark Ages," *Electronic Intifada* (blog), July 14, 2006, http://electronicIntifada.net/v2/article5010.shtml.

39. Z., "Who's to Blame?," *urban_memories [the unfinished polaroids]* (blog), July 31, 2006, http://urban-memories.blogspot.com/2006_07_01_archive.html.

40. "Sheba'a Farms," *Wizard of Beirut* (blog), August 7, 2006, http://wizardof beirut.blogspot.com/2006/08/shebaa-farms.html.

41. Hilal Chouman, *Lebanese Blogger Forum* (blog archive), July 31, 2006, http://lebanonheartblogs.blogspot.com/2006_07_01_archive.html.

42. "Lebanese President Accuses Israel of Using White Phosphorous Bombs in Lebanon," *Democracy Now!,* July 25, 2006, https://www.democracynow.org /2006/7/25/lebanese_president_accuses_israel_of_using.

43. Stefan Christoff and Mohammed Shublaq, "Photostory: Damage after Israeli Bombing of Southern Suburbs on Thursday Night," *Electronic Intifada* (blog), July 14, 2006, https://electronicintifada.net/content/photostory-damage -after-israeli-bombing-southern-suburbs-thursday-night/6109.

44. *Tears for Lebanon* (blog), August 2006, https://tears.for.Lebanon/word press.com; "Tears for Lebanon," *Flickr,* https://www.flickr.com/photos/57029367 @N00/.

45. "July War 2006," AlMashriq, August 14, 2006, https://almashriq.hiof.no /lebanon/300/350/355/july-war/index.html; "Google Earth Map of Attacks in Lebanon," *The Arabist* (blog), August 16, 2006, https://arabist.net/blog/2006/8/16 /google-earth-map-of-attacks-on-lebanon.html.

46. "The Qana Massacre," *Wizard of Beirut* (blog), August 2, 2006, http:// wizardofbeirut.blogspot.com/2006/08/qana-massacre.html.

47. Hilal Chouman, *Lebanese Blogger Forum* (blog archive), July 31, 2006, http://lebanonheartblogs.blogspot.com/2006_07_01_archive.html.

48. Simon Jeffery, "Watching, Blogging . . . Bombing," *Guardian,* July 18, 2006, https://www.theguardian.com/news/blog/2006/jul/18/watchingbloggi; Sarah Ellison, "In the Midst of War, Bloggers Are Talking across the Front Line," *Wall Street Journal,* July 28, 2006, https://www.wsj.com/articles/SB11540 5208096220028; Paul Mason, "What the Blogosphere Thinks about Lebanon," Talk about Newsnight, BBC News, July 17, 2006, http://www.bbc.co.uk/blogs /newsnight/2006/07/what_the_blogosphere_thinks_about_lebanon.html.

49. Bahador conducted a frame analysis of the television news coverage on ABC, CBS, NBC, CNN, and Fox and notes that on July 30, 2006, there was an

11–20 percent increase in news images that focused on the injuries to Lebanese civilians. Babak Bahador, "Framing the 2006 Israel-Hezbollah War" (paper presented at "Bridging Multiple Divides," Forty-Ninth Annual Convention, International Studies Association, Hilton San Francisco, San Francisco, Calif., March 26, 2008). Also see Amnon Cavari and Itay Gabay, "Coverage of Foreign Events on US Local Television News," *Israel Studies Review* 29, no. 1 (2014): 62–89; Gaber, Seymour, and Thomas, "Is the BBC Biased?," 27; and Roland Schatz and Christian Kolmer, "The Portrayal of War in the Middle East: Media Analysis of News Coverage by ARD and ZDF," *Relations*, n.s., 2 (2006): 139–50.

50. Jonathan Steele, Rory McCarthy, and Simon Tisdall, "Israel to Suspend Air Attacks for 48 hours after Qana," *Guardian*, https://www.theguardian.com/world/2006/jul/31/israel.syria1.

51. Zahera Harb, "The July 2006 War and the Lebanese Blogosphere: Towards an Alternative Media Tool in Covering Wars," *Journal of Media Practice* 10, no. 2–3 (2009): 255–58.

52. Interview by Kristin Shamas, Beirut, April 2008.

53. Interview by Kristin Shamas, Beirut, November 2006.

54. Interview by Kristin Shamas, Beirut, April 2008.

55. Ghulam Qadir Khan Daur, *Cheegha: The Call from Waziristan, the Last Outpost* (Sweden: Wisehouse Imprint, 2014).

56. Agamben, *Homo Sacer*, 17.

57. Daur, *Cheegha*.

58. Ronald Shaw, Ian Graham, and Majed Akhter, "The Unbearable Humanness of Drone Warfare in FATA, Pakistan," *Antipode* 44, no. 4 (2012): 1497.

59. "Hunt for Al Qaeda Leaders Proving Elusive," *Dawn*, March 31, 2004, https://www.dawn.com/news/355185.

60. Shaheryar Popalzai and Niha Dagia, "Explore the Data: Drone Strikes in Pakistan," *Express Tribune* (Karachi), February 9, 2018.

61. Shaw, Graham, and Akhter, "Unbearable Humanness of Drone," 1500.

62. "12 Killed in Drone Attack on Damadola," *Dawn*, May 15, 2008, https://www.dawn.com/news/302874.

63. Salman Masood, "Pakistan Says It Killed 80 Militants in Attack on Islamic School," *New York Times*, October 31, 2006, https://www.nytimes.com/2006/10/31/world/asia/31pakistan.html.

64. Sahibzada Bahauddin, "Anger after Apparent U.S. Missile Strike in Pakistan," Reuters, May 14, 2008, https://www.reuters.com/article/us-pakistan-missile/anger-after-apparent-u-s-missile-strike-in-pakistan-idUSISL11945920080515.

65. Bahauddin.

66. "12 Killed in Drone Attack."

67. Rifatullah Orakzai, "No Easy Answers after Bajaur Raid," BBC News, May 19, 2008, http://news.bbc.co.uk/2/hi/south_asia/7408927.stm.

68. Bahauddin, "Anger after Apparent U.S."

69. Bahauddin.

70. "12 Killed in Drone Attack."

71. Orakzai, "No Easy Answers."

72. Mikkel Fugl Eskjær, Stig Hjarvard, and Mette Mortensen, *The Dynamics of Mediatized Conflicts* (New York: Peter Lang, 2015), 232–50.

73. Dag Tuastad, "Neo-orientalism and the New Barbarism Thesis: Aspects of Symbolic Violence in the Middle East Conflict(s)," *Third World Quarterly* 24, no. 4 (August 2003): 591–99.

74. "What does Israel hope to achieve in slaughtering babies, other than the repugnance of all civilised human beings?" "The Qana Massacre," *Wizard of Beirut* (blog), August 2, 2006, http://wizardofbeirut.blogspot.com/2006/08/qana -massacre.html.

75. Mimi Sheller, "Media, Materiality, Mobility: Understanding Geomedia as Infrastructure Places," in *Geomedia Studies: Spaces and Mobilities in Mediatized Worlds*, ed. Karin Fast et al. (New York: Routledge, 2017).

76. Mbembe, "Necropolitics."

77. Divya P. Tolia-Kelly, "The Geographies of Cultural Geography I: Identities, Bodies, and Race," *Progress in Human Geography* 34, no. 3 (2010): 364.

CHAPTER 10

Drones versus Drones

Ambient and Ambivalent Sounds
against Remote Warfare

OWEN COGGINS

Drone Sound and Drone Violence

Several examples have recently emerged in which protests against drone warfare employ drone sound (long, constant tones, often of low pitch, with *drone* also sometimes denoting music that prominently features these extended tones). In February 2013, a Drone Not Drones protest began with a controversial set at a Minneapolis music festival by alternative rock band Low. Rather than the expected alternative rock songs, the band performed a long version of their track "Do You Know How to Waltz?," playing essentially a single extended note for twenty-eight minutes with a brief slow, melodic interlude. The performance ended with the phrase "Drone, Not Drones!" pronounced from the stage, and produced a decidedly mixed response.[1] The slogan was subsequently used as the name for a series of twenty-eight-hour concerts of overlapping drone music sets, raising money for Médecins sans Frontières in response to casualties of drone warfare. Drones against Drones in Montreal was a collaborative drone performance in May 2014 and then a digital compilation album, some tracks incorporating audio from military communications about drone strikes.[2] Also in May 2014, a website appeared promoting a Drones against Frontex event at a music festival in Nuremburg, Germany, soliciting drone pieces from musicians to be played simultaneously (without the musicians present) in protest against the European border agency Frontex and its use of surveillance drones.[3] Drone against Drones marches were held in Hastings in the United Kingdom in September 2014 and July 2015, with protesters invited to participate in noisy droning while marching against the U.K. government's involvement in drone attacks.[4] In December 2015, a record was released entitled *A Study into 21st Century Drone Acoustics*, which included audio of domestic and military drones and advice on avoiding drones.[5]

The homonymic relation between *drones* and *drones* lends itself to slogans that make their point through consonant or repetitive sound, but activist uses go beyond this coincidence in several ways: highlighting moral contrasts through linguistic homonyms; offering accessibility and community in response to the destructive, divisive, and antisocial effects of military or surveillance drones; symbolically and literally turning military hardware against itself and deploying the sounds of war drones against war drones; instantiating a sense of ineffability and ambivalence that draws attention to the uncertainties and moral failures of drone logic; or presenting noise that interrupts complacency, insisting that we are all "target audiences" of a creeping drone warscape.

Drone music is sometimes described as something to be endured rather than enjoyed, the sonic experience evoking a sense of violence that can, for some listeners, contribute to the witnessing of or participation in something significant.[6] Drone sound can be mobilized against drone warfare as an ambivalent intervention in a military-entertainment nexus of warfare, surveillance, information, and media, for which "domestic" and "foreign" populations alike are "target audiences." Drone protests produce a disruptive ambivalent ambience that instrumentalizes its own uncertainty and even failure, resisting clear, stable, intelligible messages or positions. Such conceptual indeterminacy may seem vague, its purpose by definition unclear. But in combination with an insistent sonic ambience that pervasively yet invisibly occupies space, ambivalence can become provocative in its uneasy indecipherability. Drone soundscapes can critically echo the ambient and ambivalent manifestations of violence produced by drone warfare, creating temporary but powerful sonic fields that disconcert audiences, demand attention, and refuse to be smoothly resolved. Drawing on the ambivalent affordances of music and noise, drone protests produce investigations of the shifting modalities of violence for the target audiences of that drone culture, making productively ambivalent uses of the disruptive ambience of drone sound.

Protesting Drones

Unmanned aerial vehicles have occupied the imaginations of military strategists since the early twentieth century, as Michael Zeitlin details in this volume, and were in military use at least as early as the First World War.[7] Dummy vehicles used for target practice developed into tools for surveillance and then for firing missiles, constituting "an eye turned into a weapon."[8] The term *drone* may derive from the sonic drone of buzzing engines, or from the yellow-and-black paintwork on early examples that evoked drone bees, nonworkers destined to be killed like the early airborne drones that were "made to be shot down."[9]

Drone use in anti-immigration border patrols and aerial attacks in Gaza and Yemen have attracted the concern of protesters, but a particularly contested area of drone use has been in U.S. "counterterrorism" surveillance and missile attacks in Pakistan. Strategy in the War on Terror shifted between U.S. administrations, from the George W. Bush regime of extraordinary rendition, torture, and detention without trial, to the Barack Obama administration's total surveillance and remote killing (an attempt to decenter emphasis on the Guantanamo Bay prison camp, which Obama pledged to close during his campaign but which remains open). Addressing effects of U.S. drone strikes in northwest Pakistan is the report *Living under Drones,* by the International Human Rights and Conflict Resolution Clinic at Stanford Law School and the Global Justice Clinic at the New York University School of Law.[10] With information gathered by interviewing residents and reviewing journalistic data, the report found the official narrative of accurate counterterrorism strikes to be completely false. Four areas of major concern were outlined: high civilian casualties, psychological trauma, counterproductivity, and erosion of international law.

Civilians are frequently killed or injured despite the claimed accuracy of drone strikes. Drones killed between 2,500 and 3,300 people in Pakistan from June 2004 to September 2012, of whom between 484 and 881 were civilians, including at least 176 children. However, the Obama administration categorized any adult male as a combatant unless posthumously proved otherwise, a reclassification that is highly unlikely when deaths are almost never investigated: a retrospective logic in which whatever gets hit was the target.[11] Drones also kill in "signature strikes," where unidentified targets are attacked, likely together with bystanders, based on supposedly suspicious behavior determined by U.S. personnel watching drone surveillance footage, a "predatory antihermeneutics," as described by Jens Borrebye Bjering and Andreas Immanuel Graae in their chapter in this volume. Official figures for civilian deaths are therefore extremely and unrealistically low. Drones inflict psychological trauma, anxiety, and fear on civilian individuals and communities. There is a strong sonic component to this violence, as the presence of drones overhead is marked by the continuous buzzing sound of engines, "a constant reminder of imminent death."[12] Deliberate U.S. strategies exacerbate these indiscriminate psychological attacks, such as the "double-tap" practice of firing a second missile shortly after a strike, apparently to make killing terrorists more likely. Bystanders running to help are often killed, so would-be helpers and emergency professionals keep away in fear, increasing civilian death tolls while sadistically punishing anyone trying to assist the injured. Meetings of elders are targeted, damaging community relations by disturbing dispute-resolution and problem-solving traditions. Drone missiles have destroyed schools, severely disrupting education. Drone bombing of funerals (often for drone victims) dissuades participation in public rituals crucial for collective trauma processing. Drone-induced fears of traveling, congregating, or even going outside disrupt economic and social life. Drone attacks are counterproductive even regarding their supposed purpose of making the United States and its allies safer. As Canadian journalist Taylor Owen describes, "You can always hear it. . . . You are told the robot is targeting extremists, but its missiles have killed family, friends, and neighbors. So . . . you likely start hating the country that controls the flying robot."[13] For Grégoire Chamayou, the remote launching of drone strikes reverses traditional roles by protecting military personnel at the expense of endangering civilians, with the result that a "state that uses drones tends to divert reprisals toward its own population."[14] Drones erode respect for the rule of law, recognizing no national boundaries and requiring no formal declarations of war. Activists express concerns about the geographical, psychological, and symbolic distances between drone command centers and the places where their horrific effects are felt.[15] This disconnect, together with the secrecy around drone command centers, leads to poorly delineated areas of operation and to unplanned, unauthorized, or unmonitored expansion of drone uses that already "push the bounds of ubiquity in modern warfare."[16] Warfare overlaps with surveillance in the policing of European borders by Frontex drones as far away as the coastlines of Senegal and Brazil, with drone violence in some cases contributing to motivations for migration.[17] Rather than technological development being driven by operational necessity, instead new drone capabilities drive warfare through what is possible, regardless of utility or justification.[18] Critics have raised concerns that normalizing supposedly safe and moral drone warfare exposes domestic populations to the further creep of drone surveillance and violence and, as Nike Nivar Ortiz observes in this volume, an increase in the practice of treating citizens as enemies of the state.[19]

Sonic Target Audiences

Drone protests and the drone practices that they protest against are all situated within what Stephen Stockwell and Adam Muir have called the "military-entertainment complex."[20] Rephrased by Steve Goodman, this is "the idea that target populations in wartime are also media audiences [and] refers to the migration of technologies and processes developed in the military sphere to everyday media culture."[21] For Stockwell and Muir, the first Gulf war "was different to previous wars in one major way: this war was waged as entertainment," and they point out that military and media technologies were combined and conflated as army propaganda was directed largely at the domestic U.S. population.[22] The "target audience" for drones in the military-entertainment complex therefore includes both those under military occupation and those "at home" who are subject to an information war through news media.

Paul Virilio has traced how technologies developed for military purposes find their way into entertainment media—for instance, in the development of cinema from aerial reconnaissance techniques.[23] A sonic example is the vocoder, originally designed to disguise military communications before it appeared in popular music.[24] In contemporary warfare, popular media culture also informs military technology.

In a military-entertainment feedback loop, the video games *Doom* and *Quake*, in part military inspired, were adapted by the U.S. Army for use in training, with the adaptations subsequently sold to mainstream consumers as "authentic military training game[s]."[25] Other examples, outlined by Michael Richardson in this volume, include Pentagon-produced games used for recruitment, training, and propaganda. As Stockwell and Muir describe, "The US war machine has learnt much from the entertainment industry and is now pursuing battle plans that treat the 'enemy' as the audience."[26] While discussion of a "Playstation mentality" in real but mediated warfare conditions has been criticized as simplistic and not representative of the attentional dynamics of either games or drone war, there is nevertheless overlap between military and entertainment media.[27] The U.S. military also reportedly draws on the expertise of television sports analysis in dealing with multiple data streams and works with Disney experts because of their knowledge of virtual-reality environments.[28] Dissemination of military propaganda by news media (for example, about fantasies of ethical precision in drone warfare) is a prominent instance in which audiences are targets in the military-entertainment complex.[29]

This blurring of distinctions extends beyond audiences and enemies. Despite no declarations of war, there is still war. Soldiers are "in action" abroad without leaving their home country, and drones disregard international borders by targeting those in sovereign nations. The United States has deliberately killed its own citizens abroad in unconstitutional and illegal drone strikes, and it acts as an occupying army in communities within its own territory.[30] Instead of a reduction or avoidance of war, this is a total diffusion of warfare that extends everywhere, making it "difficult to distinguish between civilian and combatant, warzone and workplace," where combat is everywhere and nowhere, and distance and intimacy become confused.[31] Apparent endpoints for war, such as the killing of Osama bin Laden, end up affirming its perpetuation; resistance only perpetuates the drone logic of death, and in paradoxical but violent absurdities the bizarre becomes commonplace.[32] The confusion is also manifested sonically, as Martin Daughtry observes in war-zone soundscapes when "the resonant properties of sound produce situations in which the differences between soldier and civilian, native and foreigner, are almost completely elided."[33] Drone use conflates the domestic and foreign, civilian and combatant, friend and enemy into a global target audience for the noise and violence of drone war.

In raising concerns over the expanding target audience of the military-entertainment complex, however, it is important to recognize the shockingly cruel imbalances that still obtain, as Vita Kirchenbauer reminds us: "What in the West can be intellectualised as the interaction of individual and collective experiences on the dramatic level of death, elsewhere actually means death."[34] Choosing whether to pay attention to a war in which your country is engaged is a mark of privilege.[35] Attempting to challenge this, activists sonically evoke the endless buzz of drone engines as signifiers of the threat of unpredictable and deadly attack, or directly employ recordings of aerial drones in music, drawing on the ambient and ambivalent possibilities of drone sound to protest drone violence.

Drone Protests

Drone music has a long history. Many traditional and ancient forms of music use notes of long duration and constant pitch, such as chanting in Tibetan Buddhist or Bon ritual, pipe drones underpinning folk music of northern Europe, or the single-string tanpura drone foundation of Indian ragas. More recently, drones have appeared in classical compositions and popular music, sometimes drawing on older folk and religious connotations. In the late 1960s, avant-garde rock group the Velvet Underground employed loud, distorted guitar and viola drones in their pop-art-inspired rock deconstructions. Meanwhile, interest in the perceived mysticism of Indian culture attracted other countercul- ture musicians to incorporate aspects of raga music, mostly superficial but sometimes extending to include drone sounds. In a similar period, composers such as Eliane Radigue and La Monte Young, as well as jazz musicians like Alice Coltrane and Sun Ra, investigated drones, in each case with significant if sometimes idiosyncratic religious trappings. These musical experimenters in extension and repetition in turn influenced subsequent generations of marginal and experimental musicians in a variety of styles, such as the electronic ambient music of Tim Hecker or Stars of the Lid; the extreme maximalist/mini- malist heavy metal of Earth, Sunn O))), or Bong; or the dynamic and drawn-out postrock of bands such as Swans and Godspeed You! Black

Emperor. Drone music often prompts divided responses, with some listeners reporting a sense of alterity, seriousness, and even meditative transcendence in powerful drone resonance, whereas others are bored or agitated, hearing no musical value in extremes of dirge-like monotony.

Drone Not Drones, Minneapolis, February 2013 Onward

The phrase "Drone Not Drones" was coined on Twitter in February 2013 by Luke Heiken, a music promoter in Minneapolis, who tweeted, "I am going to make a bumper sticker that says DRONE NOT DRONES," tagging his friends the Minnesotan alternative rock band Low.[36] Four months later, on June 15, Low performed at the festival Rock the Garden in Minneapolis. As a local report put it, "Instead of giving an audio tour of its latest release, the band 'filled its entire 27-minute set with one song, expanding the 14-minute 1996 tune 'Do You Know How to Waltz?' by nearly double. As if by way of explanation, Low front man Alan Sparhawk concluded the set with three now-infamous words: 'Drone, not drones.'"[37] Building on media attention surrounding the performance, Heiken set up a Drone Not Drones website, selling stickers, shirts, and posters bearing the slogan to raise money for Médecins sans Frontières "to help the innocent victims of the War on Terror."[38] In February 2014, an unusual twenty-eight-hour fundraising performance was organized, featuring an array of musicians playing hour-long drone sets, each overlapping with the next for the duration of the event. Subsequent twenty-eight-hour drone fund-raisers have been held annually from 2015 to 2018, with some recordings available to download from the music-streaming website Bandcamp for a donation. In 2014, U.K. postrock band 65daysofstatic digitally released a nine-minute track titled "Drone Not Drones" that appeared otherwise unrelated to the Minnesota-based protest.[39]

Drones against Drones, Montreal, May 2014

In May 2014, a compilation recording "Drones against Drones" was released on Bandcamp tagged with the location Montreal, coinciding with a National Drone Day promoted by a Canadian arts organization and involving small music events across the country.[40] The online album featured an image of a Predator drone, clearly juxtaposing drone music with military drones.[41] The sixteen tracks feature diverse approaches to drone music, including long ambient electronic passages and hushed gospel songs. Several tracks include speech samples, from recordings of drone operators and from the covertly recorded trial of Chelsea Manning, "who traded her life and freedom to expose military atrocities" in leaking materials related to drone strikes. Track titles include "I Can Count Them through My Riffle [*sic*] Scope" and "No One Looks down during a Launch." The site stated plans to donate proceeds to the defense fund for Chelsea Manning and to other organizations "specifically directing aid to victims of drone strikes in Pakistan."[42]

Drones against Frontex, Nuremburg, May–October 2014

A similar action also appeared in Germany in May 2014, labeled Drones against Frontex: A Noise Protest. A website advocated using drone sound to protest against the European Union border agency Frontex and its militarized use of drones.[43] Acting as far away from Europe as West Africa and South America, Frontex has been accused of contravening the Geneva Convention and disregarding human rights, prioritizing "border control" over rescuing drowning people and thereby directly contributing to migrant deaths.[44] At the Endzeit festival in Nuremburg in October 2014, a Drones against Frontex installation played sound files of drone music contributed by musicians across Europe through separate amplifiers (with musicians not in attendance), accompanied by visual and text projections critical of drones. This was billed as the "first instalment" of an "ongoing project/protest," though no other actions have been documented and the website was last updated in October 2014.[45]

Drone against Drones, Hastings, September 2014 and June 2015; Liverpool, October 2015

In September 2014 and June 2015, Drone against Drones protests were organized by antiwar and Palestinian solidarity groups in Hastings on the south coast of the United Kingdom. Participants were invited to march along the seafront with musical instruments, noisemakers, or just their own voices: "Everyone will play (or sing) a single note for as long as they possibly can," aiming to raise awareness about drone strikes.[46] An audiovisual clip of the first march was posted online to encourage participation in the second protest, interspersing footage from the march with text from news reports about drone strikes and information about the United Kingdom's involvement.[47] A leafleting event, also named Drone against Drones, was organized in Liverpool in October 2015 by the Merseyside Campaign for Nuclear Disarmament and the pacifist Catholic organization Liverpool Pax Christi, protesting the University of Liverpool's involvement in drone research and development, though no further information was available about the event.[48] In October 2014 a "noisy protest" took place in Lichfield, near Birmingham, against a factory alleged to be manufacturing drones for the Israeli army. The protest involved making noise at the factory gates, including by banging on a piece of metal from an old war plane that had been purchased at an auction by a peace activist and brought to the protest for creating noise.[49]

A Study in 21st Century Drone Acoustics Record, London, December 2015

In December 2015, Gonçalo F. Cardoso and Ruben Pater released an album on Cardoso's U.K. record label Discrepant. The album, *A Study in 21st Century Drone Acoustics,* on one side features field recordings of seventeen different military and commercial drones, which indeed make droning noises. The other side features "a soundscape . . . inspired by the abusive and destructive power of drone technology. The composition focus[es] on the conceptual (sound) life and death of an aerial drone machine in the 21st century."[50] While production of a musical commodity contributes less obviously to activism and protest, the recording is clearly presented in critical opposition to drone warfare. Text on the cover notes the psychological effects of drone noise on civilians in Pakistan and wryly contrasts the use of bird silhouettes by wildlife enthusiasts with the identification of drones by shape. The album cover is made from reflective foil, which can reportedly be used to counter the visual sensors of drone aircraft. A "Drone Survival Guide" included in the packaging was produced by one of the artists involved, with physical copies of this guide also donated to the Minnesota-based Drone Not Drones fund-raising efforts.

Why Drone Sound in Drone Protest?

Homonyms, Juxtapositions, and Moral Binaries

In the five examples outlined, several themes emerge in the ways that drone sound and drone warfare are contrasted and juxtaposed. Evidently an initial impulse is the homonym, lending catchy, curious, or memorable phrasing to Drone Not Drones, Drones against Drones, and Drone against Drones. Proof of the appeal of rhyming structures can be found in the names of other small protests that were part of wider campaigns, Scones against Drones (an action at a U.K. drone base) and Crones against Drones (a march in Minneapolis). While these phrases might appear to be mere wordplay or trivial linguistic coincidences, it should be remembered that rhyming itself relies on repetition and resonance, sonic characteristics that relate closely to drone. In fact, the Scones against Drones and Crones against Drones events both included sound, the former "creating the noise of a drone . . . and sharing information and scones" and the latter featuring marchers who sang to draw attention to the cause.[51] Crones represent female-gendered subject positions while hinting at alternative wisdom and ambivalent power, and scones symbolize the communal provision of food, both coded positively against the negative aspects of drones. In rhyme, homonym, and word sound, such slogans deploy oppositions where verbal similarities highlight moral contrast. A similar juxtaposition appeared in a Fly Kites Not Drones protest, with the two flying objects deployed to contrast associations of playfulness and recreation with violence against children. The *21st Century Drone Acoustics* record deliberately evoked a bird-spotting guide by displaying the silhouettes of birds next to drones, highlighting the difference between appreciating birds in the natural world and needing to watch for drones as a survival technique. The tight linguistic relation of *drones* and *drones* starkly contrasts with the moral distinction of one kind of drones being "against" or "not" the other kind of drones.

Directly presenting this contrast, rock band 65daysofstatic posted its song "Drone Not Drones" on hosting site Soundcloud, accompanied only by the text "Drone is good. Drones are not," and the Montreal-based Drones against Drones compilation was labeled as "a celebration of drones, the musical form, and a condemnation of drones, the vehicles of murder."[52] Elsewhere *drone* may colloquially describe boring or annoying sound, and this connotation may be used in protests to cause disruption or attract attention. For Low, 65daysofstatic, and others, however, drones are elements of experimental music practice, suggesting a serious or atmospheric quality that eschews the perceived simplicity of verse-chorus constructions. Drones in music can even be associated with ideas about transcendence, spirituality, and mysticism, and the imposition of droning ambience can therefore provoke consideration of a related moral binary that contrasts the power of drone sound as a meditative encounter with the sacred (an interpretation perhaps available especially for audiences in the West), with drone sound as a pervasive hovering threat of indiscriminate violence, inflicted by the airborne avatars of the United States and the United Kingdom. In sonic experience as well as in linguistic doublings, then, a moral contrast is emphasized between drone music and drone warfare.

Participation, Accessibility, and Sonic Community in Dislocation

Music in protest and activism has long been used to promote group cohesion, boost morale, express ideas or emotion, communicate nonverbally, or simply provide something to do. As a participatory, communal form of art or culture, music can also claim a kind of moral authority in opposition to the object of protest. Singing or chanting can be particularly effective in promoting communal solidarity, requiring no further equipment than the bodies of protesters creating and feeling the same resonance. The creation of drone music can have lower barriers to participation and greater accessibility than other kinds of music, which might be perceived to require tunefulness, equipment, or higher skill levels. As a social media post promoting the Hastings event put it, "No musical ability is required for this action, just concern about this new way to wage warfare and the rising death-toll it's causing."[53]

Three of the other protests also involved overtly participatory and collaborative elements. The Montreal-based online compilation foregrounded diverse participation by including tracks from sixteen different artists, which varied widely in length, style, and reference points in artists' names and song titles. The annual twenty-eight-hour Drone Not Drones performances have featured as many as fifty artists on each occasion. Organizer Luke Heiken emphasized that all musicians were

contributing to a single thing, with connections in sound representing connections between people: "All this music coming together to
form one continuous song speaks to the connectedness between communities. . . . It's a way to feel less hopeless and less alone and realize
you're not crazy for thinking things are so messed up, and that other
people feel the same way you do."[54]

Drones against Frontex also invoked collaboration as protest, in a
temporary and overtly dislocated manner, subtly presenting the geographical diversity and symbolic incorporation of participants who did
not know each other and would not meet in person, against the exclu-
sionist organization they were protesting. "Nearly 20 artists teamed up
under the alias Drones Against Frontex. . . . Musicians from all over
Germany and other European countries joined in. From Oslo to Mu-
nich soundfiles were mailed and exchanged, and at the Endzeit festival this final installation of guitar amps, tape recorders, computer boxes
and other sound sources will start to sound."[55] Drone sound can
promote inclusivity by emphasizing low barriers to participation
(simply the ability to make any kind of noise), with the continuity and
connectedness of drones also asserting a kind of symbolic community. Similarly, a physical space in which drones are sounding can feel
inhabited by a communally felt presence, even through sounds created by people who are not physically in attendance, such as when
drone contributions from different individuals were combined in one
place to symbolically defy the violent containment and segregation of
people via the aggressive drone-defended policies of the European
border agency. Drone can produce a kind of solidarity in sound, where
people at a protest march experience sound together, in opposition to
the dislocation of drone operator soldiers who are removed from the
danger of the humming, noise-accompanied violence that they are in-
flicting on their targets.

Machinery of War Turned against War

Drone protests may symbolically turn military technology against itself, recontextualizing elements of military equipment to alter perceptions or disrupt their functions. One explicit instance is the 2014 "noisy
protest" against a drone factory in Shenstone in the United Kingdom,
which was connected through nationwide antiwar organizations to the
Drone against Drones march in Hastings. A group assembled by the

factory gates, made noise on bells and whistles, and hammered on a large metal panel that was previously part of a military jet. The method of creating noise was a multiply symbolic repurposing: the sound was created by literally attacking military equipment with hammers, while at the same time the piece of military equipment was being used as a tool to protest the creation of more military equipment.

The organizers of the Hastings marches created and released a video on their social media page, the clip combining amateur footage of the 2014 marchers with snippets from news articles and facts about the effects of drone attacks, while the soundtrack "include[d] a recording of a drone strike."[56] A social media user commented on the webpage, reporting his feelings on watching the video: "It gives you a feel for the oppressiveness of having drones overhead and how people must feel in Afghanistan and Palestine."[57] The *21st Century Drone Acoustics* record also contains recordings of drone engines, presented ambiguously as music or as a dystopian bird-spotter's guide to recognizing airborne drones. While the sounds of drone engines are not a primary purpose of their deployment in war (though, as the *Living under Drones* report identifies, they do have damaging psychological effects on target populations), in drone protest they are amplified and redirected, used to oppose drone violence in attempts to communicate or provoke reflection about the experience of drone victims abroad. This is not to say that hearing recordings or abstract representations of drone soundscapes reproduces for Hastings residents or *21st Century Drone Acoustics* listeners anything like the experience of violent drone warfare. Rather, the sonic by-products of the machinery of that warfare are recontextualized in these new sonic presentations, which aim to prompt reflection on their complex implication in distant violence. The *21st Century Drone Acoustics* record performs another repositioning with its shiny silver cover, which, the liner notes report, can be used as a defense against the heat sensors with which drones "see" people on the ground. This reflective foil was developed by the same industry that developed military rockets and other hardware: a product of space-age military technology is used in defiance of and defense against technologies with a similarly belligerent origin. In another echo, the label on one side of the record displays a kind of dial as if from a cockpit or control panel, suggesting that the record itself is in a sense a piece of equipment, quasi-militaristic yet set against military drones.

In the case of the Drones against Drones compilation, the circulation of military information is rerouted in protest. The opening track features gently distorted ambient droning, together with an audio clip of Chelsea Manning reading a statement at the 2013 military tribunal at which she was convicted and sentenced to thirty-five years' detention in military prison (though she has since been released, pardoned in the last days of the Obama administration). Another track, "Collateral Murder (Trigger Warning)," includes audio clips from a video of the same title that was leaked by Manning to WikiLeaks and widely publicized. The sounds are radio chatter concerning drone strikes that killed children and journalists, and deliberately targeted wounded individuals, while the added ominous, thrumming tones highlight threat and violence. Here there are several intersecting redeployments of military information. Manning, a U.S. soldier and information analyst, shared data in an unauthorized redirection of military information in order to challenge some military behavior for ethical reasons. Recorded sound material from those leaks was further repurposed on the Montreal compilation. The military tribunal at which these issues were discussed was unofficially recorded, the sound files were (briefly) shared online by news outlets, and a clip was used on a Drones against Drones track. Manning's trial for unauthorized leaks, including of sound recordings, was itself covertly recorded and used in an unsanctioned way to draw attention, and then further reused in the Montreal project supporting Manning and continuing the protest against drone warfare. The manipulation and dissemination of audio clips from military-related sources subverts the military's control over the circulation of sound and information in the drone war context while challenging the authority and justice of its actions.

Ambivalence, Ineffability, and Failure

Drone sound can disrupt expectations, conventions, and understandings of order, using evocations of ambivalence, ineffability, and failure for activist purposes. The Drone Not Drones social media page for the twenty-eight-hour drone in 2014 introduces droning as a response to and continuation of powerlessness and lack of language: "We don't have the right words to stop 'targeted killings' or 'collateral damages' or 'illegal assassinations.' All we can do is drone on and on about it: DRONE NOT DRONES."[58] The inability to speak represents disempowerment for critics of drone attacks, and organizers acknowledge their weakness yet respond by "droning on." This phrase refers to the planned action of playing drone music for long periods, while also suggesting speech that is lengthy, perhaps boring and repetitive, yet also persistent, hinting at the tenacity in the face of dismissal that is required in many protest campaigns.

Related sentiments are expressed in a review of the twenty-eight-hour concert in 2015. Drone music produces a field of ambivalence, an appropriate feeling when grappling with the difficult-to-imagine realities of the distant violence and diffuse geopolitical impacts of drone strikes: "Drones may or may not kill innocent people in countries we're ostensibly not at war with. It's hard to know how to feel. We know they exist, but we don't quite know how to interact with them. In this respect they're not all that different from drone music."[59] Though it is well established that drones kill innocent people, the uncertainty displayed here is significant in understanding how the open-ended presence of drone sound can be productively though ambivalently provocative. While often connected with ineffability, and described (paradoxically) as impossible to describe, drone sound can be "a statement that says this is something—this is here," even if meaning and purpose are undefined.[60] A forceful ambivalence, while risking failure as protest, may at least prompt strong feelings of unease and discomfort in response to an issue kept deliberately undercover by authorities. Regarding this, J. Halberstam has outlined how, "under certain circumstances failing, losing, forgetting, unmaking, undoing, unbecoming, not knowing may in fact offer more creative, more cooperative, more surprising ways of being in the world."[61] This kind of connection with failure and ambivalence is explicitly stated by Drones against Frontex: "Why Drone/Noise? Without going too deep into that, we think this kind of music is a music that fails, in a positive way. It fails at getting instrumentalised by, excuse the generalisation, mainstream media and industry. It fails at giving out simple answers and slogans. It fails at satisfying listening habits. And by doing that, it opens up room for interpretation, as listening to music is a process as creative as making music."[62] Failure and ambivalence are useful ways of hearing the tension between drone sound as confrontational noise and drone sound as background ambience: drone sound is often physically felt as a presence without determined meaning, or as a strange combination of movement and stasis, where a tone is unchanging but ongoing vibration offers a sense of dynamic involvement. Pointing out, for example, the too easily ignored background of violence elsewhere that underpins the "home" cultures of the United States and United Kingdom, this provocative, insistent uncertainty and ambiguity can provide a foundation for a protest intervention of unstable but powerful potential.

Disruptive Noise and Sonic Consciousness

While drone sound can evoke accessibility and openness, it can also be inaccessible, resistant, and opaque. After Low's performance, a journalist observed that the drone, despite being presented in an "artful, low-keyed, actually rather peaceful manner," nevertheless "served as a jolt to some listeners who had expected something rather different," with those listeners having their "expectations of accessibility" disrupted.[63] The aim of any protest is to alter certain behaviors by certain actors or institutions, and disruption can therefore be a powerful point of intersection between symbolism and real results. Disruption may include interfering with people's ordinary patterns of behavior so as to raise questions of tacit consent, instantiating unusual situations to prompt critical reflection on norms and conventions, or actually obstructing the functioning of those engaged in problematic activities. While noise may often be used antagonistically, with music used comparatively more in creating, communicating, and motivating solidarity between protesters, these uses (and even categorizations of "music" and "noise") are neither stable nor fixed.

A report after the Hastings event identified the effect of noise in drawing notice, while also contrasting music and warfare in the choice of the word *armed*: "A group of people armed with musical instruments gathered on Hastings seafront and played, or sang, sustained notes for as long as they could. The resulting drone drew the attention of passers-by and gave an opportunity to raise awareness of this issue and create a media splash."[64] Low's twenty-seven-minute drone performance at the Rock the Garden festival also disrupted expectations while creating attention for the phrase "Drone Not Drones." Discussion in online comment threads was extensive, while news articles ruminated about the band's responsibilities to its audience and collected extreme responses from social media: that the audience had not received what they had paid for, that the band was ungrateful for the opportunity to perform at the festival, or that it was outrageous that the band had not performed a conventional set of songs.[65] Responses that referred to the "Drone Not Drones" statement were limited to a few apparently approving repetitions of the phrase, countered by one commentator who sarcastically called for drone strikes on the festival and band and mentioned a "failed abortion of a political statement."[66] The performance certainly generated coverage of the phrase, which then became the central focus for more traditional forms of activism such as benefit concerts (albeit unusual ones) and merchandise sales.

Ambivalence in interpreting drone music is indicated in the contrast between descriptions of Low's example as disruptive and controversial and descriptions of the reportedly relaxing, even soporific ambience of the twenty-eight-hour drone shows: attendees brought pillows and sleeping bags, and the snoring was reportedly sometimes louder than the music.[67] Drone sound can be a disruptive, noisy intervention that causes concern and even anger yet conversely can appear as an ambient hum that may be comforting or relaxing. As one response to the twenty-eight-hour concert asserts, the context of drone sound is important: "Imagine if 'Drone Not Drones' went down outside the Capitol, or the Minneapolis police headquarters, or the entire recording [was played] live on [local radio station] 89.3. It would get noise complaints and disrupt morning commutes and generally ruin peoples' [sic] days. And maybe that would be kind of awesome. It would be a protest, not just a charity event. Or not a protest, but a forced presence."[68] Another comment mentioned the airing of Low's performance on a local radio station: "If you tuned into The Current right now and didn't know it was Low playing Rock the Garden you would assume you were having an acid trip."[69] These and another response describing Low's set as "meditative" underscore the importance of context, expectation, and the orientation of listeners in appreciating, considering, or being confronted by drones.[70] Even though presented humorously, the comparison between unprepared listening and being under the influence of strongly psychoactive substances suggests the profoundly challenging and potentially transformative effects of drone music, particularly when presented in new or unexpected settings. These effects are mobilized by protesters attempting to confront the problematic circumstances and impacts of drone warfare.

Resistant Ambi(val)ence

As Paul Virilio points out, "Weapons are tools not just of destruction but also of perception."[71] Weaponized drones have had radical implications for the relation between perception and violence in warfare, and it is perhaps for this reason that their impact has been understood through contrasts between vision and aurality. Foreshadowing later discussions of military drone surveillance, Virilio writes that "the function of the weapon is the function of the eye."[72] Visual features are frequently cited as the centrally important elements of drones—for example, by Sunny Moraine: "Here's what I think a drone is, and what a drone is is what a drone does: it *watches*."[73] Nasser Hussain explores how this emphasis affects drone users and audiences differently, pointing out the distinction between the droning noise heard and felt by civilian victims and the silence of visual monitor screens seen by the drone operators. Hussain finds here a perceptual basis for the psychological distancing of those soldiers from their execution of deadly attacks. "In the case of the drone strike footage, the lack of synchronic sound renders it a ghostly world in which the figures seem unalive, even before they are killed. The gaze hovers above in silence. The detachment that critics of drone operations worry about comes partially from the silence of the footage."[74]

This should not tempt us into an overly simplistic polarity where sight would represent a detached, militaristic, neocolonial, and violent gaze and sound would conversely stand for an ethical, bodily conscious humanism, however much we might sympathize with the latter orientation. "Using a sight/sound dichotomy to represent imperialist power hierarchies oversimplifies both how perception works and how imperialism works. *Power and agency are certainly asymmetrical, but they are not so cleanly dichotomized.*"[75] The sonic dimensions of drone warfare do, however, have particular effects on target audiences. So too does drone sound, which, in comparison with more explicitly musical or verbal sounds, has particular affordances, capacities, and potentials that relate and respond to this diffuse warscape. Drone sound is deployed (though ambiguously) in opposition and resistance to those aggressive hierarchies and vast power inequalities, the very ambiguity and ambivalence of droning noise aimed at prompting responses to mediated, distanced violence and to complicity in oppressive systems.

For Moraine, "the gaze of a drone is intrinsically penetrative. The gaze of a drone *burrows*," a formulation that lends to vision the ability of sound to vibrate, to get inside a material body.[76] Drone sound is undeniable when it vibrates in physical space, as it burrows and penetrates, as it sounds from within as well as from around the body. Yet it is simultaneously ambivalent and unpredictable in its ephemerality, estranged from language and not easily reduced to safely legible frameworks of reason and law.

In protests the uses of drone sound bear a deep, committed ambiguity, refusing a supposed certainty that sees good and evil, judges with death, and proclaims itself precise, efficient, and fair. Instead, drone sound demands consciousness of diffusion, vagueness, uncertainty, failure, fragility, and the reality of violence on the body. This transgresses the purported division that Hussain observes in the perceptual rhetoric of drone warfare: "Sight on one side and sound on the other. Focus on one side and diffusion on the other. It is precisely this distribution of senses that produces the assertion of pinpoint accuracy and the disavowal of widespread harm."[77] Absorption in drone sound refuses to disavow this harm and, in ambiguous engagement with noise, evokes violence against the body, denouncing the psychological violence done to other bodies by drone sound, as well as the physical violence that drone sound threatens.

Drone noise, drone music, or drone sound prompts reflection on moral binaries brought together by sonic quirks of resonance and repetition in language, introducing consciousness of moral difference in repetition of apparent similarity. While this is initially introduced at the arbitrary level of linguistic coincidence, it may prompt deeper disruptions of unexamined moral and political continuities and complacencies. Drone noise is accessible yet inaccessible: it welcomes participation and community but marks them as requiring work. It can flow through borders, though it needs materiality, often of human bodies, in which to vibrate. It may appear unannounced and slowly seep into vibrating awareness, or demand attention in wild clamor, resistant in both cases to reductive explanation. Drone can therefore provoke the troubled reflections necessary for political critique, crucially disallowing final resolutions and instead calling for unending, conscious concern. It can be disturbing, even alienating, simultaneously demanding and frustrating attempts to articulate why it aggravates.

Drone noise is and is not violence: it is a sensory sign of drone-launched missiles, yet the sound can itself also do serious physiological and psychological damage to individuals and communities. Drone sound represents the threat of violence for those living under military drones, with this threat represented again by those who imitate or reproduce the sound in protesting against that threat. Drone music can instantiate a sonic representation and echo of drone warfare for audiences in the domestic populations of governments that are military aggressors abroad. By bringing "home" the ambiguous, droning sounds of uncertain, threatening aerial terror, such sounds can challenge complacent notions of safety and lack of responsibility through the intimate strangeness of vibrations inside bodily consciousness. At the uncertain borders of music and noise, drone sound can offer, even in disruption, a potentially reflective but uneasily ambiguous sonic space, the supposed precise, rational certainty of drone warfare radically questioned by the atmospheres of ambivalence projected in drone sound.

Notes

1. At the time of publication, full audio and video of the performance was available online: The Current, "Low—Do You Know How to Waltz? (Live at Rock the Garden)," YouTube video, 28:06, posted July 3, 2013, https://www.youtube.com/watch?v=zI5-MuV5NSo.

2. Drones against Drones, "Drones against Drones," Bandcamp, May 10, 2014, https://drxnes.bandcamp.com/releases.

3. "Drones against Frontex: A Noise Protest," Drones against Frontex homepage, accessed September 1, 2017, https://dronesagainstfrontex.wordpress.com/.

4. Post by Lynda Murray on Hastings against War Facebook group, "Drone against Drones," Facebook, August 8, 2014, https://www.facebook.com/search/top/?q=Hastings%20Against%20War%20drone%20against%20drones&epa=FILTERS&filters=eyJycF9jcmVhdGlvbl90aW1lIjoie1wibmFtZVwiOlwiY3JlYXRpb25fdGltZVwiLFwiYXJnc1wiOlwiexcXCJzdGFydF9tb250aFwxXC XC I6XFxcIjIwMTQtMDhcXFwiLFxcXCJlbmRfbW9udGhcXFwiOlxcXCIyMDE0LTA4XFxcIn1cIn0ifQ%3D%3D (first entry); "Drone against the Drones," Hastings Online Times, June 1, 2015, http://hastingsonlinetimes.co.uk/hot-topics/campaigns/drone-against-the-drones.

5. Gonçalo Cardoso and Ruben Pater, *A Study into 21st Century Drone Acoustics*, Discrepant Records, 2015, LP.

6. Owen Coggins, *Mysticism, Ritual and Religion in Drone Metal* (London: Bloomsbury Academic, 2018), 137–70.

7. Grégoire Chamayou, *Drone Theory* (London: Penguin, 2013), 27.

8. Chamayou, 13.

9. Medea Benjamin, *Drone Warfare: Killing by Remote Control* (London: Verso, 2013), 13; Chamayou, *Drone Theory*, 26.

10. *Living under Drones: Death, Injury, and Trauma to Civilians from US Drone Practices in Pakistan* (Stanford, Calif.: International Human Rights and Conflict Resolution Clinic, Stanford Law School; New York: Global Justice Clinic, New York University School of Law, September 2012), https://chrgj.org/wp-content/uploads/2012/10/Living-Under-Drones.pdf.

11. Michael Zeitlin, this volume.

12. David Rohde quoted in *Living under Drones*, 70.

13. Taylor Owen, "Buzz Kill: What Does Constantly Being Watched Sound Like?," OpenCanada.org, March 12, 2013, https://www.opencanada.org/features/buzz-kill/.

14. Chamayou, *Drone Theory*, 77.

15. Vita Kirchenbauer, "Infrared Dreams in Times of Transparency," accessed February 28, 2020, http://www.vk0ms.com/infrared_dreams.html.

16. Owen, "Buzz Kill."

17. "Third Countries," Frontex European Coast and Border Agency, September 3, 2017, https://frontex.europa.eu/partners/third-countries/ (webpage no longer available as of February 28, 2020; see archived page at https://web.archive.org/web/20171109215931/https://frontex.europa.eu/partners/third-countries/).

18. Chamayou, *Drone Theory*, 2; Kirchenbauer, "Infrared Dreams."

19. Chamayou, *Drone Theory*, 189.

20. Stephen Stockwell and Adam Muir, "The Military-Entertainment Complex: A New Facet of Information Warfare," *Fibreculture Journal* 1 (November 1, 2003), http://one.fibreculturejournal.org/fcj-004-the-military-entertainment-complex-a-new-facet-of-information-warfare.

21. Steve Goodman, *Sonic Warfare: Sound, Affect and the Ecology of Fear* (Boston: MIT Press, 2010), 197.

22. Stockwell and Muir, "Military-Entertainment Complex."

23. Paul Virilio, *War and Cinema: The Logistics of Perception,* trans. Patrick Camiller (London: Verso, 2009).

24. "Cultures of Sound and the War without End," SensingWar.org, February 28, 2015, http://www.sensingwar.org/ (webpage no longer available as of February 28, 2020; see archived page at https://web.archive.org/web/20150409084216/http://www.sensingwar.org/).

25. Rob Riddell, "Doom Goes to War," *Wired,* April 1, 1997, https://www.wired.com/1997/04/ff-doom/.

26. Stockwell and Muir, "Military-Entertainment Complex."

27. Chris Cole, Mary Dobbing, and Amy Hailwood, *Convenient Killing: Armed Drones and the "Playstation" Mentality* (London: Fellowship of Reconciliation, 2010); Richardson, this volume; Chamayou, *Drone Theory*, 107, 120; Benjamin, *Drone Warfare,* 86.

28. Chamayou, *Drone Theory,* 40; Stockwell and Muir, "Military Entertainment Complex."

29. Benjamin, *Drone Warfare,* 182.

30. "Islamist Cleric Anwar Al-Awlaki Killed in Yemen," BBC News, September 30, 2011, https://www.bbc.co.uk/news/world-middle-east-15121879; "Al-Aulaqi v. Panetta—Constitutional Challenges to Killing of Three U.S. Citizens," ACLU, June 4, 2014, https://www.aclu.org/cases/al-aulaqi-v-panetta-constitutional-challenge-killing-three-us-citizens; Tim Jelfs, this volume.

31. Kirchenbauer, *"Infrared Dreams"*; David Buchanan, this volume; Ann-Katrine S. Nielsen, this volume.

32. Annika Brunck, this volume; Syed Irfan Ashraf and Kristin Shamas, this volume; Brittany Hirth, this volume.

33. Martin J. Daughtry, "Belliphonic Sounds and Indoctrinated Ears: The Dynamics of Military Listening in Wartime Iraq," in *Pop When the World Falls Apart: Music in the Shadow of Doubt,* ed. Eric Weisbard (Durham, N.C.: Duke University Press, 2012), 113.

34. Kirchenbauer, "Infrared Dreams."

35. Nielsen, this volume.

36. Paul Schmelzer, "'Drone Not Drones': Behind the Slogan That Capped Low's Infamous 27-Minute Set," Walker Art, July 12, 2013, https://walkerart.org/magazine/drone-not-drones-behind-the-slogan-that-capped-lows-infamous-27-minute-set.

37. Schmelzer.

38. Drone Not Drones, "Drone Not Drones: The Live 28-Hour Drone," Facebook event, February 7–8, 2014, https://www.facebook.com/events/571807126237581/?ref=3&ref_newsfeed_story_type=regular.

39. 65daysofstatic, "Drone Not Drones," Soundcloud, 2014, https://soundcloud.com/65daysofstatic/dronenotdrones.

40. Wyrd Arts Initiatives homepage, accessed September 1, 2017, https://wyrdartsinitiatives.org/droneday.

41. Drones against Drones, "Drones against Drones."

42. Drones against Drones.

43. "Drones against Frontex."

44. "Third Countries"; *The EU's Dirty Hands: Frontex Involvement in Ill-Treatment of Migrant Detainees in Greece* (New York: Human Rights Watch, September 2011), https://www.hrw.org/sites/default/files/reports/greece0911webwcover_0.pdf; Kate Ferguson, "EU Leaders 'Killing Migrants by Neglect' after Cutting Mediterranean Rescue Missions," *Independent,* April 17, 2016, https://www.independent.co.uk/news/world/europe/eu-leaders-killing-migrants-by-neglect-after-cutting-mediterranean-rescue-missions-a6988326.html.

45. "Drones against Frontex."

46. Hastings against War, "Drone against Drones."

47. Voices for Creative Non-violence, "Drone against Drones," YouTube video, 2:33, posted March 26, 2015, https://www.youtube.com/watch?v=XRD-sbYpR9k.

48. "Drone against Drones Leafleting," Network for Peace, October 15, 2015, http://www.networkforpeace.org.uk/calendar/merseyside-cnd/2015/oct/drone-against-drones-leafleting.

49. Alex Keller, "Protesters Set to Target Village Factory Again," *Lichfield Mercury*, no. 11,905, October 16, 2014, 13.

50. Cardoso and Pater, *Study*.

51. Drone Wars (@Drone_Wars_UK), "Scones Not Drones! Drone campaigners plan protest at RAF Waddington on 3 Oct #GroundtheDrones," Twitter, August 16, 2015, https://twitter.com/drone_wars_uk/status/632976562065944576; Michael McIntee, "Crones against Drones, the Wily Women of the WAMM," YouTube video, 3:55, posted June 24, 2011, https://www.youtube.com/watch?v=H-daHj2tA4U.

52. 65daysofstatic, "Drone Not Drones"; Drones against Drones, "Drones against Drones."

53. Hastings against War, "Drone against Drones."

54. Luke Heiken quoted in Simone Cazares, "'A Way to Feel Less Hopeless': Drone Not Drones Returns for a Fourth Year," The Current, February 24, 2017, https://blog.thecurrent.org/2017/02/drone-not-drones-returns-for-a-fourth-year/.

55. "Drones against Frontex."

56. Voices for Creative Non-violence, "Drone against Drones."

57. Jim W., comment on Voices for Creative Non-violence, "Drone against Drones."

58. Drone Not Drones, "Drone Not Drones."

59. Ben Tuthill, "Drone Not Drones: The New Protest Music," City Pages, February 2, 2015, http://citypages.com/music/drone-not-drones-the-new-protest-music-6651078.

60. Tuthill.

61. J. Halberstam, *The Queer Art of Failure* (Durham, N.C.: Duke University Press, 2011), 2.

62. "Drones against Frontex."

63. Philip Bither, "Low: Rock the Garden's Own *Rite of Spring?*," Walker Art, June 18, 2013, https://walkerart.org/magazine/low-rock-the-garden-drone.

64. "Drone against the Drones."

65. Andrea Swensson, "The Audacity of Low: What Does a Band 'Owe' Us When We Pay to See Them Perform?," The Current, June 18, 2013, https://blog.thecurrent.org/2013/06/the-audacity-of-low-what-does-a-band-owe-us-when-we-pay-to-see-them-perform/; Reed Fischer, "Low's One-Song Set at Rock the Garden Totally Ruled," City Pages, June 17, 2013, http://citypages.com/music/lows-one-song-set-at-rock-the-garden-totally-ruled-6633646.

66. Ted (@grateful_ted), "Thought someone slipped a few xanax into my drink . . . Call the Pentagon we need a drone strike #low #rockthegarden" Twitter, June 16, 2013, https://twitter.com/grateful_ted/status/346042145070792704; Ted (@grateful_ted), "Pirating my next low album so I can recoup some

$$ I just waisted [*sic*] paying to see the failed abortion of a political statement #rockthegarden" Twitter, June 16, 2013, https://twitter.com/grateful_ted/status /346075215807270912.

67. Josh Keller, "Live Blog: Drone Not Drones," Reviler, February 24, 2017, https://www.reviler.org/2017/02/24/live-blog-drone-not-drones/.

68. Tuthill, "Drone Not Drones."

69. Matt K. quoted in Fischer, "Low's One-Song Set."

70. Swensson, "Audacity of Low."

71. Virilio, *War and Cinema*, 8.

72. Virilio, 26.

73. Sunny Moraine, "All Watched over by Machines of Loving Grace," Cyborgology, October 15, 2013, https://thesocietypages.org/cyborgology/2013 /10/15/all-watched-over-by-machines-of-loving-grace/.

74. Nasser Hussain, "The Sound of Terror: Phenomenology of a Drone Strike," Boston Review, October 16, 2013, http://bostonreview.net/world/hussain-drone -phenomenology.

75. Robin James, "Drones, Sound and Super-panoptic Surveillance," Cyborgology, October 26, 2013, https://thesocietypages.org/cyborgology/2013/10/26 /drones-sound-and-super-panoptic-surveillance/, emphasis in original.

76. Moraine, "All Watched Over," emphasis in original.

77. Hussain, "Sound of Terror."

CHAPTER 11

Bombs and Black Humor

Aerial Warfare and the Absurd

BRITTANY HIRTH

"The battlefield is a bizarre place," Chris Kyle declares in his autobiography, *American Sniper*.[1] The adjective that Kyle chooses, *bizarre*, vaguely describes the battlefield and also invites connotations such as *unusual* or *unconventional*. These terms all invoke the realm of the absurd. Once a popular literary method of representation for soldiers-turned-novelists, such as Kurt Vonnegut and Joseph Heller, the absurd is described within literary criticism as a nonconformist approach to narrative structure and language. In defining the absurd, Robert A. Hipkiss claims that the absurdist author "finds life's experiences so contradictory and unresolvable that he can only admit to confusion and express the need for a nonrational means of knowing."[2] The language of the absurd continues to demonstrate the difficulty for veterans to find referential language to represent their wars. Arguably, inserting elements of absurdity enables a veteran-writer to express a confusing, traumatic experience that would otherwise challenge conventional, narrative representation. Although Anthony Swofford's *Jarhead* (2003) and Chris Kyle's *American Sniper* (2012) are categorized as memoir, this chapter demonstrates how two veterans-turned-writers pull from the absurd literary tradition to shape their stories about battle in the age of remote warfare.

From the First World War into the present, continued technological advancements in warplanes, jets, drones, and weaponry have led to the increasing incorporation of aerial bombing. In his chapter in this volume, Sajdeep Soomal explains that U.S. drone strikes have pervasively continued since the first successful strike in 2001 in Afghanistan. The techniques of remote warfare, such as targeted bombing and the use of long-distance rifles, have removed soldiers from the intimate, human experience of face-to-face combat. This shift to remote warfare may result in veterans who are uncertain of their roles as ground combatants. In particular, snipers provide ground support in cities and villages by eliminating insurgents, but manned planes and drones acquire the major targets with bombs. By inserting elements of absurdity into their memoirs, veteran-writers can illustrate that aerial assault complicates their perceptions of their roles in technologically advanced war. Specifically, this chapter analyzes how the absurd narrative techniques of parody and black humor elucidate the veteran-writers' perceptions of their roles and reveal their counternarratives to the broadcast media's portrayal of "clean," remote warfare.

Parody is a common narrative tool within the absurd literary tradition, and Swofford and Kyle employ it to comment on their wars, as "contemporary novelists of the absurd often turn to parody."[3] Parody is a subversive narrative technique that exaggerates another style or form, usually for comedic effect, and exposes the author's commentary on a theme or event through the exaggeration. For example, Swofford and Kyle insert parody to exaggerate the gamelike features of war and their participation as players in order to draw attention to their diminished role as ground combatants in the age of remote warfare. Also, by parodying the ground sniper's role in wars that were mostly won by precision bombing, Swofford and Kyle emphasize that destruction and violence are still facets of war, despite the mainstream perception that remote warfare precisely targets only insurgents. In their chapter in this volume, Syed Irfan Ashraf and Kristin Shamas describe the civilians who are subjected to American drone strikes in Lebanon and Pakistan. These civilians offer their accounts of the child casualties and resulting damage to their neighborhoods on their blogs, which Western media coverage often does not explicitly report. In his contribution, Owen Coggins also affirms the destruction of drone warfare by citing the high civilian casualties, even with the assumed pinpoint accuracy of drone strikes.

Although technological advancements in remote warfare can reduce the number of deployed combatants, these advancements do not eliminate the potential for ground soldiers to develop battle trauma. Throughout the early to mid-twentieth century, war mostly entailed a conventional battlefield on which soldiers hauled heavy machinery, marched on the opposing army, and engaged in close-range shooting. This labor-intensive fighting meant that soldiers only spent weeks in the war zone. If artillery was limited, soldiers only spent hours on the battlefield. But a twenty-first-century solider is now exposed to *months* of active combat because drone bombing can quickly and efficiently acquire the targets (thereby reducing some of the labor-intensive combat). However, these technological advancements in remote warfare do not assuage battle trauma. Dave Grossman claims that the "physical and logistical capability to sustain combat outstripped [soldiers'] psychological capacity to endure it."[4] As soldiers stay in the war zone and in bodily danger for longer periods of time, the rate of their development of posttraumatic stress disorder likely increases.

Writing about the psychological dimensions of war, particularly posttraumatic stress disorder, becomes especially complicated for the veteran-writer, as traumatic events seemingly resist representation. Psychiatrist and trauma theorist Dori Laub claims that "massive trauma precludes its registration; the observing and recording mechanisms of the human mind are temporarily knocked out, malfunction."[5] Consequently, trauma eludes representation because the victim fails to psychologically process, or record, the event in real time. As trauma seemingly eludes representation, the insertion of black humor can mark the author's departure from representation in favor of an artistic response that acknowledges the trauma of warfare.

Veteran-writers can express the physiological aftereffects of service through black humor, which makes comedy of the taboo or painful. Mark Hewitson contends that war instigates a "classic case of black humour," which is humor "deriving from a confrontation with suffering or death" that combines the "darkness of experience" with "the lightness of the comic."[6] By crafting a story with black humor, Swofford and Kyle can confront battle trauma in a manner that enables them to communicate the psychological aftereffects without explicitly representing the trauma. The conclusion of this chapter demonstrates that Swofford's and Kyle's memoirs are especially poignant for their affirmation of battle trauma—the *human,* psychological dimensions of war—that manifests even in an age of remote warfare.

The Gulf War: The Air Campaign, Media Broadcasts, and Swofford's Counternarrative

The Persian Gulf War, which occurred between August 1990 and February 1991, consisted of Operation Desert Storm (the combat phase occurred January 17–February 28, 1991), a military response to Iraq's invasion and unlawful annexation of its petroleum-rich neighboring country Kuwait. For this war, aerial bombing became the most efficient means of acquiring and destroying targets, and the air campaign had several objectives: destroy the Iraqi air defense system and air force; cripple the electric systems; ensure the destruction of Iraq's nuclear, chemical, and biological warfare programs; and attack Iraq's political command and control system.[7] These objectives were necessary to prevent Saddam Hussein from ordering chemical attacks, to make certain that the Iraqi air force would not be able to conduct airstrikes (as the Iraqi air force had been launching Scud attacks in Israel in an effort to weaken diplomatic relations between the United States and Israel), and to generally render Iraq without electricity. This air campaign largely eliminated the possibility of Iraq's initiation of battle with the United States, which quickly led to Iraq's surrender.

The Gulf War's designation as a "clean" war was due to the advanced weaponry that decimated key targets. A couple of the defining features of the Gulf War were its short length (as the war ended a mere one hundred hours after the ground campaign was launched) and the new developments in stealth jets and precision-guided bombs. Stacey Peebles offers impressions of this "show of overwhelming American force and technology" in *Welcome to the Suck*. She writes, "Civilians at home watched round-the-clock, real-time coverage of smart bombs gliding soundlessly into their appointed targets. The United States could do anything, it seemed, even conduct a painless war with surgical precision."[8] However, the American advancements in warfare, when matched against the Iraqis' outdated tanks and Soviet-era Scud missiles, created an impression, at least for Jean Baudrillard, that American "victory" would be achieved before the air campaign even began. Baudrillard states in *The Gulf War Did Not Take Place*, "It is as though there was a virus infecting this war from the beginning which emptied it of all credibility. It is perhaps because the two adversaries did not even confront each other face to face, the one lost in its virtual war won in advance, the other buried in its traditional war lost in advance."[9] He further claims, "Since this war was won in advance, we will never know what it would have been like had it existed. . . . But this is not a war, any more than 10,000 tonnes of bombs per day is sufficient to make it a war. Any more than the direct transmission by CNN of real time information is sufficient to authenticate a war."[10] The Gulf War was not a war as the term had been defined in earlier decades, when it was understood to mean the direct engagement with another country in active combat. Instead, Baudrillard argues that the media crafted a narrative of a war that was won before it even began because Iraq's outdated weaponry was no match for the United States' overwhelming advancements in war technology.

Aside from the brevity of the Gulf War, which was partially due to the United States' show of force and technology, the strict media censorship of the war zone was another defining feature of the war. In her essay "Site Unseen," Mimi White clarifies the role of the media as having brought the "first war fought 'live' on television" into American homes, but the news reporting was also "highly managed and restricted by the U.S. government."[11] CNN broadcasts mainly offered what Douglas Kellner describes as "extremely positive images of the U.S. troop deployment" that depicted "an incessant flow of pictures of troops, airplanes, ships, tanks, and military equipment, with interview after interview of the troops and their military spokespeople."[12] These images and censored interviews with troops offer a problematically simplistic portrayal of this war.

John J. Fialka, a frontline reporter for the Gulf War, further investigates governmental censorship and the media's abbreviated narrative of the Gulf War in *Hotel Warriors*. He writes, "Much of what [correspondents] wrote and videotaped out there remains unread and unseen to this day because the '100-Hour War' was presented to most viewers and readers in a tidy, antiseptic package. It was a finely orchestrated burst of high-tech violence where smart bombs landed precisely on the cross hairs; where generals made Babe Ruth style predictions that came true in real time; where the 'news' and its accompanying imagery were canned, wrapped, and delivered before the shooting was over."[13] Fialka importantly describes the reporting as conveying an "antiseptic," packaged narrative for this war before it even ended. In fact, about 1,600 journalists were sent to Saudi Arabia to cover the war, but only 10 percent of them were allowed in the field. Most journalists were "provided with the heightened illusion of being near the war" in hotels where they had access to televised briefings, the pool reports from returning in-field journalists, and CNN.[14] Although it would seem that the media constructed an accurate war narrative from in-field journalists and broadcast clips from the "front lines," the majority of reports and footage collected by correspondents who were allowed into the field remains "unread and unseen."

The media's antiseptic packaging of this war into a narrative suitable for broadcasting to the public problematically obscures the physical and psychological impacts of precision bombing and "clean" warfare. Specifically, Geoffrey Wright states that "during the war, the Pentagon teamed up with cable networks to inundate the American public with spectacles of Stealth bombers, Scud missiles, Patriot missiles, Tomahawk missiles, and smart bombs in action. The highly censored media coverage obscured the region's geography and erased the suffering of combatants as well as civilians."[15] By concentrating on the war machines and censoring the human victims, the media coverage becomes antiseptic, as it omits the destruction to land and people that results from bombing.

Swofford's *Jarhead: A Marine's Chronicle of the Gulf War and Other Battles* depicts the bodily risk and psychological trauma that soldiers endure in an age of remote warfare. He narrates his service in a U.S. Marine Corps Surveillance and Target Acquisition (STA) platoon during the Persian Gulf War. Swofford's mission *should have* entailed acquiring and sniping enemy targets. Instead, Swofford narrates the ironic rigor of the elite marine training for the monotony of cleanup missions while the bombs acquired the targets.

In *Jarhead*, Swofford's portrayal of soldiers parodying their roles and their "scripted" actions emphasizes that the media's reports ludicrously simplified the war and obscured the collateral damage inflicted by American bombing. In particular, Swofford narrates a football game that his platoon is ordered to play for reporters, which illuminates the absurdity of the decision to report on his platoon playing in the desert instead of broadcasting the reality of the bombing campaign. The parody of battle in the football game also elucidates the absurdity of Swofford's deploying to a war that was mostly aerially conducted. However, despite the limited role for a ground combatant in the age of remote warfare, Swofford's insertion of black humor at the end of the parodic football scene nevertheless underscores the threat of death for the ground soldiers.

The absurdity within *Jarhead* exposes the problematic nature of the media's portrayal of the Gulf War: as a result of the in-country but censored real-time barrage of decontextualized images of aircraft and bombs, as well as the chaperoned and limited reporting on the soldiers, the underlying impression of Gulf War coverage is that "there was no way to combine these isolated sequences into even a passing narrative of war."[16] Swofford addresses the media and accentuates the real-life absurdity of reporters who were meant to observe and inform the public but merely reinforced the approved governmental rhetoric. Swofford describes a scene involving correspondents who arrive at their camp: "Knowing the reporters will arrive soon, we shave for the first time in a week, pull new cammies from the bottoms of our rucks, and helmet-wash. . . . We've known about the press for a few days, and Sergeant Dunn has already recited a list of unacceptable topics. We're prohibited from divulging data concerning the capabilities of our sniper rifles or optics and the length and intensity of our training. *He's ordered us to act like top marines,* patriots, shit-hot hard dicks, the best of the battalion."[17] These soldiers who wash and put on clean uniforms are given the stage direction to "act like top marines," complete with a script of acceptable topics, which indicates that they will function as actors more than soldiers in their interactions with the media. The freshly uniformed and conscripted-to-be-confident marines are a media-friendly image to broadcast on the civilian networks rather than the dirty, overheated, and bored soldiers of whom Swofford often writes.

For the reporters, the marines are then instructed to play football in their full combat gear and gas masks.[18] The sergeant orders this football game to demonstrate the effectiveness of the new MOPP (Mission-Oriented Protective Posture) suits and the ease with which the soldiers can play football. The inherent absurdity in this scene is, of course, within the illogicality of an order to play a game in the middle of the scorching desert while wearing full combat gear. This scene begins with black humor as the marines take turns lamenting the malfunctions in their suits before the football game starts: one of Swofford's platoon mates, Kuehn, yells, "I'm fucking dead already. The cap is broken on my canteen. If I drink this, I'm gonna drink some fuckin' mustard gas." To which another marine, Vegh, replies, "My drinking tube is broken. I'm not going to break the seal on my mask, because that would kill me. I'll die of dehydration. Sir, thank you, sir." Finally, Swofford chimes in, "I requested a new gas mask four months ago. My drinking tube fell off in the gas chamber at the Palms and Kuehn stepped on it. And we have unserviceable filters in our masks. We're all dead. We are the ghosts of STA 2/7."[19] The succession of soldiers who tell the sergeant about the malfunctions in their suits and equipment progresses into black humor as the dialogue continues: Kuehn begins with a simple statement that his equipment has a break in the seal, consequently negating the mask's protection against mustard gas. Vegh adds a slight joke to his narration of the defects by claiming that he would rather die of dehydration than let the hypothetical mustard gas seep into his suit. By the time that Swofford adds to the dialogue, the malfunctions in the suits have a tinge of both physical and black humor as he states that clumsy Kuehn stepped on and broke his drinking tube in training and concludes that the faulty filters in the suits are going to kill them if used during a chemical attack. The black humor is clearest when Swofford articulates that the sergeant is looking at the "ghosts" of the battalion.

Even after lamenting that their gear is faulty, the soldiers are still ordered to play the football game, which quickly turns into a brawl that parodies their combat readiness. What starts out as a traditional football game devolves into marines punching each other and then a pileup as "the half-speed fight degenerates into a laughter-filled dog-pile, with guys fighting their way from the bottom to climb back to the top, king of the pile, king of the Desert."[20] The staged scene of playing football for the reporters, which becomes a parody of demonstrating the effectiveness of the gear in battle, regresses into a childhood game of "king of the mountain" and further exaggerates the image of combat-ready marines.

The end of the press scene also reinforces the black humor that complements the soldiers' modeling of the combat gear. When the soldiers are done performing for the reporters, the sergeant promptly orders them to strip off their suits and throw them in a trench to light them on fire. Before striking the match, Kuehn says, "May God please save us, because these MOPP suits won't."[21] The football game concludes with soldiers joking about the defective equipment that could lead to their deaths.

This football scene, which began with the ridiculousness of wearing combat gear while playing a game in an effort to give reporters material to write about (likely to demonstrate the soldiers' preparation for chemical attacks), also implies that the equipment serves as a mere symbol of war without the war. Baudrillard describes journalists donning their gas masks while sitting in Jerusalem studios as "images of masks, of blind or defeated faces, images of falsification" and "no[t] images of the field of battle."[22] Swofford's articulation of the ineffectiveness of the gas masks underscores that the media broadcast "images of falsification," as these masks were never used (Hussein never engaged in chemical warfare against American soldiers). The only "combat" that Swofford and his platoon experience occurs when their football game derails into a playful brawl. The narration of faulty gas masks and brawling marines not only parodies their combat readiness and the ridiculous simplicity of the material that the correspondents recorded but also highlights the ineffectual role of the ground combatant in a war conducted mostly aerially.

Moreover, Swofford's description of the football scene staged for the press is not the only place in which he refers to his role as an actor. In writing about running their base-camp perimeter, Swofford describes their exercise: "Our boots slap the sand with the sound of a theater curtain falling. And we are actors running around the stage. We are delivering our lines as we run. We are proving to the great theater director of All Time that we are ready for war or whatever."[23] Through language such as "theater curtain," "actors," "delivering our lines," and "theater director," Swofford relates his service in the desert to a constant rehearsal that never culminates in the final production of war. As such, he portrays the rehearsal for the war that Baudrillard claims did not take place because of the air campaign that quickly ensured a U.S. "victory." Distinctly, Swofford refers to "war or whatever" to imply his confusion regarding whether he experienced "war" at all.

For Swofford, combat becomes harder to understand as an enlisted sniper who never fires his weapon because of the changing strategies for remote warfare, which alter a soldier's perception of his role in battle. He explicitly writes, "To be a marine, a true marine, you must kill. With all of your training, all of your expertise, if you don't kill, you're not a combatant, even if you've been fired at."[24] Swofford's inability to fire his weapon and his ensuing confusion over his battle experience become evident in the climactic scene of the book.

In this scene, Swofford radios for approval to snipe Iraqi soldiers in an air control tower. The captain tells him no, because if Swofford and his partner snipe some of the Iraqis, the airfield will not surrender. Swofford writes that the captain's assertions are untrue, stating that he knows that "certain commanders, at the company level, don't want to use us because they know that two snipers with two of the finest rifles in the world and a few hundred rounds between them will in a short time inflict severe and debilitating havoc on the enemy, causing the entire airfield to surrender"; following this assertion, Swofford assumes that he has not received approval because "the captains want war just as badly as we do."[25] The scene resolves without engagement of the snipers as Swofford watches an infantry assault company move into the airfield. Swofford describes watching "grunts [move] like mules" and listening to the "confusion" over the frequency: he claims that it "sounds as though a few grunts have shot one another, that one fire team rounded a corner of a building and shot up their buddies, because they couldn't see to know that the movement they heard came from their own platoon."[26] This scene demonstrates that with the human factor of the grunts infiltrating the Iraqi airfield, confusion and error ensue as, according to Swofford's description, it sounds as though two teams have shot each other in the low visibility. Further, Swofford describes the infantry as looking like "mules," animals that serve as a primitive form of transportation and labor—an image that similarly relegates the infantry to the role of rudimentary tool of war as the bombs level the airfield. Ultimately, it is the bombs that ensure "victory."

In another scene, Swofford's confusion about his role in war as a deployed but unengaged sniper becomes especially apparent: after testing one of their newer rifles, his platoon mate states, "Hell, I don't know if *we'll* be needed. The war's going to be moving too fast."[27] Swofford writes, "He's brought up what everyone else was talking about—the possibility of our obsolescence."[28] The initial moment of confusion for Swofford is the order for him to not complete the mission that he was assigned. This is a particularly baffling order to receive because the marines "consider [them]selves highly trained and [their] talents indispensable."[29] But Swofford is also failing to secure the sniper's head shot, which proves that the marine has been well trained and has fulfilled a *purpose*. For Swofford, "the medulla shot, pink mist, [is] the confirmation that the sniper's training and history and tactics are not all for naught."[30] When the captain denies Swofford his chance at achieving the "pink mist," the implication is that Swofford's training is meaningless. The "medulla shot" that results in "pink mist"—the shot that kills an Iraqi—would confirm Swofford's training and talent, but it is the bombs that level the airfield. This sentiment that "all [is] for naught," combined with the description of grunts who potentially shoot each other in the low visibility of the ground assault, reveals that highly trained snipers may not be needed for wars that are fought with precision bombing.

Swofford's uncertainty about his purpose as a combatant remains to the end of the book, when STA is deployed to Kuwait in a "freelance operation" to sweep Iraqi barracks.[31] As part of the cleanup mission after the bombing campaign has ended, Swofford's platoon is told that they can discharge Iraqi weapons in approved shooting zones.[32] Significantly, Swofford's platoon mates are not firing *their* weapons in the war zone. Swofford writes, "I fire, and next to me my platoon mates fire, from the hip, with no precision, as though we are famous and immortal and it doesn't matter that we'll likely hit nothing firing from such an absurd and unstable position, but we burn through the magazines."[33] This final act of emptying enemy gun chambers does not even result in an act of accurate target practice—STA's training is utterly wasted.

In this scene and occasionally in other statements, such as his declaration that "it's absurd to be in the desert and at the same time confined" to their base camp, Swofford actually uses the word *absurd* to describe his service.[34] He also mentions reading absurd texts (while deployed and after his service), such as Albert Camus's *The Stranger* and *The Myth of Sisyphus* and Louis-Ferdinand Céline's *Death on the Installment Plan*.[35] In addition to reading absurd authors, Swofford also replicates the same commentary as the absurdists in his book. Charles B. Harris claims that absurdists "comment upon the artificiality not only of art, but of life as it is usually lived, of mass society."[36] Swofford demonstrates the absurdist's vision of artificiality when he writes, "I remade my war one word at a time, a foolish, desperate act. . . . What did I hope to gain? More bombs are coming. Dig your holes with the

hands that God gave you."³⁷ This excerpt exemplifies the artificiality
of the art, as Swofford "rema[kes] [the] war one word at a time, a foolish, desperate act." He also comments on mass society when he claims
that "more bombs are coming." Like absurdist authors who "tend to see
history as repetitive," Swofford suggests that the history of Americans
waging war is repetitive and perpetual as more bombs are inevitably
"coming."³⁸ Swofford's commentary on the Gulf War not only indicates
America's proclivity for waging war but also critiques the media's representation of it. Through the language and artistry of the absurd, Swofford can offer his counternarrative to the public's perception of a "clean"
Gulf War as he elucidates the violence inflicted by precision bombs
and his resulting trauma from witnessing such destruction.

Kellner explicates that, despite the broadcast media's narrative of the
war, the damage to infrastructure and bodies during the Gulf War was
inflicted by the most relentless bombing campaign since the Second
World War: "The U.S. dominated multinational coalition systematically destroyed Iraq's military and economic infrastructure and inflicted terrible suffering on the Iraqi people. The Pentagon worked to
project an image of a clean, precise, and efficient technowar war, in
which the U.S. military was controlling events and leading the coalition inexorably to victory."³⁹ However, after the war, the Pentagon admitted that "70 percent of the bombs missed their targets," which led
to significant numbers of civilian casualties and destruction of nontar-
get infrastructure.⁴⁰ In addition, Peebles states, "Media coverage assured
the public that the war was just, efficient, and, after late February, over
and done with. Subsequently, reports and images would leak out that
indicated otherwise: the carnage on the Highway of Death, the collateral damage of misdirected attacks."⁴¹

Swofford corroborates these accounts of the destruction inflicted by
the military but obscured by the media as he writes, "They're forgetting the mission of the military: to extinguish the lives and livelihood
of other humans. What do they think all of those bombs are for?"⁴² He
explicitly describes the effects of the bombing that were not reported
by the journalists. After passing a site of bombing, Swofford states, "I've
never seen such destruction. The scene is too real not to be real. Every
fifty to one hundred feet a burnt-out and bombed-out enemy vehicle lies
disabled on the unimproved surface road, bodies dead in the vehicles or blown from them."⁴³ He exposes the sheer force of the American

military and the resulting collateral damage as he writes, "What has happened? Bombs, bombs, big bombs and small bombs."[44] As he walks through "the epic results of American bombing, American might," he claims, "The filth is on my boots."[45] By describing the destroyed vehicles and the Iraqi bodies that he witnessed and alluding to the trauma that he experienced, Swofford writes a counternarrative to the clean-war rhetoric that the media and government sought to construct about precision bombing. He figuratively refers to his trauma as "the filth," a word choice that directly opposes the implied "cleanliness" of the bombing.

Swofford does not explicitly name battle trauma but rather refers to the "mirage" that appears a handful of times throughout the book. For example, he writes, "The mirage interferes, even long after the Gulf War," and the mirage is "unknowable."[46] A mirage in a desert is an illusory perception of objects or people; Swofford describes his experience in the Gulf War as a mirage to indicate his confusion as to whether he experienced combat. The mirage, as an abstracted and allegorical concept, fittingly symbolizes a war that never seemed to commence for him, though the violent effects of bombing appear in the desert.

Allegorical devices appear within absurd texts, as Martin Esslin states: an "age-old tradition present in the Theatre of the Absurd is the use of mythical, allegorical and dreamlike modes of thought—the projection into concrete terms of psychological realities."[47] In line with the absurdists, Swofford attempts to give his memory a label that is somewhat concrete: a mirage calls a real-life referent to mind for the audience while simultaneously not labeling a trauma. Laub claims that "trauma survivors live not with the memories of the past, but with an event that could not and did not proceed through to its completion, has no ending, attained no closure, and therefore, as far as its survivors are concerned, continues into the present and is current in every respect."[48] The mirage-as-psychological-turmoil accentuates the representational issues for the veteran-turned-author, who selects the recurring word *mirage* to denote his trauma, which resists closure, as opposed to directly naming posttraumatic stress disorder. For Swofford to write that the "mirage" continues to "interfere" "long after the Gulf War" indicates that his war memories resist closure as they continue to reemerge as the illusory mirage. The mirage becomes allegorical for the memories that Swofford cannot, or will not, remember.

Toward the conclusion of his memoir, Swofford relates trauma to "a wreck in your head, part of the aftermath, and you must dismantle the wreck. . . . It took years for you to understand that the most complex and dangerous conflicts, the most harrowing operations, and the most deadly wars, occur in the head."[49] Swofford indicates that a "wreck" must be dismantled, which implies that the "war" he now experiences is in fighting the psychological postwar effects. More than merely recognizing that even the "clean" war resulted in trauma, Swofford conveys that he still attempts to figure out, to dismantle, the war experience. Significantly, the word *wreck* draws to mind a mangled machine: the same wreckage that reminds him of the targets that the machines acquired for the highly trained but ineffectual sniper.

Swofford was one of the first snipers to deploy alongside fighter jets and precision bombs, and he articulates his confusion about the diminishing role of the combatant amid remote warfare through the language of the absurd. Aside from emphasizing his confusion about his role in war, Swofford's parody of battle illustrates the censorship that rendered the reporting on the war ridiculous as journalists recorded soldiers playing football but did not report the collateral damage of bombing. This unreported collateral damage encompasses not only material destruction but also the psychological effects soldiers suffer after witnessing bombing. Analysis of Swofford's inclusion of allegorical symbols to name his distress and the black humor that attests to his traumatic experience reveals how a veteran can narrate war even when battle trauma can complicate the act of writing.

War in Iraq: Black Humor, Bullets, and Kyle's *American Sniper*

In 2003, the United States began a second war in Iraq. In his speech to the United Nations on September 12, 2002, President George W. Bush outlined three justifications for preventative war in Iraq: "to pre-empt possible use of weapons of mass destruction; the frequent, flagrant and continuing violation of international law, and the on-going violation of human rights."[50] Kyle does not address the role of the media in his memoir; however, akin to the Gulf War reporting, the media coverage of the 2003 invasion of Iraq also corroborated governmental rhetoric and "avoided the depth of controversy the war incited and focused instead on appealing to the audience through a number of strategies. One of the most significant strategies was the retelling of the official narrative the government used to justify war."[51]

Like Swofford's, Kyle's role is to engage in war at a distance by sniping. Unlike Swofford, Kyle frequently snipes insurgents, and he attained notoriety as the most lethal sniper in American history: the Pentagon officially confirmed more than 150 of Kyle's kills, which broke the previous American record. Kyle's autobiography, *American Sniper,* narrates his years of training and his four tours in Afghanistan and Iraq. It also features two other listed authors, Scott McEwen and Jim DeFelice, but Kyle clearly claims the memoir as his own in his "Author's Note" that prefaces the book: "The Department of Defense, including high-ranking U.S.N. personnel, reviewed the text for accuracy and sensitive material. Even though they cleared the book for publication, this does not mean they like everything they read. But this is my story, not theirs." Kyle alludes to the governmental censorship that prevents soldiers from revealing too much information about the military, although he indicates that this book presents *his* perspective of the war.

Just as Swofford uses narrative absurdity in his memoir, Kyle illuminates the psychological effects of his service by including black humor and parodying combat by describing it as a game. The metaphor of war as a game appears in literature by veteran-writers such as Tim O'Brien, Joseph Heller, and James W. Blinn, among others, who fictionalized their war experiences. Although a war memoir is aesthetically different from a work of fiction, all these veteran-writers turn to the game metaphor to illustrate their wars. Elaine Scarry also notably claims that war is a contest. The term *game* fittingly characterizes the war experience, which is based on "rules," such as the rules of engagement and strategic planning, and requires targets to be acquired and eliminated to "win." However, Swofford and Kyle exaggerate the game-like features of their wars, such as in Swofford's parodying of combat readiness with a football game and Kyle's description of "bagging" insurgents.

In an absurd scene, Kyle describes insurgents who attempt to cross a river by floating on oversize beach balls with all of their equipment. Kyle plays a "game" of sniping one ball and watching the insurgents panic as they swim to and cling to another ball. Once Kyle has sniped all the beach balls, the insurgents sink under the weight of their equipment and drown, prompting Kyle to proclaim, "Hell—it was a *lot* of fun."[52] Kyle's sniping of the beach balls and his declaration that it is "fun" parody the concept of conventional battle. Kyle plays target practice with beach balls instead of directly engaging the insurgents, which undercuts the seriousness of battle. In the act of sniping beach balls, which are traditionally symbols of recreation and leisure, entertainment is juxtaposed with killing. Thus, the beach ball scene reads like a parody of a firefight during which Kyle has "a lot of fun" drowning insurgents.

In another scene, Kyle's narration of combat portrays a firefight as similar to a "game" in which points are acquired. He recounts, "When the bad guys were hiding, we tried to dare them into showing themselves so we could take them down. One of the guys had a bandana, which we took and fashioned into a kind of mummy head. Equipped with goggles and a helmet, it looked almost like a soldier—certainly at a few hundred yards. So we attached it to a pole and held it up over the roof, trying to draw fire one day when the action slowed. It brought a couple of insurgents out and we bagged them."[53] This scene is another instance in which Kyle's sniping appears more as an act of play than combat. The description of the "mummy head" also juxtaposes death symbolism with an act of play. As with the beach ball scene, the mummy-decoy scene seems like a parody of battle in which soldiers are playing as opposed to killing. The end of the scene, in which Kyle is able to "bag" some of the insurgents, also reads like the description of a game in which Kyle has accumulated some points for acquiring the targets.

The absurdity of war emerges from Kyle's descriptions of war as a game and also in his word choices. Although Kyle does not overtly write the word *absurd* as Swofford does, he frequently inserts the adjective *bizarre,* which similarly denotes unconventionality. In one such instance, Kyle lists misplaced items that he would find on his building searches, such as a car tire on a roof in Fallujah or a goat in the bathroom of a Haifa Street apartment. He claims that he would see these items and then "spend the rest of the day wondering what the story was. After a while, the bizarre came to seem natural."[54] Kyle's reliance on the word *bizarre* continues to emphasize the inexplicable experience of his war service, as it is a word that not only has the connotation of "strange" but also remains ambiguous in its lack of precision. In other words, Kyle's imprecise wording suggests that conventional language cannot always represent the war experience.

In addition to describing strange scenes of misplaced items, Kyle also implies that contemporary war is inherently absurd in its excessive precision. He writes of his war, "It became so predictable, it seemed to happen according to a time schedule. Around about nine in the morning you'd have a firefight; things would slack off around midday. Then, around three or four in the afternoon, you'd have another. If the stakes weren't life and death, it would have been funny. And at the time, it *was* funny, in a perverse kind of way."[55] The idea of war as adhering to a schedule with the same inanities and repetitions as daily life seems innately absurd. But Kyle also refers to the ludicrous nature of war, which renders this repetitiveness and predictability funny—or at least funny in a black-humor sort of way, because losing this "game" results in death.

In a more overt instance of black humor, Kyle writes that the Iraqis had deployed some Scuds before the war officially started. He relates that even though most of them have been eliminated by Patriot missiles, "one got through. Wouldn't you know it took out the Starbucks where we'd hung out during our prewar training? That's low, hitting a coffee place. It could have been worse, I guess. It could have been a Dunkin' Donuts. The joke was that President Bush only declared war when the Starbucks was hit. You can mess with the U.N. all you want, but when you start interfering with the right to get caffeinated, someone has to pay."[56] In these sentences, Kyle employs black humor to comment on war's political factors: his perception of the ineffectual United Nations as an acceptable target, the unacceptable bombing of a beloved coffee store, and the seemingly arbitrary declaration of war in Iraq by President Bush. Kyle also jokes about the bombing of the Starbucks by expressing his relief that at least the Dunkin' Donuts was not hit. These instances of black humor acknowledge the violence to which Kyle is subjected in a war zone and also convey its psychological impact, a point discussed in the conclusion.

Attesting to Trauma through Black Humor

Swofford and Kyle were two snipers deployed to a war in Iraq by two President Bushes to provide ground support in an age of aerial warfare.

The absurd lens exposes another similarity between these snipers: Kyle was deployed to secure an Iraqi oil field that was previously set ablaze in the Gulf War.[57] However, he cannot secure the oilfield, and air support is called. Just as absurdist authors "tend to see history as repetitive," Kyle describes war history as absurdly repeating in his memoir, as Swofford's prediction that more "more bombs are coming" materializes in Kyle's war when the same oil fields that were bombed in the Gulf War are also bombed in the Iraq War.[58]

As veteran-writers, Swofford and Kyle illustrate that remote warfare is not so "clean." Their parodies of battle and insertion of black humor reveal some of the ethical stakes of their wars: the media's problematically "sanitized" portrayal, recirculated governmental rhetoric, the underreported collateral damage of bombing in Iraq, and the under-acknowledged impact of remote warfare on soldiers' psyches. Humans in the crosshairs of rifles become points, and bombs are dropped on blurry figures with heat signatures, but obscuring humanity does not assuage the trauma that can, and usually does, emerge postservice. By specifically inserting black humor into their narratives, Swofford and Kyle crucially describe the most difficult battle for a veteran: posttraumatic stress disorder.

In his concluding pages, Kyle addresses the psychological impact of war: "I'm not the same guy I was when I first went to war. No one is." This leads him to conclude that "war definitely changes you."[59] He claims that his "continually going to war" indicates that he "gravitate[s] to the blackest parts of existence," a statement that indicates that Kyle acknowledges the psychological and emotional stress of his war service.[60] For the soldiers who deploy to wars that increasingly rely on methods of remote warfare and later write of their experiences, black humor enables them to comment on the bodily danger to which they are still subjected but that is obscured by the broadcast media. Importantly, Kyle's and Swofford's black humor reminds the reading audience that soldiers can develop battle trauma even in an age in which war seems to be surgically conducted with precision bombing and sniping.

Swofford's and Kyle's dark jokes seemingly enable them to attest to their traumatic experiences without explicitly representing those moments, as black humor can serve as an emotional analgesic for the veterans who must write of violent scenes. Kyle mentions the need for black humor when he writes, "People back home, people who haven't been in war, or at least not that war, sometimes don't seem to understand how the troops in Iraq acted. They're surprised—shocked—to discover we often joked about death, about things we saw."[61] Kyle continues, "We saw terrible things, and lived through terrible things. Part of it was letting off pressure or steam, I'm sure. A way to cope. If you can't make sense of things, you start to look for some other way to deal with them. You laugh because you have to have some emotion, you have to express yourself somehow."[62] Kyle alludes to traumatic experiences as "things," which are reminiscent of Tim O'Brien's "things" to carry. *Things* is an unspecified word that Kyle repeats twice in just one sentence, which is similar to Swofford's articulation of trauma as the amorphous "mirage." Although Swofford and Kyle name their trauma "thing" and "mirage," the vague quality of this language indicates that their battle trauma cannot be represented in conventional language. However, they persist in sharing their stories through the unconventional language of the absurd tradition, which enables them to offer a figurative illustration of trauma.

While writing the absurd parody of battle that was the Gulf War may assist Swofford in "dismantl[ing] the wreck" and fighting the "most deadly wars [that] occur in the head," the black humor Kyle uses to describe the sniping "games" that he engaged in similarly enables him to "express himself somehow."[63] By crafting jokes and parodying their deployments, Swofford and Kyle can find the words to express traumatic experiences and reveal the violent realities of their wars. Posttraumatic stress disorder is still a mostly unspoken battle, an imperceptible "thing" that comes to light in a dark joke.

Notes

1. Chris Kyle, *American Sniper* (New York: HarperCollins, 2012), 313.
2. Robert A. Hipkiss, *The American Absurd: Pynchon, Vonnegut, and Barth* (Port Washington, N.Y.: Associated Faculty, 1984), 3.
3. Charles B. Harris, *Contemporary American Novelists of the Absurd* (New Haven, Conn.: College and University Press, 1971), 24.
4. Dave Grossman, *On Killing: The Psychological Cost of Learning to Kill in War* (New York: Back Bay Books, 2009), 44–45.

5. Dori Laub, "Bearing Witness, or the Vicissitudes of Listening," in *Testimony: Crises of Witnessing in Literature, Psychoanalysis, and History,* by Shoshana Felman and Dori Laub (New York: Routledge, 1992), 57.

6. Mark Hewitson, "Black Humour: Caricature in Wartime," *Oxford German Studies* 41, no. 2 (2012): 216.

7. Williamson Murray, *War Strategy, and Military Effectiveness* (Cambridge: Cambridge University Press, 2011), 273.

8. Stacey Peebles, *Welcome to the Suck: Narrating the American Soldier's Experience in Iraq* (Ithaca, N.Y.: Cornell University Press, 2011), 35.

9. Jean Baudrillard, *The Gulf War Did Not Take Place,* trans. Paul Patton (Bloomington: Indiana University Press, 1991), 62.

10. Baudrillard, 61.

11. Mimi White, "Site Unseen: An Analysis of CNN's War in the Gulf," in *Seeing through the Media: The Persian Gulf War,* ed. Susan Jeffords and Lauren Rabinovitz (New Brunswick, N.J.: Rutgers University Press, 1994), 122.

12. Douglas Kellner, *The Persian Gulf TV War* (Boulder, Colo.: Westview, 1992), 87.

13. John J. Fialka, *Hotel Warriors: Covering the Gulf War* (Baltimore: Johns Hopkins University Press, 1991), 1–2.

14. Fialka, 55.

15. Geoffrey A. Wright, "The Desert of Experience: *Jarhead* and the Geography of the Persian Gulf War," *PMLA* 124, no. 5 (2009): 1677.

16. Tom Engelhardt, "The Gulf War as Total Television," in Jeffords and Rabinovitz, *Seeing through the Media,* 90.

17. Anthony Swofford, *Jarhead* (New York: Scribner, 2003), 13–14, emphasis added.

18. Swofford, 17.

19. Swofford, 20.

20. Swofford, 20.

21. Swofford, 22.

22. Baudrillard, *Gulf War Did Not,* 40.

23. Swofford, *Jarhead,* 73.

24. Swofford, 247.

25. Swofford, 230.

26. Swofford, 230–31.

27. Swofford, 158.

28. Swofford, 159.

29. Swofford, 85.

30. Swofford, 57.

31. Swofford, 237.

32. Swofford, 244.

33. Swofford, 244.

34. Swofford, 72.

35. Swofford, 90, 113.

36. Harris, *Contemporary American Novelists,* 23.

37. Swofford, *Jarhead,* 254.

38. Hipkiss, *American Absurd,* 3.

39. Kellner, *Persian Gulf TV War,* 186.

40. Kellner, 234.

41. Peebles, *Welcome to the Suck,* 35.

42. Swofford, *Jarhead,* 172.

43. Swofford, 221.

44. Swofford, 222.

45. Swofford, 222.

46. Swofford, 75, 83.

47. Martin Esslin, *The Theatre of the Absurd* (New York: Anchor, 1961), 301.

48. Laub, "Bearing Witness," 69.

49. Swofford, *Jarhead,* 247–48.

50. James Turner Johnson, "Just War Thinking in Recent American Religious Debate over Military Force," in *The Price of Peace: Just War in the Twenty-First Century,* ed. Charles Reed and David Ryall (Cambridge: Cambridge University Press, 2007), 84.

51. Deborah Lynn Jaramillo, *Ugly War, Pretty Package: How CNN and Fox News Made the Invasion of Iraq High Concept* (Bloomington: Indiana University Press, 2009), 39.

52. Kyle, *American Sniper,* 203.

53. Kyle, 309–10.

54. Kyle, 214.

55. Kyle, 280–81, emphasis in original.

56. Kyle, 92.

57. Kyle, 85.

58. Hipkiss, *American Absurd,* 3; Swofford, *Jarhead,* 254.

59. Kyle, *American Sniper,* 428.

60. Kyle, 429.

61. Kyle, 312.

62. Kyle, 312.

63. Swofford, *Jarhead,* 247–48; Kyle, *American Sniper,* 312.

CHAPTER 12

An Architecture against Dacoits

On Drones, Mosquitoes, and the Smart City

SAJDEEP SOOMAL

Hovering more than thirty thousand feet above ground level, military drones differ from earlier regimes of American aerial power. Invisible to the naked eye and only perceptible on the ground by their "low-grade, perpetual buzzing," drones are routinely described sonically as *machar* (mosquitoes) by residents living in the Federally Administered Tribal Areas (FATA) of northwestern Pakistan.[1] The bleak observation gives affective texture to how drones arrive silently and suddenly into the everyday social realities of ordinary people living in the tribal areas of Pakistan. It is also a reminder that the U.S. drone strike program does not exist in a vacuum in Pakistan; the sky, the atmosphere, the blueness hold multiple, interlocking vectors of terror. Across the country, thunder roars. Mosquitoes indiscriminately spread dengue fever. The monsoon, now erratic and temperamental, heralds life-destroying rains. Toxic pollutants flow into old rivers. The economy crashes. Cunning birds trick generous fish. There is no easy way to capture—let alone sense or apprehend—the charged, atmospheric tensions that shape life in the Pakistani borderlands and to understand how military drones have arrived within and altered that landscape.

The carnage of drone warfare itself has been difficult to document. Unlike previous on-the-ground American counterinsurgencies, where war was among the people and drew media attention, drone warfare elides the same type of visual documentation by remotely using "surgical precision" and "laser-like focus" to "cleanly" obliterate insurgents.[2]

303

Public intellectual Mark Bowden explains that as a result, we do not
see any of the carnage of drone killings. "There are no pictures, there
are no remains, there is no debris that anyone in the United States ever
sees," he tells us. "It's kind of antiseptic."³ Accounts of drone warfare
often start from this sanitized aftermath, in hard statistics, chilling
testimonies, and cold reportage. In this representational void, there has
been a litany of artists, writers, and cultural producers from across
South Asia, the Middle East, Africa, and its diasporas who have put
forward drone warfare otherwise. Their projects—ranging from the
#NotABugSplat campaign in the Khyber Pakhtunkhwa region of
Pakistan to Iraqi American artist Wafaa Bilal's digitally mediated
performances—have drawn international attention to the impact of
drone warfare and have been studied by a number of American studies scholars, including Matt Delmont, Keith Feldman, Inderpal Grewal,
Ronak Kapadia, and Anjali Nath.

Thinking in line with these scholars, this chapter was initially conceived in early February 2015 as an exploration of diasporic Pakistani
cultural productions about drone warfare for a yearlong graduate seminar on American empire led by historian Shanon Fitzpatrick at Mc-
Gill University. Looking for texts that refused the logics of American
militarism, I quickly landed on a familiar song in my iTunes library:
Punjabi American rapper Heems's debut single, "Soup Boys (Pretty
Drones)." Released on November 1, 2012, the song unveils and subverts
the logics of American racial and military imperialism using seemingly
absurdist lyrics and imagery. I initially wrote about how the music
video explores the affective similitudes between death and heartbreak,
reveals the entanglements between mainland U.S. police surveillance
and drone strikes in Pakistan, and showcases the promises of getting
stoned as a way of living under militaristic American imperialism. In
her article "Stones, Stoners and Drones: Transnational South Asian Visuality from Above and Below," Anjali Nath takes up the same vein of
thinking to consider the "possible strategic interventions of irreverence,
satire, and inebriation" offered in the music video.⁴ For her, "Soup Boys
(Pretty Drones)" confronts the racial gaze of the drone with an inebriated look that blurs distinctions between the War on Terror and the
War on Drugs, asking us instead to "cast a stoned glance toward the
sky."⁵ Nath explains that in its willful incoherence, the music video puts
forward a visuality from below that escapes narrative cogency, eliding

categorization as a solely "anti-drone" text by considering drone warfare alongside other facets of U.S. imperialism.[6]

I heard the song live when Heems performed at Bar Le Ritz PDB in Montreal in the summer of 2015. Outside the concert, I talked with friends about the necessary drama around his continued use of the *n* word, while we laughed about how exactly those pretty drones would sexually dominate him. We wondered why the pretty drones—figureheads of contemporary American militarism—were women in the first place. Nath aptly writes about how Heems paints the American Predator drone as "an irrational and an unruly femme fatale, and relies on worn sexist, gendered tropes to assert a form of resistance."[7] Thinking along those lines, there was consensus on the sidewalk that he was a *philosobro*, that his inebriated assessment of politics, love, and life itself was rather a common brand of dissociative masculine ramblings about the current state of affairs.

At that point, I started thinking about Heems's work within the gendered history of diasporic Punjabi music. In *Impossible Desires: Queer Diasporas and South Asian Public Cultures,* Gayatri Gopinath studies the British Bhangra movements of the 1980s and 1990s and the post-Bhangra Asian Underground music scene, demonstrating how its male artists and groups held deep investments in militant masculinity, genealogical descent, and heteropatriarchal reproduction.[8] Unlike his predecessors, Heems is invested in a softer type of philosobro masculinity from the subcontinent, one that is found among poets, fakirs, qawwali singers, worshippers of Lal Shahbaz Qalander, and men who are not really Men. In his other songs, Heems draws out nonbiological syncretic lines of masculine genealogical descent by venerating and mimicking popular philosobros from the subcontinent, including the popular poet Shiv Kumar Batalvi and qawwali singer Aziz Mian. Rather than championing militancy, these artists herald intoxication and ecstasy (substance driven, religious, or otherwise) as generative strategies to deal with male heartbreak, state violence, and other problems that plague the minds of men.

It was only after repeated attempts to meet with an intoxicated Heems when he performed in Montreal that I took a step back from writing about the music video. At that event, I was forced to reckon with the complex realities behind the promises of getting stoned. Intimately familiar with the impact of addiction within my own family and in

Punjabi communities more broadly, I suddenly saw the inebriated gaze and meditative intoxication that Heems and his predecessors put forward in a more common and less revolutionary light. That point became clearer later that fall when life circumstances led me back home to southwestern Ontario to visit my dying grandfather. As I sat in the hospital chair, I listened to my grandfather reflect on the decades that he lived as an alcoholic, his decision to convert to *Namdhari* Sikhism, and his dismay that not even God could fix his kidneys. When there was nothing left to say and death was hanging in the air, he started reciting Punjabi folktales from my childhood. For the first time, I spent time considering the narrative forms and unruly lessons of these folktales while reacquainting myself with some disturbing cultural tropes and an unending cast of anthropomorphized animals. Enchanted by this mode of storytelling from South Asia, I started looking for contemporary folkloric accounts of drone warfare in Pakistan.

With that approach in mind, I stumbled upon the first text that forms the bedrock of this chapter: an Urdu-language cartoon titled "Kabhi Dengue, Kabhi Drone" (Sometimes Dengue, Sometimes Drone) that stages a conversation between a dengue-carrying mosquito and an American Predator drone. Produced in 2011 by Pakistan's most popular television station, Geo TV, the video shows the drone and mosquito duo flying, talking, and colluding together. Unlike the femme fatale drone in "Soup Boys (Pretty Drones)," the drone and his interlocutor in this text are presented as subcontinental men of a different sort: *dacoits* (bandits). In my analysis of "Kabhi Dengue, Kabhi Drone," I explore how the cartoon obfuscates the threats of American Predator imperialism and dengue fever by ballooning and displacing those threats onto a local figure of terror: the Dacoit. Emerging from the subjection of criminal tribes under British colonial law, the figure of the Dacoit is best captured in popular cinematic portrayals of morally depraved rural outlaws. Studying representations of dacoity in Indian cinema, I describe how dacoit characters were remade as "Indian savages" after American Western films—with their prototypical Cowboy and Indian storylines—circulated to South Asia in the 1970s. To better understand the implications of this cross-cultural encounter, I turn toward the work of Chickasaw scholar Jodi Byrd, who draws out how the recurring figure of the "merciless Indian Savage" put forward in American Western film functions as the stencil for what Jasbir Puar defines as Islamic monster-terrorist-fags.[9] It is through the reproduction of a paradigmatic, merciless Indianness in the United States–led War on Terror against monster-terrorist-fags, accordingly to Byrd, that the American empire identifies, remakes, and manages its terrorist enemies, transiting across the globe to places like the FATA. Building on that line of thinking, I suggest that the contemporary Global War on Terror arrives in the FATA with ease because the Pakistan state simultaneously identifies, remakes, and manages its terrorist enemies through the reproduction of an analogous, local variant of the "merciless Indian savage," namely the outlaw figure of the Dacoit. In my close reading of "Kabhi Dengue, Kabhi Drone," I show how dacoity functions as a powerful psychic stencil in South Asia, one that can be mobilized to shape Predator drones, dengue-carrying mosquitoes, and other threatening forces into local, villainous dacoits. When postcolonial states like Pakistan psychically collapse new threats such drone warfare into older, ongoing fights that subject Indigenous and tribal peoples as dacoity does, I contend that the shaky foundation upon which those postcolonial states base their rights to sovereignty is once again revealed. These reflections set the stage for the second inquiry of this chapter: If not in the postcolony, then where can we find shelter from the drone?

New media artist and writer Hiba Ali has been asking this question for a few years. I first met Ali while I was working at the South Asian Visual Arts Centre in Toronto. The nonprofit, artist-run center supports artists of color to produce art that offers challenging, multifarious perspectives on the contemporary world. The organization programs artwork beyond the constricting economies of sexism, racism, and classism that have shaped programming paradigms for work by artists of color in the Canadian art world since the rise of liberal multicultural politics in the 1970s and 1980s. It is within this context that I first met Ali and learned about her experimental architectural proposal for a drone-proof smart city. A collaborative effort with architect Asher J. Kohn, *Shura City* is a provocation to think about the possibilities and pitfalls of defensive architecture in the contemporary moment. Using the smart city and the drone as its conceptual starting point, the proposal explores the possibilities of an architectural build for a new postcolony, one that will protect its occupants from the carnage of drone killings. In this chapter, I consider one iteration of their proposal: a satirical, corporatized presentation for potential investors to fund the drone-proof smart city. Thinking through the short video pitch, I demonstrate how paradigms of speculation, securitization, extraction, privacy, and surveillance are endemic to the architectural imperatives of contemporary smart-city development projects. In their pitch for Shura City, the artists reveal how a seemingly subversive, drone-proof smart city can quickly turn into its own technosecuritized, neoliberal state—one that is destined to replicate the same structuring logics as the old postcolony. An architecture against drones quickly turns into an architecture against dacoits. Considering the project as an experiment in architectural thought, I end by reflecting on conversations with Ali about her emerging music practice and how to dream architecturally in the midst of military drones, dengue-carrying mosquitoes, ever-expanding neoliberal states, and unresolved antagonisms.

Folkloric Skies

On September 28, 2014, John Oliver delved into America's drone strike program on HBO's award-winning late-night talk and news satire television program *Last Week Tonight with John Oliver.* Garnering nearly twelve million views on YouTube, the episode was covered in popular liberal media outlets including the *Rolling Stones, Slate, Esquire,* and *Huffington Post.* In the thirteen-minute segment, Oliver explores what political geographers Ian Shaw and Majed Akhter call the "dronification of national security" in the United States.[10] The terror of the drone—we are told—is unparalleled in contemporary Pakistan and elsewhere on the edge of empire. Like other news media, Oliver's reportage draws on sanitized statistics, brute analyses, and somber testimonies to reveal the political life of the U.S. drone strike program. This data reportage about the drone is broken up by unlikely comedic and satirical commentary that places the drone within other, overlapping worlds. For Oliver, drones are not only a "specter of imminent death" but simultaneously the "third most annoying thing in the sky after mosquitoes and plastic bags caught in the breeze."[11]

Toward the end of that segment, Oliver shares a clip from the folkloric cartoon that I take up in this chapter: "Kabhi Dengue, Kabhi Drone" (Figure 12.1). After screening the "weird, satirical cartoon," as he calls it, Oliver defends the clip to his American audiences by assuring

FIGURE 12.1. In this episode about drones on *Last Week Tonight,* John Oliver presents the folkloric Pakistani cartoon "Kabhi Dengue, Kabhi Drone."

them it would be a lot funnier if they "spoke Urdu and lived in constant fear of being murdered by a drone." Oliver uses the cartoon to explain how drones have become "a routine feature of life in Pakistan." As Oliver continues on to other damning testimonies about the everyday impact of drone warfare in Pakistan, he sidesteps the "weird, satirical cartoon" that I use in this chapter to explore the complexities around how American drone warfare is psychically digested in the subcontinental postcolony.

Referencing the successful 2001 Bollywood family drama *Kabhi Khushi Kabhie Gham* (*Sometimes Happiness, Sometimes Sadness*), the title of the cartoon "Kabhi Dengue, Kabhi Drone" locates drone strikes and dengue infections within the ups and downs of daily life in Pakistan. The cartoon was first aired to the Pakistani public on a number of local channels, including Geo News and the popular sports channel Geo Super. Subsequently uploaded to YouTube by various Pakistani users, the online videos have garnered a modest twenty thousand views in total.

During the opening title scene and throughout the video, the song "Marenge Ya Mar Jayenge" ("We Will Hit It and It Will Die") from the hit 1983 Bollywood film *Pukar* (*Cry Out to the World*) plays in the background, situating the fight against American Predator imperialism against another South Asian anticolonial struggle. The film *Pukar* delves into the liberation struggle in Goa against the Portuguese government that continued past 1947, the year when the British Raj collapsed in South Asia. By selecting a song from that particular anticolonial film, the producers place the cartoon within a *longue durée* of political struggles against European imperialism across the subcontinent. The refrain of the song featured in the cartoon—"Marenge ya mar jayenge. Wo dhamaka kar jayenge. Dekho dekho hor se dekho" (We will hit it and it will die. We will make that explosion. Look, look, look some more)—sardonically comments on the visual sadism of American aerial militarism by compelling viewers to consider the gaze of the drone. Lev Grossman explains, "A drone isn't just a tool; when you use it, you see and act through it—you inhabit it."[12] Military drone technology—typified by the asymmetrical embodiment of sight between the hunter and the target (where the drone operator has the capacity to see without being seen)—reconfigures how enemy combatants are identified, processed, and killed. As Derek Gregory explains, looking through the eye of the drone, military analysts see objects as rifles, prayer as a "Taliban signifier," civilians as "military-aged males," and children as "adolescents."[13] In this cartoon, the playful instruction to "look, look, look some more" in the song emphasizes what Gregory identifies as the unending, searching gaze of the drone, one that is designed to find enemies where there are not any.

The opening scene of the animated short transports the viewer to the seemingly empty and inhospitable mountain ranges of Pakistan, somewhere along the postcolonial frontier. The sandy, desertlike, hilly landform signifies either the Pothohar Plateau or the Salt Range, suggesting the area is in the heartland of Pakistan somewhere between Punjab, Khyber Pakhtunkhwa, and the FATA, where the drone and mosquito might practically crossover. Against the backdrop is an animated rendering of a Predator drone. Colored light blue with black and white accents, the drone seems to be camouflaged to blend into the clear blue sky. On the back panel, where the aircraft number is usually inscribed, you can make out the marking "US420."

The marking urges us to consider in more depth the deceptive tactics of the U.S. military state. In northern India and Pakistan, the term *420* (pronounced "char-so-bees") is popularly used when someone cheats or cons you.[14] It refers to what Michelle Murphy calls the "infrastructures of gaslighting," where powerful neoliberal states, corporations, and individuals seek to sow the seeds of doubt in affected or targeted populations.[15] It is not coincidental that the cartoon was first released in late 2011, months before the Barack Obama administration—after decades of public statements that denied the existence of a drone program—finally publicly admitted to having used drone strikes in Pakistan since 2004. Drone technology first emerged during the Cold War in the 1950s with unlimited funding from the U.S. National Reconnaissance Office, which meant that drones did not have to compete with fighters, bombers, or other military agents for financial resources. Diplomatic historian Robert Farley explains that the Predator drone's later success in the 1990s and onward hinged on the emergence of a "robust, reliable data system for linking drones and operators," as well as on bandwidth and data storage capacities that were unimaginable to those who first conceived of the drone in secret in the 1950s.[16] As drone capabilities improved, the Obama administration secretly ordered a total of 193 strikes from 2009 until mid-2011—a stark contrast to the 52 drone strikes carried out under the George W. Bush administration. After investigative journalist Jane Mayer first reported on CIA-authorized drone strikes in Pakistan in 2009 and the wreckage of the strikes themselves accumulated over the following years, the Obama administration was finally compelled to end its gaslighting tactics and publicly acknowledge its decades-old drone program in January 2012.[17]

As the US420 marking disappears, the drone continues loudly snoring while a dengue-carrying mosquito creeps up behind him. As the mosquito approaches, the buzzing gets louder and louder until it startles the drone awake. The American drone screams out, "Kon hai?!" (Who is it?!), frantically attempting to flap his wings and get away while heavily panting. "Hello brother," the quick-talking mosquito says in a high-pitched voice, flicking about. "Mujhe pehchante main kon hoo?" (Do you recognize who I am?).[18]

The dengue-carrying anopheles mosquito has been present in Pakistan since the mid-1990s. The first outbreak of viral fever from dengue-carrying mosquitoes in Pakistan happened in the port city of Karachi from June 1994 to September 1995, but it was not until 2006 that dengue epidemics became an annual occurrence.[19] In 2011, dengue mosquitoes reportedly infected 21,314 people in Punjab alone, causing 337 deaths—the most of any Pakistani province.[20] While there are no writings about how exactly the dengue-carrying mosquitoes came to Pakistan, it is worth interrogating further how the mosquito's movement is directly linked to the circulation of capital along the infrastructure of empire. Instructive here is Timothy Mitchell's historical research that documents how British colonial expansionism involved the incidental transportation of disease-ridden mosquitoes across its imperial geographies, turning the mosquito into a harbinger of death across the Commonwealth.[21] After reading through Mitchell's work, it was unsurprising to find out that the dengue-carrying mosquitoes arrived in the port city of Karachi in the mid-1990s through the global supply chains that connect Pakistan to the Indian Ocean world economy.

After the drone correctly identifies his new friend as the infamous Pakistani dengue mosquito, he laments, "Tu mujhe to janta ho main kon hoon" (You must know who I am). Naming him as an "American drone airplane," the mosquito remarks that the drone's "target koi hota hai, aur thook kisi hor nu dehta hai" (target is one person, but he ends up hitting the other one). The awkward, uncoordinated drone proudly exclaims, "Yeh tho Amereek di style hai!" (That is the American way!). The tricky, clever mosquito informs his friend about his own style of killing. "Chup se ke teeka lagate hoon" (Quietly I give them a small injection), he says proudly. "Jab pathe chalta hai ke dengue kata hai to marne te dho din pehlan hi marjahte hai" (When they finally realize that the dengue mosquito has bitten them, they die two days before they are supposed to).[22]

The mosquito-borne viral disease entered the public lexicon in the 2010s as epidemiological researchers and nongovernmental organizations in Pakistan attempted to address the fatal rates of dengue infection. Published in 2013, the first major study on the domestication of the viral disease in Pakistan by postcolonial epidemiological researchers critiqued the lack of government-funded intervention into the spread of dengue.[23] Public awareness infomercials produced by local NGOs have proliferated during this time, warning the Pakistani

FIGURE 12.2. In this still from the folkloric Pakistani cartoon "Kabhi Dengue, Kabhi Drone," the dengue-carrying mosquito colludes with the American Predator drone.

public about the dangers of dengue-carrying mosquitoes. Presumably because of their small size and almost invisible presence, the mosquitoes featured in these infomercials are consistently animated as larger-than-life figures.

Bishnupriya Ghosh traces the history of animating mosquitoes to Winsor McCay's six-minute line-drawn animation "How a Mosquito Operates" (1912). For Ghosh, the mosquito is "planetary, here before us, and perhaps . . . after us."[24] Narrowing in on the atmospheric threat that disease-carrying mosquitoes have posed to human life, she offers the example of malaria, reminding us that it was named after bad air (*mal aria*).[25] Ghosh compels us to consider that the anopheles mosquito is always already a threatening force that is all-encompassing, fully atmospheric. The ambient presence that the mosquito invokes is strikingly similar to the looming drone. And yet, in "Kabhi Dengue, Kabhi Drone," the drone and mosquito are not visualized as atmospheric at all. Quite the opposite: they are presented as two men—shamelessly flying, talking, and colluding over the skies of Pakistan (Figure 12.2.). There is something decisively abnormal yet familiar about the two men in the cartoon, those two flying dacoits.

As the drone and mosquito continue to plot, we get to see the duo up close. The new wide angle showcases the out-to-lunch drone's chubby, childish face and light skin. His deep, masculine voice makes it apparent that the drone—with his blunt, inaccurate killing style—is the dim-witted, big guy, the muscles or the brawn of the two. His interlocutor, the darker-skinned mosquito, is a skinny, quick-talking, sinister character. With clever comebacks and a high-pitched, effeminate laugh, the mosquito is the mastermind, the brains behind their evil operations. And it is not incidental that neither speaks Urdu, the national language of Pakistan. When the drone reveals that he speaks Pashto, the mosquito confesses that he speaks Punjabi.

The cartoon casts the drone and mosquito as dacoits: criminal outsiders up to no good. To better understand the racial undertones of dacoity, it is worth considering how British colonial policy toward criminality transformed as the corpus of colonial thought about caste in South Asia grew. In *Castes of Mind: Colonialism and the Making of Modern India*, Nicholas B. Dirks explains how the institutionalization and naturalization of Brahmanical caste orders through colonial administrative rule by the British facilitated the rise of intense caste politics in the late nineteenth century and throughout the twentieth.[26] Considering criminality as a caste-defined hereditary profession in South Asia, similar to weaving or carpentry, British colonial officials came to believe that criminal behavior was genetically inherited rather than socially learned.[27] This shift from social determinism to biological determinism laid the groundwork for the imposition of the Criminal Tribes Act in 1871. The act grouped various ethnic and social communities (vagrants, nomads, Adivasis, *hijras,* and some lower-caste groups) into a single legal category: criminal tribes. The British colonial state used these criminal-by-birth laws to control, dispossess, and persecute over thirteen million people by designating them as dacoits.

The separation of Indigenous peoples along the lines of criminality during British rule in the subcontinent has meant that postcolonial states in South Asia largely operate with two figurations of indigeneity: the Dacoit and the Adivasi. Emerging as a result of political self-organization in the 1930s, Adivasi struggles in South Asia gained international recognition during the 1990s within the context of the global Indigenous movement.[28] While the term Adivasi is derived from the Hindi words *adi* and *vasi,* meaning "first inhabitants," now it is widely used to represent all Indigenous and tribal peoples in South Asia. Demonstrating how the contemporary political figure of the Adivasi has been cobbled together by NGOs, anthropologists, and international law, Amita Baviskar explains how circulating images of "the loincloth wearing Adivasi playing the flute or dancing" reinforce essentialist ideas of Adivasis as "ecologically noble savants."[29] This new rendering of the docile Adivasi emerges against decades of proliferating images of dacoity, typified by popular cinematic images of rural bandits running wild and wreaking havoc in the forests and hills of the postcolonial frontier in South Asia.

Predictably, the criminal outsider figure of the Dacoit has left a lasting cultural imprint in the subcontinent. Dacoits crop up as villains in a litany of artistic, filmic, and literary cultural texts from across India, Pakistan, and its diasporas. In Bollywood, there is an entire genre dedicated to them: the dacoit film genre. Discussing the wide impact of the genre, scholar Rosie Thomas explains that in the 1970s and 1980s, South Asian tourists visiting resort towns in the subcontinent would even "frequent photographers' stalls to pose for their photographs in *dacoit* outfits—cowboy-style fringed jackets, turbans, moustaches, guns—clearly inspired by film imagery."[30] Notably, the 1975 action-adventure dacoit film *Sholay* was a definitive reworking of the genre. Heralded as an Indian classic, it was the highest-grossing film in India for nearly twenty years. Blending the conventions of older dacoit films with the techniques of the American Western and its derivative works, *Sholay* became the first "curry Western." The transnational circulation of the Western as a filmic style in the twentieth century brought the structural antagonisms of U.S. settler colonialism to bear on other political contexts. In South Asia, the curry Western replaced the "Indian savages" of the American Western film with a new cast of dacoit characters.

Understanding the contemporary ways that the racialized figure of the Dacoit functions in South Asia requires further consideration of the Western film genre and its antagonistic Indian characters within the historical context of U.S. settler colonialism. Working through Indigenous presence in a swath of literary, cultural, and political contexts, Jodi Byrd demonstrates that U.S. empire does not discretely transit across "Alaska Native villages, American Indian nations, unincorporated, insular, and incorporated territories, Hawai'i, Iraq, Okinawa, and Afghanistan" through the remapping of a "detachable . . . *frontier* or *wilderness*" but rather through the continuous reproduction of "Indianness."[31] Tracing how the production of a paradigmatic Indianness functions as a mode of transit for the propagation of U.S. imperialism, Byrd reveals how this single, racially defined Indianness collapses indigeneity into another minority population within U.S. liberal multiculturalism while serving as the mold for remaking foreign subjects under U.S. imperial authority. Placing Indianness at the center of American statehood and empire, Byrd explains that the "non-discriminating, proto-inclusive 'merciless Indian Savage' stands as the terrorist, externalized from 'our frontiers,' and functions as abjected horror through whom civilization is articulated oppositionally." For Byrd, this figure is "the paranoid foundation for what Jasbir K. Puar defines in *Terrorist Assemblages* as Islamic 'monster-terrorist-fags.'"[32] If this timeless figure of the "merciless Indian savage" functions as the route of transit for the propagation of U.S. imperialism as Jodi Byrd contends, then dacoity functions as the route of transit for the consolidation and propagation of postcolonial state power in the subcontinent. Collapsing multiple peoples into a single population for expedited political management, dacoity now serves as a mold to remake and manage subjects externalized and deemed antinational by the postcolonial state, such as Muslims and Dalits in India. In the peculiar case of "Kabhi Dengue, Kabhi Drone," it is the Punjabi-speaking mosquito and the Pashto-speaking drone who are imagined through dacoity as a violent subset of Indianness, as terrorists operating in the borderlands of the Pakistani state.

If the American figure of the terrorist—and its foundational figure of the "merciless Indian savage"—is both monster and fag, then so too is the figure of the Dacoit in South Asia. Studying representations of dacoity in Indian cinema, Rosie Thomas writes about how dacoit characters are routinely presented as morally depraved and sexually uncontrollable.[33] Imagined along these lines, the two dacoits in "Kabhi Dengue, Kabhi Drone" are improperly masculine, hyperracialized, deformed, and sexually threatening to the reproduction of ordinary, everyday heteropatriarchal life in Pakistan. Whereas the hypermasculine drone is presented with a deep voice, light skin, and a wide body, the mosquito is rendered effeminate through his high-pitched voice, dark skin, and disappearing body. If one reads further into the gendered dynamics and sexual undertones of the cartoon, the queer subtext is striking: the innocent, dumb, hypermasculine drone is seduced by the cunning mosquito, who charms him with his sharp wit, effeminacy, and slender body. The cartoon fosters an amplified sense of threat at the hands of the drone and mosquito: the foreign, flirtatious queer couple become harbingers of civilizational death. While the anopheles mosquito and the Predator drone pose real, material threats to human life in Pakistan, the stencil provided by dacoity flattens these complex and debilitating atmospheric phenomena.

When the drone inquires whether the mosquito enjoys living in Pakistan, the dengue-carrying mosquito responds defiantly. "Kesa lagda hai?" (How do I like it?), he retorts. "Are mera than poura kaandaan bulaya hai!" (I brought my entire extended family here!). The mosquito continues celebrating with the drone, informing him that the Pakistani government has not even released any official reports about the dengue endemic. The drone responds in a sinister tone. "Isi lai to hum Pakistan main mauj kar rahe hai!" (That's why we're living it up in Pakistan!). On that note, the short ends with the evil mosquito and drone maniacally laughing together as they fly off into the distance to continue terrorizing the good people of Pakistan.

Calling out officials for neglecting to address and intervene in drone warfare and dengue epidemics across the country, the cartoon is a powerful indictment of the Pakistani government for its inaction. As such, the cartoon urges us to consider how Pakistani state operatives and American military officials have colluded to facilitate American drone strike operations in the FATA since 2004. While the Pakistani government has remained publicly opposed to America's drone strike program, the presence of clear airspace whenever strikes are issued lends credence to the popular idea that the Pakistani government struck a deal with U.S. officials, permitting them to carry out attacks against targets such as al-Qaeda and the Taliban in exchange for assistance with attacks against other domestic opponents of the Pakistani government.[34] Although it is critical to acknowledge the asymmetrical power that undergirds U.S.–Pakistan relations, it is worth further considering how their joint War on Terror transits to the FATA by reproducing the paradigmatic figure of the Indian savage and the merciless Dacoit respectively. This political cooperation between the United States and Pakistan reveals how drone warfare is less of a clear-cut American imperial affair than it is the newest instantiation of a timeless global war on monsters, Indians, terrorists, fags, illegal immigrants, dacoits, antinationals, and everyone else who gets in the way of powerful states. In the end, the folkloric cartoon makes us laugh at the inefficacy of the postcolonial state while providing an opening for us to consider living beyond the postcolonial frontier. But living beyond the frontier in places like the FATA means living in a dark geography, in a place where you are excised from the global citizenry and subject to the full brunt of the Global War on Terror. What do safety and security look like in practice when you are living among dacoits, under the watchful evil eye of the drone? Where do you hide when the drone is overhead?

Architectural Imperatives

On November 14, 2001, the United States completed its first successful drone strike operation. Taking off from an American air force base in Uzbekistan, an American Predator drone crossed the Afghani border to track a convoy of vehicles carrying Mohammed Atef—the military chief of al-Qaeda and son-in-law to Osama bin Laden. When the vehicles stopped in front of a building, officers from the Central Intelligence Agency issued two consecutive Hellfire missile attacks from the Predator drone overhead. The first strike blasted off the back half of the building, while the second brought the entire structure to the ground, killing Atef, among other civilians. Realizing that buildings are static choke points where insurgent cells congregate, CIA operatives have strategically turned toward using domestic buildings as primary targets during drone strike missions to increase success rates. An ongoing joint investigation by the Bureau of Investigative Journalism, Forensic Architecture, and SITU Research reveals that approximately 65 percent of drone strikes in Pakistan have targeted buildings.[35] Lacking their purported surgical precision and laser-like focus, drones routinely obliterate noncombative buildings in an attempt to kill insurgents, maiming civilians, animals, and other forms of life in the process. To put it plainly, architecture is not incidental but rather central to the tactics of America's targeted drone strike program. In this section, I question whether it is possible to find refuge from the bombs above without going into hiding, whether we might build a place that does not replicate the racial dynamics of technosecuritization that plague American imperialism and postcolonial statehood. With that objective in mind, I study the speculative architectural project *Shura City*. Conceived by architect Asher J. Kohn and new media artist and writer Hiba Ali, the collaborative experimental architectural proposal for a drone-proof smart city was put together shortly after the Obama administration first publicly acknowledged its covert drone strike program.

I met Ali while she was completing an artist residency at the South Asian Visual Arts Centre in June 2017. It is within this context that I first got the opportunity to chat in person with Ali about her work and learn about her collaborative project *Shura City*, delving into the layered meanings of the project and her thoughts on some of the conundrums that stifle clear-cut political action against drones. She explained that the project developed from an image-text originally drawn up by Kohn that envisioned a creative, hopeful response to the persistence of drone strikes. Published on *Chapati Mystery*, a "quaint" digital publication that started out "wondering what T. E. Lawrence and Bhagat Singh would talk about over dinner," the architectural project took as its starting point the failure of the law to protect civilians against drone warfare.[36] Thinking outside the bounds of legal recourse, Kohn turned toward architecture, exploring the potential for buildings to accomplish what international law could not. The result was a rhetorical thought project: What would an entire city designed with the violence of drones and the Global War on Terror in mind look like? Concerned by the arms-race logics at the heart of defensive architecture, Kohn decided against armoring the city as a way to deflect American ballistics. Instead, the smart city took magical deception as its operative logic. It is designed as a sleight of hand, in a "now you see me, now you don't" way. "Inscrutability is its armour," Kohn writes.[37]

After stumbling upon the guest post on *Chapati Mystery*, Ali initiated the collaboration with a short email to Kohn. Ali explained to me that as the thought-turned-art project developed through discussion, two latent problems started brimming to the surface. On the one hand, there seemed to be no way to escape speculative financial capital and its authority over the imagining, drafting, branding, financing, operationalizing, and marketing of any large-scale architectural build. On the other hand, the proposed city was shaping up to be a modernized medieval fortress at its base. As a result, Ali and Kohn flipped the proposal on its head, developing a short video that would better elucidate how speculative financial capital is mobilized to build modern, securitized smart cities that reproduce nearly universal, racially encoded antagonisms: life/nonlife, fort/surround, citizen/terrorist, settler/native, lightness/darkness, civilization/wilderness. Reading the video as an experiment in politicized architectural thinking, I explore the productive openings that the artists have offered for rethinking the paradigms of security that continue to underpin contemporary approaches to defensive architecture.

The corporatized video presentation, set to an audio track by the experimental techno DJ 界+ 界CHAiT, opens with an animated Predator drone taking flight into modern cyberspace.[38] Remaining out of the frame, its terror lurks in the atmosphere. As the military drone glides off-screen, the camera pans to reveal the logo—"Shura City"—sprawled across the ground and stylized in large holographic, three-dimensional English and Arabic block letters. Mimicking a flashy, high-end, large-scale corporate presentation, it is the perfect pitch for a modern Gulf capitalist looking to finance a smart city in the desert. As the drone flies across the screen, the architectural crisis is disclosed: "With the goal to eliminate a single person or a small group, [drones] scoff at conventional architecture." Laying out how "architecture against drones is a contemporary imperative," the enterprising duo clarify that "such creations are not needed for the John Connors but for the Abdulrahman al-Awlakis." The geopolitics are clear: *Shura City* is a project for those targeted by drones. Thoughtfully selected, the name John Connor is drawn from the American science-fiction film series *Terminator*. In the series, John is a messianic young boy who successfully leads resistance efforts against synthetic intelligence and its genocidal robots. On the other hand, Abdulrahman al-Awlaki is the name of the fourteen-year-old boy and U.S. citizen who was killed in a drone strike in 2011. Born to an al-Qaeda operative, he was robbed of life, innocence, and the messianic possibilities that are given to prototypical white American boys like John Connor. Unlike

John Connor, Abdulrahman al-Awlaki will not be the superhero who fights off the drones and saves the day. And neither will his eight-year-old sister, who died during a raid approved by the U.S. government in early 2017. The message is clear: the al-Awlaki children and their Muslim brethren need a modern, smart defense system. And Shura City is the ideal solution—all it requires is your funding.

In the video, the drone-proof city is visualized as an anti-imperial project. Shura City strategically incorporates Islamic architectural features into the future postcolony, including minarets. Minarets are tall, slender towers that typically form part of a mosque. As the place from which a muezzin calls Muslims to prayer, it is an integral component of religious life in Shura City. Compelled to include minarets in light of "the Switzerland ban," the smart city's creators neatly situate it within a long-standing anti-imperial contest between Euro-American Christianity and the Islamic world. The commentary refers to a popular initiative to prevent the construction of mosque minarets in Switzerland that turned into a successful referendum in November 2009 when it was confirmed by 57.5 percent of participating voters. The defiant minarets of Shura City are colored green in traditional Islamic fashion. Used as a marker of "freedom of expression," as well as "a symbol of the beliefs of the inhabitants and their pride in them," the minarets offer a dream of religious unity for potential investors, bypassing concerns about divisions between different sects and practitioners of Islam. By defining its community along ethnoreligious terms, the minaret-decorated smart city situates itself in opposition to the Christianization project of Euro-American imperialism.

Covered in an ultramarine dome, the city emerges in the middle of a never-ending desert. Elizabeth Povinelli explains how the desert is imagined as a place denuded and inhospitable to life to maintain and exacerbate the distinction between life and nonlife for the proliferation of capitalist extraction projects (oil, carbon, and so on) and development projects (plastics, cities, and so on).[39] Against the imaginary, emptied desert, the three-dimensional digital model rendering of Shura City glimmers as a fantasy of technoscientific modernity. Intended to maximize both "external confusion and internal livability," Shura City is designed in the image of a traditional fortress. Analyzing enduring images of the "surrounded fort," Stefano Harney and Fred Moten explain how the core (settler society) makes incursions into the surround

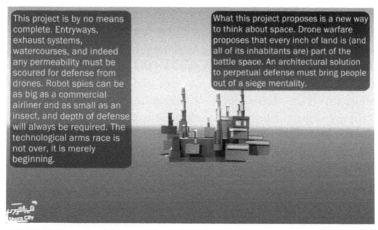

This project is by no means complete. Entryways, exhaust systems, watercourses, and indeed any permeability must be scoured for defense from drones. Robot spies can be as big as a commercial airliner and as small as an insect, and depth of defense will always be required. The technological arms race is not over, it is merely beginning.

What this project proposes is a new way to think about space. Drone warfare proposes that every inch of land is (and all of its inhabitants are) part of the battle space. An architectural solution to perpetual defense must bring people out of a siege mentality.

FIGURE 12.3. In this final scene from the video pitch for *Shura City,* artists Hiba Ali and Asher J. Kohn flip the smart-city proposal on its head.

(native land) through incursions and land grabs, highlighting how "the surround antagonises the laager in its midst."[40] The core holds the political, the settler commons, the capitalist state that is the real danger.

"Knowing that there is something between them and the unspeakable darkness outside," the artists sardonically remind us in the video that "the [dome] roof allows people to feel comfortable meeting and mixing." Throughout the video we see drones, domes, minarets, and QR codes, but human life is missing from the proposed smart city. Avoiding the task of visualizing fallible humans, the video satirically envisions a perfectly calculated robotic, machinic future that promises to keep "inhabitants" secure from the malleable, shifting "darkness outside." Racially amplifying and localizing the atmospheric threat of the drone, the video compels us to think about how those outside the new city, beyond the polis, are rendered as terrorists in the name of collective security. With its objective to protect those living in the dark geographies of U.S. imperialism, the drone-proof city quickly becomes a technosecuritized, neoliberal city-state itself, with its own dark geographies and, by extension, its own dacoits.

With one final disclaimer that the project is "by no means complete" and requires thinking about "entryways, exhaust systems, [and] watercourses," the video presents investors with what "next steps" might look like if funding is secured (Figure 12.3). It is in this last scene that the artists drive home their point and flip the entire project on its head. "The technological arms race is not over," they instruct, "it is merely beginning." By situating the smart city within a continuum of rivalistic, nationalist movements to "armament," the artists place the proposal to build a drone-proof city within a global history of technosecuritization, revealing the racial logics of fear, security, and safety that have long structured conflicts within the well-worn circuitry of Anglo-American political hegemony. The project proposes "a new way to think about space," telling us that any effective architectural solution must "bring people out of a siege mentality," out of the medieval fortress. Straddling the liminal space between speculative fiction and satire, the proposal for Shura City speaks to the deep dejection felt by people whose kin have been murdered by American Predator drones and hunted down by modern postcolonial nation-states like Pakistan. The video leaves us without answers, left looking for an elsewhere without drones.

"What if some Gulf capitalist actually builds the city?" Ali offered, laughing, during our discussion. "What a nightmare that would be." While the afterlives of Shura City are not foreclosed, Ali explained that the project was only meant as a proposal, a provocation to think about how the paradigms of speculation, security, privacy, and surveillance that continue to underwrite so many architectural futures can so easily be turned against anyone. When I asked Ali if dengue-carrying mosquitoes would ever infiltrate Shura City, she lamented, "The powerful will always find a way to protect themselves and condemn the rest." As Ali suggests, perhaps it is time to slow down, to momentarily put aside the drone while we focus our attention on all the ways that power reproduces itself. Once architecture is wrestled away from those powerful, ever-expanding neoliberal states, corporations, and individuals, we might stumble upon a different set of architectural imperatives for those lands under occupation by the postcolony, ones that do not subjugate dacoits.

Notes

I would like to thank Hiba Ali, Shanon Fitzpatrick, Indu Vashist, Joshua Falek, Yasmine Mosimann, Bhavani Raman, Kevin Coleman, Brian Jacobson, Rupali Morzaria, Khaleel Grant, Zohar Freeman, Tammy Lam, Sam Kessler, and of course David

Kieran and Rebecca Adelman for their substantive and generative commentary on this chapter as it has developed over the past few years.

1. Nasser Hussain, "The Sound of Terror: Phenomenology of a Drone Strike," *Boston Review,* November 5, 2013, http://bostonreview.net/world/hussain -drone-phenomenology.

2. Ian Shaw, "Predator Empire: The Geopolitics of US Drone Warfare," *Geopolitics* 18, no. 3 (2013): 550.

3. Mark Bowden, "The Killing Machines," *Atlantic,* August 14, 2013, http:// www.theatlantic.com/magazine/archive/2013/09/the-killing-machines-how -to-think-about-drones/309434/.

4. Anjali Nath, "Stones, Stoners and Drones: Transnational South Asian Visuality from Above and Below," in *Life in the Age of Drone Warfare,* ed. Lisa Parks and Caren Kaplan (Durham, N.C.: Duke University Press, 2017), 242.

5. Nath, 254, 256.

6. Nath, 257.

7. Nath, 255.

8. Gayatri Gopinath, *Impossible Desires: Queer Diasporas and South Asian Public Cultures* (Durham, N.C.: Duke University Press, 2005), 32.

9. Jodi A. Byrd, *The Transit of Empire: Indigenous Critiques of Colonialism* (Minneapolis: University of Minnesota Press, 2011), xxi.

10. Ian Shaw and Majed Akhter, "The dronification of state violence," *Critical Asian Studies* 46, no. 2 (2014): 211.

11. LastWeekTonight, "Drones: Last Week Tonight with John Oliver (HBO)," filmed September 28, 2014, YouTube video, 12:56, posted September 28, 2014, https://www.youtube.com/watch?v=K4NRJoCNHIs.

12. Lev Grossman, "Drone Home," *Time,* February 11, 2013, http://content .time.com/time/magazine/article/0,9171,2135132,00.html.

13. Derek Gregory, "From a View to a Kill: Drones and Late Modern War," *Theory, Culture and Society* 28, no. 7–8 (2011): 201.

14. The expression references Section 420 of the Indian Penal Code, which deals with dishonesty and cheating.

15. Michelle Murphy, "Data Justice across Environmental Publics" (lecture, Monday Night Seminar, McLuhan Centre for Culture and Technology, University of Toronto, November 27, 2017).

16. Robert M. Farley, "Drone Warfare," in *Grounded: The Case for Abolishing the United States Air Force* (Lexington: University Press of Kentucky, 2014), 146.

17. Jane Mayer, "The Predator War," *New Yorker,* October 26, 2009, https:// www.newyorker.com/magazine/2009/10/26/the-predator-war.

18. Geo News, "Kabhi Dengue, Kabhi Drone," my translation.

19. S. B. Rasheed, R. K. Butlin, and M. Boots, "A Review of Dengue as an Emerging Disease in Pakistan," *Public Health* 127, no. 1 (2013): 14.

20. Rasheed, Butlin, and Boots, 13.

21. Timothy Mitchell, *Rule of Experts: Egypt, Techno-politics, Modernity* (Berkeley: University of California Press, 2002).

22. Geo News, "Kabhi Dengue, Kabhi Drone," my translation.

23. Rasheed, Butlin, and Boots, "Review of Dengue," 15.

24. Bishnupriya Ghosh, "Animating Uncommon Life: U.S. Military Malaria Films (1942–1945) and the Pacific Theatre," in *Animating Film Theory,* ed. Karen Beckman (Durham, N.C.: Duke University Press, 2014), 265.

25. Ghosh, 264.

26. Nicholas B. Dirks, *Castes of Mind: Colonialism and the Making of Modern India* (Princeton, N.J.: Princeton University Press, 2011).

27. Sanjay Nigam, "Disciplining and Policing the 'Criminals by Birth,' Part 1: The Making of a Colonial Stereotype—The Criminal Tribes and Castes of North India," *Indian Economic and Social History Review* 27, no. 2 (1990): 131–64.

28. Daniel J. Rycroft and Sangeeta Dasgupta, *The Politics of Belonging in India: Becoming Adivasi* (New York: Taylor and Francis, 2011), xiv.

29. Amita Baviskar, "Indian Indigeneities: Adivasi Engagements with Hindu Nationalism in India," in *Indigenous Experience Today,* ed. Marisol De La Cadena and Orin Starn (New York: Berg Publisher, 2007), 289.

30. Rosie Thomas, "Melodrama and the Negotiation of Morality in Mainstream Hindi Film," in *Consuming Modernity: Public Culture in a South Asian World,* ed. Carol Appadurai Breckenridge (Minneapolis: University of Minnesota Press, 1995), 178.

31. Byrd, *The Transit of Empire,* 150, 27.

32. Byrd, xxvi.

33. Thomas, "Melodrama and the Negotiation of Morality," 169, 171.

34. Farley, "Drone Warfare," 148.

35. "Most Drone Strikes in Pakistan Have Hit Buildings," Forensic Architecture, March 8, 2017, https://forensic-architecture.org/new-research-drones-targets-pakistan/.

36. "About – Chapati Mystery," Chapati Mystery, accessed July 22, 2017, http://www.chapatimystery.com/about.

37. Brian Anderson, "To Drone Proof a City," *Vice News,* January 30, 2013, https://www.vice.com/en_us/article/9aavjd/to-drone-proof-a-city.

38. "A Proposal for Anti-Drone Architecture: Shura City," accessed September 27, 2013, https://vimeo.com/75626208. Find DJ♀+♀CHAiT on Instagram @ nusoil88: https://www.instagram.com/nusoil88/?hl=en.

39. Elizabeth Povinelli, *Geontologies: A Requiem to Late Liberalism* (Durham, N.C.: Duke University Press, 2016).

40. Stefano Harney and Fred Moten, *The Undercommons: Fugitive Planning and Black Study* (New York: Minor Compositions, 2013), 17.

Contributors

Rebecca A. Adelman is professor in the Department of Media and Communication Studies at the University of Maryland, Baltimore County. She is the author of *Beyond the Checkpoint: Visual Practices in America's Global War on Terror* and *Figuring Violence: Affective Investments in Perpetual War.*

Syed Irfan Ashraf is assistant professor in the Department of Journalism and Mass Communication, University of Peshawar, Pakistan.

Jens Borrebye Bjering is postdoctoral researcher of comparative literature at the University of Southern Denmark.

Annika Brunck is assistant professor at the University of Tübingen, Germany.

David Buchanan is associate professor of English and fine arts at the U.S. Air Force Academy, where he also serves as an instructor pilot in the academy's Powered Flight program. He is the author of *Going Scapegoat: Post-9/11 War Literature, Language, and Culture.*

Owen Coggins is honorary associate in the Religious Studies Department at the Open University. He is the author of *Mysticism, Ritual, and Religion in Drone Metal* and coeditor of *Sustain//Decay.*

Andreas Immanuel Graae is assistant professor at the Royal Danish Defence College. He works in the interdisciplinary intersection between cultural studies, military technology, and security politics. He earned his PhD from the University of Southern Denmark; his dissertation, *The Cruel Drone: Imagining Drone Warfare in Art, Culture, and Politics,* explored the cultural, historical, and political imaginaries of drone warfare.

Brittany Hirth is assistant professor of English at Dickinson State University.

Tim Jelfs is assistant professor of American studies at the University of Groningen. He is the author of *The Argument about Things in the 1980s: Goods and Garbage in an Age of Neoliberalism.*

David Kieran is assistant professor of history at Washington & Jefferson College. He is the author of *Forever Vietnam: How a Divisive War Changed American Public Memory* and *Signature Wounds: The Untold Story of the Military's Mental Health Crisis.*

Ann-Katrine S. Nielsen is a PhD student in Scandinavian studies at Aarhus University.

Nike Nivar Ortiz is a postdoctoral scholar and teaching fellow at the University of Southern California (USC). He received his PhD in comparative media and culture from USC, where he was awarded the 2016–18 Andrew W. Mellon–USC Digital Humanities PhD Fellowship. He also holds graduate certificates in visual studies and digital media and culture.

Michael Richardson is senior research fellow in the School of the Arts and Media at the University of New South Wales. He is the author of *Gestures of Testimony: Torture, Trauma, and Affect in Literature* and coeditor of *Traumatic Affect.*

Kristin Shamas is postdoctoral researcher in the Department of History at the University of Oklahoma.

Sajdeep Soomal is a doctoral student in history at the University of Toronto and research assistant at the Montreal Museum of Fine Arts.

Michael Zeitlin is associate professor in the Department of English Language and Literatures at the University of British Columbia. He is the author of *Faulkner, Aviation, and Modern War* (forthcoming) and the coeditor of *Soldier Talk: The Vietnam War in Oral Narrative.*

Index

Abbas, Malath, 138
absurdism, 20, 159, 260, 281–82, 298, 299, 304; in *American Sniper,* 295–97; in *Jarhead,* 287, 291–94. *See also* black humor; parody
Acar, Numan, 91
Acosta, Jim, 1
actor-network theory, 154, 155–58, 168
Adivasis, 314–15
aerial warfare, 14, 33. *See also* airstrikes; bombing
affect: and drone strikes in Pakistan, 303–4; in *Homeland,* 87–88, 89, 92, 93; theory, 204–6; traumatic, 17, 128–29, 131–32, 134–36, 138, 142, 144–45, 147–48, 149; and veterans, 18, 202–3, 209, 210, 211, 214–21
affective arrangement, 135
affective atmosphere, 132
affective design, 134
Afghanistan, U.S. War in (2001–), 45, 69, 181–90. *See also* War on Terror
Agamben, Giorgio, 105–6, 121–22, 234, 240
agency: of the body, 11; of the individual, 13, 55, 62, 63, 142, 147, 155, 163; of objects, 154–56; and power, 273
Ahmed, Sara, 217

Air Force (U.S.), 5, 14, 32, 58, 59, 133; Academy, 72
airstrikes, 5, 15, 19, 24n21, 32, 34–35; in First World War, 38; at Gernika, 39–41; in Iraq, 20, 45, 284; in Lebanon, 235; in Pakistan, 242; portrayal of in *Homeland,* 91; in Second World War, 39–41, 50–51n62. *See also* bombing; drone warfare
Akhter, Majed, 308
al-Awlaki, Abdulrahman, 320–21
Alfred, Taiaiake, 67, 69
Ali, Hiba, 20, 307, 308, 319, 320, 323
Alizadeh, Kathi, 155, 156
Allen, Robertson, 131
al-Qaeda, 183, 189, 190, 191, 241, 242, 243, 245, 317, 318, 320
"alternative facts," 63
al-Zawahiri, Ayman, 242
American Rust (novel), 158
American Sniper (memoir), 20, 56, 281–82, 283, 294–99
America's Army (game series), 130–31
Amnesty International, 7
Andersen, Carrie, 130
Anderson, Ben, 132
Apache helicopter, 44, 45
Arab-Israeli War, 234

Lightning Source UK Ltd.
Milton Keynes UK
UKHW021826221020
372056UK00009B/465